THE JEWISH PEOPLE IN AMERICA

THE JEWISH PEOPLE IN AMERICA

A Series Sponsored by the American Jewish Historical Society

Henry L. Feingold, General Editor

A Time for Healing
American Jewry since
World War II

THE JEWISH PEOPLE IN AMERICA

A TIME FOR HEALING

American Jewry since
World War II

Edward S. Shapiro

The Johns Hopkins University Press

Baltimore and London

Second printing, 1992

The Johns Hopkins University Press
701 West 40th Street
Baltimore, Maryland 21211-2190
The Johns Hopkins Press Ltd., London

Library of Congress Cataloging-in-Publication Data

Shapiro, Edward S.
A time for healing : American Jewry since World War II /
Edward S. Shapiro.
p.   cm. — (The Jewish People in America ; v. 5)
Includes bibliographical references and index.
ISBN 0-8018-4347-2 (alk. paper)
1. Jews—United States—History—20th century.
2. Jews—United States—Intellectual life. 3. Jews—United
States—Cultural assimilation. 4. Judaism—United
States—History—20th century. 5. United States—
History—1945-   6. United States—Ethnic relations.
I. Title. II. Series.
E184.J5S435 1992   74308
973'.04924—dc20   91-38385

In Honor of My Father
and in Memory of My Mother

CONTENTS

Contents

SERIES EDITOR'S FOREWORD

OVER the generations, there has been much change in the content of Jewish culture. Some writers argue that in the benevolent and absorbent atmosphere of America, Jewish culture has been thinned beyond recognition. But one ingredient of that culture—a deep appreciation of history—continues to receive the highest priority. The motto on the seal of the American Jewish Historical Society enjoins us, "Remember the Days of Old." It is taken from the Pentateuch, itself a historical chronicle.

Indeed, the Jewish community boasts almost one hundred local historical societies and two professional archives for preserving source material. The cherishing of its history goes beyond any biblical or cultural injunction. History is especially important for Diaspora communities because corporate memory rather than territorial space ultimately ensures their survival. That is what Bal Shem Tov, founder of the Hasidic movement, may have meant when centuries ago he counseled his followers that "memory is the key to redemption."

The American Jewish Historical Society offers this history of the Jews in America to both the Jewish community and the general reading public as a repository of memory. For Jewish readers this series provides an opportunity to enrich their self-understanding, quickening Jewry's energies and enhancing its potential for survival. We hope to remind the general reading public that, at a time when the American dream may be found wanting, the American Jewish experience is evidence that the promise of America can still be realized. Without the opportunities, freedom, and openness found in this land, American Jewry would not have been able to realize its energies and talents and become what it is today.

How that has happened over the generations is a story the American Jewish Historical Society is committed to tell. In fact, the society could think of no better way to honor its historical task and its rich hundred-year history than by recounting that story through this series. No single volume by a single historian can do justice to the multilevel historical experience of American Jewry. Drawing on the talents of five historians with a common vision and purpose, this series offers a historical synthesis at once comprehensible to the intelligent lay reader and useful to the professional historian. Each of these volumes integrates common themes: the origins of Jewish immigrants, their experience of settling in America, their economic and social life, their religious and educational efforts, their political involvement, and the change the American Jewish community experienced over time.

Predictably, the project encountered many conceptual problems. One of the most vexing stemmed from the difficulty of classifying American Jewry. To treat American Jews solely as members of a religious denomination, as was once the practice of the Reform branch, was a distortion, because most American Jews are not religious in the sectarian sense. And though some sociologists have classified Jews as a race, clearly that category does not adequately describe how they differ from other Americans. More than other ethnic communities, American Jewry is influenced by two separate historical streams: the American and the Jewish. To be sure, American Jewry is but one of the many ethnic groups woven into the American national fabric. Yet it is something beyond that as well. It is part of an evolving religious civilization that has persisted for millennia. This persistent tension between assimilation and group survival—the will to remain part of the universal community of Israel—is well evinced in the volumes of this series.

In this final volume, Edward S. Shapiro throws new light on American Jewry's leap to prominence and affluence during the postwar years. He notes how success in the temporal sphere coupled with acceptance by the host culture presented new survival problems as the demands of the accommodation process led to a thinning of the content of Jewishness in the religious and cultural spheres. The decades after World War II, he concludes, were good for Jews but problematic for Judaism.

On behalf of the society, I thank the many participants of this venture, which had its beginnings over fifteen years ago as a way of commemorating the society's 1992 centennial. Dr. Abraham Kanof, Rosemary Krensky, and the late David Lubart provided initial support for the project. Dr. Kanof has been repeatedly generous in his financial contributions over the years, while the Max and Dora L. Starr Foundation has provided additional welcome assistance. The authors, Eli Faber, Hasia R. Diner, Gerald Sorin, and Edward

S. Shapiro, deserve special thanks. In addition, we are grateful to Ruth B. Fein and the late Phil Fine for their efforts on behalf of the project. For their technical and legal expertise in making publishing arrangements for the series, Robert L. Weinberg and Franklin Feldman need to be singled out. Words of thanks also go to Henry Y. K. Tom, executive editor of the Johns Hopkins University Press, and to his colleagues for their dedication and professionalism in bringing the society's dream to realization. Last, a special appreciation is in order for the society's untiring staff, particularly Bernard Wax and the late Nathan M. Kaganoff, for their administrative support.

Henry L. Feingold
General Editor

PREFACE AND ACKNOWLEDGMENTS

THIS HISTORY of American Jewry after 1945 has two broad themes. One is the rapid social and economic mobility of American Jews. By the 1980s, American Jewry was the nation's only major ethnic group without a significant working class component. This *embourgeoisment* began prior to World War II and quickly accelerated after the war's end, encouraged by a booming economy and the decline of anti-Semitism. The other major theme is the adaptation of Jews to unprecedented conditions of affluence and freedom. Values, ideologies, and identities forged under conditions of deprivation and discrimination in Europe and the immigrant ghettos of America now existed within a different context. The history of American Jewry after 1945 provides many examples of what sociologists call cultural lag, the failure of individuals and movements to modify their thinking to accommodate new social, economic, and political circumstances.

As the disabilities of being Jewish lessened, the external pressures on Jews to identify in any significant way as Jews and to associate with the Jewish community also weakened. The most important question facing Jewish survivalists in the postwar era was whether Jews would choose voluntarily to maintain their Jewish identity at a time when there were few obstacles to complete assimilation. While there were signs of vitality within American Jewry, such as the day school movement and pro-Israel philanthropy, there was also evidence of decline, such as religious apathy, the sagging membership of B'nai B'rith and other Jewish organizations, and a rapidly increasing intermarriage rate. For every person who saw the glass of the American Jewish future as half full, there was another who saw it as half empty. The somber tone of the book's final two chapters indicates to which group I belong. Just as George Will's conservative instincts were honed by watching the Chicago Cubs as a youth, so perhaps my pessimism can be traced to those years while growing up in Washington, D.C., when I rooted for the hapless Washington Senators and the equally hopeless Washington Redskins. In the 1960s, the Senators moved to Minnesota and the Redskins became respectable, but this came too late to save me from perpetual gloom.

No book could possibly encompass all aspects—cultural, economic, social, intellectual, religious, political—of postwar American Jewish history within the restrictions of space laid down by the sponsors and the publisher of *The Jewish People in America.* I was forced to slight many worthwhile topics such as religious thought, the history of Jewish organizations and federations, the debate among Jewish intellectuals over the desirability of Jewish survival, and the relations of Jews with other ethnic and racial groups. I will consider this book a success if it encourages others to fill in its blank spaces. I would be particularly gratified if my pessimism about the American Jewish future is proved unwarranted.

In writing this book I have accumulated many debts. First there is the leadership of the American Jewish Historical Society for having the vision and patience to undertake this project and for tolerating for over half a decade the idiosyncracies and procrastinations of five different authors. Stephen Whitfield of Brandeis University, one of the doyens of modern American Jewish culture, took valuable time away from his own important work to give the manuscript an unusually close and intelligent reading. Only he and I know the extent to which his suggestions improved the content and style of the book and how much I value his friendship. The manuscript also benefited from the comments of Henry L. Feingold, the general editor of *The Jewish People in America.* Naturally, any errors of fact and interpretation are my own. Although he did not read the manuscript, Marshall Sklare's name should be included in this preface. He, more than any other person, has shaped my understanding of contemporary American Jewry. Sklare, the leading authority on American Jewish sociology, has shown me how a commitment to Jewish survival can be combined with the highest standards of modern scholarship.

Chapters 1 and 3 were greatly improved because of the suggestions of Ralph Walz and Susan Minzter of the Seton Hall University history department. I value my conversations with Ralph and with Dermit Quinn, who is also in the Seton Hall history department; their good humor and common sense is a rare commodity in academia. Anthony Lee, Richard Stern, and the other reference librarians of the Seton Hall library were very patient in responding to numerous queries. Grants from the Seton Hall University

Faculty Research Council and the Lucius N. Littauer Foundation speeded the research and writing of the book. Seton Hall University, a Roman Catholic institution, provided a congenial and supportive academic environment for working in American Jewish history, disproving George Bernard Shaw's assertion that a Catholic university is a contradiction in terms. I am also grateful to the editors of *Amerian Jewish History*, *Congress Monthly*, *Judaism*, *Midstream*, and the *World and I* for allowing me to try out some of my ideas on their unsuspecting readers. The manuscript was improved immeasurably by the staff at Johns Hopkins University Press, including designer Edward King, and my editors Diane Hammond, Jane McGarry, and Carol Zimmerman.

Finally, there is my family. My wife, Daryl, was helpful in keeping my household responsibilities down to a minimum while I completed the manuscript. My four sons—Marc, Alan, David, and Evan—also did their part by getting me on occasion to leave the computer and to concern myself with what was taking place in the "real" world, such as Little League baseball, the New York Yankees, high school basketball, and P. J. Carlesimo's Seton Hall Pirates. Thankfully, however, they disagreed with the words of Ecclesiastes (chapter 12, verse 12), "And furthermore, my son, be admonished: of making many books there is no end; and much study is a weariness of the flesh."

A Time for Healing
American Jewry since
World War II

CHAPTER ONE

THE AFTERMATH OF THE WAR

THE JOY felt by American Jews in 1945 as a result of the Allied victory over the Axis was tempered by sadness and forebodings not experienced by other Americans. As the impact of the Holocaust became more fully known, American Jews confronted the fact that many had lost close relatives and friends in Europe and that the world's most vibrant Jewish cultural and intellectual center had been destroyed. They realized also that they had escaped the fate of European Jewry only because they and their ancestors had decided to emigrate from Europe. Never did the Jewish folk saying "it is hard to be a Jew" appear truer than in the 1940s.

In the postwar era, the major responsibility for the economic and social rehabilitation of the survivors of the Holocaust necessarily rested primarily with American Jewry. But before assuming this task, American Jews had to answer the question of whether, in the aftermath of the Holocaust, Jewish existence continued to have any purpose. A minority of American Jews concluded that the price of identifying with the Jewish people had simply become too high. For them, the gas chambers of World War II meant the end of Jewish history. Would it not be better for everyone—Jews and Gentiles alike—if Jews disappeared rather than live under the shadow of virulent anti-Semitism? What rational case could be made, they asked, for affirming a Jewish identity after Auschwitz?

The classic answer of Jewish survivalists to such despair was theological. God had chosen the Jewish people for his own purposes. But the concept of the Jews as God's chosen people appeared absurd in the aftermath of World War II. God should choose some other people for a change and give the Jews a respite. The Holocaust also led some American Jews to doubt the existence of God. They were faced with the same problem that had confronted philosophers and theologians for centuries and would con-tribute to the "God is dead" thinking of the 1960s. Theologians termed this attempt to reconcile a just and all-powerful God with suffering and injustice *theodicy*. The question of theodicy had never been more troubling for Jews than in the years after World War II. How could God have allowed the slaughter of nearly six million Jews, over a million of whom were children? If God was not dead, at least he appeared deaf to the cries of the Jewish people.

Perhaps the most remarkable aspect of American Jewish life after 1945 was the rejection of this gospel of despair by the vast majority of American Jews. As a result of the decimation of European Jewry, the United States had become the most important Jewish community in the world. Nowhere else was there a Jewish population with its numbers, wealth, and intellec-tual resources. The burdens of world Jewish leadership had crossed the Atlantic and rested with these upstart Americans, most of whom were immigrants or the children of immigrants. Their tasks included not only succoring the remnants of European Jewry and aiding the struggling Jewish community in Palestine, but also creating a vibrant Jewish life in the United States that could give the younger generation a reason for continuing to identify as Jews. From a contemporary perspective, the most striking fact regarding the postwar American Jewish experience has been its success in fulfilling these responsibilities, the most awesome ever faced in the three centuries of American Jewish life.

For American Jews, World War II was a confrontation with reality in its bleakest form. Novelist Meyer Levin recounts in his autobiography the day he entered the Ohrdruf concentration camp in western Germany as a war correspondent accompanying American troops. "We had known. The world had vaguely heard. But until now no one of us had looked on this. It was as though we had penetrated at last to the center of the black heart, to the very crawling inside of the vicious heart." Samuel Glasshow, a Jewish soldier who had helped liberate the Woebbelin camp in northern Germany, responded similarly. "This horror was of such a nature that I couldn't wait to get away . . . and get that smell out of my nose and wipe the dirt off my feet and yet I went back. . . . I don't know what I went back for, I don't know, maybe to get a souvenir or bring it back to have something tangible to think about."[1]

Although the encounter of Jews back in the United States with the Holocaust was not as immediate, they were depressed by the picture of Nazi bestiality conveyed by movies and photographs. Critic Susan Sontag vividly remembered her reaction as an adolescent in California to photographs of Belsen and Dachau. "I felt irrevocably grieved, wounded, but a part of my feelings started to tighten; something went dead; something still is crying."[2]

For American Jews, the vulnerability of the Jewish condition was accentuated by the realization that the fate of European Jewry had mattered little to the victorious Allied powers. Military strategists had not been swayed by the need to liberate the Nazi death camps and to end the slaughter of the Jews as soon as possible. Neither the United States nor Great Britain had favored admitting a significant number of Jewish refugees either before or after 1939, and England adamantly opposed a large Jewish immigration into Palestine. Even the proposal presented to the U.S. Congress in the late 1930s to admit a mere twenty thousand Jewish children from Germany could not be passed without crippling amendments. In 1939 nearly two-thirds of Americans opposed special quotas for Jewish children from Europe, despite the fact that the alternative for them was remaining on a continent that Hitler dominated.

Wartime surveys of public opinion disclosed that even Chinese immigrants, the erstwhile "yellow peril," were viewed as more desirable than Jewish immigrants. The surveys also reveal that 80 percent of Americans rejected the immigration of large numbers of refugees, no matter who they were. European Jews at least had the solace of knowing, for what it was worth, that the American public did not differentiate between them and non-Jewish refugees. Both were considered undesirable. The reluctance of the Roosevelt administration to press for the liberalization of American immigration policy is understandable. Even if immigration had been a priority of the New Deal, President Franklin D. Roosevelt would not have expended valuable political capital on a doomed cause.[3]

Jews suspected that the Holocaust had not changed the attitude of the great powers and their citizens toward Jewish victimization. After the war the borders of Palestine remained closed to Jewish survivors. Even Roosevelt, a revered figure among American Jews, had remarked upon returning from the Yalta Conference of February 1945 that his brief meeting with the King of Saudi Arabia had finally clarified to him the Palestine controversy. If Palestine was not to be an option, where could the survivors of the Holocaust resettle? Few wanted to return to eastern Europe, where anti-Semitism remained strong. After 1945 Jews continued to be murdered in Poland. Furthermore, there was little likelihood of a change in American immigration policy to admit a significant number of displaced European Jews.

The revelations of the Holocaust did not have a significant impact on American public opinion immediately after the war. The award-winning movie *Stalag 17* (1953), for example, portrayed the conditions in a prisoner-of-war camp in Germany without once mentioning anti-Semitism or the fate of Europe's Jews. Movies and books on the Holocaust would not make an impact in the United States until at least a decade after the war's end. Evidently during the cold war the American public could be concerned with only one totalitarian power at a time. The threat from the Soviet Union preempted interest in the horrors of Nazi Germany, while the status of West Germany as an American ally made Americans reluctant to embarrass Germans by drawing attention to their recent past.

American attitudes toward immigration reflected public indifference to the Holocaust. Most Americans remained opposed to the admission of large numbers of refugees, Jewish or otherwise. Sixty percent of the respondents to one 1948 poll believed a "special limit" should be placed on the number of Jewish displaced persons allowed to immigrate to the United States, while only 10 percent supported unrestricted immigration. Whether the public's attitude toward immigration was primarily shaped by anti-Semitism or by a general dislike of all immigration is difficult, if not impossible, to determine. Some opponents of immigration were undoubtedly motivated by the widespread but mistaken perception that the overwhelming number of displaced persons were Jews. Other Americans emphasized that immigrants might take jobs from native Americans. Certainly the public was far more sympathetic to eastern and central European Christians who fled Communist tyranny during the 1940s and 1950s than it had been to those who had attempted to escape from the Nazis during the 1930s and World War II.[4]

The public attitude regarding the Palestine question was also not without anti-immigrant overtones. The vast majority of Americans favored the Jewish cause and supported the creation of a Jewish state in Palestine. Americans believed the Holocaust had demonstrated the need for a Jewish homeland, and most believed the Jews had religious, legal, and historical claims on Palestine. Christian fundamentalist groups saw a Jewish homeland as a harbinger of the Second Coming. A Jewish state, Americans believed, would also relieve the United States of any responsibility for absorbing large numbers of Jewish displaced persons.

Nativism continued to shape postwar American immigration policy. William Chapman Revercomb, a West Virginia Republican and one of the most influential and fervent senatorial opponents of immigration, claimed that the European displaced persons were procommunist, a curious charge since none of them wished to settle in the Communist states behind the Iron Curtain. "Many of those who seek entrance into this country have little concept of our form of government," Revercomb said in 1947. "Certainly it would be a tragic blunder to bring into our midst those imbued with a communistic line of thought when one of the most important tasks of this Government today is to combat and eradicate communism from this country."[5]

American Jews feared that the widespread domestic anti-Semitism of the 1930s and World War II would continue after 1945. Public opinion polls in 1938 reveal that, while Hitler was very unpopular among Americans, most believed that Germany's Jews were partially responsible for their own persecution by the Nazis, and only a small majority supported their government's official protest of the Crystal Night riots in Germany in November 1938. According to polling data, American anti-Semitism reached its peak *during* the war. This was despite the efforts of the national and local governments to eradicate anti-Semitism. The two most important World War II novels written by American Jews—Norman Mailer's *The Naked and the Dead* and Irwin Shaw's *The Young Lions*—both discuss the presence of anti-Semitism within the military.[6]

Efforts to instill a sense of national unity, exemplified by the song "When Those Little Yellow Bellies Meet the Cohens and the Kellys" and by Hollywood war movies featuring servicemen who were identifiably Jewish, were unable to stem the growth of anti-Semitism during the war. Although most Americans interpreted the struggle between the United States and Germany as a conflict between democracy and totalitarianism, this did not lead to a revulsion from anti-Semitism, the most salient element within Nazi ideology.[7]

Before and during the war a large percentage of Americans accepted anti-Semitic stereotypes. Public opinion surveys of the late 1930s and early 1940s disclose that nearly two-thirds of Americans believed Jews had "objectionable traits" such as being mercenary, clannish, pushy, crude, and domineering. The most important stereotype featured the unscrupulous and greedy Jewish businessman. Over one-half of Gentile Americans believed Jewish businessmen to be less honest than other businessmen, while only 3 percent believed them to be more honest.[8]

Such attitudes constricted economic and social opportunities for Jews. A survey of employment advertisements appearing in 1942 in the *New York Herald* and *New York Times* reveal that almost a third of the firms seeking employees wanted only Christian applicants. Prejudice was particularly widespread in heavy industry, utilities, and—contrary to the common view of Jewish dominance in finance—in banking. Presumably even the Jewish owners of the *Times* would have had difficulty finding employment in companies advertising in their own paper. This did not prevent them from running such ads. At the same time, young Jews experienced difficulty in gaining admission to elite universities and to medical and law schools.[9]

While most of the anti-Semitic stereotypes in this era were ancient, a new aspect was the image of the Jew as warmonger. The most famous example of this was Charles Lindbergh's September 1941 speech, "Who Are the War Agitators?" Given before an America First audience in Des Moines, Iowa, this speech differentiated between "us," namely Americans who wished to stay out of World War II, and "them," those disloyal groups agitating to bring America into the European conflict. They included America's Jews. While Jews could not be blamed "for looking out for what they believe to be their own interests," Lindbergh said, "we also must look out for ours. We cannot allow the natural passions and prejudices of other peoples to lead our country to destruction."[10]

Lindbergh's picture of Jews conspiring to drag the United States into war reflected the widespread belief that American Jews were too powerful. In 1941, isolationist Senator Burton K. Wheeler of Montana cautioned native Americans about the pro-war propaganda of immigrant and largely Jewish "Hollywood Hitlers." "Gifted in the arts of corruption and bribery," the movie moguls have "debauched legislatures; they have elected and controlled governors. The tentacles of this octopus reach not only into the state legislatures but at times into the Congress of the United States." This exaggeration of the power of American Jews was common. During World War II, from one-third to two-thirds of Americans believed America's Jews had too much political and economic influence. In 1944, American Jews were considered to be a greater national "menace" than German-Americans or Japanese-Americans.[11]

The belief that Jews were warmongers became more significant after 7 December 1941. Jews were a convenient scapegoat for the frustrations and deprivations of wartime life. Jewish businessmen were accused of profiteering, Jews were charged with shirking military service, and Jewish soldiers were accused of avoiding dangerous duty and of being cowardly under fire. Wartime surveys disclosed that over a quarter of Americans believed Jews to be less patriotic than other Americans, while over a third believed they were reluctant to serve in the military. This anti-Semitism would dissipate with the relaxation of wartime stresses after 1945.[12]

Modern American anti-Semitism peaked in 1944. One-third of the respondents to a poll that year said they would join or at least sympathize with an anti-Semitic political campaign. But, it must be noted, when offered this opportunity they failed to take advantage of it. Gerald L. K. Smith ran for president in 1944 as a third-party candidate on a blatantly anti-Semitic platform. While Roosevelt won 25.6 million votes and his Republican opponent Thomas Dewey got 22 million votes, Smith received the grand total of 1,781 votes. He had managed to get on the ballot only in Michigan and Texas. Smith's dismal showing is typical of the failure of anti-Semitism to become an important force in American politics. Without a system of proportional representation, voters have been reluctant to waste their ballots on doomed third-party candidates. In addition, more visible minorities, such as blacks and Asians, have deflected prejudice away from Jews.[13]

With the end of the fighting, American Jews debated how they should respond should anti-Semitism continue at or near its wartime level. Previously, Jews had gone out of their way to be as inconspicuous as possible, hoping to persuade Gentiles that they presented no threat to American culture. Jewish entertainers such as Nathan Birnbaum (George Burns), Julius Garfinkle (John Garfield), Marion Levy (Paulette Goddard), and Betty Perske (Lauren Bacall) had anglicized their names. (Gentile performers such as John Wayne and Cary Grant also had changed their names.) Other Jews had changed their noses, while Danny Kaye had dyed his hair. This assimilationist impulse also resulted in the widespread phenomenon of Jews hanging stockings and placing trees in their homes at Christmas.

In a 1941 article titled "Red, White, and Blue Herring," Jerome N. Frank, a former chairman of the Securities and Exchange Commission and Harvard Law School professor, attempted to reassure the readers of the *Saturday Evening Post* that Jews posed no threat to the United States. American Jews, he said, did not endanger other Americans because Jews were too differentiated economically, socially, and culturally to comprise a unified interest group. According to Frank, Jews overwhelmingly rejected traditional Judaism, Zionism, and all other ideologies that isolated them from other Americans.

Zionists were mere "sojourners" in America and had little support among America's Jews. Only immigrants continued to accept traditional Judaism, while thankfully the native-born "have rejected all or most of the old Jewish customs." Furthermore, Jews did not possess any unique characteristics that would prevent their rapid and complete assimilation. "The proportion of intellectuals or duds or bores or incompetents or mediocrities among American Jews is just about the same as one would find if he took any group selected at random—say, all red-headed or blue-eyed Americans." Whether many people were convinced by this dubious venture into pop ethnography is questionable. In any case, the readers of the *Saturday Evening Post* would soon be concerned with other matters. Frank's article appeared in the magazine's 6 December 1941 issue.[14]

American Jews had no reason to be optimistic that the efforts of Frank and others to reassure the Gentiles would be successful. On the contrary, they feared that anti-Semitism would increase after 1945. This expectation was based on the overwhelming importance they attributed to economic factors in causing anti-Semitism. It was no coincidence, they believed, that Hitler had assumed power in Germany at the very depth of the Great Depression. The spread of the second Ku Klux Klan and the racist immigration legislation of the 1920s had occurred at a time of economic hardship in much of rural America. Anti-Semitism flourished, it was believed, only during hard times, when it provided the economically ravaged with scapegoats.

The economic prognosis for postwar America was not favorable. Virtually every economic pundit predicted a postwar recession at least as bad as that which had occurred after World War I. Modern war, it was believed, was so disruptive of economic relationships that a postwar recession was virtually inevitable. Furthermore, the depression of the 1930s had demonstrated that capitalism was inherently unstable. Without the taming of the business cycle, there was no assurance that future depressions along the lines of that of the thirties would not take place. If Germany, the most socially and culturally advanced nation in Europe, could succumb to an orgy of anti-Semitism led by so unlikely a figure as Hitler, what assurance was there that the United States was invulnerable? Certainly the data from the wartime public opinion polls were not sanguine.

Less than one week after the official Japanese surrender on 2 September 1945, an event took place in Atlantic City, New Jersey, that belied these fears and, although American Jewry did not realize it at the time, prefigured their postwar condition. On 8 September, Bess Myerson of the Bronx became the first (and until now, only) Jewish Miss America. There could be no more dramatic contrast between the status of Jews in the United States and in Europe than Myerson's victory, coming exactly four months after the defeat of Nazi Germany. A Jew had received the most important American award for beauty at the same time that the remnants of continental European Jewry were attempting to recover from the greatest tragedy in Jewish history. The selection of Bess Myerson as Miss America signaled the postwar movement of American Jews into the American mainstream.

Myerson had entered the Miss New York City contest almost on a lark. She was then studying music, and her father, a house painter, could not afford to buy a good piano. One of her sisters encouraged Bess to enter the contest in the hope of making enough money to purchase one. After winning the New York City competition, Myerson moved on to the Atlantic City pageant, where the winner would receive a five-thousand-dollar scholarship. If successful, she planned to use the scholarship to further her music education.

Myerson's triumph was important for Jews not merely because she was Jewish but also because of the type of Jew she was. She was not a product of a gilded ghetto and an assimilated family. Her parents were part of the Jewish immigrant, working-class, left-wing culture of New York City. Myerson's family spoke Yiddish at home, she briefly attended an afternoon socialist Yiddish school (the Sholem Aleichem Folkschule), and she had participated in demonstrations in behalf of radical causes. Her family lived in the Sholom Aleichem Cooperative Houses, an apartment complex inhabited by Jewish radical families, which was located in a solidly Jewish neighborhood. Here the favorite adult avocation was debating the relative merits of socialism and communism.

Myerson further endeared herself to America's Jews because she rebuffed suggestions by some of the Miss America pageant officials that she call herself Beth Meredith or some other name not so obviously Jewish. For many Jews, Myerson was "one of us," and her fate became entwined with their own. Complete strangers came up to Myerson during the week of competition at Atlantic City and told her how much they were pulling for her and how important her victory would be for them personally and for Jews everywhere. A New York clothing manufacturer provided her with all her evening gowns at no cost so that she could represent American Jewry in style.

With her triumph, Myerson became the most famous contemporary Jewish woman. "Bess Myerson was the most important female image in your life," one Jewish woman, then a teenager, recalled. "We didn't just know about her. We *felt* her." Every young American Jewish girl could now strive to follow in Myerson's footsteps, to become, like her, a true Jewish American princess. (A decade later, young Jewish girls would model themselves after the heroine of Herman Wouk's novel *Marjorie Morningstar*.) The residents of the Sholom Aleichem Houses and other left-wing Jews, for whom bathing beauty contests exemplified the decadence and sexism of capitalism, rooted as hard for Myerson as did more acculturated Jews. The news that a Jew had been chosen Miss America even caused celebrations among Jewish refugees in the European displaced persons camps and made them even more determined to relocate to the golden land of America, where a Jew could become a female icon.

The selection of Bess Myerson as Miss America of 1945 was incongruous. It was remarkable for a Jew—especially the child of poor, radical, New York immigrants—to become the exemplar of American womanhood at a time of anti-Semitism and opposition to large-scale immigration of Jewish refugees. This, of course, was why American Jews were so enchanted by Myerson. Her individual triumph was also their collective victory over bigotry. Myerson symbolized the promise of American life, and she made them prouder as Jews and more confident about their future as Americans. Seemingly, there was nothing in America to which they could not now aspire. This amalgam of ethnic pride, social mobility, and acculturation that infused the events of September 1945 foreshadowed the postwar American Jewish experience, while Myerson's own career exhibited that hunger for social and economic mobility and disdain for the values of the world of her fathers that was so characteristic of the second generation of Jews. For the next four decades, Myerson was a beloved figure among American Jews. Her endorsement was eagerly sought by ambitious New York City politicians since it supposedly carried great weight among the city's Jews who remembered the night of 8 September 1945 as one of the most memorable and meaningful in their lives.[15]

American Jews had another cause for celebration during September 1945. On 30 September, the last day of the major league baseball season, Hank Greenberg hit a ninth inning grand slam home run against the St. Louis Browns to win the American League pennant for the Detroit Tigers. "Goddam that dirty Jew bastard, he beat us again," muttered one member of the runner-up Washington Senators. Greenberg went on to lead the Tigers to victory over the Chicago Cubs in the World Series, hitting over .300 and two home runs and batting in seven runs.

French-born Jacques Barzun, a distinguished Columbia University professor, once remarked that "to know the heart and mind of America one must learn baseball." As part of their acculturation, Jews became great baseball fans. They passionately supported their home teams, and many leading baseball writers have been Jews. Novelists like Bernard Malamud, Philip Roth, Chaim Potok, and Mark Harris wrote about the sport. One reason for this fascination with the national pastime has been the belief of "greenhorns" that a knowledge of the game would transform them into real Americans. The road to Americanization led through Yankee Stadium, the Polo Grounds, and Fenway Park.

For Jewish baseball fans, World War II unofficially ended on 14 June 1945, the day Greenberg made his triumphal return to baseball after over four years in the military. He was the first major league veteran to return to the big leagues, and no player had ever successfully resumed his major league career after such a long hiatus. Fans wondered whether Greenberg could be the first. He surprised the skeptics by hitting .311 in seventy-eight games. Among his eighty-four hits were thirteen home runs. He would have won the league batting championship had he been at the plate more often.

To know the heart and mind of American Jews in 1945 one had to be familiar with their love affair with Hank Greenberg. He became bigger than life to them from the moment he entered the major leagues in 1933, and during the next dozen years a hagiography transformed him into a Jewish demigod. Greenberg was the long and fervently anticipated Jewish baseball star whose accomplishments would demonstrate that Jews could master this most American of games.

Greenberg's background was familiar to American Jews. Most lived in areas similar to his Crotona Park neighborhood in the Bronx, not far from Bess Myerson's home. They more readily identified with him than with, for instance, Buddy Myer, the second baseman of the Washington Senators who had been born in Ellisville, Mississippi. Greenberg's success in a sport dominated by players from America's small towns, particularly those of the South, endeared him to Jews familiar with the nativist complaints about the aliens who lived in the tenements and high-rise apartments of New York City.

From 1933 through 1947 Greenberg was by far the most prominent

American Jewish athlete and arguably the nation's most famous Jew. He was the American League's Most Valuable Player in 1935 and 1940 and, in 1956, became the first Jew elected to the Baseball Hall of Fame. (Sandy Koufax is the only other Jewish member of the Hall of Fame.) Greenberg captured the nation's attention in 1938 when he almost surpassed Babe Ruth's 1927 record of sixty home runs in a season. Greenberg remained ahead of Ruth's home run pace of 1927 until the final week of the season. He finished with fifty-eight home runs. His challenge to the most hallowed record in American sports took place against the backdrop of the approaching European war and the rapid growth of anti-Semitism in the United States and abroad. Greenberg's glorious 1938 season symbolized to Jews the opportunities of American life, particularly since Detroit was home to both Henry Ford, America's leading anti-Semite of the 1920s, and Charles E. Coughlin, the notorious anti-Semitic radio priest of the 1930s.

Greenberg realized the significance of his assault on the Babe's record. "Sure, there was added pressure being Jewish," he recalled. "How the hell could you get up to home plate every day and have some son of a bitch call you a Jew bastard and a kike and a sheenie and get on your ass without feeling the pressure?" Greenberg knew he was a Jewish standardbearer. "I just had to show them that a Jew could play ball. . . . I came to feel that if I, as a Jew, hit a home run, I was hitting one against Hitler."

For Jews, the most important aspect of Greenberg's popular image was his seeming pride in being Jewish. His finest moment for them took place at the end of the 1934 season. That year he played in 153 of 154 games. Greenberg refused to play on 19 September because it was Yom Kippur. Overnight he became renowned throughout America. Americans admired his decision. Edgar Guest's poem "Speaking of Greenberg" praised the slugger:

> Came Yom Kippur—holy fast day world wide over to the Jew—
> And Hank Greenberg to his teaching and the old tradition true
> Spent this day among his people and he didn't come to play.
> Said Murphy to Mulrooney, "We shall lose the game today!
> We shall miss him on the infield and shall miss him at the bat,
> But he's true to his religion—and I honor him for that!"

Future Jewish ballplayers, most notably Sandy Koufax, would follow Greenberg's example and also not play on Yom Kippur.

Much to his surprise, Greenberg was applauded when he appeared in a

Detroit synagogue on the Day of Atonement. Jews chose to overlook the fact that he had played on the first day of Rosh Hashanah on 10 September, when the Tigers were in the midst of a hot pennant race with the New York Yankees. In fact, he hit two home runs that day to defeat the Red Sox, 2–1. Gentile fans, particularly in Detroit, saw this as a sign of divine approbation of Greenberg's decision to play. In contrast to Greenberg, Barney Ross, the Jewish world welterweight boxing champion, refused that year to allow a rained-out title fight to be rescheduled for Rosh Hashanah. Jews also ignored the fact that, by the time of Yom Kippur, the Tigers had clinched the American League pennant, their first one in a quarter of a century, and that Greenberg's absence from the lineup had little significance.

Nevertheless, nothing could tarnish the Jews' image of Greenberg. Shirley Povich, the longtime Jewish sports writer for the *Washington Post,* described the Tiger slugger as "the perfect standard-bearer for Jews. Hank was smart, he was proud, and he was big." Greenberg refused to be intimidated by anti-Semitic taunts. The epithets directed at him included "Jew bastard," "pants presser," and "kike son of a bitch." The heckling of Greenberg was so vicious during the second game of the 1935 World Series that the home plate umpire threatened to throw several of the Chicago Cubs out of the game if they did not desist. For American Jews, Greenberg's struggle against anti-Semitism was their struggle, and his victory over hatred and injustice was theirs also.

In 1941, Greenberg's stature among Jews and the general public grew even further. He was the first important ballplayer to be drafted into the armed forces. Though mustered out of the army a few days before Pearl Harbor, he promptly enlisted into the army air force, the first major leaguer to do so after 7 December 1941. Greenberg served in the military for forty-nine months and came out of the service a hero. Americans admired him for sacrificing his baseball career to serve his country. Jews pointed to Greenberg as proof that Jews did not shirk their military obligations.

A few months after the 1945 season, Greenberg married Carel Gimbel, the daughter of Bernard Gimbel, the New York City Jewish department store magnate. The wedding, performed by a justice of the peace in Brunswick, Georgia, and not by a rabbi, was more indicative of Greenberg's true Jewish identity than the mythology that had enveloped him for over a decade and was a forecast of the Greenbergs' future relationship with things Jewish.

Greenberg became an executive with the Cleveland Indians after his playing days ended in 1947. Uninvolved in Jewish affairs, the Greenbergs never joined a synagogue or even a Jewish country club while in Cleveland. Hank's interests focused on making the Indians a pennant contender, and Carel's were focused on the city's cultural life. Greenberg sought to shield his three children from the prejudice he had experienced in the thirties. The Greenberg family never attended religious services or celebrated any Jewish festivals, and the children did not receive any Jewish education. In fact, they were scarcely conscious of even being Jewish. Steve Greenberg, one of the two Greenberg sons, attended a New England prep school. When he entered Yale and was asked his religion, he responded, "Congregational."

Hank Greenberg's attitude toward Judaism and Jewishness was not uncommon among second-generation Jews, the so-called lost generation. Growing up in heavily Jewish neighborhoods, they took being Jewish for granted and saw little need to dwell on this fact. They were torn between the Jewish world of their parents and the American world of the streets. Greenberg was alienated from Judaism at an early age. He was completely bored by Hebrew school, and he resented the time it took away from playing ball. He identified Judaism and Jewishness with the drab immigrant life of his parents. How could these compete with the alluring world of baseball? He eventually concluded that all organized religion, including Judaism, was a con game. After divorcing his first wife, Greenberg married an actress, Mary Jo Tarola. It was of no concern to him that she was not Jewish. Not surprisingly, there was no Jewish element in the memorial service at his funeral in 1986.[16]

Greenberg, however, never changed his name or denied being Jewish. He was always quick to confront anti-Semites. Although he never visited Israel, he prized the Jewish state. Most of his charitable contributions went to Jewish causes. He thought that Jews should give to Jewish institutions and Christians to Christian institutions. The children of immigrants who rooted for Hank Greenberg knew what they were doing, for he was one of them in ways other than simply ethnic background. His huge ambition, his eagerness to make the most of America's opportunities, his secularism and disdain for the ways of his parents, his admiration for Israel, and his ambivalence regarding his Jewish background stamped Greenberg as a prototypical member of the second generation. He and Bess Myerson provided American Jews with heroes at a time when they were sadly in need of them.

In 1979, Andrew Kopkind, a staff writer for the *Village Voice,* reflected on what Myerson and Greenberg had meant to him in 1945. At that time,

Kopkind was ten years old and living in New Haven, Connecticut. "I can think of no public personages in all the succeeding years whom I've followed with such fawning," he wrote. They were

> secular saints, . . . symbols of a sudden legitimacy which my family
> and friends seemed to sense in a nation under reconstruction. Hank
> and Bess were winners, like DiMaggio and Grable—only smarter.
> They were as American as apple pie and the Fourth of July—and as
> Jewish as *knishes* and Yom Kippur. They belonged to a race of victors,
> not victims. . . . For the first time, the Jews had successfully crossed
> over from ethnic favorites to national heroes without being isolated or
> absorbed: they had arrived without being assimilated or stereotyped.

September 1945, Kopkind claimed, saw the revenge of these eastern European Jews on their German Jewish detractors. For three-quarters of a century, America's German Jews had sought to "civilize" these crude, backward, and poor immigrants from eastern Europe. "More polish and less Polish" was supposedly the unofficial motto of New York's Harmonie Club, a bastion of the city's "Our Crowd." Now eastern Europeans, according to Kopkind, had achieved social parity with their snooty critics. "The *Deutsche* were defeated on all fronts; the hour of the Litvak had struck."[17]

Philip Gleason, the prominent University of Notre Dame authority on American ethnic history, persuasively argued that "cultural pluralism in all its ambiguities and complexities is the critical legacy of World War II in respect to American identity." Certainly this was true of American Jews. "The experiences of the war years," Lucy S. Dawidowicz wrote, "had a transfiguring effect on American Jews and on their ideas of themselves as Jews."[18]

World War II was the great watershed in the history of American Jewish identity. Military service broadened the cultural perspective of Jewish servicemen, and American Jewry emerged from the struggle convinced that they were no longer an exotic ethnic and religious minority but an integral part of American culture. At least in their own eyes, they had finally arrived, both as American Jews and as Jewish Americans. Bess Myerson and Hank Greenberg were proof that, contrary to the fears of the pessimists, America really was different.

Prior to World War II, this notion would have seemed bizarre to some American Jews. In 1922, for example, the eminent Harvard philosopher Harry Austryn Wolfson had suggested that Jews accept the permanence of

American anti-Semitism. Writing at a time when Congress was busy restricting the flow of Jews into America and the Ku Klux Klan was growing rapidly, Wolfson stated that being Jewish was a disability to be endured forever. "There are certain problems of life for which no solution is possible," he wrote in a pamphlet with the apt title *Escaping Judaism*. "Because of our Judaism we must be prepared to give up some of the world's goods even as we must be prepared to make sacrifices because of other disadvantages with which we may happen to be born." Not all men are born equal. "Some are born blind, some deaf, some lame, and some are born Jews." The common lot of Jews, even in America, was "to be isolated, to be deprived of many social goods and advantages." Even the president of Wolfson's own institution would soon suggest that restrictions be placed on the number of Jews admitted to Harvard College.[19]

After 1945, the Jews who agreed with Wolfson's gloomy analysis declined in number. The war had diminished any conflict they might have perceived between their identities as Americans and as Jews. As servicemen and civilians, they had made important contributions to this greatest of all American undertakings. The war saw the merging of Jewish and American fates. Nazi Germany was the greatest enemy of both Jewry and the United States. For Jews, participation in the war effort was an ethnic and religious as well as a patriotic imperative. Anti-Semitism was no longer merely one of many American prejudices. Since anti-Semitism was the key element in the ideology of Nazi Germany, the American anti-Semite was in effect allying himself with America's mortal foe.

To Jews of the postwar era, their longstanding claim that anti-Semitism was un-American appeared more convincing than ever. They no longer viewed anti-Semitism as an inevitable aspect of American life, as did Wolfson. They now saw it as an aberration, an anachronism, a deviation from fundamental American principles. Jews now sought to eliminate anti-Semitism completely rather than to contain its influence. After the Holocaust, anti-Semitism meant not merely the exclusion of Jews from clubs, exclusive neighborhoods, and elite colleges. It also involved mass murder. To accept quietly any form of anti-Semitism, many believed, would be a cowardly betrayal of the six million European Jewish victims of Hitler.

Predictably, Jews exhibited a new militancy regarding anti-Semitism and a new unity in opposing it. The American Jewish Committee, the American Jewish Congress, the Anti-Defamation League of B'nai B'rith, and the various local community relations councils joined together in a crusade against anti-Semitism. In 1944 the various national and local Jewish defense agencies established the National Community Relations Advisory Council to coordinate their activities and to act as a clearinghouse in the campaign against bigotry. After the war, these agencies sponsored research in the social and psychological roots of anti-Semitism, lobbied on the state and federal levels for antidiscriminatory legislation, pressured colleges and professional schools to admit more Jews, challenged discriminatory behavior in the courts, and sponsored local programs to overcome prejudice.[20]

Jewish leaders tried to make sure that the rest of the country would not forget the wartime contributions of Hank Greenberg and other Jewish servicemen. This was not the first time that Jews had publicized their wartime exploits. Haym Salomon after the American Revolution and Washington, D.C., attorney Simon Wolf after the Civil War had compiled lists of Jews who had fought in the recent wars. In 1946 the Jewish Welfare Board published a two-volume work describing the Jewish contribution to the war effort. It listed over half a million Jews who had served in the armed forces, eleven thousand who had died in combat, twenty-four thousand who had been wounded, and thirty-six thousand who had been decorated. The most important of these casualties was Rabbi Alexander Goode.[21]

Rabbi Goode was one of the four chaplains killed in action in 1943 when the military transport SS *Dorchester* was torpedoed in the north Atlantic. After giving their life preservers to others on board, the chaplains went down with the ship, supposedly with their arms linked together. A 1948 U.S. postage stamp commemorating the heroism of the four chaplains bolstered the claim of Jews for complete equality. The stamp showed the faces of the four chaplains, a sinking ship, and a life preserver floating in the water. The stamp's legend read, "These IMMORTAL CHAPLAINS . . . INTERFAITH IN ACTION."[22]

The major purpose of this stamp and the JWB's volumes was to emphasize the multiethnic makeup of the American military. They rebutted the anti-Semitic accusation that Jews had shirked their military responsibilities and had profited from the war. In view of their great sacrifices, could Jews now be denied any of the benefits and burdens of American citizenship? American popular culture asked the same rhetorical question during and after the war.

In the 1949 film *The Sands of Iwo Jima,* starring John Wayne, a Jew dies in battle while saying the *Sh'ma,* the declaration of religious faith. *The Sands of Iwo Jima* was one of the many "platoon" movies that appeared during or shortly after World War II. These films argued the case for tolerance by emphasizing the heterogeneity of the American military. The military unit in a platoon movie contained a cross section of Americans: a Texas cowboy, a southern farmer, a Boston Irishman, a Pole from Chicago, a rich Anglo-Saxon New Englander, and a Brooklyn Jew. In a few of the platoon movies, it is the Jew who defines the meaning of the war. In *Action in the North Atlantic* (1943), Chip Abrams praises the American cause. In America "you've got a right to say what you want. That's what we're fighting this war for. The Czechs and Poles, they didn't have a chance to say or do what they wanted."

The presence of the Jew in wartime and post–World War II films reversed the "de-Semitizing" of Hollywood movies of the thirties. During the Great Depression, Hollywood film executives, who were mostly Jews, feared that films with Jewish characters and Jewish themes might exacerbate anti-Semitism and be unpopular at the box office. When novels were brought to the screen, the names of Jewish characters were frequently anglicized. Even anti-Nazi films such as *Confessions of a Nazi Spy* (1939) and *The Mortal Storm* (1940) did not stress the persecution of Germany's Jews.[23]

Because it assumed that platoon films would help the war effort, the federal government's Office of War Information encouraged their production. Jewish characters appeared in *Air Force* (1943), *Bataan* (1943), *Guadalcanal Diary* (1943), *The Purple Heart* (1944), *Winged Victory* (1944), *Objective Burma* (1945), and *A Walk in the Sun* (1945). Among the most important of these films was Warner Brothers' *Pride of the Marines* (1945).

At one point in *Pride of the Marines,* Lee Diamond, a wounded Jewish marine played by Dane Clark, describes his hopes for an America in which everyone will have a fair shake. "One happy afternoon when God was feeling good, he sat down and thought up a beautiful country and named it the USA. . . . Don't tell me we can't make it work in peace like we do in war. Don't tell me we can't pull together." These words are accompanied by the strains of "America the Beautiful" in the background. At the film's end, Diamond says, "Maybe some guys won't hire me because my name is Diamond and not Jones. 'Cause I celebrate Passover instead of Easter. . . . We need a country to live in where no one gets booted around for any reason."[24]

Nineteen forty-seven was the pivotal year in the history of Hollywood's portrayal of Jews. In that year there appeared *Crossfire* and *Gentleman's*

Agreement, Hollywood's two most significant films on American anti-Semitism. Their popularity led to the appearance in 1948 of *Open Secret* and *Prejudice,* two other movies on American anti-Semitism. The theme of *Crossfire* was that anti-Semitism was un-American because of the Jewish contribution to the war effort. Although its director, producer, and screenwriter were Gentiles, the film would not have been made had not Dore Schary, the head of production at RKO, enthusiastically supported the project.

Crossfire was based on Richard Brooks's novel *The Brick Foxhole,* which describes the experiences of a homosexual in the military. The victim in the film version is Joseph Samuels (Sam Levene), a Jew and decorated war hero, who is murdered by the anti-Semitic Sergeant Montgomery (Robert Ryan). This change in persona reflected not only Hollywood's reluctance to make a homosexual heroic but also its postwar willingness to have Jewish characters and topics appear on the screen.

Montgomery justifies his antagonism to Jews by claiming that they had shirked their military obligations during the war. "I've seen a lot of guys like Samuels, guys who played it safe during the war, scrounged around keeping themselves in civvies, had swell apartments and swell dames. Some are named Samuels and some got funnier names." Sergeant Kelley (Robert Mitchum) responds to Montgomery's bigotry. "He ought to look at the casualty list some time. There are a lot of funny names there too." When Montgomery is arrested for Samuels's murder, Kelley says to him, "My best friend, a Jew, is lying back in a foxhole at Guadalcanal. I'm gonna spit in your eye for him because we don't want people like you in the USA. There's no place for racial discrimination now." While some critics panned *Crossfire,* Bosley Crowther of the *New York Times* described it as "a frank and immediate demonstration of the brutality of religious bigotry." He gave the film an "unqualified *A* for effort."[25]

Crossfire was nominated for the 1947 Academy Award for best picture. The winner was Twentieth Century Fox's *Gentleman's Agreement,* which, to Fox's surprise, was also its most profitable film for the year. Ironically, influential Jews had tried to prevent the release of both *Crossfire* and *Gentleman's Agreement* because they feared an anti-Semitic backlash. *Time* magazine claimed that *Gentleman's Agreement* was "an almost-overpowering film"; the *Hollywood Reporter* called it "a profound occurrence in the history of the motion picture industry"; and the *New York Times* drew attention to its "dramatic forcefulness."

Gentleman's Agreement was based on Laura Z. Hobson's best-selling novel of the same name. It is Hollywood's finest and best known film about American anti-Semitism. In contrast to *Crossfire, Gentleman's Agreement* focused on the genteel anti-Semitism of the American upper crust who would never think of murdering a Jew. But neither would they think of living or working alongside one. The film implicitly argues that anti-Semitism would disappear if not for this tacit acquiescence of the upper class.

The hero of *Gentleman's Agreement* is Phil Green (Gregory Peck), a magazine writer whose editor has assigned him to write an article on contemporary American anti-Semitism. Green's research technique is novel. He pretends to be a Jew, and his article is titled "I Was Jewish for Eight Weeks." (Two decades later, John Howard Griffin used the same technique in researching his book *Black Like Me.*) When asked by his young son to tell him something about Jews, Green responds: "There are lots of different churches. Some people who go to them are Catholics. People who go to other churches are called Protestants. Then there are others who go to still different ones, and they're called Jews, only they call their churches synagogues and temples. . . . You can be an American and a Protestant or a Catholic or a Jew. Religion is different from nationality." This statement was typical of the postwar interfaith movement's simplistic belief that Jews were merely a religious group like Methodists or Presbyterians.

At the end of the movie, Green's mother praises her son's article. "Wouldn't it be wonderful, Phil," she says, "if it turned out to be everybody's century, when people all over the world, free people, found a way to live together?" Other persons received a different message from the film. A stagehand working on *Gentleman's Agreement* told Moss Hart, one of its scriptwriters, that he had loved the movie's moral lesson. "I'll never be rude to a Jew again because he might turn out to be a Gentile."[26]

Probably the most famous, and certainly the most popular, attempt to relate America's involvement in World War II to the struggle against anti-Semitism was Herman Wouk's 1951 novel, *The Caine Mutiny. The Caine Mutiny* won the 1952 Pulitzer Prize for fiction, has sold over three million copies, and has been published in seventeen foreign languages. It was made into a successful play, *The Caine Mutiny Court-Martial,* and into a very popular movie starring Humphrey Bogart, Van Johnson, and Fred Mac-Murray.

Wouk, an Orthodox Jew and a fervent American patriot, was a naval veteran of World War II. He participated in eight Pacific invasions and won four campaign stars. One of the central themes of his fiction is a dislike of deracinated intellectuals who undermine valuable religious and national traditions and social institutions. To readers unfamiliar with Wouk's outlook, Lt. Barney Greenwald's defense of Captain Queeg—"Old Yellowstain"—and his attack on the mutineers aboard the *Caine* seemed incongruous since most of the book had described Queeg's incapacity for command.

It is no coincidence that the leading advocate of the military virtues of discipline, honor, loyalty, and duty in *The Caine Mutiny* is the mutineers' Jewish lawyer. Greenwald's vigorous cross-examination of Queeg reveals the commander's demented mental condition and results in the acquittal of the mutineers. At a cocktail party celebrating the courtroom victory, a half-drunk Greenwald surprisingly turns on his erstwhile clients and accuses them of betraying their captain. Here Wouk emphasized the relationship between the American involvement in World War II and the struggle against anti-Semitism.

"See, while I was studying law 'n' old Keefer here was writing his play for the Theatre Guild and Willie here was on the playing fields of Prinshton," Greenwald says, "all that time these birds we call regulars—stupid Prussians, in the Navy and the Army, were manning guns." It was the efforts of people such as Queeg that had prevented the Nazis from turning the Jews of America into soap. "Yes, even Queeg, poor sad guy, yes, and most of them not sad at all, fellows, a lot of them sharper than any of us, don't kid yourself, best men I've ever seen, you can't be good in the Army or Navy unless you're goddam good. Though maybe not up on Proust 'n' *Finnegan's Wake* and all." Greenwald is ashamed for having helped destroy Queeg. "Thass why I'm drunk. Queeg deserved better at my hands. I owed him a favor, don't you see? He stopped Hermann Goering from washing his fat behind with my mother."[27]

In later books, Wouk would continually return to this theme of the intertwining of American and Jewish destinies. In *This Is My God,* his only book on theology, he compared Jews and American sailors. "I have always thought that the Jewish place among mankind somewhat resembles the position of navy men among other Americans," he wrote. "Are the sailors and officers less American because they are in the navy? They have special commitments and disciplines, odd ways of dress, sharp limits on their freedom. They have at least in their own minds, compensations of glory, or of vital service performed. The Jews are not cut off from mankind by their faith, though they are marked different."[28]

Wouk continued to explore the relationship between Jewish and American fates in *The Winds of War* (1971) and *War and Remembrance* (1978). Both novels were best-sellers. Tens of millions of viewers also became familiar with the Wouk saga as a result of two lengthy television series based on the two books. Wouk's story follows the Christian Henry and Jewish Jastrow families through the 1930s and World War II. The families are related through the marriage of Byron Henry and Natalie Jastrow. While Byron Henry and his father Pug, two naval officers, fight the Axis in the Pacific and Europe, Natalie Jastrow and her uncle Aaron Jastrow are stranded in Hitler's Europe. Both are sent to Auschwitz, where Aaron dies and Natalie barely survives. Wouk emphasized the Jewishness of the Jastrows. Aaron, a former religious skeptic, returns to the Orthodoxy of his youth shortly before entering the gas chamber. *War and Remembrance* ends with the American victory over Hitler, the liberation of Natalie, and the flight of the remnants of European Jewry to Palestine, where they will help create the new state of Israel.

In 1980, Wouk wrote the introduction to *Self-Portrait of a Hero,* an English edition of the letters of the Israeli soldier Jonathan Netanyahu. The American-born Netanyahu was killed in July 1976, during Israel's rescue of over one hundred Jewish hostages held by pro-Palestinian terrorists at the Entebbe (Uganda) airport. The only Israeli to die in the operation, Netanyahu became a national hero in Israel. The rescue and Netanyahu's death occurred at the very moment when Americans were celebrating the two hundredth anniversary of the Declaration of Independence; the publication of Netanyahu's letters took place while American officials were being held hostage in Iran by the Ayatollah Khomeini. These coincidences were not lost on Wouk.

In his introduction, Wouk described the Entebbe raid as a beacon in the "dense gloom" in the struggle of civilization against terrorism. Netanyahu had died fighting or the freedom of all men. He had demonstrated that "love of country is noble, that self-sacrifice is rewarding, that to be ready to fight for freedom fills a man with a sense of worth like nothing else." The United States, Wouk said, had a thousand men similar to Netanyahu who were willing to sacrifice their lives for their country. America would need them "to stand guard in the night" if she was to "remain . . . the promise to the hundreds of millions of the oppressed that liberty exists, that it is the shining future, that they can throw off their tyrants, and learn freedom." Netanyahu's letters, Wouk concluded, "may tell us Americans, in the greatest land of the free, something about honoring our own young guardians in the night."[29]

In 1985, Wouk published *Inside, Outside,* a semiautobiographical novel. It recounted the life of David Goodkind, an American patriot and a fervent supporter of Israel. This "good kind" is an American on the "outside" and a Jew on the "inside." For Wouk, being a good American and a good Jew are simply different sides of the same coin. He makes this point crystal clear when he has Goodkind's year-long mourning period after the death of his father begin on 7 December 1941.

By the 1970s, Goodkind is a successful New York tax lawyer. Over the opposition of his wife and friends, he takes a temporary leave of absence to work in the White House during the last days of the Nixon administration. He is grateful to the president for his support of Israel during the 1973 Yom Kippur War, and he tells Nixon that the Jewish people will honor him for shipping arms to the Jewish state during its time of peril. Nixon in turn praises Goodkind for not having deserted him during the Watergate affair. "You've stayed aboard while some others were jumping ship. It's been appreciated." This struck some readers of *Inside, Outside* as a craven and undemocratic deference to authority. Goodkind, however, does not betray the president for the same reason that Barney Greenwald berates the mutineers on the *Caine*. Wouk valued duty and loyalty and wished to preserve intact institutions of tradition and stability such as the navy and the presidency.

World War II influenced other American Jewish writers and intellectuals besides Wouk. Some were induced to reconsider the stance of alienation fashionable during the 1930s and to see the creative possibilities in a symbiosis between American and Jewish identities. The earliest and most important manifestation of this occurred in November 1945, when the first issue of the monthly magazine *Commentary* appeared.

Commentary was sponsored by the American Jewish Committee, which had also funded its predecessor, the *Contemporary Jewish Record.* The AJC staff and lay leadership believed American Jewish writers and intellectuals had something important to say to the rest of the nation and that the time had finally come for the American Jewish community to contribute to the nation's intellectual life. The AJC's role in this grandiose goal was to subsidize a more ambitious and less parochial magazine than the *Contemporary Jewish Record,* one that would explore issues of importance to both America and American Jewry.

During its first decade, *Commentary* reflected the outlook and interests of Elliot E. Cohen, its first editor. Born in Mobile, Alabama, in 1899, Cohen was named after the English writer George Eliot, and grew up in a family in which ideas, books, and literature were taken seriously. Jewish topics were frequently discussed at the Cohen table. (The family's Creole cook even learned to make jambalaya with *gribenes,* a favorite eastern European Jewish dish, instead of with shrimp.) This early acquaintance with Jewish concerns influenced Cohen's choice of a career as an editor of Jewish magazines. From 1923 to 1931 he was the managing editor of the *Menorah Journal,* and in 1945 he became editor of *Commentary.* His main objective at both magazines was to treat Jewish issues seriously, to demonstrate that an involvement with Jewish matters could be reconciled with a commitment to the life of the mind. Cohen welcomed the opportunity of being the mentor to the secular Jewish writers who wrote for the *Menorah Journal* and *Commentary,* hoping that he could bring them back within a Jewish ambience.[30]

Despite its neutral title, there was never any doubt that *Commentary* was a Jewish publication. "The main difference between *Partisan Review* and *Commentary,*" Cohen once remarked, "is that we admit to being a Jewish magazine and they don't." Among the magazine's initial group of contributing editors were Salo W. Baron and Jacob R. Marcus, the two most distinguished historians of the Jewish people then living in the United States. Cohen presented his rationale for *Commentary* in his editorial "An Act of Affirmation," which appeared in the magazine's initial number.

Commentary, Cohen asserted, was an "act of faith" of post-Holocaust American Jewry "in the intellect, in the visions of visionary men, in the still, small voice of poets, and thinkers, and sages." Some outsiders viewed this "act of faith" as foolhardy, since the Holocaust had seemingly demonstrated the power of irrationality to triumph over the power of intellect. These doubters questioned whether Jewish identity would survive Auschwitz. They also wondered whether *Commentary*'s Jewish but nonparochial orientation would offend both universalists and Jewish tribalists. And would American Jews take time off from their rapid economic mobility and assimilation into the American mainstream to contemplate a serious treatment of Jewish topics?

Cohen argued in response that it was particularly incumbent on Jews to make this leap of faith since they, more than any other group, had experienced the hatred and irrationality threatening modern civilization. Because of the devastation of European Jewry, the responsibility of carrying forward the "common Jewish cultural and spiritual heritage" necessarily rested with American Jewry. The founding of *Commentary* was a vote of confidence in the intellectual maturity of the Jewish community, in Jewish "possibilities" in America, and in the prospect of shaping a creative American Jewish culture. "We have faith," Cohen concluded, "that out of the opportunities of our experience here, there will evolve new patterns of living, new modes of thought, which will harmonize heritage and country into a true sense of at-home-ness in the modern world. Surely, we who have survived catastrophe, can survive freedom, too."[31]

Cohen's use of the word *faith,* a term generally associated with religion, perhaps reflected a pessimism about the likelihood of *Commentary*'s success. Certainly there was no guarantee that Gentiles would take the magazine seriously or that Jewish intellectuals would want to write for it. And as Cohen well knew, it was still problematical whether there was a sufficient number of Jews who were interested in serious ideas and, at the same time, wished to remain Jews "in freedom." A successful *Commentary* would augur well for the future of American Jewry.

According to Norman Podhoretz, who succeeded Cohen as *Commentary*'s editor, Cohen had a "Grand Design" for the magazine. He wanted *Commentary* to increase the influence of American Jewish intellectuals by lessening their estrangement from the American Jewish establishment and from the national mainstream. This "modern-day Moses," in Podhoretz's words, wanted to lead the Jewish intelligentsia out of "the desert of alienation . . . and into the promised land of democratic, pluralistic, prosperous America where it would live as blessedly in its Jewishness as in its Americanness, safe and sound and forevermore, amen." Jewish writer Judd L. Teller believed that Cohen's grand design had been successful. By providing Jewish intellectuals with a forum for grappling seriously with Jewish concerns, *Commentary* had been responsible for a shift of posture "from Jewish self-consciousness to Jewish self-awareness."[32]

Commentary's staunch anticommunism during the 1940s and early 1950s stemmed in part from Cohen's goal of ending the alienation of the Jewish intelligentsia from the American mainstream. Jews, he believed, must be in the forefront of those defending America. As long as Cohen was its editor, *Commentary* described the Soviet Union as a totalitarian power, remained skeptical of Russian intentions, questioned whether a thaw had really taken place in American-Soviet relations after Stalin's death in 1953, advised Americans to maintain a strong military, and warned against the spread of neutralist sentiment in the Third World. During these years, *Commentary* also generally avoided drawing attention to America's social and economic failings.

One of the most eloquent dissenters from *Commentary*'s celebration of the status quo was Irving Howe, the eminent literary and social critic. Howe was a leading member of the New York Jewish intelligentsia and wrote frequently for both *Partisan Review* and *Commentary*. In 1946, *Commentary* published his semiautobiographical essay, "The Alienated Young Jewish Intellectuals." By the early 1950s, however, Howe had become dismayed by what he perceived to be the knee-jerk anticommunism of *Commentary* and the rightward drift of *Partisan Review*. He was particularly disturbed by *Partisan Review*'s 1952 symposium, "Our Country and Our Culture," which revealed the eagerness of former radicals to join in the national mood of celebration. Most writers, the editorial statement prefacing the symposium declared, were no longer alienated and now wished "to be a part of American life."

In 1954, *Partisan Review* published Howe's lengthy response titled "This Age of Conformity." This was a full-barreled attack on American intellectuals for allowing themselves to be co-opted by American capitalism and the war economy, for becoming partisans of bourgeois life, and for enlisting in the defense of American foreign policy. He urged intellectuals to return to the ranks of the outsiders, to remain true to the ideal of the intellectual as social critic. Howe believed *Commentary*'s obsession with the threat of communism had blinded it to the danger of McCarthyism and to a national mood of mindless conformity and self-satisfaction. *Partisan Review,* according to Howe, was not much better. Its editors seemed more concerned with atoning for their radical past than with providing a forum for discussing America's real problems. From Howe's perspective, there was an obvious need for an alternative magazine that would subject the status quo to fundamental criticism from the Left. Howe's most important contribution to puncturing the smugness of the Eisenhower era occurred in 1954 when he helped establish a new independent democratic socialist quarterly, appropriately titled *Dissent*.33

Dissent never fulfilled its founders' hopes of becoming a serious rival of *Partisan Review* or *Commentary,* although it did achieve a circulation of four thousand within three years. Sociologist Nathan Glazer wrote in *Commentary* that *Dissent*'s first issue had been a "disaster." In part, *Dissent* was a victim of circumstances over which it had no control. It was established at a time when socialism had lost most of its élan. *Dissent*'s editors knew, of course, that the prospects for socialism in America were bleak at best and that their prospective radical constituency was tiny. Even the editors themselves rejected most of the economic and political specifics of socialism. They preferred to describe themselves as "independent radicals" and to offer hazy prescriptions for the country's ills.[34]

To add to *Dissent*'s problems, by the early 1960s it faced competition on the Left from a revamped *Commentary*. Cohen, depressed for several years, committed suicide in May 1959. Norman Podhoretz became the magazine's new editor as of the February 1960 issue. This number featured the first installment of Paul Goodman's *Growing Up Absurd,* and this foreshadowed Podhoretz's determination to place *Commentary* on the port side of the social and political spectrum. In "The Issue," his introductory editorial which appeared in the February 1960 issue, Podhoretz made clear his rejection of *Commentary*'s previous hard-line anticommunism and sunny view of America. As editor, he was going to "take a fresh look at all the weary ideas and attitudes whose constant reiteration in the *Commentary* of the recent past . . . had made it so predictable." Ironically, the same charge of predictability would be directed at Podhoretz's *Commentary* during its neoconservative period commencing in the late 1960s.

Podhoretz hoped *Commentary* could play an important role in the revival of radical social criticism, which he correctly anticipated was on the horizon. The magazine's circulation skyrocketed from twenty thousand in 1960 to sixty thousand by 1966. The next year, war broke out between Israel and its Arab neighbors, and *Commentary* embarked upon a new phase of its history.[35]

Nineteen sixty-seven was a crucial year in the development of American Jewish consciousness. Twenty-two years after the end of World War II, American Jewry was confronted with the possibility of the destruction of a community containing nearly one-quarter of the world's Jews. The response of America's Jews, including intellectuals such as Podhoretz, to the Six-Day War of 1967 is inexplicable without considering World War II's historical legacy. The dramatic social and economic strides of American Jewry had not stilled the memories of World War II. America's Jews knew that Jews could no longer take their physical existence for granted. In the aftermath of World War II, Jewish survival became the most important Jewish imperative, even if this meant, as in the case of *Commentary,* a radical restating of Jewish interests.

CHAPTER TWO

THE DECLINE OF ANTI-SEMITISM

Among the most important aspects of the post–World War II history of America's Jews was their movement into the nation's social, cultural, and economic mainstream. Never were they more prosperous, culturally creative, and secure than in the postwar decades. After 1945, other Americans no longer viewed the Jews as merely another of the many exotic groups within America's ethnic and religious mosaic. Instead, they were now seen as comprising one of the country's three major religions. The years after 1945 also saw the emergence of Jews as an interest group that politicians courted as avidly as steel manufacturers, school teachers, and real estate speculators. American Jewry had entered its golden age.

American Jews witnessed a lowering of economic and social barriers after 1945 unprecedented in American history. However, because of their memories of the anti-Semitism of the 1930s and World War II, they continued to view Gentiles, in the words of the title of Jerome Weidman's popular postwar novel, as "the enemy camp." So strong was this lag in perception that Stuart E. Rosenberg, a rabbi and historian in Rochester, New York, entitled one of his books *America Is Different*. This effort at reassurance appeared in 1964, the same year in which, for the first time in history, a major political party selected as its presidential candidate a person with a Jewish background. (Barry Goldwater's father, Baron, was a Jew who had married a Protestant and raised his son as a Christian. One Jew quipped in 1964 that he always knew the first Jewish candidate for president would be an Episcopalian.) Of all the questions confronting American Jewry after 1945, few were more important than determining precisely how "different" America really was.

American Jews were ambivalent regarding their postwar situation. On the one hand, they conducted their lives seemingly oblivious to anti-Semitism. They made rapid economic and social strides, and they immersed themselves in all aspects of American culture. Some even became arbiters of American popular mores. Jews taught Americans how to dance (Arthur Murray), how to behave (Dear Abby and Ann Landers), how to dress (Ralph Lauren), what to read (Irving Howe, Alfred Kazin, and Lionel Trilling), and what to sing (Barry Manilow and Barbra Streisand).

America's Jews baffled Zionist ideologues. The most important element in Zionist ideology and the major rationale for the state of Israel was the belief that only a Jewish state could be free of anti-Semitism, which supposedly was endemic and permanent throughout the Diaspora. Surely, Zionist spokesmen and Israeli politicians asserted, America's Jews would eventually realize this and relocate en masse to Israel. Their refusal to do so could only be explained as a temporary hankering for the fleshpots of America. Jews, however, remained in America despite contributing billions of dollars to Israel, and even though the nurture of the Jewish state was an important element in their Jewish identity. American Jewry was perhaps the greatest of all Zionist failures. The aliyah (immigration to Israel) of America's Jews numbered not in the millions, or even in the hundreds of thousands, but in the thousands, and these came mainly from the ideological and religious fringes of American Jewish life. The American Jewish theme song was not "Hatikvah" but "God Bless America," a song written by Irving Berlin, a first-generation product of New York's Lower East Side.

On the other hand, despite the euphoria engendered by Bess Myerson and Hank Greenberg, American Jews exhibited a psychological insecurity that was never far from the surface. If their response to the option of immigration to Israel reflected the optimism of American Jews, their attitude toward postwar American anti-Semitism revealed their pessimism. They were convinced that anti-Semitism was pervasive and, at times, even growing, and they contributed large sums of money to B'nai B'rith's Anti-Defamation League and to other organizations fighting anti-Semitism. They looked askance at those who tried to calm their fears. This insecurity enabled the Simon Weisenthal Center of Los Angeles to run during the 1980s the most successful fund-raising operation of any domestic Jewish organization. With the exception of some Jewish intellectuals, there were few American Jews who dissented from this siege mentality, particularly during the immediate postwar decades.

Columbia University economist Eli Ginzberg, the son of Louis Ginzberg, an eminent Judaic scholar at the Jewish Theological Seminary, was part of this minority. In his 1949 volume, *Agenda for American Jews,* he warned American Jewry that a Jewish identity revolving around anti-anti-Semitism lacked a positive content and could not be the basis of a vibrant Jewish community. "Today at least among large numbers of American Jews," he wrote, "the 'defense activities' have usurped a position of priority. This was more or less inevitable since many of these Jews have lost all interest in positive Jewish values: their entire adjustment is externally oriented."[1]

Most American Jews viewed with disbelief the public opinion surveys of the 1940s and 1950s indicating that a dramatic decline in American anti-Semitism had taken place since 1945. This skepticism was understandable. Optimistic reports regarding the demise of anti-Semitism were not new. The most recent example had been that of Germany. The amelioration in the social and economic condition of German Jewry during the late nineteenth and early twentieth centuries had prompted some observers during the 1920s to predict the eventual end of anti-Semitism in Europe's then most cultured nation. Germany's subsequent history had demonstrated that it was more dangerous to underestimate than overestimate anti-Semitism, and that hatred of Jews could occur at unexpected times and in unanticipated places.

Because of Jewish history and their own experiences with prejudice and discrimination, American Jews exaggerated the extent and depth of postwar American anti-Semitism. Many exhibited what social psychologists termed *cognitive dissonance.* This is the conflict between perception and reality that occurs when people are confronted with facts that clearly contradict important beliefs. Religious groups that have predicted the imminent end of the world and Communists of the 1930s and 1940s who claimed that the Soviet Union was a progressive state and Stalin a democratic ruler are examples of groups who manifest cognitive dissonance. Students of such groups have shown that their convictions remain unchanged, and often are strengthened, when they encounter conclusive evidence refuting deeply held beliefs.

The cognitive dissonance of America's Jews was far more understandable. They were living in the shadow of the Holocaust and had themselves lived through an era during which American anti-Semitism had crested. They were continually reminded by American Jewish leaders of the hostility of the Gentiles and of the virulence of anti-Semitism. In 1947, for example, Isaiah M. Minkoff, the executive director of the National Community

Relations Advisory Council, warned that the seeming decline of anti-Semitic activity merely camouflaged the fact that the anti-Semites were "involved in their own postwar reconversion, seeking for and experimenting with new avenues of attack, exploring the possibilities of exploiting new issues, now that peace had deprived them of their war-time pretexts." Discrimination persisted against Jews in employment, housing, education, and at resorts, Minkoff said, while the public opinion polls indicated that there still existed "much latent anti-Semitic sentiment."[2]

This willingness to believe the worst about anti-Semitism continued throughout the postwar years. Meir Kahane, a Brooklyn rabbi with a checkered past, exhibited this type of thinking in its most intemperate form. In 1968, Kahane helped found the Jewish Defense League and later became its leader. In his books *Never Again!* and *Time to Go Home,* and in newspaper articles and speeches, Kahane emphasized the dangers facing America's Jews and pleaded with them to flee to Israel before it was too late. Kahane appealed mainly tò Jews living in declining lower-middle-class Jewish neighborhoods in New York City, many of whom were readers of the *Jewish Press,* a weekly Brooklyn Anglo-Jewish paper catering to religious zealots and right-wing Zionists. The *Press*'s lurid headlines constantly drew attention to the latest report of real and imaginary anti-Semitic incidents in the United States. The paper also carried advertisements for Kahane's Museum of the Potential Holocaust, located in Jerusalem. A typical advertisement declared that anti-Semitic movements were "growing quickly in membership and influence in America. They are gaining the sympathy and support of many of your neighbors. Hitler is their patron saint. Learn about them. The lesson might save your life."[3]

These notices were published in the 1980s, at a time when the economic, social, and political status of America's Jews had never been more secure and elevated. While the vast majority of American Jews did not support the politics of Kahane and the *Jewish Press,* a surprising number shared their forebodings. Every report of an anti-Semitic incident, whether serious or trivial, seemed to confirm the vulnerability of Jews, the hostility of the Gentiles, and the fatuousness of those claiming that anti-Semitism had ceased to be a major problem. During the 1940s and 1950s, this bleak view was not restricted to the uneducated and the gullible but was even shared by supposedly sophisticated scholars.

The migration of Jews from Germany during the 1930s included a small number of sociologists and social psychologists known collectively as the Frankfurt School. They included Theodor Adorno (half Jewish), Max Horkheimer, Leo Lowenthal, and Herbert Marcuse. The Frankfurt scholars fervently wished for the obliteration of fascism and anti-Semitism, which had driven them from Europe. Heavily influenced by Marxism, they argued that the destruction of anti-Semitism required the overthrow of the liberal capitalist society that had supposedly spawned fascism. Ironically, this liberal capitalist society had provided them with a refuge in the New World. "He who does not want to speak about capitalism," Horkheimer wrote in his 1939 essay "The Jews and Europe," "should also remain silent about fascism." Fascism was "the truth of modern society."[4]

During the war, several members of the Frankfurt School attended a conference hosted by the American Jewish Committee to examine religious and racial prejudice. This conference led to the creation of a Department of Scientific Research within the AJC. Horkheimer became the department's first director. His greatest achievement while heading the department was planning its five-volume series *Studies in Prejudice*. The most important and best known of these volumes was Adorno's *The Authoritarian Personality* (1950), written with Austrian psychologist Else Frenkel-Brunswik and Americans Daniel Levinson and Nevitt Sanford. The object of this book, as Horkheimer noted in his introduction, was to help eliminate prejudice by discovering its sources.

Three years before the appearance of *The Authoritarian Personality*, Adorno and Horkheimer had published *Dialectic of Enlightenment*. This volume contains a chapter called "Elements of Anti-Semitism," which anticipated some of the themes of *The Authoritarian Personality*. "Elements of Anti-Semitism" is an example of the tendency of European social scientists in the 1940s and 1950s to base their conclusions on abstract conceptualization rather than on historical and statistical data. Adorno and Horkheimer argued, for example, that modern anti-Semitism did not stem from mass discontent but from the injustices of liberal capitalism. German fascists, they wrote, were "liberals who wanted to assert their anti-liberal opinions."

"Elements of Anti-Semitism" was concerned with the danger of fascism in the United States rather than in postwar Europe, despite the fact that at no time in American history had the level and virulence of anti-Semitism come close to that of its European counterpart. If anti-Semitism was a product of liberal capitalism, and since the United States was the liberal capitalist society par excellence, then it followed that American Jews had more to fear from anti-Semitism than did European Jews. This syllogistic reasoning was a triumph of ideology over reality. In the actual world of the 1940s, Jews were infinitely less secure in Europe than in the United States.

Adorno and Horkheimer argued that in America the hatred for Jews had assumed a new shape, which they called the "ticket mentality." This was the tendency of Americans to vote the straight ticket of "aggressive big business." Equating capitalism with fascism and support for big business, they claimed that anyone who "subscribed to the destruction of the trade unions and the crusade against Bolshevism automatically subscribes also to the destruction of the Jews."[5]

The Authoritarian Personality is one of the most notable books in the history of psychology. It is deeply flawed, however, by its authors' unfamiliarity with, and lack of sympathy for, American social and cultural life. *The Authoritarian Personality* claims that the tensions and contradictions of American capitalism were responsible for the emergence of an authoritarian personality, which, in turn, was a major source of American prejudice, particularly anti-Semitism. As described by Adorno, a person with an authoritarian personality has a low tolerance for ambiguity and admires fascist and anti-Semitic movements. The authoritarian personality is frequently found among those with strong religious feelings and among those who had a rigid and repressed childhood.

Despite its conceptual brilliance, *The Authoritarian Personality* remains unconvincing. Its positing of an authoritarian personality as the cause of anti-Semitism seemed to be contradicted by suggestions that anti-Semitism could be combated simply by education without any radical changes in American society. At best, modification of personality is a long, difficult, and problematic process, particularly when one is concerned not with the personality of an individual but with personality traits found among a large number of persons. In addition, most of the book's readers concluded that, in explaining American anti-Semitism, it had unduly emphasized the subjective factor of personality at the expense of American history and the characteristics of the American economic, social, and political systems. Finally, as University of Chicago sociologist Edward Shils pointed out, *The Authoritarian Personality* was wrong in assuming that authoritarianism and dogmatism were to be found only among those on the political Right.[6]

If anti-Semitism stemmed largely from personality maladies, as *The Authoritarian Personality* argued, then a decrease in anti-Semitism would seem to require the alleviation of these disorders. By the time *The Authoritarian Personality* appeared in 1950, public opinion polls had revealed a significant decline in American anti-Semitism from its wartime levels. It was unlikely that the authoritarian personality, if in fact it actually existed, could have changed rapidly enough to be responsible for this decline. If not, then other factors must have been responsible. The personality thesis could be salvaged only if it was assumed that the polls had greatly underestimated the extent of anti-Semitism. This approach, of course, harmonized with the congenital pessimism of American Jews regarding anti-Semitism. In any case, the value of *The Authoritarian Personality* depended on whether it could accurately predict behavior, and for this it could not have been published at a more opportune time.

In the years immediately after the publication of *The Authoritarian Personality,* a popular anticommunist demagogue would emerge, two American Jews would be executed for spying for the Soviet Union, American racial tensions would intensify, and a war in the Middle East in 1956 would find the United States government opposing the government of Israel. Much to the surprise of American Jews, and certainly to the amazement of the Frankfurt scholars, anti-Semitism actually declined during this period.

In February 1950, Senator Joseph R. McCarthy began his career of national demagoguery with a speech in Wheeling, West Virginia charging the State Department with knowingly harboring Communists. This would be followed by other McCarthy speeches repeating these unsubstantiated and wild accusations. Jews feared the Wisconsin senator, not because they were procommunist, but because they worried that he might be the long-dreaded American demagogue who would lead the neofascist movement the Frankfurt scholars believed to be on the horizon. Many persons had predicted that, if and when fascism came to America, it would be disguised as anticommunism, and American Jews were familiar with the close historical relationship between fascism and anti-Semitism.

It was certainly possible to discover whether McCarthy and his followers manifested an authoritarian personality and to test the validity of the Adorno book. Scholarly examinations of McCarthyism could also reveal whether there was a deep reservoir of anti-Semitism in America and whether rightist and anticommunist politics could be correlated with anti-Semitism. For these and other reasons, few American social phenomena have been subjected to such intense field investigation as McCarthyism.

McCarthy possessed precisely the background and outlook that social scientists and Jews had associated with the anti-Semitic rabble-rouser. The senator was a native of rural Wisconsin, where populist fears of Jewish bankers were supposedly widespread. His appeal derived from attacking radicals, many of whom had a Jewish background. He had a conservative voting record on social and economic issues while in the Senate. Finally, his constituency contained many isolationists and German-Americans. Arnold Forster, then general counsel of the Anti-Defamation League, remembered the fears of Jews during the Great Red Scare of the early 1950s that they would be victimized by McCarthyism. "Jews in that period were automatically suspect," he said. "Our evaluation of the general mood was that the people felt if you scratch a Jew, you can find a Communist."[7]

Despite the concerns of American Jews, the memories of Forster, and the authoritarian personality thesis, neither Senator McCarthy nor his followers proved to be anti-Semitic. The targets of McCarthy's witch-hunts were not Jews but Anglo-Saxon Protestants, particularly graduates of elite colleges. Cambridge, Massachusetts, Berkeley, California, and Morningside Heights in Manhattan had more to fear from McCarthy than did the Lower East Side of New York or the Brownsville–East New York section of Brooklyn. McCarthy never attacked Jews as Jews. His leading advisors included Roy Cohn, and one of his most enthusiastic supporters was Rabbi Benjamin Schultz of Clarksdale, Mississippi, the head of the American Jewish League Against Communism. In fact, Gerald L. K. Smith, the leading American anti-Semite of the day, accused McCarthy of betraying America by not emphasizing the relationship between Jewry and communism. As for McCarthy's followers, one 1954 public opinion survey concluded that they actually were more likely to vote for a hypothetical Jewish candidate for Congress than were the senator's enemies.[8]

Five months after McCarthy entered the national spotlight, an event took place in New York City that shook American Jewry to the core. On Monday, 17 July 1950, the Federal Bureau of Investigation arrested Julius Rosenberg and charged him with transmitting classified information regarding the atomic bomb to the Soviet Union. Rosenberg's arrest had been preceded by the arrest of Harry Gold and David Greenglass, Rosenberg's brother-in-law, and was to be followed three and a half weeks later by the arrest of his wife, Ethel. The three-year Rosenberg case culminated in their execution on Friday, 19 June 1953, just minutes before the onset of the Jewish Sabbath. J. Edgar Hoover called the Rosenbergs' offense "the crime of the century." If it was not that, it certainly led to one of the great American trials of the century, and was a cause célèbre of the cold war.

For Jews, the most important aspect of the Rosenberg case was the

Jewish background of all four of the major defendants (five, if Morton Sobell is included). All had obviously Jewish names. American Jews feared the Rosenberg trial would be a godsend to anti-Semites. What better proof could there be of the communist sympathies of Jews and their support for the Soviet motherland? Never in American history was the hoary anti-Semitic association of Jews with communism more believable than in the early 1950s.

The fear that the Rosenberg case would exacerbate anti-Semitism was heightened by the emphasis of European and American Communists on the couple's Jewish background once it became clear that they were not going to talk. Anti-Semitism, their supporters charged, was behind the government's prosecution and execution of the Rosenbergs. The Rosenbergs' defenders wondered why the New York City jury that convicted the Rosenbergs did not contain one Jew, even though the city's population was 30 percent Jewish. They also noted that, even if the Rosenbergs were guilty as charged, their crime had been committed during World War II when the Soviet Union was not an enemy of the United States. At the worst, the Rosenbergs had provided information to an ally, and this did not warrant the death penalty.

For the left-wing defenders of the Rosenbergs there was a bitter paradox in claiming that they were victims of anti-Semitism. Stalin was then in the midst of his murderous campaign to destroy Jewish culture behind the Iron Curtain, the so-called black years of Soviet Jewry. Noncommunists pointed out that the accusation that the Rosenbergs were martyrs to anti-Semitism was designed to deflect attention away from the real campaign of anti-Semitism then being waged in eastern Europe.

Jewish leaders immediately attempted to contain any damage resulting from the Rosenberg case. They launched a propaganda campaign to convince the general public that American Jews were not tainted with communism and that the Soviet Union was hostile to Jews, Judaism, Jewish culture, Zionism, and Israel. Testifying before the House Committee on Un-American Activities, a representative of the American Jewish Committee emphasized that "Judaism and communism are utterly incompatible." The Anti-Defamation League, the American Jewish Committee, and the Jewish War Veterans cooperated with HUAC and opened their files to the committee.[9]

The Jewish establishment was careful to distance itself from the Jewish Left and to make sure that Jewish communal leadership rested safely in the hands of staunch anticommunists. The American Jewish Committee assigned a full-time staff member to investigate Communist infiltration into Jewish communal life. The Jewish Welfare Board strongly urged Jewish community centers not to allow radical speakers to use their facilities. Mainstream Jewish organizations refused to help the Rosenbergs, and they vehemently denied the charge of Herbert Aptheker, Howard Fast, and other Communists that the Rosenberg case was an American Dreyfus affair. The National Community Relations Advisory Council—made up of the American Jewish Committee, the American Jewish Congress, the Jewish War Veterans, the Jewish Labor Committee, and the Union of American Hebrew Congregations—accused the National Committee to Secure Justice in the Rosenberg Case (the Rosenberg Committee) of being a Communist-front organization and of fomenting hysteria among Jews by claiming the Rosenbergs were victims of anti-Semitism.[10]

Convinced of the guilt of the Rosenbergs, the American Jewish Committee openly supported their execution. Rabbi S. Andhill Fineberg, a member of the AJC's staff, wrote a long exposé entitled *The Rosenberg Case: Fact and Fiction* (1953), which strongly championed the jury's finding of guilt and the judge's sentencing of the Rosenbergs to death. Future historian Lucy S. Dawidowicz also argued against clemency for the Rosenbergs. Her 1952 article in the *New Leader*—"The Rosenberg Case: 'Hate-America' Weapon"—warned America's Jews not to be duped by the Communists into supporting a "war against America." The failure to go through with the execution of the Rosenbergs, she wrote, would mean that the American judicial system had caved in to the Communists' "moral blackmail." Dawidowicz's essay "'Anti-Semitism' and the Rosenberg Case: The Latest Communist Propaganda Trap" was an even more powerful indictment of the "insidious campaign" of the Rosenberg supporters to equate anticommunism with anti-Semitism. It appeared in the staunchly anticommunist *Commentary*. Dawidowicz concluded with a solemn warning to Jews: "It is well to be on guard; we have seen how similar campaigns of identification and accusation have strengthened the hands of anti-Semitic forces elsewhere."[11]

Even Jewish periodicals that opposed the Rosenbergs' death sentences emphasized that they had no quarrel with the jury's decision. The *Reconstructionist* as well as the *Daily Forward* and the *Day*, two Yiddish dailies, agreed that the Rosenbergs were guilty but maintained that the death sentence was too harsh, particularly in view of the jail terms received by the English atomic spies Klaus Fuchs and Allan Nunn May.[12]

The Rosenberg case weakened the American Jewish Left, particularly that small number of American Jews who were Communist party members or fellow travelers. Coming at the same time as the murder of Jewish writers in the Soviet Union and the Slansky trial in Czechoslovakia, it undermined the efforts of Jewish radicals to weld Jewish culture to "progressive" politics. Jewish leftists were now ostracized by other Jews, denied employment by Jewish organizations, and subjected to legal attacks by the federal and local governments. Three years after the execution of the Rosenbergs, the old Jewish Left finally received its fatal blow when Soviet Communist party head Nikita Khrushchev gave his famous speech on the crimes of Stalin at the Twentieth Party Congress.

After the revelations of Khrushchev, even the most committed Jewish Communists recanted. "How could we reconcile anti-Semitism with communism?" one former Communist who had been imprisoned under the Smith Act asked. "Our whole world was falling apart. . . . As an American and a Jew, I had become a Communist, and in time these parts of my social being had become fused. Now the unity had been shattered; as some of us sensed forever." For him the future was clear. "Now I could think of my Jewish origins, the emotions engendered by the plight of the Jews in Europe, the epic of the Warsaw Ghetto, and know with certainty that whatever my political beliefs now or in the future, I was a Jew." Some radicals asserted this newly discovered Jewishness through Zionism, an erstwhile "bourgeois nationalism," while others reverted to a Judaism they barely remembered.[13]

The Rosenberg case neither resulted from nor increased anti-Semitism. Both Irving Saypol, the federal attorney who prosecuted the government's case, and Irving R. Kaufman, who presided at the trial, were Jews. (The maiden name of Kaufman's wife was Rosenberg.) Revelations in the 1980s that the FBI and the prosecuting attorney were in contact with Judge Kaufman prior to his sentencing of the Rosenbergs to death have led to questions regarding the fairness of the trial. Nevertheless, no evidence has ever materialized that the jury's decision or the sentence would have differed had the Rosenbergs been Gentiles. Nor is there any evidence that the Rosenberg case created an anti-Semitic backlash.

Polls taken in November 1950, in July 1953, and in November 1954 among twelve hundred white Americans by the University of Chicago's National Opinion Research Center showed that the percentage of persons naming "Jews" as one of the "kinds of people in the United States who are more likely than others to be Communists" actually declined from 4 percent to 1 percent during these four years. In another survey during this period, twice as many people named "actors" and four times as many selected "Puerto Ricans" than "Jews" as persons likely to be Communists. This can be compared to the situation prior to World War II, when anywhere from one-quarter to one-half of Americans believed Jews to be more radical than other Americans. "The notion of the Jew as a congenital radical," sociologist Charles H. Stember wrote in 1966, "seems to have come close to extinction in the postwar decades."[14]

Its demise was merely one aspect of the general decline of American anti-Semitism after the war. Pressured by local and state governments and by the courts, universities repealed quotas on Jewish students, corporations increased their hiring of Jews, and previously restricted neighborhoods opened their borders to Jews. By 1949, Connecticut, Massachusetts, New Jersey, New York, Oregon, Rhode Island, and Washington had banned employment discrimination, and bills had been introduced in the legislatures of other states forbidding such practices. A bill was even introduced in Congress making anti-Semitism a crime. All of the veterans organizations officially condemned bigotry as un-American, magazines and radio shows frequently discussed anti-Semitism, clergymen often preached against religious (and racial) intolerance, and Laura Z. Hobson's novel *Gentleman's Agreement* was a best-seller.[15]

Public opinion surveys taken between 1940 and 1962 reveal a sharp decrease in the percentage of Gentile Americans who believed Jews had too much power, were "unscrupulous," and had other objectionable traits. The number of Americans who claimed that Jews lacked culture and good breeding, for example, decreased from 15 percent to 4 percent. Polls taken only after World War II disclose the same trend of diminishing anti-Semitism. While over one-fifth of the respondents to a 1948 poll said they did not want Jews as neighbors, only 2 percent of those polled in 1959 objected to Jewish neighbors.[16]

The polls also reveal a greater tolerance for Jews in politics. As early as 1949 the Anti-Defamation League, much to its surprise, discovered a "comparative absence of anti-Semitic activity" during the 1948 elections. A poll taken in 1959, the year before the election of the first Roman Catholic president, reveals that slightly more Americans were willing to vote for a Jew for president than for a Roman Catholic, and a far greater number would have voted for a Jewish man than for a Gentile woman. In 1981, three-quarters of Americans claimed they would vote for a qualified Jew for president.[17]

By 1962, three-fourths of Americans said they would vote against an anti-Semitic candidate solely because he was anti-Semitic. Conversely, the percentage of those who said they would vote *for* a candidate because he was anti-Semitic had declined sharply. According to one 1962 poll, only one in twenty-five Americans would have supported an anti-Semitic candidate because of his anti-Semitism. The lessened importance of political anti-Semitism paralleled a sharp decrease in the number of Americans who feared Jews. By the 1960s, only one Gentile in a hundred believed Jews to be a national menace. Since World War II, Earl Raab observed in 1969, "there has been no serious trace of political anti-Semitism in America." Raab, a prominent San Francisco Jewish spokesman, declared that suggestions that "it could happen here" have "an antique flavor and would be widely branded as phobic, paranoid, and even amusing."[18]

As Congressman John E. Rankin discovered, it was a political kiss of death to be known after the war as an anti-Semite. Rankin, Congress's most blatant anti-Semite during the 1940s, had represented a solidly Democratic district in northeast Mississippi since 1921. Politically impregnable, he was able to voice his hatred of Jews with impunity. In 1939, for example, he warned his congressional colleagues that, while "99% of the Christian people of America" wanted to stay out of the European war, "a certain international element that has no sympathy for Christianity was spending money by the barrel" in order to commit the United States to the support of England. These were the same people, he said two years later, who controlled the world's gold supply and who had "crucified" Germany.

During and after the war, Rankin blamed Jews for communism, finance capitalism, and the plight of Christianity. Thirty million white European Christians had been murdered by "the same gang that composed the fifth column of the crucifixion," he declared. For nearly two thousand years, Jews had attempted "to destroy Christianity and everything that is based on Christian principles. They have overrun and virtually destroyed Europe. They are now trying to undermine and destroy America. God save our country from such a fate." The issue facing America, simply put, was "Yiddish Communism versus Christian civilization."

The most important reason for Rankin's hatred of Jews was his belief that northern "long-nosed reprobates" were behind the civil rights agitation in the South. Jews, he contended, were bent on mongrelizing the South, and

Jewish Communists were responsible for the rape and murder of white girls by "vicious Negroes." He particularly was incensed by a bill to eliminate segregation in the District of Columbia, which had been introduced by a Jewish congressman from Hartford, Connecticut. Rankin predicted the passage of this bill would encourage "brutal Negroes to assault white women in every section of the city," force whites to relocate to the suburbs, and frighten law-abiding blacks. The bill was part of the Jewish-Communist plot to "force Negro equality upon the white people of the South" and to destroy American civilization.

Rankin's vision of a Jewish conspiracy of race mixers, Communists, and gold bugs was too much even for the electorate of Mississippi. He finished last among five candidates in the 1947 primary election to choose a successor to the deceased Senator Theodore G. Bilbo. Five years later, he lost his own congressional seat when reapportionment forced him into a runoff with another incumbent. The demise of Rankin meant the virtual end of anti-Semitism in Congress.[19]

The fate of Rankin was not lost on other southern politicians. Much to the surprise of northern Jews, George Wallace, the flamboyant segregationist governor of Alabama, did not exploit anti-Semitism in his 1964, 1968, and 1972 campaigns for the Democratic nomination for president. In fact, much as Bilbo had done two decades earlier, Wallace emphasized the opposition of southern Jews to the civil rights movement and to any outside tinkering with southern racial mores. A large minority of Jews in Mobile and other Alabama cities supported Wallace. When speaking to northern audiences, Wallace would trot out Jews from Alabama to testify to their loyalty to the southern white gospel of race relations.

Israel was widely admired throughout the South, and this had a spill-over effect on the region's stance toward Jews. The southern attitude toward Israel stemmed from the proto-Zionism of Old Testament–oriented southern Protestantism, the South's respect for Israel's martial virtues, and the South's esteem for the Jewish state's opposition to the spread of communism in the Middle East. As the only part of the country to have experienced military defeat, the South empathized with Israel's determination to survive under difficult conditions. The situation of Israel, southerners believed, resembled that of the white South. Both were beleaguered regional minorities threatened by hostile outside forces. Israel was also highly regarded in other regions besides the South, as was the assistance provided to the Jewish state by American Jews. During the 1956 Middle East war, when the Eisenhower administration successfully pressured Israel to vacate the Sinai, the American public did not believe that the support of American Jews for Israel manifested dual loyalty.[20]

The most important potential source of anti-Semitism in the South was the help provided by northern Jews for the civil rights movement. The warnings of southern Jews that the activities of northern Jews on behalf of blacks could cause an anti-Semitic backlash in the South had little effect. Northern Jews continued to play a major role in the struggle against segregation. Jack Greenberg headed the legal arm of the National Association for the Advancement of Colored People, Kivie Kaplan and other Jewish philanthropists contributed generously to black causes, and a disproportionate percentage of the white college students involved in the civil rights protests of the 1960s were Jewish.

Southern Jews cautioned that these activities threatened their personal security and economic well-being. They feared that, in the eyes of local whites, the Jew could come to symbolize the alien forces seeking to revolutionize southern racial patterns. These forebodings seemed to be confirmed in 1958 by a series of bombings of southern synagogues. The bombings were widely condemned throughout the South, however, and they were not indicative of southern opinion. Only a small percentage of southern whites blamed Jews for the region's racial difficulties. In part, this was because of the role that some southern Jews, most notably Charles Bloch of Macon, Georgia, had played in the defense of racial segregation. Also, southern white Gentiles underestimated the bonds between southern and northern Jews.

Southerners believed Jews constituted one of the South's many religious sects and not a religio-ethnic people. Just as Baptists were divided into southern and northern branches, so, southerners surmised, Jews were also divided regionally. Southern Jews were believed to be no more responsible for the activities of northern Jews than southern Baptists were responsible for those of northern Baptists. Because of their important economic position and their long historical presence in the South, their assimilation into southern society, and their caution regarding racial matters, southern Jews were viewed as having little in common with the race mixers of the North. The great social divide in the South was never between Christians and Jews. It was between whites and blacks.

The absence of any southern anti-Semitic backlash was also due to the white South's failure to fully comprehend the extent of northern Jewish support for the civil rights movement. Because of the work of the Roman Catholic hierarchy in behalf of civil rights, particularly in New Orleans, white and black southerners alike mistakenly believed that Roman Catholics were more strongly committed to racial integration than were Jews. White southerners also assumed that labor unions were a greater danger than northern Jews. But the white South's greatest concern was with black organizations, especially the National Association for the Advancement of Colored People and the Southern Christian Leadership Conference. They correctly perceived that the source and energy of the civil rights movement came from within the black community.[21]

The surest sign of the acceptance of Jews after the war was the increasing willingness of Gentiles to marry them. Between 1964 and 1981, Gentiles who would accept the marriage of a child to a Jew increased from 55 to 66 percent. "Since marriage would seem to constitute the ultimate degree of acceptance," Charles Stember noted, "the lessening resistance to Jews as potential wives or husbands probably is even more significant than the simultaneous lowering of barriers in other fields."[22]

Perhaps the most important finding of the postwar polls on American attitudes toward Jews was the change in their economic image. For centuries the foremost element in anti-Semitic demonology had been the notion that the Jew was mercenary and dishonest. This was the source of the most famous anti-Semitic incident in American history—General Ulysses S. Grant's order number eleven in 1862 commanding all Jews to leave the territory then under his military control. Grant issued this order because he believed Jews were responsible for the smuggling of contraband to Confederate forces in Tennessee. The order was countermanded by Lincoln.[23]

The stereotype of the dishonest Jewish businessman became even more widespread after the Civil War. In American popular culture, the word *jew* was used frequently as a verb and an adjective to denote unsavory business practices. In a 1939 poll, one half of Americans claimed that Jewish businessmen were less honest than other businessmen. By 1962, however, only 18 percent said this, while 70 percent asserted that Jewish and Gentile businessmen were equally honest (or dishonest).[24]

Anti-Semitism in the United States, a 1981 report prepared for the American Jewish Committee by the Yankelovich, Skelly, and White polling company, noted that the decline in anti-Semitism had been particularly evident "when it comes to traditional negative images of Jewish character such as those relating to dishonesty, shrewdness, assertiveness or willing-

43

ness to use shady business practices." These negative images tended to be found particularly among the less educated, poorer, and older Americans. The report predicted that anti-Semitism would decline even more as the country became more prosperous and as the older generation yielded to a better-educated younger generation.[25]

Accompanying this decline in anti-Semitic prejudice was a decrease in discrimination against Jews. Fewer and fewer Americans favored restrictions against Jews in employment, housing, and college admissions, and most supported the efforts of local governments to ensure that hiring practices conform to the principle of merit. In 1940, over a quarter of Americans had not wanted to work alongside of Jews. By the 1960s, hardly anyone in the general population supported job discrimination against Jews. Such fields as insurance, commercial banking, and automotive manufacturing that previously had few Jewish employees were now hiring them in large numbers. Elite private universities followed the example of Harvard and dropped their quotas for Jewish students, even though the price of this was the transformation of their student population.[26]

Not all observers, however, were convinced that the position of Jews in America was as favorable as it appeared on the surface. These skeptics claimed that the polls were wrong in portraying a dramatic decline in anti-Semitism. Those polled, the critics charged, were often reluctant to indicate their true feelings to pollsters, particularly regarding a sensitive issue such as anti-Semitism. As Thomas F. O'Dea, a Columbia University sociologist, wrote, "We do not doubt that the polls accurately reflected the expressed attitudes of the moment. We question, rather, whether survey responses can be accepted as evidence of deeper sentiment when they deal with a phenomenon of the psychological depth and historical longevity of anti-Semitism."[27]

Ben Halpern, a professor of Jewish history at Brandeis University, agreed. For him the polls only revealed what the respondents *thought* they believed, or thought they *should* believe, or were willing to tell the pollsters. The polls were unable to convey what those polled actually believed within the inner recesses of their minds. Nor could the polls forecast how people would respond when faced with an actual situation rather than with a hypothetical question. At best, Halpern claimed, the polls indicated only that the respectability of anti-Semitism had declined, not that anti-Semitism itself had diminished.[28]

But even if the polls were believable, Jews were warned not to let down their guard. The polls had not measured how intensely Americans opposed anti-Semitism. The findings of the polls could be interpreted as indicating indifference rather than antagonism toward anti-Semitism. The history of Nazi Germany had demonstrated that an apathetic and indifferent majority was powerless against a deeply committed minority of bigots. Furthermore, the polls did show that a sizable number of Americans remained prejudiced. In 1981, two-fifths of those polled believed "Jews stick together too much," and over a third claimed "Jewish employers go out of their way to hire other Jews." Also, during the 1970s and 1980s the polls charted an increase in the number of Americans who believed that Jews "have too much power in the United States" and "are more loyal to Israel than to America."[29]

The public opinion surveys had their defenders as well as detractors. These people asserted that the polls' conclusions were not invalidated by the fact that some people might have lied to the pollsters. One could safely assume that approximately the same number would have lied to the pollsters in 1946 as in 1987. That some people might have been too embarrassed to reveal their prejudice to the pollsters was itself significant. It showed the diminished respectability of anti-Semitism.

While the postwar polls did not measure the intensity of anti-Semitism, they did indicate that it was not as widespread as hostility toward business corporations, labor unions, the news media, the federal government, Arabs, Asians, blacks, Hispanics, and the Catholic church. Anti-Semitism was usually just one of the many biases of a prejudiced person and generally not the most important. Also, bigots often had an ambivalent attitude toward Jews. They might dislike them for sticking together and for being too rich, but at the same time they admired them for being hardworking, religious, and family oriented.

In 1987, Seymour Martin Lipset, a world-renowned sociologist and a leading authority on American public opinion, claimed that public opinion data disclosed that there was no more prejudice against Jews than against other white ethnic groups. Jews were seen as being "just as honest, just as unobjectionable as neighbors or co-workers, and just as supportable for high public office as white Catholics or mainline Protestants." They were even viewed more favorably than fundamentalist Protestants. "Their energy and achievements are viewed with admiration," Lipset concluded. "Jews have arrived."[30]

And yet, Lipset wrote in 1990, Jews were "full of foreboding," despite their wealth, power, and repute. Wildly exaggerating the hostility of Gentiles, they lived "under a permanent cloud." Jews felt "anxious, rejected and worried." As proof, Lipset noted the results of a poll of San Francisco Jews in which one-third of the respondents claimed that a Jew could not be elected to Congress from the Bay area. This was asserted at the same time that the two state senators from San Francisco were Jewish, the mayor of San Francisco was Jewish, and the three congressmen representing the districts in and adjacent to San Francisco were Jews. Jews, Abba Eban once quipped, are a people who can't take yes for an answer.[31]

The findings of Steven M. Cohen, a sociologist at Queens College in New York, reinforced Lipset's. Cohen's 1989 survey of Jewish attitudes revealed that three-quarters of American Jews believed anti-Semitism to be a serious problem. The same percentage disagreed with the statement that "virtually all positions of influence in America are open to Jews." They maintained this even though the chairman of the Federal Reserve System, the U.S. secretary of commerce, eight U.S. senators, several U.S. congressmen from New York City, the chairman of the President's Council of Economic Advisers, the mayor of New York City, and the president of Columbia University were Jews. Cohen answered in the affirmative the question he posed in the title of a 1989 article: "Undue Stress on American Anti-Semitism?" Every recent serious study of anti-Semitism, he wrote, has "documented a retreat from earlier, higher levels of anti-Semitic prejudice and discrimination."[32]

Jewish professional workers had more reason than the man in the street to be aware of this decline in anti-Semitism. But even they had difficulty accepting it at face value. While they admitted that the nature of anti-Semitism had changed during the postwar years, they still argued that it continued to threaten Jewish interests. During the 1940s and 1950s, Jewish professionals had been concerned with the anti-Semitism menacing Jewish lives and property and impeding Jewish social and economic mobility. The books of Arnold Forster (*A Measure of Freedom* [1950]) and Benjamin R. Epstein (*The Trouble Makers* [1952]), both officials of the Anti-Defamation League, focused on social and economic discrimination and the importance of the country's anti-Semitic demagogues and hate groups. By the 1970s, however, overt discrimination against Jews was no longer significant, and the few vocal anti-Semites were to be found only on the lunatic fringe.

A new interpretation of American anti-Semitism was required if the Anti-Defamation League and other such agencies were to salvage their mission and if the struggle against anti-Semitism was to remain an important item on the American Jewish agenda. In 1974, Forster and Epstein published *The New Anti-Semitism*. They admitted here that American Jews now had "a greater degree of economic and political security and social acceptance than has ever been achieved by any Jewish community since the Dispersion." But, they contended, American Jews were being lulled into a false sense of security. Forster and Epstein pointed to a "new anti-Semitism" that involved neither physical assaults on Jews and their property nor economic and social discrimination.

The new anti-Semitism was instead "a callous indifference to Jewish concerns," a failure to appreciate "the most profound apprehensions of the Jewish people," and "a blandness and apathy in dealing with anti-Jewish behavior." It was particularly evident in the "widespread incapacity or unwillingness" of Gentiles to understand the importance of Israel for Jewish security. Forster and Epstein's expansion of the definition of anti-Semitism was troubling. Was it realistic to expect non-Jews to understand "the most profound apprehensions of the Jewish people"? How could Gentiles be expected to empathize with Israel in the way that Jews did? Was this a manifestation of anti-Semitism, or was it simply the normal indifference of persons toward a country not their own? Forster and Epstein implied that the new anti-Semitism was the inability of Gentiles to love Jews and Israel enough.[33]

If indifference to Jewish concerns was to be the litmus test for anti-Semitism, then by definition virtually the entire world was anti-Semitic. By the same token, Forster and Epstein could be described as anti-Christian for not appreciating the profoundest apprehensions of Christians. Critics of *The New Anti-Semitism* accused Forster and Epstein of engaging in political blackmail by insisting that the price of not being called an anti-Semite was steadfast support for Israel. By taking Jewish sensitivity regarding anti-Semitism to an extreme conclusion, *The New Anti-Semitism* bent the meaning of anti-Semitism all out of shape.

Nathan and Ruth Ann Perlmutter's *The Real Anti-Semitism in America* (1982) elaborated on this new definition of anti-Semitism. Nathan Perlmutter, an official with the Anti-Defamation League, and his wife asserted that the real threat to Jews now came not from "crude" anti-Semitism but from indifference to Jewish interests by persons who did not think of themselves as anti-Semites. "Jews today," the Perlmutters wrote, "face greater jeopardy from quarters which though innocent of bigotry, nonetheless pose us greater danger than do our long time, easily recognizable, anti-Semitic nemeses."

The Jews' enemies included radicals, black militants, pro-Arab spokesmen for mainline Protestant churches, businessmen eager for trade with the Arab world, neo-isolationists, opponents of a strong national defense, and supporters of affirmative action.[34]

The Perlmutters emphasized the paradoxical nature of American Protestantism. While Methodist, Presbyterian, and Episcopalian denominations had a less anti-Semitic membership than the more fundamentalist churches, their leaders were far less supportive of Israel than fundamentalist churchmen. This meant that the mainline denominations were, to a certain extent, objectively anti-Semitic, despite their protestations to the contrary. Not surprisingly, the Perlmutters were more supportive of Jerry Falwell's Moral Majority than of the National Council of Churches.

The New Anti-Semitism and *The Real Anti-Semitism in America* sought to keep American Jews vigilant despite what appeared to be a sharp diminishing of anti-Semitism. These books had a sympathetic audience. It was difficult for Jews to admit that American anti-Semitism had dwindled to the point of insignificance. Their memories of anti-Semitism were so clear, their image of the suffering Jew so potent, and the definition of their own Jewish identity so inextricably intertwined with the combating of anti-Semitism that it was virtually impossible for them to believe what the polls and sociologists were saying. Jews had invested too much emotional capital in the struggle against American anti-Semitism to recognize that the contest was virtually over and that they had won.

During the Arab oil embargoes of the 1970s, there were reports of bumper stickers blaming Jews and Israel for the shortage of gasoline. They supposedly read "burn Jews, not gasoline." Jews feared the United States was on the verge of an anti-Semitic backlash fueled by anger over the long lines at the service stations. Polls, however, revealed that only 1 percent of Americans blamed Jews and Israel for the scarcity of gasoline, while most thought the Arabs were responsible for the energy crisis. Despite the efforts of Arab propagandists and political radicals, 70 percent of Americans continued to believe that the survival of Israel was a vital American interest.[35]

The Wall Street scandals of the 1980s also frightened American Jews. They worried that the involvement of Ivan Boesky, Michael Milken, and other Jews would revive the old anti-Semitic image of the mercenary and dishonest Jew. The case of Boesky was particularly embarrassing because of his high profile within the Jewish world. He had headed the Federation of Jewish Philanthropies of New York, and he was a generous benefactor to

Jewish causes. The library of the Jewish Theological Seminary had been named for him and his wife. There is no evidence, however, that the Wall Street scandals increased anti-Semitism. The public was largely unaware that a disproportionate number of the culprits were Jews, and the more informed did not dwell on this fact.

During the 1980s, Jews on the lookout for anti-Semitism focused their attention on the plains of the West as well as on the canyons of Wall Street. At a time of growing economic difficulties in the farm belt, alarming reports appeared of violent anti-Semitic fascist groups in the Middle West and the Rocky Mountain states preparing to take over the country. Jews took these stories very seriously. The anti-Semitism of the 1930s had accustomed them to attributing the hatred of Jews to economic discontent, while Oscar Handlin, Richard Hofstadter, and other historians had emphasized the rural origins of American anti-Semitism. The reports of rural anti-Semitism became more credible after right-wing extremists murdered Alan Berg, a popular and controversial Jewish radio talk show host in Denver in June 1984. Attention was further focused on western, rural anti-Semitism by the release of three Hollywood films on this subject—*Talk Radio, Betrayed,* and *Dead Bank.* In order to alleviate the danger of agrarian anti-Semitism, Jewish organizations lobbied for increased government aid to farmers and sponsored conferences on the economic distress of rural America.[36]

Daniel Levitas, research director of Prairiefire Rural Action, Inc., claimed that anti-Semitism had "spread to an ever wider strata of the rural population and has become increasingly sophisticated. . . . the threat of organized anti-Semitic activity remains very real." In 1986, the Anti-Defamation League commissioned the Lou Harris polling company to survey attitudes toward Jews in Iowa and Nebraska. While the pollsters did discover the existence of anti-Semitic stereotypes in the Midwest (27 percent of the respondents agreed with the statement "Farmers have always been exploited by international Jewish bankers"), they had difficulty locating any members of these paramilitary anti-Semitic groups. Furthermore, 80 percent of those polled had not even heard of these gangs. Even Levitas admitted that there were at most no more than five thousand hard-core members of Posse Comitatus, the Populist party, and other such groups.[37]

More indicative of the actual status of Jews in the American heartland during the 1980s was the election of Edward Zorinsky as a U.S. senator from Nebraska. Jews were elected to high office from other states as well.

The only Jewish U.S. senator in 1952 had been Herbert Lehman of New York, and the few Jewish members of the House of Representatives were from New York City, Chicago, Philadelphia, and other cities with sizable Jewish populations. By the 1980s, in contrast, there were eight Jews in the Senate and thirty or so in the House of Representatives. As striking as this increase were the areas these politicians represented. Jewish senators came from Michigan, New Jersey, Ohio, Connecticut, Florida, and Pennsylvania, states with large Jewish populations, but they also came from New Hampshire, Nevada, Wisconsin, Minnesota, and Nebraska, which had few Jews. Jews represented congressional districts in Brooklyn, Chicago, Philadelphia, Miami, and Los Angeles. But they also represented districts in Alabama, Colorado, Georgia, Kansas, and Texas. No longer were Jewish members of Congress exclusively urban liberals. They were now to be found along the entire political spectrum. While the majority were liberals, there were also conservatives such as the Republican senators Chip Hecht of Nevada and Warren Rudman of New Hampshire.

Jews became politically more prominent on the local level as well. Few cities had had Jewish mayors prior to the 1960s. During the 1930s, Minneapolis had been the unofficial capital of American anti-Semitism. In the 1960s, Arthur Naftalin was the city's mayor. Jews were also elected mayors of Atlanta, Kansas City, New York City, Omaha, San Francisco, and Portland, Oregon. Jewish politicians benefited enormously from the election of John F. Kennedy in 1960. The selection of the nation's first Catholic president rendered obsolete many American political taboos. Kennedy's cabinet contained the first Polish-American and Italian-American members of the cabinet, as well as two Jews of eastern European extraction, Arthur Goldberg and Abraham Ribicoff. In 1973, Henry Kissinger became the first Jewish secretary of state.

Anti-Semitism did not disappear in the postwar years, but what remained was largely social—the exclusion of Jews from private clubs, resorts, and a limited number of cooperative apartment houses and neighborhoods. Anti-Semitic conversation was relegated to locker rooms and living rooms. The reluctance of some Gentiles to enter into close social relationships with them was not a burning issue for most Jews, who actually preferred associating with other Jews. Nor did it present significant obstacles to their social and economic advancement. They were more concerned with employment and professional opportunities and with getting their children into prestigious universities and professional schools, than in breaking down what came to be known as "the five o'clock shadow," the social separation between Jews and Gentiles once the workday ended. In "Lakeville," the pseudonym of an affluent and tolerant middle western suburb that was closely studied by Jewish sociologists in the 1960s, relations between Jews and Gentiles were described as existing on "the edge of friendliness." The contacts between Jews and Gentiles tended to be functional and casual, in contrast to the close and warm relationships among Jews.[38]

While vestiges of anti-Semitism in the workplace remained, the situation had improved enormously by the 1970s and 1980s. Jews were now employed in the highest echelons of Bank of America, Chrysler, Disney, Du Pont, McDonald's, and other major American corporations. They also had important positions in the major New York law firms, banks, investment companies, and insurance companies. While the anti-Semitism of the executive suite, which so preoccupied the American Jewish Committee in the 1950s, had not completely disappeared by the end of the 1980s, it was on the verge of extinction.

In his speech accepting the 1976 Democratic nomination for president, Jimmy Carter promised a war against prejudice. The time had finally come, the former Georgia governor declared, "to guarantee an end to discrimination because of race and sex." Carter's failure to include religious or ethnic discrimination was not as remarkable as the fact that few people noted, much less commented, on this omission. Carter would not knowingly have antagonized an important bloc of voters and financial contributors to the Democratic party. Apparently, Jews were no longer perceived as an oppressed minority requiring special treatment.

Outsiders found incongruous the Jews' continued concern with anti-Semitism in light of their rapid cultural, political, social, and economic progress. Gentiles failed to realize the way anti-Semitism had shaped the Jewish understanding of history. Nor did they recognize the great emotional stake that many Jews had in the struggle against anti-Semitism. These Jews were often ignorant of Jewish belief and uninterested in Jewish culture, and yet they wished to identify strongly with the Jewish people. For them, being Jewish meant fighting anti-Semitism by supporting organizations such as the Anti-Defamation League and the Simon Wiesenthal Center and by being continually on the alert for traces of anti-Semitism. It was difficult for them not to exaggerate the extent of American anti-Semitism. Otherwise they would have had either to admit that the most important element in their own Jewish identity was no longer relevant or redefine their Jewish identity in more positive ways. Another element in this continuing concern of American Jews with anti-Semitism was their interpretation of the conflict in the Middle East between Israel and the Arabs. For them it was not a struggle among rival nation-states or between opposing nationalist movements, but the latest chapter in the history of anti-Semitism.

By the 1960s, the decline of overt anti-Semitism had become obvious to most Americans. Gentiles believed that a permanent change had taken place in Jewish-Gentile relations. Professor John Higham of Johns Hopkins University, for example, a leading authority on American ethnic history, speculated that this was due to the cultural assimilation of Jews. The Jewish immigrant population had gradually died out, while the second and third generations had melted into the middle class. The dream of nineteenth- and twentieth-century Zionists for the normalization of the Jewish social condition had seemingly come true in the New World.[39]

Certainly the absorption of native-born Jews into the national mass culture had diminished their ethnic and religious distinction. Fewer Jews spoke Yiddish or worshipped in Orthodox synagogues. The flight of Jews to suburbia attenuated their association with the metropolis, especially with "Jew" York, while their movement into the professions and into government, academic, and corporate bureaucracies had weakened the association of Jews with petty commerce. In this new social and economic environment, the image of the Jew as the sharp trader as well as other anti-Semitic stereotypes had less saliency. The "old hostile imagery evidently is fading at last," Thomas O'Dea concluded. "We appear to be witnessing an historical change."[40]

The acculturation of Jews meant that the differences between Jews and Gentiles increasingly involved religion. According to public opinion polls, the percentage of Americans who believed Jews made up a religion rather than a race or ethnic group increased after the war. These same polls also revealed that Gentiles exaggerated the religiosity of Jews. This was a logical corollary to the belief that Jews constituted a religion. If religion was the main factor dividing Jews and Gentiles, then Jews must be religious. If not, then what differentiated Jews from non-Jews?[41]

Jews benefited from the public's high esteem for religion and the right of religious expression. The practice of rabbis offering communal prayers alongside ministers and priests accustomed the public to viewing Judaism as a legitimate American faith and Jews as an integral part of American life. As Gregory Peck said in *Gentleman's Agreement,* an American could be a Protestant or a Catholic or a Jew.

Will Herberg's 1955 book, *Protestant-Catholic-Jew: A Study in Religious Sociology,* revealed just how far the normalization of Jews and Judaism had gone. Written by a former Marxist who had returned to Judaism after World War II, *Protestant-Catholic-Jew* was one of the most influential postwar volumes in the sociology of American religion. Its thesis concerned the perennial question of American identity. Herberg claimed that the coming of age of the grandchildren of the immigrants of the nineteenth and twentieth centuries had changed the way Americans answered the question "Who am I?" Instead of describing themselves as Irish, Italians, or Swedes, most Americans now preferred to identify themselves in religious terms. They were either Protestants, Catholics, or Jews. According to Herberg, Americans viewed each of these three religions as equally valid expressions of what had come to be known as the American Way of Life. "Our government makes no sense unless it is founded in deeply felt religious faith," president-elect Dwight D. Eisenhower said in 1952, "and I don't care what it is."[42]

For Jews, the implications of Herberg's thesis, if correct, were incredible. Gentiles now no longer considered Jews, who made up only 3 percent of the nation's population, an exotic ethnic and religious minority. Jews had achieved parity not only with Catholics but with Protestants as well. Bolstering Herberg's argument was the widespread use during the postwar years of the adjective *Judeo-Christian* rather than *Christian* to describe the country's moral and spiritual values. This indicated that Gentiles were willing to accord Jews an important role in the saga of American development. They no longer thought of the United States as an exclusively Christian nation.

The Judeo-Christian definition of America served to bind Americans more tightly together in the confrontation with atheistic Russia, as religion, including Judaism, was mobilized in the struggle against communism. The same impulse was behind the growing popularity of the interfaith movement. Most Jews supported interfaith activities such as religious dialogues and the exchange of pulpits by rabbis and Christian clergymen that had begun in the 1920s. In order to foster interfaith work, Jewish organizations forged close relationships with their Christian counterparts, assigned personnel to this area, and even hired Christians to be interfaith emissaries to their fellow Christians. For Jews, the interfaith movement confirmed their status within the American mainstream. For the same reason, Jews were also pleased by the emphasis of Christian theologians and historians on the Jewish roots of Christianity.[43]

With Jews no longer relegated to the social and economic margins of American life, the mysterious aura that had enveloped them dissipated. This process had already begun during the war. Gentiles had been in close proximity to Jews while in the armed forces, and this helped undermine anti-Semitic stereotypes. By 1950, according to one poll, less than one-tenth of American Gentiles objected to friendships with Jews. The war had also undermined much of the appeal of anti-Semitism because of its identification with America's wartime foe, Nazi Germany, and because the Holocaust had demonstrated where anti-Semitism could lead. Finally, American Jews benefited from the public's positive attitude toward Israel.[44]

Except for political extremists on the Left and the Right and persons with economic and cultural ties to the Arab world, most Americans admired Israel. They believed the Holocaust had made the need for a Jewish state self-evident, they applauded Israel's tenacity in the face of overwhelming odds, and they were comfortable with Israel's democratic and prowestern character. Israel disproved the anti-Semitic canard, popular during World War II, that Jews were cowards and poor soldiers. In fact, the image of a militarist Israel became popular among fringe elements on the political Left.[45]

Despite their tendency to exaggerate anti-Semitism, Jews during the postwar years recognized that they were living under unprecedented conditions of freedom and openness. In 1965, for the first time in its sixty-year history, the *American Jewish Year Book* replaced its discussion of anti-Semitism in its lead articles with a section titled "Civil Rights and Intergroup Tensions." Local and national Jewish "defense" agencies, whose major mission had been combating anti-Semitism, now defined their responsibilities more broadly as "community relations." Community relations involved a concern with the larger community and denoted a more sophisticated approach to the defense of Jewish interests. It included encouraging harmonious ethnic and race relations. The activities of the American Jewish Committee were particularly important. Beginning in the late 1960s, the AJC sponsored publications and conferences publicizing the complaints and plight of white ethnic groups. The AJC feared that white ethnics had become embittered by the focusing of the attention of the government and the university on the problems of blacks, Indians, and Hispanics.

One measure of the new sense of security was a noticeable lessening of Jewish defensiveness. The Jewish reluctance to stand out in a crowd gave way to a willingness to publicize one's Jewishness. During the 1930s, Jews had kept their religious and ethnic commitments private. Few Jews built succahs, the booths in which Jews eat during the holiday of Succot. Only infrequently did Orthodox Jews wear skullcaps on the street. Ramaz, an Orthodox school in Manhattan, told its students that the skullcap was an "indoor garment." After World War II, however, the wearing of skullcaps, the Star of David, and other Jewish accoutrements became common. Jews organized mammoth parades in New York City in support of Israel and Russian Jewry. The age-old fear of "what will the Gentiles think" was replaced by a militant espousal of Jewish interests. This was particularly evident in the new Jewish prominence in matters of church and state.[46]

Because of their experiences in Europe and the United States as a religious minority, Jews traditionally supported the wall of separation between church and state. They feared they would be adversely affected if government supported religion. But at first, Jews were not in the forefront of the campaign to ensure that religion remain a private matter. This task was performed by Protestants such as Paul Blandshard, the author of *American Freedom and Catholic Power* (1949), who opposed the efforts of the Roman Catholic church to secure government funds for its institutions, especially its parochial schools. In the 1950s, however, secular Jewish organizations, most notably the American Jewish Congress, became prominent in the legal efforts to construct a towering and impenetrable wall of separation between church and state.

These organizations took an absolutist position on church-state issues, opposing virtually all proposals to provide state support to nonpublic schools through direct subsidies, supplementary educational programs, educational vouchers, and the funding of transportation. Jewish organizations also objected to the displaying of religious symbols, including menorahs, on public property, and to the saying of nondenominational prayers in public schools. In the early 1960s, the Jesuit magazine *America* warned Jews that their church-state position could lead to increased anti-Semitism. Jews refused to back down and accused *America* of attempting intimidation. If anything, Jewish organizations became even more committed to ensuring that religion not overstep its proper bounds.

After 1945, no one was more important than Leo Pfeffer in developing this strict separationist dogma. For over four decades, Pfeffer was either a member of the American Jewish Congress's legal staff or a special consultant to the congress on church-state matters. He argued more church-state cases before the Supreme Court than anyone else in history and wrote several significant books on the church-state question. At first glance, the relationship between the American Jewish Congress and Pfeffer appears incongruous. The congress was a social action and secular organization that had been founded in 1918 by Stephen S. Wise, a Reform rabbi and social firebrand. Pfeffer, in contrast, was an Orthodox Jew. His father was an Orthodox rabbi, he had received a traditional religious education, he observed the Jewish dietary laws, and he attended synagogue on a regular basis. The union of the American Jewish Congress and Pfeffer reveals the extent to which the strict separationist faith encompassed the broadest spectrum of American Jewry.[47]

The willingness of America's Jews to make their political weight felt publicly also manifested itself in their response to the March 1987 conviction of Jonathan and Anne Pollard for espionage. Jonathan Pollard, an employee of the navy, had been charged with providing Israel with classified documents, and his wife had been accused of assisting him. The Pollards became involved in espionage as a result of ideological and more mundane considerations. From his youth, Jonathan Pollard had had an intense emotional attachment to the Jewish state. The Pollards also seemed to be chronically short of money. Unfortunately, there were Israeli officials in America willing to gratify Jonathan Pollard's Zionist fantasies and to provide the couple with the money they constantly requested. In contrast to the Rosenbergs, the Pollards pled guilty in the hope of mitigating their sentences. They were unsuccessful. Jonathan Pollard received life imprisonment and his wife a five-year prison term.

The Pollard case was potentially embarrassing for American Jews. Here was seeming confirmation of the anti-Semitic claim that the Jews' ultimate loyalty was to international Jewry and to the Jewish state. Israel's supporters in the United States told Israeli officials in no uncertain terms of their anger at being placed in such a difficult position and of their disappointment that Israel's representatives would act so foolishly and arrogantly in encouraging the Pollards' treason. The American Israel Public Affairs Committee (the "Jewish lobby") feared that the Pollard case would seriously injure American-Israeli relations. In order to reassure the American public of the loyalty of America's Jews, the head of the Conference of Presidents of Major American Jewish Organizations publicly supported the life sentence handed out to Jonathan Pollard.[48]

In a famous letter published in the 21 March 1987 issue of the *Jerusalem Post* (international edition), Israeli historian Shlomo Avineri charged that the response of American Jews to the Pollard case exhibited the typical Diaspora insecurity that Zionism had sought to extirpate. Writing to an imaginary "American Jewish friend," Avineri perceived in American Jewry "a degree of nervousness, insecurity and even cringing . . . which runs counter to the conventional wisdom of American Jewry feeling free, secure and unmolested in an open and pluralistic society." This anxiety, he wrote, is "deep in your soul," and deep in the soul of every other Jew living outside of Israel. Avineri's letter went to the heart of the American Jewish condition. He was correct in asserting that the Pollard case had brought to the surface the insecurity of some American Jews. But it also brought to the surface the confidence of other Jews.[49]

Much to the surprise of Jews, the Pollard case did not increase anti-Semitism. The public's indifference to and ignorance of the Pollards was impressive. A *New York Times* poll revealed that 82 percent of Americans did not even know for whom Pollard had spied. An equally high number did not realize that he was Jewish. The relation between the actions of the Pollards and Zionism was not dwelled upon except by fringe groups such as the American Council for Judaism, which was exhumed in the wake of the Pollard affair. Few Americans changed their attitude toward Jews or Israel because of the Pollards.

In responding to the Pollard case, some Jews exhibited a sense of security as Americans and as Jews, which contrasted dramatically with the mentality of their parents during the early 1950s. Jewish spokesmen were not reluctant to come to the aid of a convicted spy and to run the risk of being charged with dual loyalty. In April 1989, for example, Rabbi Avi Weiss of the Hebrew Institute of Riverdale, New York, and fifteen other Jews participated in a "freedom seder" in front of the federal prison in Marion, Illinois, which housed Jonathan Pollard. Weiss protested Pollard's incarceration and demanded the release of this "Jewish political prisoner."

In contrast to Weiss's group, the majority of Jews readily admitted that the Pollards were guilty. (The Pollards had, after all, admitted their guilt.) Their objections centered instead on the life sentence handed out to Jonathan Pollard and on the government's treatment of the couple while they were in prison. The members of the Walker spy ring, which was unmasked in the 1980s, had received lighter sentences than the Pollards even though they had spied for an enemy of America and had endangered American security far more than the Pollards. The executive board of the Central Conference of American Rabbis (Reform) unanimously called upon the

American government to "re-evaluate the Pollard case and to ensure that the Pollards be treated with fairness and equity during their incarceration."[50]

The literature of the Justice for the Pollards Committee compared the couple to Alfred Dreyfus. There was, of course, a crucial difference between Dreyfus and the Pollards. Dreyfus had been the innocent victim of a frame-up, while the Pollards were guilty of espionage. According to the Justice for the Pollards Committee, the couple had been victimized by an anti-Semitic cabal within the Justice Department. Herb Zweibon, chairman of Americans for a Safe Israel, claimed the Pollard case demonstrated the existence of elements within the American government "who use whatever opportunities they can to pound Israel on the head." More objective observers found this statement puzzling, since Jews had been prominent on the government's legal team that argued the Pollard case.[51]

The resemblance between the Pollard case and the Dreyfus affair was also the theme of David Biale's essay "J'Accuse: American Jews and L'Affaire Pollard," which appeared in *Tikkun,* a radical American Jewish magazine. Biale, director of the Center for Jewish Studies at the Graduate Theological Union in Berkeley, California, speculated wildly that Pollard's "extraordinarily harsh and thoroughly unexpected sentence" was an act of revenge by Edwin Meese, the attorney general, and Caspar Weinberger, the secretary of defense, against Israel's enticing of the Reagan administration into the Iranian arms scandal.

Biale predictably suggested that Jews should respond to the Pollard affair by increasing their resistance to the Reagan presidency, which "had sown terror abroad and hunger and homelessness at home." While Biale approached the Pollard case from a different political perspective than Zweibon, both were confident that the security of American Jews would not be adversely affected by their objections to the treatment of the Pollards. Neither believed these would be interpreted as disloyalty to America.[52]

The most striking example of American Jewry's sense of security took place at the White House in 1985, a few months before the arrest of the Pollards. Shortly after his reelection in 1984, President Ronald Reagan announced that he had scheduled a visit to Germany. A wreath-laying ceremony at a German military cemetery at Bitburg, a small town in the Rhineland, was on his itinerary. It was soon discovered that the cemetery contained the graves of forty-seven members of the Waffen SS. Jews, World War II veterans, and other Americans were infuriated that the president would consider honoring members of a German military unit that had participated in Nazi atrocities. The president was caught in the middle between the outrage of these Americans and the insistence of Helmut Kohl's West German government that the Bitburg visit proceed as scheduled. The president did ultimately lay the wreath at Bitburg, but he spent as little time as possible at the cemetery.

The Bitburg controversy assumed great symbolic importance for American Jews. Elie Wiesel, a survivor of Auschwitz, a prolific author, and arguably the American Jew most admired by other Jews, expressed the anguish of Jews in a dramatic televised confrontation with the president just before Reagan left for Europe. It took place at the White House, where Wiesel was to receive the Congressional Gold Medal of Achievement, the government's highest civilian honor.

Instead of politely accepting the honor, Wiesel let it be known that he was going to use the opportunity to reproach the president for planning to visit Bitburg. Fearing repercussions, American Jewish leaders attempted to dissuade him. Their pleas left the author of *The Jews of Silence* unmoved. "Compromise was impossible; Jewish dignity was at stake," he later told Charles E. Silberman. Speaking with "the sadness that is in my heart," Wiesel gently chided Reagan. The president of "the freest nation in the world, the moral nation," had no business at Bitburg. "That place, Mr. President, is not your place. Your place is with the victims of the SS." Wiesel's statement, *Newsweek* wrote, was "surely one of the most remarkable moments in the annals of the White House."

It was also, as Silberman concluded, one of the most remarkable moments in the annals of American Jewry. For a Holocaust survivor to receive the Congressional Gold Medal of Achievement was noteworthy enough. But for him to use the occasion to rebuke the president and to do this in the White House manifested a sense of security unprecedented in American Jewish history. Wiesel's words were a fitting epitaph to the age-old fear of "what will the Gentiles think." It helped, of course, that American public opinion and a large majority of Congress agreed with him. The next year Wiesel would win the Nobel Peace Prize.[53]

CHAPTER THREE

FILLING THE VOID

WORLD WAR II dramatically changed the demographic configuration of world Jewry. In 1933, the more than seven million Jews of eastern Europe made up 46 percent of the world's Jews. Eastern Europe's significance within the Jewish world was, however, more than a matter of numbers. It was also home to the most vibrant and creative of Jewish cultures, what Lucy S. Dawidowicz has called "the golden tradition." The Jews of Poland, Hungary, Romania, Lithuania, Russia, and the other states east of Germany and Austria lived within a deeply Jewish environment that, although showing signs of decay, was still powerful. The core of this culture was the Yiddish language, which most Jews in eastern Europe spoke.[1]

Yiddish literature had flourished during the nineteenth and early twentieth centuries, along with the culture of which it was a part. The leading talmudic academies, theaters, publishing houses, newspapers, Hasidic dynasties, and charitable and scholarly institutions were located in eastern Europe. Out of eastern Europe had emerged important modern Jewish ideologies, including Zionism and Jewish socialism. Most of the significant figures within the Jewish intelligentsia—religious and secular scholars, novelists, poets, and journalists—were products of eastern Europe. The Holocaust not only destroyed much of the body of world Jewry; it also destroyed most of its heart, soul, and mind.

As a result of the war, the United States replaced eastern Europe as the largest and most important center of Jewish population and culture. American Jews made up less than 5 percent of world Jewry in 1875 and only 29 percent in 1933. They were 40 percent in 1945. These five million American Jews were approximately the same percentage of world Jewry after the war as eastern European Jewry had been prior to it. Never before had one single country contained so many Jews. The United States, historian Moses Rischin would later write, had become "the greatest Jewish center in the long history of this ancient people."[2]

Even before the end of the war, Salo W. Baron, the great Jewish historian, had predicted the future significance of American Jewry. "The Jews of the United States together with the small groups in Latin America and the British Empire," he prophesied in 1942, "will decide in the next few years the course of Jewish history for generations to come." Their numbers and financial resources virtually guaranteed that American Jews would have a decisive role in determining the Jewish future. The real question was whether they would assume the burdens of leadership or abdicate the responsibilities that recent history seemingly had thrust on their shoulders. Should American Jewry assume these obligations, Baron wrote, they "would earn the gratitude of generations." Should they refuse, they "would fail . . . the Jewish people as a whole and . . . be justly called to account by mankind at large."[3]

There were good reasons for believing in 1945 that American Jews would not be equal to the task. American Jewry's role up to this point had been largely financial. It had been generous in aiding Jews overseas, but had not as yet exhibited the same dedication to ensuring its own Jewish survival. Its energies had been mainly directed at achieving economic and social mobility and adapting to American culture. Many observers were pessimistic regarding the long-term viability of the American Jewish community, and some questioned whether it could survive without some form of self-imposed isolation and without continual demographic and cultural replenishment from eastern Europe.

Prewar analyses predicting the assimilation of Jews as they moved out of the immigrant neighborhoods were common. The small number of children enrolled in Jewish schools and the small percentage of adults who attended weekly religious services, kept kosher, and observed the Sabbath, along with the seeming apathy of many Jews toward their Jewish heritage, substantiated this pessimism. Sociological studies of American Jews such as Louis Wirth's 1927 examination of Chicago Jewry, *The Ghetto,* had a dirge-like quality. Wirth and others wondered what convincing reasons Jewish survivalists could provide to the young and upwardly mobile for continuing to identify as Jews, in light of the mediocre, anachronistic, and foreign character of much of American Jewish life. Judaism, it was commonly believed, was destined to become another of America's many small cults.

Observers were particularly somber regarding the future of Jewish identity among the college-educated. The Jewish-born philosopher Sidney Hook was surprised to discover during the 1930s that the great majority of Jews in his classes at New York University regretted being Jewish and wished they had been born Christian. They viewed their ethnic and religious heritage as an onerous and unnecessary burden. Few planned to perpetuate the Jewish commitment of their parents.[4]

Even in fund-raising, where American Jewry had excelled, the years immediately after World War II did not seem to be propitious for assuming the burdens of leadership. While American Jews comprised the wealthiest Jewish community in history and under normal conditions could be expected to be generous in aiding Jews overseas, these were not normal times. It would take a while for the American economy to convert to a peacetime basis and for the hundreds of thousands of Jewish servicemen to resume their civilian occupations. Also, because of the American experience after World War I, it was widely assumed that the transformation of the economy to a peacetime footing would be difficult and marked by dislocations and perhaps by a recession. Even if the expected postwar economic difficulties did not materialize, normal employment patterns would have to be established before Jews could be expected to divert discretionary income to the United Jewish Appeal and other Jewish causes.

In addition to fund-raising, there was the additional matter of culture. Could American Jewry partially fill the great cultural void created by the destruction of eastern European Jewry, or would American Jews perceive their responsibility solely in terms of writing checks? Only they now had the financial resources and numbers to create the seminaries, schools, libraries, and other institutions to ensure the transmission of Jewish values and culture to future generations. The response of American Jews to the new role that the European tragedy had thrust upon them was not long in coming.

The reaction of American Jewry to fund-raising appeals exceeded even the most optimistic predictions of American Jewish leaders. The dramatic contrast between the sums raised by the United Jewish Appeal before and after the war indicated the impact the Holocaust had on American Jews, particularly the guilt they felt for not having done more to rescue Europe's Jews. In 1938, the separate campaigns of the Joint Distribution Committee, the United Palestine Appeal, and the National Coordinating Committee Fund (refugee assistance) had raised seven million dollars. These three organizations merged into the United Jewish Appeal in the wake of the burning of Germany's synagogues in November 1938. The UJA's first fundraising campaign in 1939 raised nearly sixteen million dollars. While more than double the 1938 total, the 1939 campaign fell four million dollars short of its goal. The 1940 campaign raised only fourteen million dollars.[5]

These figures were large in comparison to previous campaigns but small considering the needs of the postwar years. In December 1945, American Jewish philanthropy entered a new era when the National Conference of the United Jewish Appeal for Refugees, Overseas Needs and Palestine convened its first postwar conference. Uppermost in the minds of the representatives of American Jewry who gathered in Atlantic City was the enormity of the tragedy experienced by European Jewry and the perilous condition of the Jewish community in Palestine. They realized that half-hearted measures would no longer suffice. Despite the skepticism of national and local lay leaders and Jewish professionals, these grass-roots delegates unanimously voted for a campaign of one hundred million dollars, more than three times what had been raised in 1945. When the final figures of the 1946 campaign were tallied, UJA leaders were dumbfounded. Actual contributions to the campaign exceeded the goal by thirty-one million dollars.

The success of the 1946 campaign emboldened the UJA. The 1947 campaign raised nearly one hundred and fifty million dollars and the 1948 campaign, which took place during Israel's War of Independence and America's postwar economic boom, raised more than two hundred million dollars. It was during these years that the United Jewish Appeal became the preeminent American Jewish organization, and philanthropy became the most popular and important expression of American Jewish identity. American Jews became accustomed to the UJA's annual campaign of self-taxation in behalf of Jewish survival. Much to the surprise of organizations not subvented by UJA dollars, their own fund-raising efforts were not adversely affected by the UJA's success. These cultural, religious, and health and welfare organizations also set their own sights higher and raised unprecedented amounts.[6]

Fund-raising became the tail wagging the dog of Jewish organizational life. Future Jewish leaders received their basic training in the trenches of fund-raising, and the effectiveness of lay and professional leadership was measured by their abilities at solicitation. This involvement in fund-raising provided volunteers with a glimpse of Jewish organizational needs and structure, and this encouraged many to become more involved in Jewish communal life. This emphasis had its critics, particularly Jewish intellectuals, who were dismayed by vulgarities such as calling cards (the public announcement of charitable pledges) and the honoring of wealthy, but otherwise unworthy, individuals.

Intellectuals, unable to match the charitable efforts of businessmen and professionals, believed their contributions in the realm of ideas should count for as much as the dollars of the affluent. They feared that the raising and allocating of money was becoming the be-all and end-all of American Jewish life, that Jewish solicitors and donors were replacing religious and cultural leaders within the American Jewish communal pecking order, and that status was flowing from the synagogues to the federations that conducted the annual fund-raising drives. No longer were rabbis the leading spokesmen of the Jewish community. Secular federation leaders supplemented and often supplanted the rabbis as the most important voice of the community.

This emphasis on raising money did have its redeeming features. For centuries, the giving of charity had been an important Jewish value. Moses Maimonides and other Jewish sages had written treatises on the religious obligation to give charity. Although the annual United Jewish Appeal campaign lacked religious trappings, it expressed a profound spiritual commitment to Jewish survival. Critics of the UJA failed to realize the paramount role that American Jews had accorded the UJA in this sacred task. If a group's priorities are most clearly revealed by how it spends its money, then the requiems sung over American Jewry were perhaps premature.

The sole contact of some Jews with the Jewish community was their annual check to the United Jewish Appeal. "I am because I give" defined their Jewish identity. Fund-raising thus preserved a tenuous Jewish identity among individuals who were otherwise disaffected from Jewish life. Although Jews made up only 3 percent of the nation's population, the United Jewish Appeal became the most successful of all postwar American philanthropies, raising hundreds of millions of dollars annually.

Increased fund-raising was merely one aspect of the greater importance of American Jews after the war. World War II resulted in the shift of the Zionist movement from London and Berlin to Jerusalem and New York. While Zionist leaders in Palestine oversaw the economic and political development of the yishuv (the Jewish community in Palestine), Zionist leaders in New York raised funds, lobbied in Washington and other political centers, and disseminated the Zionist message to influential groups and individuals. The role of American Zionists was magnified by the postwar significance of the United States in the negotiations over the future of Palestine. The British need for American economic and diplomatic assistance increased the political leverage of the American government, and this in turn placed American Jews in a strategic position they had previously never occupied.

The United States also became the intellectual and cultural center of world Jewry because of the war. "As a result of the destruction of Eastern European Jewry," the 1948 *American Jewish Year Book* reported, "this country now holds first place in Yiddish culture and ranks second only to Palestine as a creative center in Hebrew." Remnants of the eastern European Jewish intelligentsia who had survived the Holocaust, including rabbis, librarians, writers, and scholars, resettled in America.[7]

The most important institution for the study of Yiddish-speaking Jewry was YIVO, the Yiddish Scientific Institute, which had been established in Vilna in the mid-1920s. It moved to New York City in 1940, shortly before the German invasion of the Baltic states. Once in America it changed its name to the YIVO Institute for Jewish Research. The size of its library increased dramatically after World War II when the State Department and the American military agreed that it should be the repository of tens of thousands of books and manuscripts that had been stolen by the Nazis. This increase in library holdings necessitated a move to larger quarters, and in 1945 YIVO purchased a Fifth Avenue mansion once owned by the Vanderbilts.[8]

YIVO became an important element in the intellectual life of New York Jewry. It offered courses in eastern European Jewish history and in Yiddish; it published books, pamphlets, and a scholarly yearbook; and it provided researchers with the world's most important collection of books, newspapers, and manuscripts pertaining to the history and culture of Yiddish-speaking Jewry. It was an invaluable institution in preserving the cultural legacy of eastern European Jewry. YIVO's employees and those using its research facilities viewed their work with reverence. They believed they had virtually a religious obligation to reconstruct—if only in books, essays, and archives—the vanished world of east European Jewry. Despite their valiant efforts, it was beyond the possibility of YIVO, or any other institution, to arrest the decline of Yiddish culture in America.

This decline was most noticeable in the decreasing circulation of the Yiddish press, which became evident as early as the 1920s, as eastern European Jews began moving out of the areas of immigrant settlement. The Holocaust left New York City, along with Palestine, as one of the major centers of Yiddish-reading Jews. After the war, the city had several daily Yiddish newspapers, Yiddish publishing houses, a Yiddish stage, Yiddish magazines, and Yiddish schools for the young and adults. The city was also home to what remained of the Yiddish literary establishment. Max Weinreich, YIVO's head and the foremost authority on the Yiddish language, migrated from Vilna to New York in 1940. The two most popular post–World War II Yiddish novelists—Isaac Bashevis Singer, a future Nobel Prize laureate, and Chaim Grade—also relocated to New York. The works of Singer and Grade, as well as those of other Yiddish literary figures, often appeared in serial form in the New York Yiddish press before being published as books in English.

In September 1948, representatives of the Farband Labor Zionist Order, the Workmen's Circle, the Yiddish Pen Club, and the Yiddish Writers Union, along with several east European Jewish writers and educators who had survived the war, established the Congress for Jewish Culture. Headquartered in New York City, the CJC soon became the most important American organization working to perpetuate Yiddish culture. It published the works of writers and scholars murdered by the Nazis (including Simon Dubnow's monumental ten-volume *History of the Jewish People*), reprinted the major works of Yiddish literature, promoted Yiddish education, and printed documents relating to the Holocaust. Its monthly literature magazine, *Di Tsukunft* (the future), was the most important post–World War II Yiddish literary journal.9

The CJC, however, was fighting a losing cause. The condition of Yiddish culture in New York and the rest of the country became increasingly perilous. Few of the children and grandchildren of the immigrant Jews from eastern Europe spoke or read Yiddish regularly. They identified Yiddish with the impoverished and foreign world of the immigrant generation from which they had fled (except for periodic nostalgic slumming back to the old neighborhoods and trips to the theater to see *Fiddler on the Roof*). The Yiddish-speaking population in America was elderly, and every year fewer people patronized Yiddish institutions and publications.

The fate of the *Forward,* the most prominent Yiddish newspaper, was symptomatic. Prior to World War II, the *Forward*'s daily circulation was well over one hundred thousand, and it was the most widely read foreign language newspaper in the United States. Through its reports of life in

America and the "bintel brief" (bundle of letters)—its daily advice column—the paper was an important instrument in the Americanization of Jewish immigrants. The *Forward* and other Yiddish newspapers in America experienced hard times after World War II. Its competitors folded, and the *Forward* barely survived. Circulation and advertising revenues were inadequate to meet expenses, and the paper became dependent on the generosity of friends. In the 1980s, the *Forward* became a weekly and moved uptown from East Broadway, the erstwhile Fleet Street of the Yiddish press, to midtown Manhattan. Chinese-Americans purchased the *Forward* building, a neighborhood landmark and the tallest building on the Lower East Side, and turned part of it into a Chinese church.

In 1990, plans were announced for an English language weekly edition of the *Forward* to be published in New York City with bureaus in Moscow, Washington, Paris, and New York. It was announced that Seth Lipsky, a former member of the editorial board of the *Wall Street Journal,* was to be the editor, president, and chief executive officer. The English supplement of the old *Forward* was to be eliminated. The editors of the new *Forward* hoped to attract an audience of younger Jews who were unable to read Yiddish but were interested in the news provided by the old *Forward*. The days of the Yiddish *Forward* appeared to be numbered. It was likely that its Yiddish-reading audience would have to be satisfied with a Yiddish supplement in the English edition.

The fate of the *Forward* and the Yiddish press in general was not without irony. The *Forward* began as a socialist newspaper, although it did break with its socialist allies to support the reelection of Franklin D. Roosevelt in 1936. Its masthead read "Workers of the world, unite." Its working-class, pro-union, left-wing orientation reflected the outlook of Abraham Cahan (1860–1951), who edited the *Forward* for half a century. As was true of most leading Jewish socialists, Cahan was not religious himself, although he urged his readers to treat the pious with respect. Today the success of the Yiddish press and the Yiddish language in America is dependent on Orthodox religious groups in Brooklyn, where the Lubavitch and Satmar Hasidic sects support small opposing Yiddish newspapers. One of the few places in the United States where Yiddish is still spoken is in the yeshiva, a seminary for the intensive study of the Talmud.

That the United States became a center for right-wing Orthodoxy was also ironic. Prior to World War II, Orthodox spokesmen in eastern Europe had discouraged their followers from migrating to America. The United

States, they claimed, was a godless land where Jews quickly forgot the hallowed ways of their fathers. Rabbi Israel Meier Kohen, the most revered of all eastern European Orthodox leaders of the twentieth century, argued that Jews should remain in anti-Semitic Russia, where at least they would remain faithful to religious tradition, rather than flee to the golden land of America. "A man must move away from any place which causes turning away from the way of the Lord," he said, "even if he knows for certain that he will have great economic success there." If a person was determined to seek his fortune in the New World, Kohen declared, he should at least leave his children behind so they could be immersed in Jewish traditions and values. Elazar Shapiro, the Hasidic leader of the Jews of Munkacs in Hungary, agreed with Kohen. America's Jews, Shapiro claimed, were destined for purgatory, since repentance was impossible in a pagan land where the pursuit of money was the all-consuming passion.[10]

As a result of increasing anti-Semitism in the 1930s and then the Holocaust, the United States became more attractive to eastern European Orthodox leaders. In 1937, Rabbi Moses Feinstein, a leading authority on Jewish law, migrated from Luban in White Russia to Manhattan. Four years later, Rabbi Aaron Kotler, one of the giants of east European Orthodoxy, arrived in America. He planned to stay for only a short time before traveling to Palestine, where he hoped to establish a yeshiva. Promised financial support by a small group of American Orthodox laymen if he would settle permanently in America, Kotler changed his plans and founded the Beth Medrash Govoha of America (the Rabbi Aaron Kotler Institute for Advanced Studies) in Lakewood, New Jersey. This institution would eventually become the most distinguished of American yeshivas, and the first one to provide a *kollel*—a higher institute for talmudic study—where married men could study the Talmud on a full-time basis.

The arrival of Kotler, Feinstein, and other luminaries of eastern European Orthodoxy reinvigorated right-wing Orthodoxy in America. The great eastern European talmudic academies of Telshe, Lublin, Radun, Mir, and Bialystok established new homes in Cleveland, Detroit, Manhattan, and Brooklyn. This revival of sectarian Orthodoxy in America was also seen in the history of Agudath Israel. Prior to World War II, Agudath Israel had been the most important organization in Europe of right-wing Orthodoxy. It had tried without success in 1922 to establish an American branch. It succeeded in 1939. Two years later, Agudath Israel itself moved its headquarters from London to New York.[11]

The United States also became a favorite destination for the remnants of eastern European Hasidism, a mystical movement dating from the eighteenth century. In 1940, Rabbi Joseph Schneerson, the leader of Lubavitch Hasidim, arrived in America from the Soviet Union and settled in the Crown Heights section of Brooklyn. Lubavitch flourished in the United States. It became famous for its outreach program to the nonreligious, for the Habad centers it created on college campuses, and for the piety and congeniality of its adherents. Satmar, Karlin-Stolin, and other Hasidic dynasties also established their headquarters in Brooklyn during or shortly after the war.

Just before America's entry into World War II, a sizable group of non-Hasidic but traditional Jews from western Germany under the leadership of Rabbi Joseph Breuer settled in the Washington Heights section of Manhattan. Breuer was the grandson of Rabbi Samson Raphael Hirsch, the greatest figure in nineteenth-century German Orthodoxy. K'hal Adath Jeshurun, Breuer's synagogue, was modeled on Hirsch's community in Frankfurt am Main. KAJ was a "full-service" synagogue, which attempted to meet all of the social, educational, and religious needs of its eight hundred families. Three decades after the founding of KAJ, a member of one of KAJ's families would become the first Jewish secretary of state, but that was long after Henry Kissinger had forsaken Orthodoxy for power politics.[12]

The Breuer community was part of a larger migration to America of over one hundred thousand German-speaking Jews from Germany and Austria. Approximately two-thirds settled in New York City, where they congregated in Washington Heights, Kew Gardens and Forest Hills in Queens, the West Bronx, and the Upper West Side in Manhattan. The most important area of German Jewish settlement was Washington Heights. This so-called Fourth Reich contained twenty thousand German Jewish refugees in the 1940s, many of whom were Orthodox. Max Frankel and Fred Hechinger, who became columnists for the *New York Times,* and the future sexologist Ruth Westheimer (Dr. Ruth) were raised in traditional German Jewish families in Washington Heights. During the 1950s and 1960s, most of the German-speaking Jews of Washington Heights moved to other parts of the city or to the suburbs of New York and New Jersey, due to the influx of blacks and Hispanics into the area.[13]

The destruction of Jewish culture in central Europe by the Nazis led to efforts by German-speaking Jews, particularly in the United States, to preserve the historical record of German Jewry. In 1955, the Council of Jews

from Germany founded the Leo Baeck Institute, named for the last spokesman of pre-war German Jewry. The institute established centers in London,
Jerusalem, and New York. The New York center concentrated on docu-
menting the history of German-speaking Jewry. Its library, located in the
center's headquarters on East 73d Street in Manhattan, became the major
archival repository in its field. It contained over fifty thousand books,
public records, private papers, and manuscripts of all sorts relating to the
social, political, and intellectual history of German-speaking Jewry since
the seventeenth century. The New York center published more than sixty
books pertaining to German-speaking Jewry and put out a yearbook containing important essays on the history and legacy of Central European
Jewry. The center also sponsored the Leo Baeck Memorial Lectures, an
annual lecture series given by a prominent Jewish scholar.[14]

The Holocaust created a void in the field of Jewish publishing. Most of
the major Jewish publication houses had been in continental Europe. Several Jewish publishers escaped from Europe and made their way to the
United States. The most important was Zalman Schocken, who fled Berlin
in 1934 for Palestine. In 1940, he relocated to New York and opened a
publishing house that bore his name, specializing in publishing Judaic
works in English. In addition to Schocken and other refugee publishers,
various American university presses, the Bloch publishing company, Behrman House, and the Jewish Publication Society of America also published
scholarly and popular Judaic works after the war. The postwar resurgence
of American Orthodoxy increased the number of publishers and bookstores specializing in religious books. The most prominent of the new
religious publishers was Mesorah Publications of Brooklyn, publisher of
the ArtScroll series of devotional, children's, and semischolarly books.

The destruction of the Jewish libraries of eastern and central Europe
made the Judaica collections of American libraries more important. For
Jewish scholars, the most significant American libraries were the Library of
Congress, the New York Public Library, the libraries of Columbia, Yeshiva,
Brandeis, and Harvard universities, and the libraries of YIVO, the Leo
Baeck Institute, and the Jewish Theological Seminary (JTS). The YIVO
library had the most important collection of material on east European
Jewry, while the JTS library contained the greatest collection of Jewish
manuscripts in the world. The New York Public Library had the finest
collection of Jewish books of any public library in the world, with the
possible exception of the British Museum in London. Harvard's collection

of Judaica was the most important of any American university. Its holdings of one hundred and fifty thousand volumes, including fifty thousand in Hebrew and ten thousand in Yiddish, were overseen by a librarian holding the endowed position of Lee M. Friedman Bibliographer in Judaica.[15]

Of all American universities, none played a more significant role in Jewish scholarship than Brandeis University. Its distinguished faculty included Nahum Glatzer and Alexander Altmann, two of the world's leading authorities on Jewish philosophy. Glatzer, until 1933 when he left Germany, had held the chair of Jewish philosophy and ethics at the University of Frankfurt previously occupied by Martin Buber. Altmann had been a rabbi in Berlin and a lecturer in the city's Orthodox rabbinical seminary before he fled Germany in 1938. In the 1950s, when Glatzer and Altmann joined the Brandeis faculty, the university was less than ten years old.

Brandeis's meteoric rise to academic excellence was without parallel in the history of American education. The 107 students who made up Brandeis's first class in 1948 had enrolled in an institution whose future was cloudy at best. Its campus in Waltham, Massachusetts, had previously housed Middlesex University, a defunct medical college, and its most imposing building resembled a medieval castle. The university began with a library containing only a thousand books, mostly out-of-date medical texts. With only thirty-three thousand dollars in the bank, the institution's financial condition appeared precarious.[16]

The founders of Brandeis, most of whom were from neighboring Boston, seemed to have embarked on a fool's errand. There was no assurance that American Jews in the 1940s would be any friendlier to the idea of a Jewish university than they had been in the 1920s, when Yeshiva University announced plans to establish a liberal arts college. At that time, the *American Hebrew,* the organ of the German Jewish establishment, described the idea of a Jewish college as a "preposterous proposition . . . fraught with harmful possibilities." Such a proposal indicated "a lamentable lack of confidence in the justice and fair play of the American people." Fortunately it was "not in any sense representative of the wishes of American Jewry." Judaism did not require "cloistered walls or academic seclusion to retain its integrity." Louis Marshall, the unofficial spokesman for the Jewish establishment, agreed. The establishment of a Jewish college, he predicted, would be "most unfortunate."[17]

Some opponents of Yeshiva College objected to the very idea of a Jewish college, while others opposed its control by Orthodox elements. For the latter, the name Yeshiva University was an oxymoron. Just as the British writer George Bernard Shaw had once described a Catholic university as a contradiction in terms, so they argued that an educational institution under Orthodox auspices would be too sectarian and narrow-minded to be a true university.

Most American Jews believed that Jewish collegians should not voluntarily isolate themselves from the rest of society by attending a Jewish university. This would impede their social and economic mobility and acculturation. Also, American Jews feared that the voluntary segregation of Jews in a Jewish university implied the acceptance of the inevitability of anti-Semitism in academia. From their perspective, it would be far better to destroy the anti-Semitic barriers preventing Jewish scholars from finding employment and Jewish students from attending elite institutions than to establish parallel institutions.

The establishment of Brandeis after the war was an act of faith by its founders in the willingness of wealthy Jews to support a university under Jewish auspices and in the school's ability to attract students. Brandeis was founded at a difficult time for fund-raising. The first demands on Jewish philanthropy in the aftermath of World War II were refugee resettlement and support of the struggling Jewish community in Palestine. A Jewish university appeared to be a costly luxury. Also, there was no assurance that Jews, much less Gentiles, would be attracted to an institution describing itself as nonsectarian but Jewish-sponsored.

Despite these potential problems, Brandeis's early supporters proceeded with their plans. They justified it on the traditional grounds of providing an alternative for those Jews who had been rejected by other institutions because of anti-Semitism. Albert Einstein, an early friend of the Brandeis idea, contended that "under present circumstances, many of our gifted youth see themselves denied the cultural and professional education they are longing for." This rationale, with its pessimistic assumptions regarding anti-Semitism in America, came at a time when anti-Semitism was actually declining in academia and elsewhere. Brandeis required a more positive justification if it was to get off the drawing board.[18]

Brandeis's founders thus argued that the university would enable America's Jews to repay the country for the freedom and economic opportunity it had provided them. According to Abram L. Sachar, the university's first president and guiding light during its first quarter of a century, Brandeis was to be "a corporate gift of Jews to higher education." Brandeis's founders were bolstered by their confidence in the reconciliation of Jewishness and Americanness. Brandeis was to academia what Elliot Cohen's *Commentary* was to publishing, a manifestation of the conviction that Jews had become part of the American mainstream.[19]

The title of Sachar's memoir of his long involvement with Brandeis—*A Host at Last*—expressed his assumption that, at least for Jews in America, the long history of the wandering Jew had finally ended. In America, Jews no longer lived on the fringes of national life and at the sufferance of their neighbors. But a condition of this new Jewish status was that Jews must contribute to the welfare of American society. Just as Protestants had founded Harvard and Yale and Catholics had founded Georgetown and Notre Dame, so too Jews should establish a university of their own that would be an academic host for all Americans and not, as Yeshiva College was, a haven for Jews only. A Brandeis fund-raising brochure of the late 1940s asked, "Has not the time come when the numerous and well-placed American Jewish community should make at least one symbolic contribution to higher education?" This definition of Brandeis's role proved to be irresistible when Sachar approached potential benefactors.[20]

The Brandeis president was an extremely able fund-raiser and a wise observer of American Jewry. Irving Howe, a member of the Brandeis faculty during the 1950s, recounted how Sachar had raised philistinism "to the level of genius." He "turned to Jews of East European origin who had grown wealthy during the war years, men mostly lacking in education yet worshipful of the idea of it. Sachar milked this layer of the newly rich Jewish bourgeoisie with a skill that it would have taken a heart of gold not to admire."[21]

Sachar emphasized to potential Jewish donors that their contributions to Brandeis would benefit all Americans, not only Jews. Just as American Jewry had established a network of excellent hospitals and other social institutions for the general benefit of society, it should also support at least one major university. If it was acceptable for Jews to matriculate at Protestant and Catholic universities, such as Harvard and Georgetown, then it was also appropriate for Gentiles to attend a Jewish institution. Gentiles were not reluctant to patronize Jewish hospitals and they would not be averse to attending a university sponsored by Jews, provided it was a quality institution. It was time, Sachar argued, for Jews to become part of the American academic establishment.

By contributing to Brandeis, Sachar implied, Jews would not only be aiding a deserving Jewish cause. They would also be validating their own status as Americans worthy of the gratitude of the general society. American Jews would finally achieve the social acceptance they had been seeking for three centuries when Gentiles would enroll at Brandeis. Instead of being guests in America, they would be "a host at last." For Sachar then, there was no better way for Jews to raise their status than to support Brandeis. For Jews, the American mainstream passed through Waltham, Massachusetts.

Sachar did not want Brandeis to be a parochial institution similar to Yeshiva University or to the numerous small Catholic and Protestant colleges. Instead, he envisioned Brandeis as a quality university with a national reputation. Such a university would bring credit to American Jews in general and to its financial supporters in particular. There was no reason, Sachar believed, why a diploma from a Jewish university could not be a ticket of admission into the American professional, business, and academic elite for Jews and Gentiles alike.

From its beginning, Brandeis's Jewish character was shrouded in ambiguity. While admission to the university was open to all on a nondiscriminatory basis, a policy in which the university took pride, its founders assumed that a significant part of the student body would always be Jewish. (This was a correct assumption: at least two-thirds of Brandeis's undergraduates during its first four decades were Jewish.) The nature of Brandeis's Jewish identity was much talked about during its early years. Jews were naturally confused by a university describing itself as both Jewish and nonsectarian, particularly when they were being asked to send their children and dollars to Waltham. How could a university claiming to be Jewish not profess some specific form of Judaism or Jewish culture?

Thus traditionalists strongly protested when Brandeis held its 1950 commencement on Saturday, the Jewish Sabbath. The *Jewish Forum,* the voice of modern American Orthodoxy, editorialized that, despite its awarding of an honorary degree to Eleanor Roosevelt, Brandeis was "Neither Jewish, Nor American." Its "contempt for the most sacred institution in Jewish life," the magazine wrote, was an affront to God and religious Jews. The magazine suggested that Jews, instead of aiding Brandeis because they wrongly assumed they were contributing to a worthy Jewish and American cause, "might be truer to their intentions by transferring their support to the only truly Jewish and simultaneously truly American university in existence—Yeshiva University."[22]

Although future Brandeis commencements were not held on Saturday, the obscurity of Brandeis's Jewish identity remained. It became a bone of contention during the 1987–88 school year when the school's administration suggested that the cuisine in the two main student dining rooms be "internationalized" by serving pork and shellfish. This proposal stemmed from the university's effort to raise itself into the ranks of the nation's most prestigious institutions. This, it believed, required attracting a more diverse student body, which, in turn, depended on diluting Brandeis's image as a Jewish institution.

The two main dining rooms had never been kosher, except for part of one which was reserved for Brandeis students who kept kosher. The eating of nonkosher beef and the mixing of meat and dairy dishes is as great a violation of Jewish law as the consumption of pork, crabs, and scallops. Nevertheless, the suggestion to serve pork and shellfish assumed great symbolic importance both inside and outside the Brandeis community, and it was vigorously denounced by some who did not keep kosher themselves. They assumed the administration's proposal was merely the entering wedge of a campaign by Evelyn Handler, the university's president, to dilute Brandeis's Jewish character. This charge appeared credible, since the menu change occurred at about the same time as the Hebrew word *emet* (truth) was dropped from the university's logo and a change in the school's calender replaced all references to Jewish holidays with the wording "no university exercises."

Critics of the administration saw no reason why Brandeis should water down its Jewish identity. If Notre Dame had been able to raise its academic stature while maintaining its ties to the Catholic church, why must Brandeis weaken its ties to the Jewish community to attract a more representative student body? Gentiles would come to Brandeis not because it served pork and shellfish, but because it was a quality institution. What was wrong with having Jews and Gentiles studying together in an identifiably Jewish institution? These critics believed the administration's actions reflected an assimilationist mentality that ran counter to Brandeis's historic claim that it stood for the symbiosis of the best in American and Jewish identities. By questioning whether Jews qua Jews could be a host at last, the administration had implicitly challenged Sachar's assumption that committed Jews could become part of the American mainstream.

An ad hoc student organization called the Brandeis Anti-DeJudaization Coalition urged alumni to deny financial support to the university as long as the forbidden foods were offered on campus. An airplane hired by the coalition flew over the 1988 commencement with a banner protesting the serving of pork. The university's fund-raising was adversely affected by the controversy, and a one-million-dollar pledge reportedly was withdrawn. Because of the publicity and the opposition from alumni and prospective donors, the university partially backed down. Pork chops and shrimp were not served in the dining room where kosher food was offered. *Emet* was returned to the university's logo, and Jewish holidays were specifically mentioned as such on the university calender. In 1990, Handler resigned as Brandeis's president, a move brought on in part by the backlash resulting from the maladroit attempts to change the university's image.[23]

Brandeis returned to the status quo prior to the "trefa (nonkosher) war." On the one hand, the university prized its secular character and its freedom from religious orthodoxies, and it remained determined to improve its national standing. On the other hand, its campus housed the American Jewish Historical Society and other Jewish organizations, its student body was overwhelmingly Jewish, the number of its Orthodox students was slowly increasing, it provided a range of Jewish religious services ranging from Reform to Orthodox, and it had the finest undergraduate Jewish studies program in the country.

Brandeis was not the only manifestation of the new importance of Judaism and Jewish culture in American academia. An even more significant development occurred when, beginning in the 1960s and continuing through the 1970s and 1980s, Jewish studies became part of the curriculum of hundreds of secular and religious colleges. Accompanying this development was a large increase in the number of historians, sociologists, philosophers, linguists, and literary scholars specializing in the study of Jews and Jewish culture. For the first time in history, major centers for the study of Jews and Judaism were not exclusively Jewish institutions but included universities. This breakdown in the isolation of Jewish studies from the other humanities was one of the most remarkable occurrences in the history of post–World War II American Jewry and the American university.

The rise of Jewish studies took place approximately two centuries after Brown University in Providence, Rhode Island, offered to establish a chair in "Hebrew and Oriental languages" if the Jewish merchants of Newport would fund it and send their sons to Brown. The merchants had better uses for their money and their sons. Their money stayed in their pockets, and their sons went into the family businesses. The development of Jewish studies would have to wait until Jewish benefactors were more open to such appeals for aid, the study of Jews and Judaism was accepted as a legitimate part of the university curriculum, and there were numerous Jewish under-graduates.[24]

Before 1945, there were only a handful of American academicians specializing in Jewish studies. As in Europe, Jewish scholarship was the province of specifically Jewish institutions, particularly the rabbinical semi-naries. There were few academic opportunities for Jewish scholars even in Germany, where the modern scientific and historical study of Judaism had emerged during the mid-nineteenth century. Leopold Zunz, among the most important formative figures in the Science of Judaism, was unable to secure an academic appointment in his native Prussia during this period. Jewish scholars in Europe and the United States were mainly employed by Jewish institutions. The only two university chairs in Jewish studies in American universities prior to World War II were held by Harvard philosopher Harry A. Wolfson and Columbia historian Salo W. Baron. In the absence of research institutes, academic programs, and other institutional support, Jewish studies in American academia prior to 1945 essentially involved scattered individuals working alone.

Baron himself had been reluctant to relocate to Morningside Heights from central Europe after a graduate of Columbia had endowed a chair in Jewish history in 1929 at his alma mater. Baron did not believe he would have enough graduate students, and he feared that any students he did attract would have difficulty finding employment during the Great Depres-sion. Baron might also have been concerned with the reception he would receive from the members of Columbia's history department. They had made it quite clear that they were unconvinced that Jewish history was a fit topic for study at an institution with Columbia's cachet.[25]

Prior to the 1960s, Baron, Wolfson, and the few other Judaic specialists were voices crying in the wilderness. Except for those teaching at one of the three major rabbinical seminaries—Hebrew Union College in Cincinnati (Reform), the Jewish Theological Seminary in New York (Conservative), and Yeshiva University in New York (Orthodox)—Judaic specialists had few colleagues with whom to talk shop, and there was a shortage of journals to publish their research. Their undergraduate classes were small and their graduate students few in number. They felt isolated from the academic mainstream. "Then we were alone, without a clear place, without a long tradition in our several universities, without a viable model for our courses or for our place in the curriculum," Jacob Neusner recalled just before the great expansion in Jewish studies. "Nearly all of us in my age group found that we had to invent ourselves and our careers. We had to define for ourselves not only a profession, without the academic framework, but also an ethos and a definition of professionalism." The situation of Jewish scholars within the academic community resembled the fringe position of American Jews within the larger society prior to World War II.[26]

Many academicians assumed that Jewish culture was unworthy of serious academic study. To them, the term *Jewish studies* was oxymoronic. They identified Jewish culture with the economic and social impoverishment and superstition of the ghetto. They viewed Christianity, by contrast, as the most important element in Western culture. Because of the university's disdain for the study of Jewish culture, Jewish learning in America was largely the preserve of the rabbinical seminaries and Jewish institutions such as Dropsie College for Hebrew and Cognate Learning in Philadelphia. In the foreword to his 1949 collection *The Jews,* Louis Finkelstein, chancellor of the Jewish Theological Seminary, vigorously protested this academic neglect of the Jewish experience. "It is no extravagance," he lamented, "to call Judaism the unknown religion of our time."[27]

Finkelstein's comment was published one year after the establishment of the state of Israel, which, more than any other single event, was responsible for the initial growth of Jewish studies. A harbinger of this growth was Edmund Wilson's essay "The Need for Judaic Studies." Wilson, then America's leading man of letters, had become fascinated with Jews, Judaism, and Israel, in part because of his interest in the Dead Sea Scrolls that had been unearthed in Palestine just after the end of World War II. "The Need for Judaic Studies," which appeared in Wilson's *A Piece of My Mind* (1956), recommended that the examination of Judaism and Jews become an integral part of the college curriculum. It outlined a two-year course in the literature and history of the Jews that would include the study of the Bible, the Dead Sea Scrolls, Josephus, the Talmud, Maimonides, and Hasidism. Wilson, the grandson of a Presbyterian minister, even argued that this course would have to be taught by Jews since only they would have sufficient empathy with the subject matter.[28]

Despite Wilson's imprimatur, not even the most optimistic observer could have predicted the development of Jewish studies after 1960. By the mid-1960s, according to Professor Arnold J. Band's survey of the field in the 1966 *American Jewish Year Book,* there were already over sixty full-time positions in Jewish studies in American universities, compared to only twelve two decades earlier. This expansion continued during the 1970s even though academic programs in other areas were shrinking.

Band's essay, the first comprehensive examination of Jewish studies, was ambivalent about the status of Jewish studies. With less than one thousand undergraduate majors, Jewish studies had as yet only a "vague presence" in academia. Band estimated that no more than ten thousand students had enrolled in Jewish studies courses in 1965. Jewish studies offerings were narrow and concentrated in the traditional fields of Semitics, rabbinics, Hebrew, and Bible. While Jewish history, literature and Yiddish were taught in a few places, courses in contemporary Jewish sociology, economics and politics were rare. In states such as Colorado, Georgia, Louisiana, Virginia, and Washington, no colleges offered courses in Jewish studies, and many leading universities such as Georgetown, Notre Dame, Northwestern, Rochester, Stanford, and Tulane did not teach courses in Jewish studies.

One encouraging sign noted by Band was the quality of the Jewish studies faculty. Many were young and well trained, with doctorates from such major universities as Columbia, Harvard, Johns Hopkins, and Chicago. With positions opening up throughout the country, employment prospects were bright. In contrast to the 1930s, when professors attempted to dissuade students from pursuing academic careers in Jewish studies, there was now an employee's market in the field. The United States, Band said, was "on the threshold of a new and promising period in Jewish scholarship in America." His prediction, coming one year before the Six-Day War of 1967, was prophetic.[29]

Samuel Sandmel, a professor of Bible at Hebrew Union College, was ecstatic about the future of Jewish studies. In 1969, he described the establishment of chairs of Judaica in universities as "the most significant development in modern American Judaism." But only one viewing American Jewry from the rarified heights of academia could consider Jewish studies more important than the expansion of the Jewish day school movement, the intensification of Jewish identity stemming from the Six-Day War, the decline of anti-Semitism, and the social and economic ascent of American Jews.[30]

While Jewish studies appeared to have a happy future, its practitioners still had reservations. Sixty-five positions, after all, were a mere drop in the bucket of American academia. These "talented solitary individuals," Band later recalled, were beset with "anxieties and loneliness." While the origins of Jewish studies antedated the ethnic and racial militancy of the 1960s, Jewish studies profited from the agitation of blacks, native Americans, and Hispanics for ethnic studies programs. When universities established programs in black studies, native American studies, Chicano studies, and Asian studies, it was difficult not to fund programs in Jewish studies also, particularly when the institutions were located in areas or states with sizable Jewish populations. This benefit, however, promised to be only temporary. The danger was that Jewish studies would be grouped with these other ethnic programs and come to be viewed as an academic fad.[31]

Despite these caveats, the rapid growth of Jewish studies convinced several of the major figures in the field of the need for a scholarly association. In September 1969, the Association for Jewish Studies was founded. Brandeis played an important role in the association's early history. Leon Jick, a Brandeis historian, initiated the process leading to its creation, and its first meeting was held at Brandeis under the auspices of the Lown Graduate Center for Contemporary Jewish Studies. Among those in attendance at this initial meeting were Alexander Altmann (Brandeis), Arnold Band (UCLA), Joseph Blau (Columbia), Gerson Cohen (Columbia), Lucy Dawidowicz (Yeshiva), Nahum Glatzer (Brandeis), Alfred Ivry (Cornell), Michael Meyer (Hebrew Union College), Jacob Neusner (Brown), Nahum Sarna (Brandeis), Marshall Sklare (Yeshiva), Frank Talmage (Toronto), and Yosef Yerushalmi (Harvard).

Although its founding was due in part to the vogue of ethnic consciousness and cultural pluralism of the 1960s, the AJS saw itself as a society devoted to scholarship rather than to ethnic political advocacy. It was, as one of those attending the 1969 meeting described it, a "fellowship" of scholars. The initial issue of the *AJS Newsletter* defined Jewish Studies as a "scholarly discipline which deals with the historical experience of the Jews in the religious, cultural, intellectual, and social spheres, in all centuries and countries." The association's goals included the maintenance of academic standards, the exchange of ideas, the presentation of research, and job placement. In 1976, the association began publishing a scholarly journal, the *AJS Review*.[32]

The AJS helped reduce the intellectual isolation of the Judaic scholar. No longer was he or she a lonely worker in the vineyard of Jewish studies but a member of an academic association that, by 1990, numbered around one thousand. Hundreds of these—professors and graduate students alike—came to Boston in December for the association's annual convention, where they delivered and listened to scholarly papers, renewed friendships, and interviewed for jobs.

By the mid-1970s, there was little doubt that Jewish studies had become a permanent aspect of the academic landscape. Over three hundred American universities offered at least one course in Judaica, forty had undergraduate Judaic majors, and twenty-five had graduate programs in Jewish studies. This growth continued into the 1980s. By the end of this decade, there were over six hundred academic positions in Jewish studies. The scope as well as the size of Jewish studies had increased. The classical areas of rabbinics, Semitics, Hebrew, and Bible were now supplemented by courses in philosophy, theology, history, sociology, the Holocaust, Yiddish, Hebrew, the Middle East, and literature. Often the most popular of Jewish studies undergraduate courses were in the history and literature of the Holocaust. Courses in Jewish feminism were also well received.[33]

Jewish studies appealed to Gentiles as well as to Jews, particularly in colleges outside the Northeast. Among those motivated to take these courses were Gentiles who wished to learn about the Jewish background of Christianity and non-Jews who were involved romantically with Jews. Most students enrolled in Jewish studies courses, and virtually all the Jewish studies majors, however, were Jews curious about their roots. As Robert Alter noted, the willingness of American Jews to take courses in Jewish studies indicated "a changing sense of self," a willingness of the young to go public with their Jewishness, a trait their parents had not exhibited. Some sought in Jewish studies a vicarious Jewish experience. Studying Jewish culture and Judaism was an alternative to living Jewish lives.[34]

Jewish studies benefited from the huge postwar increase in the number of Jews attending American universities. Postwar affluence enabled many young Jews to attend residential colleges. This dispersal of the Jewish college population encouraged the establishing of Jewish studies programs at institutions that previously had had relatively few Jewish students. Jewish laymen hoped that Jewish studies would provide a surrogate Jewish community for Jews living far from the influence of family and local Jewish institutions, and that the Jewish studies faculty would provide students with role models of adults who were comfortable being both scholars and committed Jews.

Jewish studies also profited from the opening up of the college curriculum during the 1950s, 1960s, and 1970s. By reducing the number of required courses in modern language, history, English, and philosophy, colleges increased the number of elective courses a student could take. This encouraged a more diversified curriculum and enabled new programs in such fields as American studies, black studies, women's studies, and Jewish studies to be offered.

In addition, area studies such as Russian studies, African studies, and Asian studies became an academic rage beginning in the 1950s because of America's new importance in world affairs. Involvement in remote parts of the world required the expertise of area specialists trained in the universities. This worked to the advantage of Jewish studies since the field also had an area focus. Jewish studies encompassed not only the Bible and medieval Jewish philosophy, but also the politics, military policy, and culture of Israel and the Middle East. The intense emotional involvement of many American Jews with the fate of Israel, particularly after 1967, encouraged the proliferation of college courses in the history, sociology, and foreign policy of Israel. Brandeis University's Jewish studies program, for example, was named the Department of Near Eastern and Jewish Studies.

The establishment of the state of Israel was among the most important factors in the rise of Jewish studies, particularly for the study of Hebrew. No longer was Hebrew merely a language of prayer. It had become the language of a living people, of a state, and of a modern literature. No one could expect to understand the culture and politics of the Middle East without some familiarity with Hebrew.

America's global confrontation with the Soviet Union, the three major wars America fought in Asia, and the nation's worldwide economic and cultural involvements widened the horizons of most Americans. By the 1940s, the *New York Times* was placing its articles on world affairs at the beginning of the paper. Americans realized they were living in a diverse world and that civilization could no longer be equated with the Christian West. This lessening of political and cultural isolationism encouraged American universities to add courses in non-Western and non-Christian religions and cultures, including Judaism, to their curriculum.

The growth of Jewish studies signified the academy's recognition that American Jews had become part of the American mainstream, that Judaism was as legitimate an American faith as Christianity, and that Jewish culture could be studied for its own sake, not merely as a prelude to Christianity. The growth of Jewish studies indicated a remarkable rise in the status of

Jews and Judaism. Even Princeton and Wellesley, not previously known for welcoming Jewish students, established Jewish studies programs.

As early as 1969, Gerson D. Cohen, a Columbia University historian and future chancellor of the Jewish Theological Seminary, was describing the status of Jewish studies as "an embarrassment of riches." This "embarrassment" would increase. "The number of scholars involved in research and teaching, the number of institutions in which serious programs in Jewish studies are available, the number and quality of publications which have appeared and continue to appear on every phase and state of Jewish civilization," Leon Jick wrote two decades later, "is astonishing."[35]

Not everyone shared this enthusiasm. Parents were naturally concerned that their children who were majoring in Jewish studies would not be equipped for employment except in the fields of Jewish communal service and academia. Qualms were also voiced that Jews majoring in Jewish studies could be denying themselves a liberal education. These students, it was argued, would experience the same narrowing of intellectual perspectives and social isolation as blacks who majored in black studies.

Academicians also questioned whether there were enough competent scholars to fill all the positions opening up in Jewish studies. Complaints were frequently voiced in the 1960s and 1970s that the shortage of qualified personnel had resulted in universities hiring unqualified rabbis and Israelis who happened to live near campus. This problem continued to plague Jewish studies throughout the 1980s. Marvin Fox, a Brandeis philosopher, noted in 1986 that there was still much in the field that was "academically shoddy, with no one to control the quality and soundness of curricula and instruction." Critics also claimed that the rapid growth of Jewish studies had occurred without sufficient thought regarding its place within the curriculum.[36]

There was no consensus within the field whether Jewish studies faculty should be part of a separate department or members of the traditional departments of religion, philosophy, and history. In 1969, Gerson Cohen voiced the concern of many regarding the haphazard growth of Jewish studies. He called for articulating in the near future "a set of standards which will clarify . . . what we conceive to be the proper scope of Judaica, what we regard as minimal requirements for a college program of Jewish studies and what are the prerequisites for graduate study in the field." This clarification never occurred.[37]

No problem was more vexing for those in Jewish studies than resolving the conflict between the ideal of objectivity demanded of them as scholars and the commitment to Jewish identity they felt as Jews. No one wished Jewish studies to degenerate into the special pleading, extreme ethnocentrism, and shoddy intellectual standards that had marred other ethnic studies programs. The problem was complicated by the fact that the financial benefactors of these programs believed one of their goals should be combating assimilation.

This objective, however laudable, ignored the fact that the university's purpose was the search for truth and not ethnic and religious consciousness-raising. Once Jewish studies left the seminaries and became part of the university, it had to relinquish any responsibility for maintaining group loyalties. Gentile scholars such as George Foot Moore and Frank Cross of Harvard would have been excluded from the field of Jewish studies if one of its purposes was to encourage Jewish identity. Jacob Neusner of Brown was so fearful that Jewish studies would degenerate into Jewish advocacy that he opposed universities accepting money from Jewish federations. "Nothing will so endanger the healthy development of Jewish learning in its various modes," he wrote, "as the exploitation of that development for other than strictly and narrowly defined university purposes."[38]

And yet it was not so easy to resolve the relationship between the scholarly and the personal commitments of Judaic scholars, the vast majority of whom were Jews. Thus, while the AJS welcomed Gentile members, all of the forty-seven persons who attended the association's initial meeting at Brandeis were Jews. Jick suggested that it was necessary for any Jew teaching Jewish studies to be both objective and committed to Jewish continuity. "Yet who, if not those immersed in Jewish culture, will demonstrate its validity and its value?" he asked. "Who, if not those with a passion for objective Jewish learning, will serve as models for students, our students, who need to be taught both Torah and in the literal sense *derach eretz*?"[39]

Sociologist Marshall Sklare, a strong proponent of Jewish survival, agreed with Jick. He believed the future of Jewish studies depended on whether it could help Jewish collegians explore their personal identity. "It follows then," Sklare wrote, that Jewish studies would not prosper "if they move too far in the direction of becoming a pure and impersonal science." The emphasis of Sklare and Jick on the maintenance of Jewish identity was understandable. (Sklare then taught at Yeshiva University and Jick at Brandeis.) This rationale for Jewish studies, however, did not take into consideration the possibility that people other than Jews would be interested in

Jewish studies, or that Jewish studies would become part of the academic mainstream to the extent that it did.[40]

Despite disagreeing over the methodology and goals of Jewish studies, Jewish scholars were naturally pleased by the growth of the field. "When I compare my 1966 article to the state of the field today," Band said in 1989, "I come to the inescapable conclusion: Jewish Studies are firmly established and seen as part of the establishment." Rabbi-historian Stuart E. Rosenberg called Jewish studies "one of the brightest spots on the 'Jewish map' of America." In 1986, Marvin Fox described Jewish studies as "a positive phenomenon of the highest value."[41]

Only in Israel were there Judaic scholars of the number and distinction comparable to those in the United States. Some of these Americans had drifted into Jewish studies from allied fields, while others were recent graduates of doctoral programs in Jewish studies, particularly those at Brandeis, Columbia, and Harvard. An important development was the increasing number of women in the field. No woman had attended the AJS's organizational meeting. Within a decade, however, women made up a significant percentage of the faculty in Jewish studies, particularly in the areas of sociology, history, and literature. Some female academicians were even researching and teaching Judaism and the Jewish experience from a feminist perspective.

Professors of Jewish studies taught on campuses with a large Jewish student body and at colleges with few Jewish students. Harvard, with its many Jewish undergraduates and its graduate program in Jewish studies, offered forty courses in Judaica, including Introduction to the Bible, Modern Hebrew Poetry, and Christians and Jews Under Islam. The chairman of Harvard's Jewish studies program was heir to a Hasidic dynasty. Isadore Twersky, Nathan Littauer Professor of Hebrew Literature and Philosophy, was the son of R. Meshullam Zalman Twersky (the Tolnaer Rebbe), the son-in-law of Joseph Dov Soloveitchik, American Orthodoxy's leading intellectual luminary, and rabbi of a small Orthodox congregation in Brookline, Massachusetts.

By contrast, St. John's University in Collegeville, Minnesota, had few, if any, Jewish students in 1970 when it became the first American Catholic university with an endowed chair in Jewish studies. The chair was a gift of the wealthy Phillips family of Minneapolis, one of whose members had married the columnist who wrote "Dear Abby." Located in a largely German Catholic area in central Minnesota, St. John's was a small liberal arts college controlled by Benedictine monks. The neighboring town of St. Cloud had less than fifteen Jewish families.

The Phillips family and other benefactors of Jewish studies programs had a variety of motives. Some believed Jewish studies was an appropriate topic for academic study, others wanted their names associated with education and prestigious institutions, and still others believed Jewish studies could combat anti-Semitism. But the most important motivation was the belief that Jewish studies could counteract the failure of Jewish families and schools to convey a sense of ethnic and religious identity to Jews in college. The philanthropists hoped Jewish studies would counteract intermarriage, stem the flight of Jewish youth to religious cults and radical politics, and project a more affirmative view of Jewish culture.

An increase in the rate of intermarriage, the seeming attenuation of Jewish identity among the young, and the appeal of the New Left led Jewish leaders in the 1960s to fear the campus as a threat to Jewish survival. Jewish collegians spent at least four years in a non-Jewish environment, where, at an impressionable age they came into close contact with Gentiles of both sexes and were taught by professors who were sometimes hostile to religion and ethnicity. With over 80 percent of Jews attending college after high school graduation, the college campus, Jewish leaders concluded, had become the battleground of the Jewish future.

Irving Greenberg's essay "Jewish Survival and the College Campus" (1968) was the most important expression of this fear of the campus. Greenberg, the rabbi of a large Orthodox congregation in the Bronx and a professor of history at Yeshiva University, described the college as a "disaster area" for Judaism and Jewish identity. "It has been said that the British Empire was lost and won on the playing fields of Eton," Greenberg wrote. "The crown of Judaism and Jewishness will be won or lost on the campuses of America."

Greenberg argued that the secular, rationalist, and universalist values of the university had caused a decrease in religious faith and observance and an increase in intermarriage among Jewish collegians. In order to deal with this problem, he proposed creating a Center for Jewish Survival funded by grants from Jewish federations. Among the center's tasks would be providing scholarships to committed Jews to go into college teaching, publishing textbooks presenting a more favorable image of Judaism, and supplying seed money for chairs in Jewish studies.[42]

In response to this widespread perception of college as a Jewish wasteland, the Lubavitch Hasidic group established dozens of religious centers near major American universities, and the campus Hillel chapters expanded their programing and fund-raising. Much of the appeal of Brandeis University stemmed from the fact that it was the only secular American university that encouraged Jewish identity. The high percentage of Jewish students at Brandeis also made the parents of Brandeis undergraduates more confident that the campus romances of their children would be with other Jews.

With Jewish philanthropists willing to pick up some of the expenses, American universities were willing to make a place in the curriculum for Jewish studies, particularly if this might lead to additional gifts. Often the seed money for Jewish studies was provided by outsiders. At Ohio State University, for example, a half-million dollar gift from the Melton Foundation led to the establishment in 1966 of what would become an extensive program in Jewish studies. Outside money was particularly important for Jewish studies in the 1960s and early 1970s. At this time these programs received approximately one-third of their funds from sources outside the university. Jewish academicians encouraged this flow of funds. As Norman Roth of the University of Wisconsin declared in 1986, "Strengthening and continuing to expand the Jewish studies programs in our colleges and universities may be the single most important task facing the American Jewish community." With the passage of time, the support of outsiders became less critical. As the programs demonstrated scholarly credibility and popularity, a larger percentage of their budgets was funded through the general university budgets.[43]

Despite the academic chairs, lecture series, and libraries provided by Jewish benefactors, Jewish studies proved to be an unsuitable instrument for counteracting assimilation. Although there were numerous examples of young men and women choosing careers in the rabbinate and other areas of Jewish communal service because of their undergraduate experience in Jewish studies, only a small percentage of Jewish undergraduates ever took courses in Jewish studies, and most of these only took one or two courses. The number of Jewish studies majors was never large enough to counteract the assimilationist pressures of the campus. Furthermore, the scholarly and dispassionate manner in which Jewish studies courses were usually taught militated against Jewish consciousness-raising. Yale historian Paula E. Hyman argued that the major contribution of Jewish studies in strengthening Jewish identity had little to do with the nature of Jewish studies or with how many Jews enrolled in these courses. The mere presence of Jewish studies on the campus enhanced

the self-esteem of Jewish students, for they need no longer see themselves
as heirs to an invisible culture—a culture of no value according to the
criteria of the university. Rather, they must become aware that the culture
and historic experience of their ancestors have become incorporated into
the Western humanistic tradition . . . This "legitimation" of Jewish
culture and history by a central institution of the larger society is an
important step in the process of full emancipation of the Diaspora Jew.44

The presence of Jewish scholars at the university also benefited neighboring Jewish communities. These scholars were committed to Jewish
survival in one form or another and, in places such as New Haven and
Hartford, Connecticut, they were valuable resources for local Jewish institutions. In more isolated locales, Jewish studies faculty were among the very
few within the local Jewish population knowledgeable in Jewish matters.

In 1987, Ismar Schorsch, chancellor of the Jewish Theological Semi-
nary, attributed the flourishing of Jewish studies to the "unheralded politi-
cal security" of America's Jews and to the "high regard for Judaism" in the
United States. Ironically, the prospering of Jewish studies had occurred at
the expense and over the opposition of the rabbinical seminaries, including
Schorsch's own institution. From the 1920s to the 1960s, JTS and the
Hebrew University in Jerusalem had been the two most important centers for
Jewish scholarship. The faculty of the Jewish Theological Seminary included
Louis Ginzberg and Saul Lieberman in Talmud, Alexander Marx in history,
Abraham Joshua Heschel in philosophy, and Israel Friedlander in Semitics.
"Rarely before, and never since, did one academy encompass just about all of
the masters of one scholarly discipline within its own walls," a JTS graduate
recalled. "It can take credit, almost single-handedly, for the transmission of
the tradition of Jewish scholarship from Europe to America."45

Jewish studies broke this near-monopoly of the seminaries in Jewish
scholarship, destroying in the process the close relationship between piety
and learning. The academy provided a less traditional education for students seeking a career in Jewish scholarship who did not want to enter the
rabbinate. While the financial rewards of academia were not equal to those
of the rabbinate, many persons found university life to be attractive, particularly in the opportunity it provided for research and writing.

The seminaries now found themselves competing for students, funds,
and faculty with the major universities. The move of David Halivni, the
renowned Talmudist, from JTS to Columbia University in the late 1980s

was symptomatic. The seminaries were further aggrieved by attacks coming from the university. Those of Jacob Neusner were the most intemperate:

> One wonders what scholarly achievements will be possible among men whose appointments depend upon criteria irrelevant to scholarship, whose educational environment will be created in dogmatic surroundings where . . . the question of relevance and the search for instant wisdom are predominant considerations . . . . Will the Jewish schools find themselves able to compete for talent, even among their own graduates, with the opening up of hitherto undreamt of opportunities for true intellectual freedom and a genuinely heterogeneous scholarly climate?[46]

The Jewish Theological Seminary responded to the challenge from the university by establishing its own graduate program in 1970 offering M.A. and Ph.D. degrees. This, however, did not restore the institution to its previous preeminent position.

Yeshiva University, the leading institution of indigenous American orthodoxy, was also adversely affected by the increased Jewish presence on the American campus. The availability of Jewish studies programs and kosher dining facilities at prominent universities, including those in the Ivy League, made it more difficult to draw outstanding students to Yeshiva. To attract superior students, Yeshiva offered scholarships for those with high Scholastic Aptitude Test scores and excellent high school transcripts, and to guarantee a sufficient number of undergraduates, the university emphasized its preprofessional programs at the expense of its liberal arts curriculum. Its premedicine and accounting programs, in particular, were very popular. The university also established the Syms School of Business in the 1980s. Yeshiva's vocational emphasis was understandable in view of its serious financial problems and its small potential applicant pool. Friends of Yeshiva feared, nevertheless, that vocationalism would undermine the university's efforts to improve its academic standing.

The rise of Jewish studies affected the graduates of the seminaries as well as the seminaries themselves. During the 1970s and 1980s, observers of the American rabbinate, whether they were sociologists or popular novelists such as Harry Kemelman, remarked on the low morale of pulpit rabbis. Rabbi Small, the discontented hero of Kemelman's mystery novels, believes he is better suited for academia than for his pulpit in suburban Boston.

One of the reasons for the dissatisfaction was the rabbis' recognition of their profession's fall in status. The rise of Jewish studies had shifted the focus of Jewish intellectual life from the rabbinate to academia. Rabbis were no longer viewed as the preeminent authorities in Jewish learning, and ordination no longer sufficed as expertise in Jewish lore. Now the possession of a Ph.D. was even more prestigious. Rabbis envied the Jewish scholars in the university, some of whom had been their classmates in the seminary. The pulpit rabbis had left the seminaries eager to be spiritual and intellectual leaders. Instead, they found themselves ministering to congregations that were often uninterested in Jewish practices and beliefs. They remembered their own years in college and the seminary with nostalgia, and they looked wistfully toward academia, where Jewish ideas were taken seriously.

This dissatisfaction was particularly noticeable among graduates of the Jewish Theological Seminary. They had been enormously influenced by the example of the scholar-rabbi provided by Ginzberg, Lieberman, and Halivni, and by JTS's emphasis on modern scholarship. The seminary's products once had hoped to join the ranks of the scholars, and many secretly disdained the life of the synagogue administrator and pulpit rabbi. Kemelman's Rabbi Small is, not surprisingly, a graduate of JTS. The seminary's graduates were disappointed and even embittered by not having followed in the footsteps of their illustrious teachers. The unhappiness of some was partially assuaged by part-time teaching at local universities. Most, however, did not have this opportunity, and they had to settle for the intellectual stimulation of self-study or of study with other rabbis. Neither option was completely satisfying, particularly when compared to the full-time immersion of the academician in books and ideas.

Dropsie College in Philadelphia was another Jewish institution that fell on hard times in the 1960s and 1970s. This occurred even though Dropsie received a university charter in 1969. In a 1980 speech at Dropsie, Jacob Neusner proposed converting the school to a postgraduate center for Jewish studies. Such a center, modeled after the National Humanities Center in North Carolina, would provide residential fellowships for senior and junior scholars. Jewish academicians, Neusner claimed, needed a place for scholarly solitude during sabbaticals and leaves of absence. "To Dropsie the people who do the work in universities may retreat for renewal, for intellectual encounter with peers, for fresh exercises in systematic learning." Neusner believed Dropsie was ideally suited to become such a center because it did not have any specific theological axe to grind.[47]

A few years later, Neusner's suggestion became reality when Dropsie was converted into the Annenberg Institute for Advanced Research through the generosity of the philanthropist Walter Annenberg, a native of Philadelphia, a former ambassador to Great Britain, and the former owner of Triangle Publications. The institute provided grants and research facilities for Judaic scholars. Its first director was Bernard Lewis, an eminent historian of Islam and a former member of the Institute for Advanced Study in Princeton, New Jersey.

Beginning in the 1960s, scholarly publications in Judaica flourished along with Jewish studies. Jewish studies journals such as *Modern Judaism* and *Prooftexts* were founded to provide publication outlets for scholars, and general journals were more willing to publish essays on Jewish topics. The publication of scholarly Jewish books also thrived. Judaic specialists now had other publishing opportunities besides Jewish publishers. The academic presses of Columbia, Harvard, Yale, Chicago, and other major universities were eager to bring out scholarly works in Judaica. Even university presses in such unlikely places as Bloomington, Indiana, and Tuscaloosa, Alabama, published extensively in the field.

One subfield within Jewish studies was American Jewish history. After 1945, American Jews professed greater interest in their past. Oscar Handlin and other Jewish historians suggested that the time had finally come for historians to examine American Jewish history with the same rigor and objectivity used when investigating other aspects of American history. Antiquarianism and special pleading would no longer do. Before this examination could occur, however, the resources of the American Jewish experience would have to be made more accessible to scholars, and journals would have to be established to provide publication outlets for researchers.

In 1947, Hebrew Union College established the American Jewish Archives on its Cincinnati campus. Jacob Rader Marcus convinced Nelson Glueck, the president of the college, of the need for such an institution to document the rise of the American Jewish community now that the United States had become the most important Jewish center in the world. The American Jewish Archives became one of the two major repositories for manuscripts and memorabilia in American Jewish history. The other was the American Jewish Historical Society. Founded in 1892, the society moved in 1968 from its cramped quarters in New York City to a new building on the campus of Brandeis University. In 1948, the society transformed *Publications of the American Jewish Historical Society* from an annual to a quarterly (later called the *American Jewish Historical Quarterly* and then *American Jewish History*). Also about this time the first course for credit in American Jewish history was offered on the graduate level at an American university.[48]

The historical consciousness of American Jewry was never higher than in 1954, the tercentenary of the first Jewish settlement in North America. The American Jewish community had grown from a handful of settlers in New Amsterdam to over five million people within three centuries. American Jews looked back on these years with a justified sense of accomplishment. Never in their three-hundred-year history had they been more secure, prosperous, and culturally creative. Both the text and title of Handlin's tercentenary history—*Adventure in Freedom: Three Hundred Years of Jewish Life in America*—reflected this triumphant mood.

The theme of achievement dominated the speeches at the various banquets held to commemorate the tercentenary. The most important of these banquets was the National Tercentenary Dinner in New York City on 20 October. President Eisenhower was the guest speaker. One item on the menu indicated the symbiotic relationship between America and its Jewish citizens. The appetizer was "traditional stuffed freshwater fish." Presumably the term *gefilte fish* was unfamiliar to the president, although it certainly was known to his hosts.[49]

Not all American Jews joined in this self-congratulation. Some emphasized that the freedom of America had not been an unmitigated blessing. The price of Jewish social and economic advancement, they argued, was the dissipation of group cohesiveness. One of the reasons for the continual stress on anti-Semitism, at a time when it was in sharp decline, was the belief that Jewish solidarity depended on keeping the dread of Gentiles uppermost in the minds of Jews. Once convinced that they had nothing to fear from the Gentile world, Jews would choose the path of least resistance and assimilate. One of the recurring debates within American Jewry during the 1940s and 1950s was whether Jewishness and Judaism could exist "without ghetto walls." For the pessimistic, the prospects of a vibrant Jewish life in the United States, which, more than any other nation, embodied the rationalist and universalist values of the Enlightenment, were bleak.

The major problem with the ghetto walls argument was that it fell on deaf ears. American Jews were unwilling to migrate to Israel, they refused to remain in cramped lower-middle-class Jewish neighborhoods when their incomes enabled them to move to better areas, and they welcomed economic opportunities even though these often led to close social relationships with Gentiles. Why would Jews choose to remain in the old neighborhoods in Brooklyn and the Bronx when the suburbs beckoned? How could Brownsville and the Grand Concourse compete with Great Neck and Scarsdale? How could Jews resist intermarriage, which resulted from the lowering of social and economic barriers, putting them in closer and more frequent proximity to non-Jews?

One affirmative answer to these questions was the third version of the film *The Jazz Singer,* which was released in 1980. Whereas the original 1927 movie starring Al Jolson had stressed the incompatibility of American and Jewish identities, Richard Fleischer, the director of the 1980 film, muted this conflict through the use of color. He used blue to represent the world of rock music and white to represent the Jewish world. Near the end of the film, the two colors come together. Jess (Neil Diamond) sings the Kol Nidre prayer at the beginning of the Yom Kippur service dressed in the traditional white robe, while a bright blue skullcap rests on his head. At the movie's conclusion, Jess, with his beaming parents in the audience, performs at a concert. He sings his own rock songs dressed in a shiny blue shirt with a white scarf resembling a prayer shawl draped around his neck.[50]

Jess's success as a rock star epitomizes the opportunities of postwar America for American Jews. This is best expressed when he sings "Coming to America," a rousing affirmation of America as a land of promise. For Jess and other American Jews, the years after 1945 were a golden age. Whether it was a golden age for Judaism and Jewishness, and whether Jess satisfactorily blends the blue of America and the white of Jewishness is, however, doubtful. His success comes only after he rejects his traditional Jewish wife, leaves New York for California, and becomes involved with a Gentile woman. The major question facing American Jewry throughout the postwar years was whether their valiant efforts to fill the cultural vacuum created by the Holocaust would prove to be sufficient; would Jewish culture and religion be sufficiently attractive so that Jews would voluntarily identify with the Jewish community and reject acculturation and assimilation? In Jess's case the answer is clearly no. Only in Israel does blue and white signify the harmonious integration of Jewish and national identities.

CHAPTER FOUR

A TALE OF TWO SHAPIROS

IN TERMS OF social and economic mobility, the years after 1945 were the best of times for American Jews. For many aspects of Jewish continuity, however, they were the worst of times. Academia and business were two areas of American life in which this simultaneous postwar improvement in the lives of individual American Jews and the general weakening of Jewish identity were prominent. The selection of Harold T. Shapiro as president of Princeton University in 1987 and Irving Shapiro as president of the Du Pont Corporation in 1973 symbolized the rapid social ascent of American Jewry. That Jews could be picked as the heads of two of the toniest institutions in America revealed, as nothing else could, the new openness of American society to Jewish aspirations. In the movie *Pete and Tillie,* the character played by Walter Matthau was asked why, since he was three-quarters Lutheran and only one-quarter Jewish, he insisted on calling himself Jewish. "I'm a social climber," he replied.[1]

Prior to the 1960s the presidency of the leading American universities had been monopolized by white Anglo-Saxon Protestant males. "The Protestant caste system," theologian Richard L. Rubinstein wrote in 1965, "remains as rigidly operative in the universities as it does in most business corporations." Rubinstein noted that it was "almost impossible for a Jew to be appointed to an administrative position at any university not sponsored by Jews." The next year, in his annual report as president of the American Jewish Committee, Morris Abram noted that there had not been one Jew among the approximately one thousand persons who had been named presidents of public colleges and universities during the preceding seventeen years.[2]

Neither Rubinstein nor Abram realized that a major change in the position of Jews in the highest rungs of American academia was about to occur. This change initially manifested itself in 1968 with the naming of Edward H. Levi as president of the University of Chicago. This was the first time a Jew had been chosen to head a major American university not under Jewish auspices. The *New York Times* article on Levi's selection mentioned that he was Jewish. The appointment of Levi was followed by the selection of other Jews for important positions within American academia, including the presidency of Indiana University. In the early 1920s, the state of Indiana had been a virtual fiefdom of the Ku Klux Klan.[3]

The new academic prominence of Jews was particularly noticeable in the Ivy League. "Dartmouth," president Ernest M. Hopkins had declared in 1945, "is a Christian college founded for the Christianization of its students." Less than four decades after Hopkins made this statement, two Jews had served as president of Dartmouth, Jews had been presidents of Columbia University and the University of Pennsylvania, a Jew had been offered the presidency of Yale, and Jews had been deans of the law schools at Columbia, Harvard, and Yale. The Ivy League, it was wryly noted, was well on its way to becoming the *oi-vey* league. In addition, Jews had served as presidents of the two most prestigious of America's scientific universities—the California Institute of Technology and the Massachusetts Institute of Technology.[4]

The selection of Harold Shapiro was significant, not because a Jew was chosen president of an important American university, but because it had occurred at perhaps the most socially exclusive of American universities. Princeton had always prided itself on its social standing. When the *Social Register* began publishing early in the twentieth century, it chose the colors orange and black for its binding. These were also Princeton's colors. This, one reporter suggested at the time, was appropriate since Princeton was then America's "most elegant university." Princeton's selective admissions policy, its informal quota for Jewish applicants, and its eating clubs reinforced its elitist reputation. The five Jews in the class of 1935, for example, made up less than 1 percent of that class, and throughout the decade the total Jewish enrollment at Princeton hovered around 2 percent. Jews were made to feel that, as a group, they lacked cachet.[5]

Two interwar novels described the difficult situation of Jewish students at Princeton. Ernest Hemingway's *The Sun Also Rises* (1926) contains a character named Robert Cohn, modeled on one of the grandsons of Meyer Guggenheim, the mining magnate. No one, Hemingway wrote, had ever made Cohn "feel he was a Jew and hence any different from anybody else until he went to Princeton." In F. Scott Fitzgerald's *This Side of Paradise* (1920), students amuse themselves by filling a "Jewish youth's bed with lemon pie."[6]

Princeton's pecking order was most evident in its system of eating clubs, where juniors and seniors ate their meals and relaxed. The clubs had begun in 1879 when the university banned Greek fraternities. The social status of undergraduates was revealed by the clubs to which they belonged. Few Jews were ever invited to join the most exclusive ones. During World War II, the university administration insisted that there must be a place in a club for every student who had applied for membership, including Jews. It would have been embarrassing for Princeton if its eating clubs blackballed Jews and other undesirables at the same time their friends and relatives were fighting in defense of Princeton and other American institutions.

This system worked reasonably well until 1958, when twenty-three students failed to receive bids from any of the seventeen eating clubs. Over half of these were Jews.[7] The resulting controversy made the national news. A headline in the *New York Post* read, "How It Feels to Be an Outcast at Princeton." Fifteen Jews who had not received bids signed a statement charging religious and ethnic discrimination, and the Anti-Defamation League promised to investigate. In the ensuing discussion it became clear that the Jews had been rejected because the clubmen considered them to be excessively bookish, lacking in the social graces, and ill at ease among their social betters. They were, it was believed, New York Jewish "nerds," graduates of what one Princeton alumnus called the "blackboard jungles." This attitude reflected the preppy anti-intellectualism that permeated much of the Princeton undergraduate student body. Jews, one Princeton undergraduate declared, were academic "grinds" and "poor mixers who did not fit well into a purely social organization."[8]

Three years after the eating club controversy, Harold Shapiro began his graduate work in economics at Princeton. A native of Montreal, he entered Princeton five years after graduating from McGill University. The death of his father had delayed his graduate studies, and he had spent the intervening period helping run the family business, Ruby Foo's, the most expensive and elegant of Montreal's Chinese restaurants. After receiving his doctorate, Shapiro joined the economics department at the University of Michigan. He later became its president. Shapiro soon became highly regarded in American academic circles. He was rumored to have been a leading candidate for the presidency of Yale before he withdrew his name from consideration after the Princeton presidency became open.[9]

The most surprising aspect of the selection of Shapiro to succeed William G. Bowen as Princeton's president was, of course, the fact that he was Jewish. And yet neither the news article in the *New York Times* announcing his selection or the paper's long profile of him the next day made any mention of this. Evidently, the *Times* believed a Jew becoming head of Princeton was not newsworthy. If so, the most remarkable thing about Shapiro's selection was that it was not considered remarkable at all.

Shapiro's Princeton differed considerably from the school he attended during the 1960s. This "country club of the Ivy League" was then believed to have had the most restrictive admissions policy regarding Jews of all the Ivy League schools. By the 1980s, Princeton had become very sensitive to Jewish concerns. In 1985, for the first time in its history, it rescheduled the opening day of classes so that it would not conflict with the Jewish New Year. By the 1980s, approximately 20 percent of Princeton's students were Jewish, and Princeton's local Hillel chapter was aiding the university's admissions office in recruiting Jewish students.

This increase in Jewish enrollment resulted in an active Jewish cultural life on campus, including a Jewish quarterly newspaper, Israeli and Yiddish film festivals, a Hebrew choir, lectures and concerts, religious services ranging from Reform to Orthodox, and a "Free Jewish University" offering a variety of courses in Jewish religion and culture. Princeton also ran one of the three kosher kitchens in the country directly operated by a university. (The other two were at Brandeis and Yeshiva University.) Princeton's kosher kitchen was dedicated in 1971 on the eve of Hanukkah, the Jewish holiday celebrating the victory of Jewish values over Hellenism.[10]

One striking example of this Jewish ascent up the ladder of academia occurred at Columbia University. Columbia was founded as an Anglican institution in the eighteenth century, and its president had always been an ex officio member of the board of trustees of the Cathedral of St. John the Divine, located a few blocks from the Columbia campus. When William J. McGill became Columbia's first Catholic president in 1970, he was probably the first Catholic to be on the cathedral's board of trustees. When Michael I. Sovern succeeded McGill in 1980, he might have been the first professing Jew in history to be a member of the governing body of any cathedral. Had Sovern applied for admission to Columbia as an undergraduate prior to World War II, he might not have even been admitted.

Members of the Ivy League and other prestigious institutions followed Columbia's example. Because of its location in New York City, more Jews applied to Columbia than to any other Ivy League institution. Fearing that future members of the American social and economic elite would not send their sons to Columbia if it became known as a haven for Jews, the university's officials had taken the lead in devising a variety of stratagems to lessen this Jewish influx. These included geographical quotas, personal interviews, tests for "character," and the requirement that applicants furnish photographs and their mothers' maiden names. Frederick S. Jones, dean of Yale College, justified restricting Jewish enrollment at Yale since Christians refused to compete for academic honors if this meant matching wits with "the greasy grind" Jews. Yale, Jones bluntly told a Jewish student, was a "Christian college."[11]

This distaste for Jews was not restricted to administrators and alumni. "Were it only a matter of scholarship," a group of Harvard students declared, "there could be no objection to Jews at all. But they do not mix. They destroy the unity of the college." A 1926 editorial in the student-run *Yale Daily News* strongly supported reducing Jewish enrollment at Yale because an admissions policy based solely on merit would transform the university into "a brains plant." Such attitudes led professor Harry A. Wolfson to suggest that Jews should "submit to fate" rather than "foolishly struggle" against prejudice. To be "deprived of many social goods and advantages," he wrote, "is our common lot as Jews."[12]

Much to the regret of the former editors of the *Yale Daily News,* merit played a larger role after World War II in the admission of students and the appointment of faculty and administrators at America's major universities, including Yale. Eugene V. Rostow was one of the lucky Jews admitted to Yale in the 1930s. Three decades later he was named dean of the university's Law School. In 1977, Yale even offered its presidency to Henry Rosovsky, a Jew who had been born in eastern Europe. Rosovsky, an economist and dean of Harvard's Faculty of Arts and Sciences, turned Yale down despite the urging of his Israeli-born wife. He stated that under different circumstances he might have accepted. By the 1970s, however, most of the barriers to Jews in academia had been eliminated, and there was nothing left to prove. Rosovsky believed it was then of little social significance for him to become Yale's president, and he wanted to complete the revamping of the Harvard curriculum. Just prior to rejecting Yale, Rosovsky had also declined an offer to head the University of Chicago. In 1985, he became the first Jewish member of the Harvard corporation. By that time, the Purim Ball had become one of the highlights of the Harvard social calendar. It was fitting that the new Hillel building at Harvard, scheduled to be completed in 1993, was to be named for Rosovsky.[13]

There were many reasons for this change in the status of Jews in academia. The impact of World War II, the postwar scientific, economic, and military competition with the Soviet Union, state laws outlawing racial, ethnic, and religious discrimination, the civil rights movement of the 1960s, and the large increase in the number of students seeking admission to college encouraged universities to emphasize intellectual distinction rather than ancestry in admissions and hiring. Unsympathetic alumni worried that their own children no longer were assured admission to their alma mater now that they had been transformed into "brains plants." The prewar proponents of Jewish quotas had admitted that academic excellence would have to be sacrificed in order to limit the number of Jewish students. They were willing to pay this price since they believed intellectual quality to be less important than the inculcation in their students of the personality traits and values suitable for future members of the American social and economic establishment.

The postwar lowering of religious, ethnic, and racial barriers in academia helped American universities move into the ranks of the world's leading educational institutions. They no longer were willing to sacrifice intellectual quality for social exclusivity, and they no longer wished to be parochial institutions catering to a small segment of the American population. Because of the prosperity of the postwar years, a wider sector of the American population could afford an Ivy League education for their children. This was particularly true of Jews.

By 1952, about one-quarter of the students in Harvard College were Jews, and this would continue over the next four decades. The percentage of Jews among the Harvard faculty was even greater. Harvard sociologist David Riesman estimated that one-third of his colleagues in the 1970s were Jews. The same developments occurred at Princeton and Yale. By the 1970s, Princeton's undergraduate Jewish enrollment reached 20 percent, and the percentage at Yale was higher.[14]

The answer of Yale's dean of admissions to a question posed by a prospective student revealed the change in Yale's attitude toward Jewish students. Asked whether eating kosher would be held against the student, the dean responded, "Absolutely not, although it's something you might want to hold against us." A few years later Yale's Whiffenpoof singers selected an Orthodox Jew to join its ranks. He wore a skullcap during concerts, much to the surprise of old Yalies and to the delight of Jews in the audience. Yale and other universities became more sensitive to Jewish concerns, such as providing kosher food for students and exempting Jews from Saturday examinations and classes. When one of Harvard's commencements in the 1980s inadvertently fell on the Jewish holiday of Shavuot, the university vowed it would never happen again.[15]

The Jews at America's elite institutions were visibly Jewish. It was common to see Jewish students in skullcaps walking across the Harvard Yard and on the Yale campus. In contrast to their parents, young Jews were not reluctant to display their Jewishness in public, whatever that might mean to them. Nor were they self-conscious about being Jewish, although for some this was due to indifference rather than to any positive Jewish commitment.

In the postwar era, America's Jews became the best educated of any major American ethnic or religious group. By the mid-1970s, according to Father Andrew M. Greeley's study *Ethnicity, Denomination, and Inequality* (1976), Jews averaged fourteen years of education. This was a half year more than Episcopalians, the American religious group with the highest social standing. While less than one-half of Americans went on to college, more than 80 percent of Jews did so, and, as indicated by the statistics from Harvard, Princeton, and Yale, Jews were more likely to attend elite institutions. In 1971, for example, Jews made up 17 percent of the students at private universities.[16]

Jews tended to do better scholastically than their Gentile classmates. They were selected to Phi Beta Kappa at a rate at least double their proportion of the undergraduate population. Jews also were disproportionately involved in the more important undergraduate organizations. The editors of Brown University's newspaper once even published a semihumorous editorial that assured Gentiles they would not meet with discrimination if they wished to work for the campus paper.[17]

The Jewish presence in academia was equally as impressive on the faculty level. Jewish academicians benefited from the explosive growth in college enrollments after the war. On the eve of World War II, college enrollment was only 2,650,000. By 1975, enrollment had soared to 8,000,000. There was a parallel growth of faculty during these thirty-five years, from 147,000 to over 600,000. Until the 1970s, academia was a growth industry, and professors were in an excellent bargaining position. At this period of growing demand for academicians, salaries and benefits increased and universities eliminated discriminatory hiring policies. Persons who under previous economic and social conditions might have gravitated to elementary and high school teaching now chose careers in academia. After 1945, tens of thousands of Roman Catholics and Jews entered university teaching. This transformed an elitist profession that had been overwhelmingly Protestant into one that more accurately reflected the ethnic and religious heterogeneity of America.[18]

The increase of Jews in academia was particularly noticeable. In 1940, only 2 percent of America's professors were Jews. By the 1970s, they were 10 percent. The postwar Jewish presence in academia was notable not only for its high proportion but also for its distinctive profile. Jewish academicians congregated in the most intellectually demanding fields—fields that emphasized abstract and theoretical reasoning—and at the most prestigious institutions. They were overrepresented in anthropology, economics, history, mathematics, physics, and sociology, and underrepresented in agriculture, education, home economics, journalism, library science, nursing, and physical education. Electrical engineering, the most theoretical branch of engineering, had a greater proportion of Jews than mechanical, civil, or chemical engineering. Medicine was a high-status profession, and Jews were disproportionately represented in biochemistry, bacteriology, physiology, psychology, and other academic fields allied to medicine.[19]

By every possible criteria, Everett Carll Ladd, Jr., and Seymour Martin Lipset wrote in 1975, Jewish academicians had "far surpassed their Gentile colleagues." At this time, Jews were one-fifth of the faculty at elite universities and one-quarter of the faculty of the Ivy League. They constituted an even higher proportion of Ivy League professors under the age of thirty-five and of faculty at the elite medical and law schools. In 1968, 38 percent of the faculty at America's elite law schools were Jews.[20]

The disproportionate number of Jews in academia was no accident. It reflected the high status accorded by Jews to scholarly achievement. Jewish professors, Ladd and Lipset reported, published more frequently, were more committed to research, were promoted at an earlier age, made more money, and were more likely to define themselves as intellectuals. Jews attributed their new status in the university to the spread of the merit principle throughout academia, and since the twenties they had vigorously advocated merit in hiring and admissions.[21]

The major challenge during the 1970s and 1980s to the merit principle came not from old-line Americans seeking to restore their prewar position, but from blacks, Hispanics, and other aggrieved minorities who sought through affirmative action to lessen the importance of impersonal test scores. Jewish spokesmen argued that affirmative action would harm Jews, lower the academic standards of the universities, devalue academic degrees, and balkanize American education into competing ethnic and religious groups. For Jews, affirmative action was reminiscent of the anti-Jewish quotas of European and American universities prior to World War II.

In the 1920s, the facility of Jews in test-taking had led universities seeking to reduce their Jewish enrollment to emphasize personality traits and other intangible considerations. Initially, however, the universities had assumed that testing would keep down the number of Jewish students. In 1912, Henry Goddard, an American pioneer in mental testing, had administered a series of tests to a large group of immigrants at Ellis Island. He concluded that 83 percent of the Jews were "feeble-minded." Today a statue of Goddard stands in front of the headquarters of the Educational Testing Service in Princeton, New Jersey. Ironically, no ethnic groups benefited more from the popularity of the impersonal examinations of ETS and other testing agencies than Jews and Asians.[22]

This ascent of Jews into the higher echelons of the American university reflected a new hospitality on the part of the American intellectual elite. In *The American Scene* (1907), novelist Henry James protested the cultural impact of the massive immigration from eastern and southern Europe that had occurred while he had been living in England for a quarter of a century. He was shocked by the immigrant ghettos that had sprung up during his absence. While disturbed by the Italian ghettos of Salem and Boston, his greatest concern was with what he termed "the Hebrew conquest of New York." The Jewish prominence in New York, America's most important center of writers and publishers, was threatening to extinguish the English language in America, James believed. "In the ultimate future," he wrote, the American language "may be destined to become the most beautiful on the globe," but "whatever we shall know it for, certainly we shall not know it for English—in any sense for which there is an existing literary measure." What Gentile can know, James asked, "what the genius of Israel may, or may not, really be 'up to'?"[23]

Within half a century, James's prediction regarding the influence of eastern European Jews had proved true. By the 1950s, Jewish literary critics, poets, and novelists had a major role in American letters. Robert Lowell, one of the most important of America's postwar poets and a relative of A. Lawrence Lowell, noted that "Jewishness is the theme of our literary culture in somewhat the same fashion that Middle Western and Southern writing occupied this position in earlier decades." When Elizabeth Hardwick left her native Kentucky for New York City, she said she was doing it in order to become a New York Jewish intellectual. Her ethnic conversion would take place in the editorial offices of the *New York Review of Books*.[24]

Henry James was wrong, however, in believing that New York Jewish intellectuals would seek to subvert the English language. They did not want to transform American culture but to become part of it. Irving Howe, Alfred Kazin, William Phillips, Philip Rahv, Lionel Trilling, and other Jewish men of letters of the 1940s and 1950s were children of immigrants, and immersion in American (and English) literature was a means for them to escape the immigrant milieu of their youth. They became Americans through its literature.

Beginning with Alfred Kazin's *On Native Grounds: An Interpretation of American Prose Literature* (1942), the major thrust of the Jewish critics was the celebration of American language and literature. Their books and essays in *Partisan Review, Commentary,* and other journals often protested the undermining of American high culture by the mass culture of advertising and middlebrow writers. Their conservative thrust was particularly noticeable in the midcentury revival of interest in Henry James himself. This was largely the work of American Jews, led by his major biographer, Leon Edel, who became the Henry James Professor of English and American Letters at New York University.

Trilling, the most elegant of the Jewish literary critics, was at the center of one of the most famous cases in the history of American academic anti-Semitism. In the 1930s, he had decided upon an academic career against the advice of friends who thought him "naive to the point of absurdity" for failing to recognize that as a Jew his prospects for a university appointment were slight. Elliot Cohen, one of his mentors, had discontinued his own graduate studies in English at Yale precisely because of these fears. At this time, the departments of English at the major universities carefully guarded the sanctity of English against contamination by upstart Jews and other immigrants who, it was claimed, could never become part of what was then called the Anglo-Saxon tradition.[25]

In 1932, Trilling became an instructor in English at his alma mater,

Columbia University. "Had his name been that of his maternal grandfather, Israel Cohen," Trilling's wife later recalled, "it is highly questionable whether the offer could have been made." In 1936, the English Department ended his appointment, telling him that as a Jew, a Freudian, and a Marxist, he would be more comfortable elsewhere. In truth, Trilling was far more at home in the university than among Jews. American Jewish culture, he later charged, was so sterile that "it can give no sustenance to the American artist or intellectual who is born a Jew." There was not one American Jew, he claimed, "with the note of authority—of philosophical, or poetic, or even of rhetorical, let alone of religious authority."[26]

Trilling convinced the department to reconsider its decision and continued teaching at Columbia. In 1939, he published his doctoral dissertation, an outstanding intellectual biography of Matthew Arnold. Trilling's book impressed Nicholas Murray Butler, Columbia's president, and Butler made sure, despite opposition within the English Department, that Trilling was appointed an assistant professor. He was the first Jew from the English Department to become a member of the Columbia faculty. This did not please all members of the department. His dissertation mentor told Trilling he hoped, now that he was a member of the department, that Trilling would not favor the hiring of additional Jews. By the time of his death in 1975, Trilling was viewed by critics of the American literary establishment as an insider, a spokesman for that Anglo-Saxon literary tradition that, it had been believed, was beyond the comprehension of eastern European Jews.[27]

The position of Jews in English departments changed after World War II. Diana Trilling never forgot her husband's grin when he came home one afternoon and reported, "We hired a new English instructor today. His name is Hyman Kleinman." Before the war, no Jew had ever received tenure in the English departments of Harvard, Princeton, and Yale. Trilling himself had been rejected for a position at Yale because of the anti-Semitism of Chauncey Brewster Tinker, Sterling Professor of English Literature. By the 1970s, Yale's English Department, which was among the most distinguished in the country, had several Jewish members.[28]

Even at Harvard, where the New England literary tradition resembled a religious cult, the teaching of early American literature was entrusted to Sacvan Bercovitch, who had deserted Columbia to fill the position once occupied by the lofty Perry Miller. At one time, Bercovitch had even taught at Brandeis. In the 1920s, President A. Lawrence Lowell of Harvard had strongly supported the execution of Sacco and Vanzetti. In the 1970s, a scholar whose radical parents had named him Sacvan for the two Italian anarchists was teaching at Harvard the literature of Lowell's Puritan ancestors.

History was another area in which Jews, after some opposition from the Brahmins in the field, made their mark. Before World War II, Jewish historians had a difficult time breaking into the academic big leagues. Even J. H. Hexter, a historian of future note, had difficulty finding employment. "I'm afraid he is unemployable," Crane Brinton of Harvard said in 1938 regarding Hexter, "but I'd like to make one last effort in his behalf." Selig Perlman, a professor of economics at the University of Wisconsin, reportedly warned Jewish graduate students in history at Wisconsin to switch to economics or sociology. "History belongs to the Anglo-Saxons," he told them in his deep Yiddish accent. This situation changed after World War II. By 1970, Jews constituted over 20 percent of the historians at America's better universities.[29]

Jews specializing in American history had a particularly difficult time getting jobs. Historians were reluctant to entrust the teaching of the nation's sacred history to such outsiders. In addition, they believed that Jews, particularly those with an eastern European ancestry, lacked gentility and were too radical. The mentors of Jewish graduate students went out of their way to emphasize to prospective employers how different their Jewish students were from other eastern European Jews. Bert Loewenberg "by temperament and spirit . . . measures up to the whitest Gentile I know," wrote Arthur Schlesinger in 1930. On another occasion, he wrote a prospective employer that Oscar Handlin "has none of the offensive traits which some people associate with his race." Such sentiments were widespread within the profession. Ironically, Schlesinger was half Jewish himself (although of central European background). He had overcome this disability, marrying into a distinguished New England family and securing a professorship at Harvard.[30]

One thinly disguised protest against the influence of Jews, particularly New York Jews, in the writing of American history was Carl Bridenbaugh's 1962 presidential address before the American Historical Association. In "The Great Mutation," Bridenbaugh questioned whether historians born after World War I could understand, much less empathize with the majority of Americans, including himself, who, prior to World War I, had grown up in a country overwhelmingly rural. This was particularly true of historians with immigrant, urban backgrounds. Such persons, Bridenbaugh argued, allowed their emotions to affect their understanding of the American past.

They find themselves in a very real sense outsiders on our past and feel
themselves shut out. This is certainly not their fault, but it is true. They
have no experience to assist them, and the chasm between them and the
Remote Past widens every hour. . . . What I fear is that the changes observant in the background . . . of the present generation will make it
impossible for them to communicate to and reconstruct the past for
future generations.

The problem was not racial but environmental. Previously "such understanding was vouchsafed to historians who were raised in the countryside
or in the small town, where the eccentricities, idiosyncracies, and individual
traits of people were allowed free play, openly, and more often than not
encouraged, because they made them more interesting." Bridenbaugh was,
of course, talking about Jews.[31]

Bridenbaugh's belief that first- and second-generation Jews could not appreciate American history appears absurd in retrospect. His speech was given
in Chicago at a time when Daniel J. Boorstin, a second-generation Jew, was
the most significant American historian in the Windy City. During the 1950s,
this University of Chicago historian had been one of the three major spokesmen for "consensus history," the belief that the central theme of American
history was continuity and homogeneity and not regional, racial, and class
conflict. The other two exponents of this conservative view of American history—Richard Hofstadter and Louis Hartz—also had Jewish backgrounds,
although Hofstadter's mother was a Lutheran. While Hofstadter and Hartz
believed intellectual consensus had impoverished the nation's social and
political thought, Boorstin believed it was the secret of American success.

Beginning with *The Genius of American Politics* (1953), Boorstin published a series of books presenting the most important post-1945 conservative interpretation of American history. These volumes included a textbook with the subtitle *A Conservative Textbook for Conservative Times*
(1981). Boorstin's place within the historical profession was an ironic commentary on the fears of historians concerning Jewish radicalism. In 1949,
for example, John D. Hicks had expressed concern over the possibility that
Armin Rappaport, a prospective member of the history department at the
University of California, "might have some of the ultra left wing tendencies
so common to the New York Jewish intelligentsia."[32]

By the 1960s, Jews were important even in Carl Bridenbaugh's own
speciality, colonial American history. The best example was Bernard Bailyn,

who taught colonial American history at Harvard. This position, one of the most prestigious in the profession, had been occupied previously by Samuel Eliot Morison. Nothing was more indicative of Harvard's commitment to merit than the change from Morison, the scion of two distinguished Boston families, to Bailyn, the offspring of Jews from Hartford, Connecticut. Oscar Handlin, a second-generation Jew from Brooklyn and the first Jew of eastern European background to be a member of Harvard's history department, had directed Bailyn's doctoral dissertation, a study of New England merchants during the seventeenth century.

Four years after Bridenbaugh's qualms surfaced, Bailyn would receive the first of his two Pulitzer prizes. A decade later Michael Kammen, a student of Bailyn who taught colonial American history at Cornell, would also win a Pulitzer. Kammen had grown up within the city limits of Washington, D.C. The examples of Boorstin, Bailyn, and Kammen were not unique. By the 1960s, scholars with Jewish backgrounds taught American history at many of America's leading universities, including Columbia (Richard Hofstadter), Princeton (Eric F. Goldman), Yale (John Morton Blum), and the University of California (Lawrence Levine). While being Jewish did not necessarily help them understand American history, it certainly did not prevent them from making significant contributions to the field.

Three-quarters of a century after James had wondered what the "genius of Israel" was "up to," the three most important American cultural institutions were directed by descendants of eastern European Jews. Conservative Republican presidents had appointed Ronald Berman to head the National Endowment for the Humanities and Daniel Boorstin to head the Smithsonian Institution and the Library of Congress because of their reputation as cultural traditionalists. By the 1970s, the "genius of Israel" was guarding the ramparts of American culture from the onslaught of cultural barbarians, some of whom were products of white, Anglo-Saxon, Protestant America.

The new prominence of Jews in American letters led to grumblings, often tinged with anti-Semitism, regarding a Jewish literary conspiracy. Truman Capote, the author of *Breakfast at Tiffany's* and *In Cold Blood,* claimed in the March 1968 issue of *Playboy* that there existed a

> clique of New York-oriented writers and critics who control much of the literary scene through the influence of the quarterlies and intellectual magazines. All these publications are Jewish-dominated and this

particular coterie employs them to make or break writers by advancing
or withholding attention. . . . Bernard Malamud, Saul Bellow, Philip
Roth and Isaac Bashevis Singer are all fine writers, but they're not the
"only" writers in the country as the Jewish mafia would have us believe.
I could give you a list of excellent writers . . . . The odds are you
haven't heard of most of them for the simple reason that the Jewish
mafia has systematically frozen them out of the literary scene.[33]

Novelist Gore Vidal seconded Capote's grievance. Vidal, who became
notorious in the 1980s for questioning the patriotism of Jewish supporters
of Israel, wrote that writers such as Malamud, Bellow, and Roth "comprise
a new, not quite American class, more closely connected with ideological,
argumentative Europe (and talmudic studies) than with those of us whose
ancestors killed Indians, pursued the whale." Saul Bellow's novel *The Victim* (1947) satirized such resentments by having an anti-Semite complain
that the author of a book on Emerson and Thoreau was named Lipschitz.
(During the 1940s, John E. Rankin, the rabid anti-Semitic congressman
from Mississippi, claimed that the radio columnist Walter Winchell was a
"loathsome" Jew whose real name was "Lipshitz" [i.e., lip-shit].)[34]

The intellectual influence of the Lipschitzs of America extended beyond American letters. In no other country in history, Ladd and Lipset
wrote, have Jews "been able to do as well intellectually as in the United
States." Charles Kadushin's *The American Intellectual Elite* (1974) reported
that, of the country's two hundred most important intellectuals, half were
Jews, and sixteen of the twenty-one most influential intellectuals had at
least one Jewish parent. Approximately three-fifths of these leading Jewish
intellectuals were professors and, Kadushin wrote, had benefited from "the
post–World War II expansion of universities and colleges and the accompanying relaxation of barriers against Jewish professors."[35]

Surveys of American scientists, musicians, and the media also revealed
a disproportionate number of Jews. According to Harriet Zuckerman's
1977 survey of American Nobel laureates raised in the United States, only
1 percent had a Roman Catholic background while 27 percent were Jews,
even though Catholics then outnumbered Jews in the United States by eight
to one. In percentage terms, there were nine times as many Jewish Nobel
Prize winners as there were Jews in the general population. This intellectual
preeminence resulted in the wry definition of a Soviet-American cultural
exchange as the Soviets sending their Jewish violinists from Kiev to the

United States and America sending its Jewish immigrant violinists from Kiev back to Russia.

At the end of World War II, Albert Sprague Coolidge of Harvard's chemistry department told a committee of the Massachusetts legislature, "We know perfectly well that names ending in 'berg' or 'stein' have to be skipped by the board of selection for students for scholarships in chemistry." It was thus ironic that William Howard Stein, a Jew, shared the Nobel Prize in chemistry in 1972. Not only did his name end (and begin) with "stein," but he had earned his bachelor's degree and had begun his graduate work at Harvard.[36]

Jews were also prominent among those in publishing, in Hollywood, and in the media who defined themselves primarily as intellectuals rather than as mass media technicians. The cerebral Walter Lippmann, a completely assimilated Jew, was the most admired American journalist of the twentieth century. Jews were more prominent within the ranks of editors and writers than among the owners of newspapers, television and radio stations, and magazines. Although large, the presence of Jews in the media elite was never as important as the fantasies of Henry Ford, Charles Lindbergh, Jr., Spiro Agnew, and Jesse Jackson presumed. While making up 6 percent of the national press in 1982, one-quarter of those employed by the *New York Times,* the *Wall Street Journal,* the *Washington Post, Time, Newsweek,* and the major television networks were Jews.[37]

Jews in the media were located along the entire political spectrum and were not involved in a conspiracy to further Jewish interests. The politics of Mortimer Zuckerman of *U. S. News and World Report* and Norman Podhoretz of *Commentary* had little in common with those of Martin Peretz of the *New Republic* and Victor Navasky of the *Nation,* while the news reports and editorials on the Middle East of the *Washington Post,* a newspaper in which Jews held important editorial positions, angered Israel's fervent supporters in America. The Jewish identity of the Sulzberger family which controlled the *New York Times* was tepid at best, and the *Times* had the reputation within Jewish circles of bending over backward not to appear too Jewish. In 1948, A. M. Rosenthal was denied an opportunity to cover a conference in Paris. "One Jew in Paris is enough," Cyrus L. Sulzberger told him. Four years later, the *Times* turned down Daniel Schorr's request for a position on its European staff because "we have too many Jews in Europe." Supposedly the *Times* used the initial *A* rather than *Abraham* in the bylines of A. M. Rosenthal and A. H. Raskin in order to play down their Jewish backgrounds.[38]

Despite their diverse areas of expertise and places of employment, most Jewish intellectuals shared a common political and religious outlook. As Jews and as intellectuals, they were members of two of the most politically liberal groups in America. The voting profile of Jewish academicians was far to the left of their Gentile colleagues and the general population. While Barry Goldwater received nearly 40 percent of the vote in the 1964 presidential election and 24 percent of the vote of Protestant academicians, only 2 percent of Jewish faculty members voted for him. One exception was Harry Jaffa, a Jewish political scientist, who wrote part of the acceptance speech that Goldwater delivered before the Republican convention. Four years later, one-fourth of Catholic academicians and 42 percent of white Protestant professors voted for Richard Nixon, compared to only 6 percent of Jewish professors. In 1972, seven out of eight Jewish professors voted for George McGovern for president, even though he got less than 40 percent of the total vote and only about one-third of the white vote.[39]

The political impact of the Jewish intelligentsia was to move American intellectual discourse further to the left. Magazines edited by Jewish intellectuals—such as the staunchly anticommunist *Partisan Review,* and *Commentary* prior to its metamorphosis in the late 1960s—generally supported the social and economic program of the American Left. David Broder, Richard Cohen, Joseph Kraft, Anthony Lewis, and most of the other Jewish political columnists have been part of the American liberal coalition. In such politically relevant academic fields as history, political science, psychology, and sociology, Jews were in the forefront of those challenging the conventional wisdom and calling for social and economic reforms to benefit the disadvantaged.

Sociologists who studied American Jewish academicians noted their alienation from the American Jewish community. This alienation was a major concern of American Jewish leaders, because a large number of Jews were intellectuals (or at least perceived themselves as intellectuals), and because Jews saw themselves as a people who valued ideas and books. Even Gentiles made invidious comparisons between Jewish intellectuality and the intellectual level of their own communities. Monsignor John Tracy Ellis's famous 1955 essay, "American Catholics and the Intellectual Life," criticized Catholic anti-intellectualism and asked where were the Catholic Einsteins, Salks, and Oppenheimers. Similarly, Richard Hofstadter, in his Pulitzer Prize-winning *Anti-Intellectualism in American Life* (1963), examined the sources of Catholic intellectual backwardness. He did not discuss any comparable phenomenon within American Jewry.

American Jews respected intellectuals and patronized cultural institutions more than other major ethnic groups. This exalted attitude toward the intellectual life helps explain the Jewish love of academia and the prominence of Jewish intellectuals in the postwar era. Postwar surveys revealed that Jews bought books, subscribed to intellectual magazines, attended concerts, purchased works of art, and went to art galleries more often than Gentiles. One way to achieve status within the postwar American Jewish community was to become part of the intelligentsia, even if only vicariously through writing a check to an educational or a cultural institution. Wealthy but uneducated Jewish businessmen gave munificent sums to art galleries, museums, research institutes, universities, and other institutions. Jews who had developed great businesses were often deferential in the presence of persons whose only claim to fame was a university position.

It was comforting for American Jews to assume that intellectuality and an affinity for the academic life were inherent in Jewish culture. The supposed dogmatism and authoritarianism of Christianity, it was argued, contrasted with Judaism's emphasis on study and the give-and-take of talmudic reasoning. But Judaism was never as compatible with the modern university and the unfettered pursuit of knowledge as Jews liked to believe. Traditional Judaism could be every bit as dogmatic and intolerant as Christianity. As readers of Chaim Potok's novels know, traditional Judaism viewed the modern university with suspicion, even when, as in the case of Yeshiva University, it was under Orthodox auspices. Right-wing Orthodox spokesmen believed the modern university was a pagan institution, and they discouraged their followers from attending college except for purely vocational reasons. They realized that most of the intellectual challenges to traditional religion had emanated from the intellectuals of the university, that the social life of the university was often libertine and decadent, and that Jewish academicians were by and large estranged from traditional Judaism.

Jewish academicians would have been surprised to learn that their choice of a career was due to a religion and culture to which they often had only the most attenuated relationship. The Jewish attraction to academia was not due to Judaism but to the secular values that Jewish immigrants handed down to their children and grandchildren. These emphasized literacy, social mobility, individual achievement, economic success, the deferral of gratification, competitiveness, professionalization, and respect for ideas. This explained the ability of Jewish professors to move ahead rapidly within academia once merit became the ruling principle. Jewish academicians were driven to become part of an academic culture that, for the most part, disdained parochial ethnic and religious loyalties.

The university, as a miniature society with its own values, traditions, and accepted modes of behavior, was a rival to and a surrogate for the Jewish community. Jewish professors readily tossed aside ethnic and religious loyalties, which many felt were anachronistic and burdensome. The things that attracted Jews to academia—its critical spirit, its distrust of authority, and its interest in abstract ideas—were precisely the same things that made them skeptical of religion and the demands of tradition. "The Jewish world is a sectarian world," one Boston-area Jewish academician said. It has "too narrow a basis, too narrow a spectrum for a man who wishes to make a contribution in international communicative ideas to feel comfortable in this group."[40]

Most Jewish professors taught at institutions with large Jewish enrollments. Inevitably they were role models for Jewish students at precisely the time when these young Jews were establishing their own identities away from the supervision of parents and community. The answer students often got from their Jewish professors to the question of what it meant to be a Jew in America was that it often did not mean very much. To be sure, there were Jewish academicians involved in American Professors for Peace in the Middle East and the Academic Committee for Soviet Jewry. These, however, were a small minority.

Most Jewish professors had only a slight relationship to Jewish culture and Judaism. Data collected by the Carnegie Commission on Higher Education in 1969 revealed that while 32 percent of professors with a Protestant background and 25 percent with a Catholic background were either indifferent or opposed to religion, 67 percent of Jewish professors were indifferent or opposed to religion. And while 16 percent of Protestant professors and 23 percent of Catholic professors considered themselves deeply religious, only 5 percent of Jewish professors defined themselves as such. In comparison to other Jews, Jewish academicians observed fewer Jewish rituals, were more hostile to religion, affiliated with Jewish communal institutions less frequently, and intermarried more often.[41]

Despite their problematical relationship with Jewish culture and religion, academicians were respected by other Jews, who viewed anti-intellectualism as a Gentile disease and an integral element of the anti-Semitic personality. Their favorite solution for anti-Semitism was more education.

It was important for American Jewry to maintain the loyalty of its intellectuals in order to validate its self-image as a community of scholars and thinkers. A Jewish community without intellectuals was simply inconceivable. Even when intellectuals supported policies hostile to Jewish interests, they were viewed as wayward sons rather than as enemies. Anti-Zionist radical sociologist Herbert Marcuse, for example, taught for many years at Brandeis University. Periodically the American Jewish establishment voluntarily subjected itself to the criticisms of intellectuals. This form of masochism reflected the need of Jewish spokesmen to win the approval of intellectuals and also the desire of Jewish leaders to be thought of as intellectuals themselves.

Just as its investment in formal education was greater, so American Jewry spent more time, energy, and money than any other American ethnic or religious group in cultivating and analyzing its intellectuals. There must be something seriously wrong with American Jewry, it was argued, if it could not retain the loyalty of its brightest and best-educated members. The alienation of the Jewish intellectual from the American Jewish community occasioned much wringing of hands. There was, however, little that could have been done to bring Jewish intellectuals back to the fold. The sermons of rabbis and the proclamations of Jewish organizations could hardly convince intellectuals and academicians to abandon their secular and universalist outlook.

For the historian, the most significant aspect of this controversy was the controversy itself. The soul-searching of Jewish leaders regarding the status of Jewish professors manifested a fear for the future of American Jewry itself. From their perspective, the university was a microcosm of the general society. In both there had been a sharp decline in anti-Semitism and an openness to the aspirations of individual Jews. Since Jewish professors had responded to the unprecedented freedom and opportunity of the campus by becoming alienated from Jewish traditions and values, would not other American Jews react the same way when faced with economic and social opportunities of their own? Would Jews maintain a Jewish identity in an open society?

Despite their prominence after World War II, academicians and other intellectuals made up only a small part of American Jewry. The primary avenue of Jewish upward social and economic mobility both before and after the war was business. Most Jewish businessmen (and women) prior to the war were involved in retail trade. While some of their businesses were fairly substantial, the great majority were of the mom-and-pop variety. Jews were prominent in the entertainment industry, especially in the production of motion pictures. In the major cities, Jews were also important in wholesaling.

Jews were scarce, however, in the most important sectors of the economy, such as commercial banking, communication, transportation, insurance, the utilities, mining, oil and gas production, heavy construction, and manufacturing. Automotive manufacturing, insurance, commercial banking, and the telephone company, in particular, had the reputation of being anti-Semitic. The basic manufacturing industries—steel, petroleum products, machine tools, automobiles—had few Jewish employees in positions of responsibility. Men's and women's clothing was one of the rare manufacturing fields with a sizable Jewish presence. Of all the anti-Semitic beliefs, none was more ludicrous than the charge that the American economy was controlled by Jews. In the early postwar years, the economy resembled academia, with white Protestants monopolizing the positions of power and prestige.

The absence of Jews from important positions in the economy was as much due to the job preferences of Jews as to anti-Semitism. Jews avoided large private business bureaucracies where advancement would depend on evaluations of superiors who might be anti-Semitic. Jews wished to control their own future, even if it meant working long hours as proprietors of retail outlets. Jewish professionals exhibited this same desire for economic independence. Jewish accountants, doctors, and lawyers preferred to be self-employed or to work for other Jews rather than be employed by Fortune 500 corporations. But the reluctance of Jews to work for large bureaucracies did not extend to government employment on the federal, state, and local levels. Such positions were relatively free of anti-Semitism and, particularly during the 1930s, offered Jews job opportunities frequently not found in the private sector.

While there had been important Jewish businessmen prior to World War II, most, such as Julius Rosenwald of Sears, Roebuck and Louis B. Mayer of M-G-M, had founded or joined their companies when they were just beginning their operations. With very few exceptions, Jews were not named the chief executive officers of already established important concerns. An exception was Gerard Swope, president of General Electric from 1922 to 1940. Swope had married a Christian and concealed the fact that he was Jewish. Surprisingly, he left the bulk of his estate of nearly eight million dollars to the Technion in Haifa, Israel's leading engineering institution.[42]

By the 1960s, there were signs that the restricted position of Jews in big business was changing. In *Today's American Jew* (1967), Morris N. Kertzer reported that, while Jews were conspicuously absent from the higher rungs of American business, merit considerations were slowly replacing "traditional clubhouse fraternalism." The great breakthrough occurred in 1973, fourteen years before Harold Shapiro was appointed president of Princeton, when the board of directors of the Du Pont Corporation chose Irving Shapiro, the son of a Lithuanian-born pants presser, to be its chairman and chief executive officer. Because of the nature of the Du Pont company, the selection of Shapiro caused much discussion in the American media and was a significant milestone in recent American Jewish history. Du Pont was then America's largest chemical company, the third largest American manufacturing concern, and the nation's oldest major corporation.[43]

Few American corporations had so illustrious (or notorious) a history. For nearly two centuries, the Du Pont family and the Du Pont company had been an important part of the American scene and the corporate establishment. The company also had an anti-Semitic personnel policy as late as the 1950s. "I could understand a Jew becoming President of the United States," the American ambassador to Great Britain said after hearing of Shapiro's appointment, "but not the chief executive officer of Du Pont." Shapiro believed that his selection in 1976 as chairman of the Business Roundtable was even more important than his becoming Du Pont's CEO. This organization of leading corporate chief executives was a major voice in behalf of the interests of big business. "The key leaders of American industry made it damn clear that I was welcome in their club," Shapiro recalled.[44]

In selecting Shapiro, Du Pont decisively broke with the polite anti-Semitism prevalent within American corporate boardrooms. The choice of Shapiro assumed great symbolic importance not merely because he was a Jew but because he refused to disguise his Jewishness to get ahead. "I accomplished all this by my deliberate decision to be myself," Shapiro told Charles E. Silberman. "I am what I am, and I can never change." During the 1940s when he was a struggling lawyer in his hometown of Minneapolis, then considered to be the most anti-Semitic American city, he had rejected the advice of professors at the University of Minnesota Law School and of other young Jewish lawyers to change his obviously Jewish last name.[45]

While working his way up through the Du Pont corporate bureaucracy, Shapiro played a prominent role in the local Wilmington, Delaware, Jewish community. He was president of the Jewish Federation of Delaware, chaired the local United Jewish Appeal campaign, and sat on the board of a Jewish old-age home. When he became Du Pont's head, he refused to join a Wilmington country club that had never had any Jewish members. "I told them that it just would not be comfortable for my wife and me to socialize there," Shapiro said. "It never occurred to them that I might say no."[46]

Shapiro was proud of the fact that his becoming Du Pont's CEO had opened the doors of big business to other Jews. But he was also wise enough to realize that he was a product of his time, and that, if not him, then another Jew would have broken the corporate barrier. "I am absolutely convinced that the situation has turned around completely," he remarked in 1983. "Jewishness is simply not a relevant factor any more in most corporations." The presence of Jews in the highest echelons of Bank of America, Chrysler, Colgate-Palmolive, Disney, Ford, McDonald's, United Airlines, and other important corporations confirmed the accuracy of Shapiro's statement.[47]

His conclusion was also borne out by an academic study sponsored in the mid-1980s by the American Jewish Committee, which examined the rate of mobility within corporate America of Jews with master's degrees in business administration. Samuel Z. Klausner, a sociologist at the University of Pennsylvania, noted that none of the seven indexes he used in the study had turned up any anti-Semitism. "The burden of proof must now fall on those who perceive a climate of employment discrimination," he concluded. Jews, he asserted, had advanced more rapidly within corporate hierarchies and had higher salaries than their Protestant and Catholic counterparts. Klausner believed the higher salaries of Jews were due to the fact that they "hold positions of greater responsibility and in part because they work for more profitable firms. The higher salaries may also be attributable in part to career strategies among Jews that include longer cultural preparation, attending better colleges, majoring in liberal arts and then pursuing administrative rather than technical positions in a variety of corporate divisions." One of the more surprising of Klausner's findings was that a higher percentage of Jewish MBAs than Gentile MBAs believed performance rather than family or personality determined success.[48]

Another barometer of the extent to which Jews had become part of the American economic establishment was the increasing number of American Jews with immense fortunes. Money, it is true, is not an infallible indicator of status and power: the president of a major bank has far more status and power than a much wealthier entrepreneur. But it is also a mistake to deny that money has no relationship to status and power. Beginning in the early

1980s, *Forbes* magazine published an annual compilation of the four hundred richest Americans. Strictly based on their percentage of the general population, there should have been about twelve Jews on this list. Instead, there were over one hundred. Jews, who constituted less than 3 percent of the American people, made up over one-quarter of the richest Americans. They were overrepresented by a factor of nine.

By contrast, ethnic groups that greatly outnumbered Jews—Italians, Hispanics, blacks, and eastern Europeans—had few representatives on the list. The higher the category of assets listed by *Forbes,* the greater the percentage of Jews. Over 30 percent of American billionaires were Jewish. The same phenomenon was also found in Canada, where the three most prominent business families were all Jewish—the Belzbergs of Vancouver, the Bronfmans of Montreal, and the Reichmanns of Toronto. It was possible that *Forbes* even underestimated the number of America's superrich Jews, since many of them had become wealthy in real estate, the most difficult of fields to gauge assets and the easiest in which to hide wealth.[49]

An even more impressive list appeared in the 22 July 1986 issue of *Financial World.* It numbered the one hundred Wall Street executives—investment bankers, money managers, arbitragers, buyout specialists, speculators, commodities traders, and brokers—who had earned at least $3 million in 1985. The list began with Ivan Boesky, who supposedly made $100 million. This was more than two and a half times the annual salaries of all senators and congressmen, but as the *Financial World* explained, Boesky had a better year than Congress. "Ivan is one of the cleverest people in the business," a vice president at Drexel Burnham Lambert declared. "He's deeply charitable and socially conscious. If you don't like Ivan, you don't like Pete Rose. It's just another sport."

Boesky would spend a couple of years in prison for financial chicanery, including insider trading. In 1989, his fellow sportsman Rose was banned from baseball for life for betting on baseball games, and the next year he was sentenced to five months in prison for income tax evasion. Boesky's earnings were dwarfed by the $500 million Michael Milken earned in a following year. Milken also was hotly pursued by the government because of a variety of purported civil and criminal offenses. Milken and Boesky were Jewish, as were half of the people mentioned by the *Financial World.* Wall Street's Jewish heavy hitters included George Soros ($93.5 million), Asher Edelman ($25 million), Morton Davis ($25 million), and Michael Steinhardt ($20 million).[50]

Jews were reluctant to advertise their financial success because of fear of bolstering the anti-Semitic accusation of vast Jewish wealth and economic power. It was much more comforting to claim that Jews were like everyone else, only more so. The inability of American Jews to recognize the extent to which they had become part of the financial (and academic) elite was due in part to its novelty. Jews were unfamiliar with status and power, and it was not surprising that they should view their situation as exceptional and temporary. History had taught them that safety lay in anonymity, that it was the raised nail that was hammered down. Thus it was not surprising that the chronicler of the wealthy American Jews was a Gentile. In *Our Crowd, The Grandees,* and *"The Rest of Us,"* Stephen Birmingham recounted the accomplishments and the foibles of America's most successful German, Sephardic, and eastern European Jews.

Jewish historians ignored or discounted the role of American Jewish economic barons. While their books discussed such figures as Mordecai Noah and Emma Goldman, they slighted the founders of Inland Steel, Federated Department Stores, Consolidated Foods, and Hyatt Hotels. A particularly egregious example was Irving Howe's *World of Our Fathers* (1976), described by its bookjacket as an analysis of "the journey of the east European Jews to America and the life they found and made." In Howe's 650 pages of text there are long accounts of labor lawyer Joseph Barondess, socialist politician Meyer London, and Yiddish literary critic Shmuel Niger. There is, however, no mention of David Sarnoff, who grew up on the Lower East Side and established the Radio Corporation of America (RCA).

For Howe, a democratic socialist and one of the editors of the independent socialist quarterly *Dissent,* the essence of the Jewish immigrant experience was "a readiness to live for ideals beyond the clamor of self, a sense of plebian fraternity, an ability to forge a community of moral order even while remaining subject to a society of social disorder." Jews could take pleasure "in having been related to those self-educated workers, those sustaining women, those almost-forgotten writers and speakers devoted to excitements of controversy and thought." But Howe slighted the most significant characteristic of Jewish immigrants—their drive for economic success and social mobility, their determination that their children, including Irving Howe, would not work in the sweatshops. In this they were largely successful.[51]

Jewish discomfiture over their social and economic success resulted from a psychology of insecurity and marginality that was incongruous with the actual status of Jews in contemporary America. Because they feared what the Gentiles might think, Jews tended to underestimate, deny, or explain away their prosperity. In his 1948 essay "The Self-Fulfilling Prophecy," sociologist Robert K. Merton discussed the absurdity of denying Jewish achievements. Jewish defense agencies, he wrote, were

> busily engaged in assuring the powerful in-group that they have not, in fact, been guilty of inordinate contributions to science, the professions, the arts, the government and the economy. . . . In a culture which consistently judges the professionals higher in social value than even the most skilled hewers of wood and drawers of water, the out-group finds itself in the anomalous position of pointing with defensive relief to the large number of Jewish painters and paper hangers, plasterers and electricians, plumbers and sheet-metal workers.[52]

Jews failed to realize that their embarrassment was inappropriate in a country where financial success and the rags-to-riches myth were crucial to the definition of national identity. The contrast between the Jewish and Gentile view of the Jewish rich was striking. Gentiles admired the Jewish economic status and attributed it to positive characteristics such as sobriety, frugality, and hard work. The achievements of the "brash and young, ambitious and daring eastern European Jewish entrepreneurs," Stephen Birmingham remarked, have been accepted by Americans "with equanimity and respect, without envy or rancor." Jews greatly overestimated the number of Americans who resented their prosperity. The 1981 study *Anti-Semitism in the United States,* prepared for the American Jewish Committee by the Yankelovich, Skelly, and White polling agency, revealed that three-quarters of American Jews believed that the majority of Gentiles felt Jews had "too much power in the business world." In fact, only one Gentile in three believed this.[53]

The Jewish wealthy were in fact quintessential Americans. John Higham, an eminent historian of American immigration and ethnicity, has argued that the competitiveness and materialism exhibited by Jews was, in fact, a "deeply ingrained" aspect of American life. While many of the Gentiles on the *Forbes* list made their money in the old-fashioned way—through inheritance—the Jews achieved success through entrepreneurial talents, determination, the successful exploitation of the tax laws, and the good fortune of having been located in areas of the country and in sectors of the economy that boomed after World War II.[54]

In *Democracy in America,* his classic commentary on American society published in the 1830s, Alexis de Tocqueville described the crucial role of money in America. "I know of no other country where love of money has such a grip on men's hearts or where stronger scorn is expressed for the theory of permanent equality of property," the Frenchman wrote. "No stigma attaches to the love of money in America, and provided it does not exceed the bounds imposed by public order, it is held in honor." In a nation without aristocratic distinctions, people were differentiated primarily by the possession of money. One usually finds, Tocqueville claimed, that "love of money is either the chief or a secondary motive at the bottom of everything the Americans do." It was thus fitting that Horatio Alger, the most famous exponent of the success myth, was employed by the German Jewish Seligman family to tutor its children.55

Jewish fortunes were to be found in many areas. Russell Berrie manufactured teddy bears, Paul Kalmanovitz owned breweries, and Arthur Sackler published medical magazines. But in no field were Jewish entrepreneurial talents more evident than real estate. Perhaps half the Jews on the *Forbes* list made their fortunes in real estate, particularly in New York City. "The Jew runs to real estate as soon as he can save up enough for a deposit to clinch the bargain," Jacob A. Riis had written in *How the Other Half Lives* (1890). Except for a few Gentile interlopers such as Donald Trump and Harry Helmsley, the most successful New York real estate developers were Jews. They included Laurence and Preston Tisch, Leonard Stern, Samuel LeFrak, and Sol Goldman. Other cities had their own Jewish real estate barons: Jerry Moore in Houston, A. Alfred Taubman in Detroit, Walter Shorenstein in San Francisco, Guilford Glazer in Los Angeles, Melvin and Herbert Simon in Indianapolis, Monte and Alfred Goldman in Oklahoma City, Frank Morgan and Sherman Dreiseszun in Kansas City, Mortimer Zuckerman and Harold Brown in Boston, Stephen Muss in Miami, Harry Weinberg in Baltimore, Neil Bluhm and Judd Malkin in Chicago, and Charles E. Smith in Washington.56

In *Beyond the Melting Pot* (1963), Nathan Glazer examined the economic and sociological reasons for this Jewish affinity for real estate. Real estate was an open field, in contrast to, say, banking and insurance. There was among Jews "an accumulation of business acumen, supported by a relatively strong family system that permits mobilization of capital (even if in small sums), and that makes it possible to move into new areas with opportunities for great growth and high profits."57

Real estate was an ideal industry for ambitious entrepreneurs who lacked capital and contacts. The Jewish attitude to real estate differed from that of other ethnic groups who also migrated in large numbers to America during the late nineteenth and early twentieth centuries. Gentiles from southern and eastern Europe believed land was sacred. Their savings went toward the purchase of houses, and they vigorously opposed the encroachments of other ethnic and racial groups into their neighborhoods. Jews, in contrast, preferred to use their savings for the education of their children or to buy businesses. Their favorite stratagem when confronted with a changing neighborhood was simply to move to other areas. Having been forbidden to own land in many societies and having been expelled from many countries, Jews never developed an attitude of reverence and permanence toward land. What was important were land values, not the land itself.

This stance toward real estate was particularly evident among Holocaust survivors. Real estate was an ideal field for these people who lacked capital but were ambitious and willing to take risks. They arrived in America at an opportune time. The depression and war had created a pent-up demand for housing that resulted in a building boom after 1945. In the decade after the war, ten million homes were built, housing some forty million people. Some of these houses and apartments were built by Holocaust survivors, many of whom became wealthy in the process. David Chase of Hartford and Laszlo Tauber of Washington, D.C., even made the *Forbes* list of the four hundred richest Americans. In no locale were survivors more prominent in real estate than in the midsize city of Elizabeth, New Jersey. Here, in the late 1940s and early 1950s, there settled a dozen or so Holocaust survivors who would later become enormously successful in land speculation and building. The "Elizabeth builders," as they came to be known, shaped a community in which real estate and Jewish philanthropy were major passions.

As Jews moved up the corporate and financial ladder, they came into closer social contact with non-Jews. As was true of Jewish academicians, it was impossible for successful Jewish businessmen to remain within a hermetically sealed Jewish social environment. The inevitable result was intermarriage and an attenuating of Jewish identity. The same studies that showed a marked improvement in the status of Jews in corporate America also reported that Jews advancing up the corporate hierarchy tended to be lukewarm in their Jewish attachments. "Once they get affluence and mingle in the non-Jewish world," Laurence Tisch, the head of Loew's Corporation and one of America's most influential and wealthiest businessmen, complained, "they think there's something socially more desirable perhaps over there." The September 1988 issue of *Moment* contained two interviews with prominent Jewish industrialists—Irving Shapiro and Alec Flamm, president of Union Carbide. While both were married to Jews, neither executive seemed particularly disturbed that their children had intermarried.[58]

Many of the most successful Jewish businessmen and financiers intermarried, including Henry Kravis and Felix Rohatyn. Among those who divorced their Jewish wives to marry Gentiles was Leonard Stern, a billionaire New York City real estate magnate. Stern's father was Max Stern, the founder of Hartz Mountain Products, a successful pet supply company. Max Stern was a generous contributor to Orthodox Jewish causes, and Stern College, the women's college of Yeshiva University, had been named in his honor. Despite his second marriage, Leonard Stern was also a benefactor of Yeshiva University and other traditional Jewish institutions.

On the basis of income and education, Jews by the 1980s were in the upper strata of American society and had moved into positions of political, economic, and social power. Beginning in the 1960s, Jews had headed some of the most important branches of the federal government, including the Federal Reserve System and the labor, commerce, state, and treasury departments. In the 1980s, eight Jews were members of the United States Senate. Jews had also become influential on Wall Street. The chief executive officer of the *Wall Street Journal,* the self-styled bible of the American dream, was a Jew named Warren Phillips. Jews had even broken into the exclusive world of American philanthropy. Few charities were reluctant to put wealthy Jews on their boards or have them participate in their fund-raising campaigns. This was particularly true in higher education. Philanthropies could not seek major gifts from Jews without according them recognition and status. New York University named its Business School after Leonard Stern because of his gift of twenty million dollars.

One barometer of how far Jews (and other ethnic groups) had come since 1945 was the American Leadership Study, conducted by the Bureau of Applied Social Research at Columbia University in 1971 and 1972. In the 1950s and 1960s, the most famous contribution of Columbia University to the study of leadership within American society was made by C. Wright Mills, a member of its sociology department. In *The Power Elite* (1956) and other books, Mills claimed there existed within America an interlocking elite that controlled American politics, the economy, and the military. The American Leadership Study, by contrast, concluded that reality was more complex than Mills had pictured. Ancestry was no longer crucial, although gender and education remained significant. The social system was sufficiently open to enable Jews to become an important part of the American elite. According to the analysis of the American Leadership Study's data by sociologists Richard D. Alba and Gwen Moore, Jews comprised over 11 percent of the American elite. "Being a male with a college degree is usually a prerequisite for admission" to the American elite, they wrote, "but British Protestant ancestry no longer is."[59]

The experience of Jews as a beleaguered and vulnerable minority made it difficult for America's Jews to fully recognize their favored position within American society. This was understandable since their situation was unprecedented. "Never has such a large number of the Jewish people in any one country of the Diaspora been counted as part of the elite," the Jewish historian David Biale wrote. Although their collective occupational and income profile surpassed that of Anglo-Saxon Episcopalians and Presbyterians, it was easier for American Jews to continue believing that they had more in common with blacks and Hispanics. Even academics such as Richard L. Zweigenhaft and G. William Domhoff (*Jews in the Protestant Establishment* [1982]) and Abraham K. Korman (*The Outsiders: Jews and Corporate America* [1988]) were skeptical about the extent of the Jewish ascent into the leadership ranks of American business and unwilling to give up the image of the Jew as the outsider. Milton Plesur asserted in 1982, nine years after Du Pont selected Irving Shapiro as its chief executive officer, that "it is virtually impossible for a qualified Jew to head a major corporation that is not already controlled by Jews." Arthur Liebman's *Jews and the Left* (1979) stressed the marginality and precariousness of the Jewish economic position and argued that socialism and not capitalism was most compatible with Jewish economic interests.[60]

These skeptics were ideologically closer to Michael Gold's *Jews without Money* (1930) than to Gerald Krefetz's *Jews and Money* (1982). In describing the economic success of Jews in America, Krefetz noted that never in modern history had Jews been as wealthy or as powerful as in the United States. "As a group they have risen to the top, and as individuals, their existence is freer, happier, and more productive than it has been for a thousand years. It may not be a Messiah's dream, but it may be the next best thing." Gold, in contrast, had experienced the poverty common to the Jews of New York's Lower East Side during the 1920s. Convinced that it was better to be dead than to be poor in America, his father had pleaded with him to become rich in order to escape from the "devil's dream" of New York's slums, where trees, grass, and flowers did not grow, "but the rose of syphilis bloomed by night and by day."[61]

Gold did not follow his father's advice. Instead, he worked for a Communist revolution that would destroy the Lower East Side and create "a garden for the human spirit." Gold's Lower East Side was destroyed, but it was destroyed by Jewish upward economic mobility, not by communism. He himself would never have considered the Jewish gilded ghettos of suburbia as gardens of the human spirit.

CHAPTER FIVE

WANDERING JEWS

WHILE few Jews after World War II became part of the American business, academic, and intellectual elite, the majority of Jewish families experienced social and economic mobility. In fact, a crucial development in the postwar history of American Jewry was their continued ascent en masse into the American middle class. After 1945, the social and economic profile of American Jews was transformed into one that closely approximated the American ideal. A larger percentage of Jews were native-born and lived in the suburbs, while fewer spoke Yiddish, resided in New York City, and worked in traditional Jewish areas such as small business and the garment industry. The transformation of American Jewry paralleled (and perhaps effected) the decline of anti-Semitism. Nativist fears regarding Jews had less saliency at a time when the vast majority of Jews had been born in the United States and were securely ensconced in the American middle class.

The census of 1940 was the first to report that a majority of American Jews were native-born. The percentage of American Jews who were immigrants continued to decrease after World War II. By 1964, only one out of seven American Jews was foreign-born. Immigration, however, remained important in the postwar era. Because of a low birth rate, increasing inter-marriage, and acculturation, American Jewry required the continual infusion of immigrants to sustain its growth. During the 1947–56 period, for example, nearly 60 percent of the increase in Jewish population came from immigration.[1]

There were three major waves of Jewish immigration as well as several smaller ripples. The first one consisted of refugees, the so-called displaced persons from Europe who settled in America in the late 1940s and early 1950s. Of the four hundred thousand refugees who relocated to America

during this period, approximately 40 percent were Jews. The Jewish survivors of the Holocaust were able, by and large, to establish a new life for
themselves in America. Tom Lantos, a survivor, and Sam Gejdenson, the
child of a survivor, were even elected to Congress. Other survivors established major businesses. The survivors' greatest achievement was overcom-
ing their horrific memories and not giving in to despair. The survivors were
remarkable, Rabbi Steven Riskin noted, not because they continue to believe
in God "but that they have children after Auschwitz; that they affirm life
and the future." By 1990, the survivors and their children constituted
approximately 8 percent of American Jewry, and their influence on the
American Jewish scene was greater than their numbers. Fiercely committed
to perpetuating the Jewishness for which they almost lost their lives, they
were generous benefactors to all sorts of Jewish causes. They were partially
responsible for reinvigorating American Orthodoxy which most observers
of the 1940s believed to be moribund.[2]

The survivors were Jews who happened to be from Poland, Hungary,
Romania, and the other countries of central and eastern Europe. The
second major wave of postwar Jewish immigration was from the Soviet
Union. Over one hundred thousand Jews from Russia immigrated to America in the 1970s and 1980s. They were, with some exceptions, Russians who
happened to be Jews. Six decades of Communist rule had attenuated the
Jewish identity of Russian Jewry. In contrast to the displaced persons and
the immigrants from eastern Europe in the late nineteenth and early twentieth centuries, the Russian immigrants of the 1970s and 1980s did not
speak Yiddish, knew little of Judaism, and tended to remain aloof from
Jewish organizations. Coming from the Soviet Union, where religion in
general and Judaism in particular were frowned upon, they perceived being
Jewish as a national and not a religio-cultural category. They distrusted
political and religious authority, suspecting that Jewish communal institutions, synagogues, and rabbis must be part of the state apparatus. But they
were Jewish enough to want to leave Mother Russia, where economic and
social opportunities for Jews were limited.

American Jewish officials realized that they were in a race against time
for the souls of the Russian Jews. They sought to Judaize the Russians
before they became completely assimilated. Studies of the Russian Jews
conducted in the 1980s indicate that these efforts had some success. The
longer Soviet Jews lived in the United States, the more their observance of
Jewish ritual and membership in Jewish organizations approximated that

of native Jews. The studies also revealed the negative attitudes many American Jews harbored toward the new arrivals. They were disappointed that, after all the trouble the Russian Jews had in leaving the Soviet Union, they preferred the fleshpots of the United States to life in the Jewish state of Israel. They were also disappointed that the Russians seemed so apathetic to Jewish concerns and so consumed with improving their economic condition and enjoying the material pleasures proffered by a consumer culture. American Jews had an excessively romantic picture of contemporary Russian Jews. They expected them to have the intense Jewish identity of their own parents and grandparents, or at least an identity stronger than the average American Jew. The Russians with whom the American Jews came in contact bore little resemblance to the heroic Jewish figures they expected.[3]

The third group of postwar Jewish immigrants were from Israel. In 1989 sociologist Chaim I. Waxman estimated that half a million Israelis and their children lived in America, with most residing in metropolitan New York and Los Angeles. Native American Jews were ambivalent toward the Israelis as well. On the one hand, they were fellow Jews. But on the other hand, American Jews were dismayed that the Israelis had abandoned the Jewish state. American Jews also did not know what to make of their lack of interest in Judaism and Jewishness. Like most Israelis, the majority of Israeli immigrants were apathetic regarding religion. They were first and foremost Israeli nationals and not Jews. Seeing themselves as temporary sojourners in America, the Israelis also tended to stay aloof from Jewish communal life.[4]

In addition to the survivors, Russians, and Israelis, smaller groups of immigrants migrated to America in the postwar decades. In the 1950s, over ten thousand Hungarian Jews came to America after the Russian suppression of the Hungarian revolution of 1956. Three years later, a couple of thousand Cuban Jews fled to the United States when Fidel Castro assumed power. After 1979, twenty thousand Iranian Jews migrated to America as a result of the overthrow of the shah of Iran by the Ayatollah Khomeini.

The ease with which the postwar immigrants adapted to life in America and the rise in the economic and social position of American Jews seemed at first glance to refute the predictions of Zionist ideologues who had argued that only in a Jewish state could the Jewish social and economic status be "normalized." By normalization, they meant a situation in which the social and economic patterns of Jews would approximate that of Gentiles. As one Zionist poet asserted, the Zionist movement could be judged a success only when a Jewish policeman would arrest a Jewish prostitute and bring her before a Jewish judge for sentencing. The ascent of American Jews into the middle class and their demographic dispersion seemed to resemble the normalization that Zionists, writing against the backdrop of growing nationalism and anti-Semitism in Europe, believed could occur only within a Jewish state. But the condition of American Jewry bore little resemblance to the Zionist model.

The Zionists claimed that the excessive orientation of European Jews toward Talmudic study and business had stunted normal social and economic development. Only if Jews became economically productive rather than middlemen and scholars, they asserted, could the Jewish national renaissance be successful and the Jews become a normal people. As was true of all other states, a Zionist nation would require farmers, laborers, and skilled craftsmen. Zionists, however, believed physical labor to be more than a necessary evil. It was the key to the remaking of the Jewish social and economic persona and to the metamorphosis of the European Jewish psyche. Through the dignity of labor, A. D. Gordon and other Labor Zionist pioneer thinkers maintained, Jews could purge themselves of the subservience and other damaging psychological traits that they had incurred living in the ghetto.

These goals of Labor Zionism had little in common with the realities of Jewish life in America after 1945. Far from being normalized, the social and economic condition of American Jewry entailed a rapid contraction of the Jewish working class, a virtual elimination of the Jewish farm population, and a lessening in the number of Jewish plumbers, carpenters, and electricians. The economic and social profile of American Jewry became more skewed than that of European Jewry. Jews exhibited a stronger drive for middle-class status, education, and professionalization than any other major American ethnic or religious group. As a result, their place on the occupational and economic ladder soon surpassed that of Episcopalians and Presbyterians, the highest status groups in American society. It was as if the Zionist ideal had been turned on its head. Much to the embarrassment of Zionist advocates, many of the cultural, educational, social, religious, and medical institutions of Israel became dependent on the financial support of American Jewish businessmen, doctors, and lawyers.

In the decades after World War II, America's Jews and Gentiles alike lived in an age of demographic revolution. What George W. Pierson, a Yale historian, called the "M factor"—migration, mobility, and movement—was strongly felt throughout all sectors of American society. Packing their belongings into modern-day Mayflowers, Americans set out in quest of economic and social opportunities. As Americans and as Jews, American Jews were part of this massive internal migration. Jews too left the small towns, the central cities, and the Northeast for the suburbs and the sunbelt.5

Although American Jewry prior to 1945 had been overwhelmingly urban, Jewish settlements could be found throughout the Northeast, South, and Middle West. On the main streets of virtually every county seat and town serviced by a railroad were stores owned by Jews or by their assimilated descendants that dated from the nineteenth and early twentieth centuries. While businessmen made up most of small-town Jewry, many towns had small contingents of Jewish doctors, lawyers, and schoolteachers. In college towns such as Chapel Hill, North Carolina, and St. Cloud, Minnesota, the local Jewish population was supplemented by academicians. Because of their economic role, the importance of small-town Jews was out of proportion to their numbers.

Many were significant political figures in their states. Sol Blatt was a fixture in the South Carolina legislature for half a century and, for much of that period, the most powerful local politician in the state. Louis Goldstein of Annapolis was important in Maryland politics for nearly five decades after World War II. Madeline Kunin served as governor of Vermont during the 1980s. The Evans's family history was paradigmatic. The father of Eli N. Evans, the author of *The Provincials: A Personal History of Jews in the South,* was a substantial merchant and the mayor of Durham, North Carolina during the 1950s at the beginning of the civil rights movement. His son graduated from the Yale Law School, worked in the White House during the 1960s, and then became president of the Charles Revson Foundation in New York City.

The economic role of small towns weakened after World War II. The decline of the farm population shrunk the clientele of small-town merchants, Jews and Gentiles alike, while the automobile, modern highways, catalogue houses, and radio, television, and other modern marketing media broke down the economic isolation of these communities. Small local merchants now found themselves in an almost impossible competition with catalogue houses, shopping centers, and chain stores such as Sears, Roebuck and K-Mart. For Jews with college degrees, there was little economic incentive to remain in the small town. The city offered more economic, cultural, and social opportunities. Movement to the city was almost a necessity if a young Jew wished to socialize with other Jews. National economic trends as well as their own ambitions encouraged younger Jews to leave the small towns for greener pastures.

According to the 1976 *American Jewish Year Book,* less than 1 percent of American Jews lived in communities where there were fewer than one hundred and fifty Jews. Other estimates used different criteria in calculating the size of small-town Jewry and found higher figures. But in none were small-town Jews more than a small percent of the total American Jewish population, and in few small towns were Jews more than a minor part of the general population. As a tiny minority surrounded by Christians, many of whom were devout evangelicals, small-town Jews had a strong sense of being Jewish. "You know, we're curiosities around town," one Jew told sociologist Peter I. Rose. "The people always heard about Jews but never met one. Then we appeared. Real live Jews. After some hesitancy they began to ask us all kinds of questions. . . . Often I wished I could answer all of them."[6]

A higher percentage of small-town Jews than their urban coreligionists were members of synagogues. However, it was often impossible for small-town Jews to express this Jewishness in a religious manner because of the lack of synagogues and rabbis and the difficulty of gathering the required ten adult men for religious services. Instead, they manifested their Jewish identity in the observance of various religious traditions, such as lighting candles at Hanukkah and participating in Passover seders; in support for the state of Israel; in membership in Jewish organizations such as B'nai B'rith and Hadassah; and in close social relationships with family and other Jews. "It's funny," one small-town Jew remarked, "but though we're really out of touch with Jews we're the ones who try to keep up the traditions."[7]

The specter of intermarriage, assimilation, and out-migration hung over small-town Jewry, which was chiefly concerned with the shortage of young Jews for their children to date. Many sent their children to Jewish summer camps and encouraged them to attend colleges with large Jewish enrollments. By the 1970s, they were also encouraging their children to spend time in Israel.

Small-town Jews liked the quiet, informality, and friendliness to which they were accustomed. Few, however, were optimistic regarding the Jewish future of their communities, as Lee J. Levinger noted in his 1952 *Commentary* essay "The Disappearing Small-Town Jew." "Their only chance for survival lies in the growth of their town, in its transformation into a suburb by the spread of a metropolitan area," Levinger wrote. "But then the town is no longer a village, and its Jews are no longer village Jews. . . . It seems that we shall soon have to write off most of the 150,000 village Jews from the roster of American Jewry."[8]

Sociologist Eugen Schonfeld disagreed. While admitting that the future of small-town Jewry appeared bleak, he strongly urged the American Jewish community not to write it off. The problems of small-town Jews, he argued, were not unique. Rather, they foreshadowed the difficulties of the rest of American Jewry. "Intermarriage, loss of identity, and declining populations," he noted in 1974, were "hardly problems exclusive with small-town Jews. If solutions can be found for the latter, they may be equally useful for American Jewry in general. Small towns thus not only presage what is happening to Jewish life, but they can also serve as a proving ground in developing solutions. They serve an indispensable function that may insure the continued existence of the Jewish people." Although Jewish organizations, particularly B'nai B'rith, evidenced some interest in and concern for small-town Jewry, little was done to alleviate its plight. Indeed, it was difficult to see what could have been done. The resources of organized Jewry were hardly sufficient to reshape the social and economic influences influencing the Jews of the small towns, even if they had been willing to serve as a laboratory for experiments in Jewish continuity.[9]

The number of Jewish farmers also precipitously declined. This mirrored the shrinkage of America's general farm population as agriculture became consolidated into fewer hands. Although they had never been a significant percentage of the American Jewish population, Jewish farmers had been important to the rural economies of New York and New Jersey. The "borscht belt"—the Jewish resort industry in Sullivan County, New York—began prior to World War I when Jewish farmers began taking in boarders in order to supplement their meager income. A Jewish farmer by the name of Max Yasgur modified this practice a half century later by renting out his farm to promoters of a musical festival. In August 1969 they held the Woodstock music festival in tiny Bethel.

The major centers of Jewish farming after World War II were in southern New Jersey near Woodbine and Vineland and in central New Jersey around Lakewood and Toms River. Jewish farming in New Jersey dates from the 1880s and 1890s, when several farm communities were established in southern New Jersey. These settlements stemmed from the same desire to normalize the Jewish social and economic condition that motivated the European founders of Zionism. Idealistic Jewish immigrants and Jewish philanthropists believed Jews should live off the land rather than remain in the slums and work in the sweatshops of New York and Philadelphia. It was preferable, they asserted, for Jews to be "sowers of oats than sewers of coats." Jewish philanthropists wished to wean eastern European Jewish immigrants away from what was perceived as an excessive involvement in commerce and a disdain for manual labor. As did the early Zionists, they wished to demonstrate that Jews could be productive farmers and craftsmen, not "parasitical" merchants and Shylocks. "Adam was placed in the garden of Eden not to trade or peddle therein," said Rabbi Bernard L. Levinthal of Philadelphia, a proponent of the back-to-the-land movement, "but to till it and to keep it, and the greatest of lawgivers, kings, and prophets in Israel came not from merchants, but from the rural population of the farmers."[10]

For a variety of reasons, southern New Jersey became the center of Jewish farming. The price of land there was cheap. The region was close to the markets and Jewish cultural centers of New York and Philadelphia and yet far enough away from these cities so that the inhabitants of the farm communities would not be continually tempted by urban life. Southern New Jersey was also near enough to be visited by Jewish philanthropists of Philadelphia and New York and by potential settlers.

Lacking capital and without experience in agriculture, New Jersey's Jewish farmers gravitated toward poultry farming, which was labor-intensive and did not require much land. One could make a living without large expenditures of money for land and machinery, and one could do it on a part-time basis. The fact that many of the poultry wholesalers in New York, Philadelphia, and other eastern cities were Jews was important, since it lubricated the process of marketing the eggs and chickens. Probably 75 percent of New Jersey's Jewish farmers were poultry farmers, a highly commercialized version of farming.

By World War II, Vineland was known as the "Egg Basket of the East" and Jewish farmers dominated the raising of the state's eggs and chickens. Through the application of the latest developments in farm technology, they transformed poultry farming into a scientific, mass-production business. Perhaps the greatest problem of New Jersey's Jewish farmers was their inability to convince their children to remain on the land. As so much in American Jewish life, Jewish farming was mostly a one-generation phenomenon. This was true of the pioneers of the 1890s as well as the farmers of the 1960s. The limited economic opportunities of agriculture combined with its low prestige could not compete with the bright lights of the city and the economic advantages of business and the professions. In addition, mechanization, higher labor costs, automation, competition from the South, and other economic changes within the poultry business made the family poultry farm somewhat anachronistic. In 1957, New Jersey's egg production was sixth among the states; by 1964 it was fourteenth. Between 1956 and 1966, 50 percent of New Jersey's Jewish farmers left agriculture.[11]

The Jewish farm population depended on immigration to counteract this continuous hemorrhaging. With the aid of loans from the Jewish Agricultural Society, a hundred German Jewish refugee families settled in Vineland in the 1930s and became poultry farmers, even though they had been professionals and businessmen in Europe. After the war, a thousand Polish Jewish refugees were relocated to central and southern New Jersey, where many became poultry farmers. In 1951, they founded the Jewish Poultry Farmers' Association. They also revived Jewish culture in Vineland. The local radio station broadcast Yiddish programs, Yiddish concerts and plays were performed, several new synagogues were built, and a Jewish day school opened in 1953.[12]

Not all American Jews found rural and small-town life unattractive. There was a small migration of Jews to rural America during the 1960s and 1970s. Influenced by the counterculture's distaste for the materialistic rat race of urban-industrial America, these refugees from the cities hoped to create a "Rocky Mountain chai" life-style that would be both radical and Jewish. In Vermont, Colorado, and other states, they founded communities combining organic cooking and Jewish rituals and established synagogues with names such as Beth Evergreen and Beth Vail. Few Jews, however, were sufficiently motivated to make such a sharp break with mainstream America, and even some of the Jewish communities in Colorado were within easy commuting distance of Denver.[13]

Many Jews who left the small towns of the South and Middle West migrated to the sunbelt cities of the West and South. The sunbelt cities also attracted Jews from New York, Chicago, and other large centers of Jewish population. In the late 1940s, over two-thirds of America's Jews, who then numbered between four and five million, lived in New England and the mid-Atlantic states. By 1990, barely half of America's six million Jews lived in the Northeast. By 1990, more Jews lived in San Francisco than in Baltimore, more in Phoenix than Pittsburgh, and there were as many in San

Diego as Detroit. Washington, D.C., was a special case. The postwar expansion of the federal government resulted in an increase in metropolitan Washington's Jewish population from less than twenty thousand in 1945 to one hundred sixty-five thousand four decades later.[14]

The fastest-growing Jewish communities after the war were in San Diego, Phoenix, Miami, Los Angeles, and other sunbelt cities. The dates when Jewish federations (communitywide organizations that oversee Jewish communal groups and conduct fund-raising drives) were established indicate the flow of Jewish population westward and southward—Sacramento (1948), Stockton, California (1948), Orlando (1949), St. Petersburg (1950), Sarasota (1959), Clearwater, Florida (1963), Orange County, California (1964), Mobile (1966), North Broward, Florida (1967), and Palm Springs, California (1971). A federation was even established in 1973 in Las Vegas, the most problematical of all American cities in which to raise money. It was also the city that, probably more than any other, needed the personal and family counseling offered by Jewish social welfare institutions.[15]

No state attracted more Jewish migrants than California. Jews had first settled in California during the 1840s as a result of the gold rush. Many of San Francisco's first families were Jews; the Sutro, Strauss, and Haas families were important in the cultural and economic life of the city. As a result, anti-Semitism was never the problem in San Francisco that it was in Los Angeles, where Jews were excluded from the country clubs and other watering holes of the city's financial and social elite.

The massive growth in California's Jewish population occurred after 1945, when tens of thousands of Jews from the East migrated westward. Some settled in the San Francisco–Oakland–San Jose region. Here, in Silicon Valley (and later in suburban Boston), Jews became part of what political scientist Daniel J. Elazar called the "metropolitan-technological frontier." The greatest number of California-bound Jews, however, ended up in the booming southern part of the state. In 1948, Los Angeles had 4.5 percent of America's Jews. Thirty years later it contained 7.9 percent. Next to New York City, Los Angeles was home to more Israelis than any other American city.[16]

By the 1980s, approximately three quarters of a million Jews lived in California. This was more Jews than in any country except for the Soviet Union, Israel, and the rest of the United States. With its increased population, California assumed a greater importance on the American Jewish scene. The Reform movement, for example, adopted its third major declaration of principles in the state. The first was in 1885 in Pittsburgh, the second was in 1937 in Columbus, Ohio, and the third was in San Francisco in 1976. There could have been no more ironic setting for the Reform movement to stress its "devotion to our particular people" and its responsibility "in building the State of Israel, assuring its security, and defining its Jewish character." The most prestigious of all San Francisco Reform congregations, which dated back to the nineteenth century, closed during the summer months, its devotion to the religious needs of its members being a ten-month affair. San Francisco Jewry had also been a bulwark of anti-Zionist sentiment prior to the establishment of the state of Israel in 1948.

Many Jews had migrated to California precisely because the hold of Jewish identity on them was attenuated. The percentage of Jews in Los Angeles who contributed to the annual federation fund-raising campaign there was low compared to other Jewish communities, while San Francisco had been laggard in establishing Jewish communal institutions. Elazar argued that the amorphousness of Jewish life mirrored the underlying California ethos. The state's extreme individualism ran directly counter to the Jewish sense of ethnic and religious community. One of the most prominent and successful efforts to overcome the anomie of California Jewry was carried out by Rabbi Harold Schulweis of Encino, a Los Angeles suburb. Schulweis transformed his synagogue into several *havurot* (fellowships) in order, he said, "to decentralize the synagogue and deprofessionalize Jewish living so that the individual Jew is brought back into a circle of shared experience."[17]

The influx into southern California shifted the center of California's Jewish life from San Francisco to its southern rival. Los Angeles now contained more Jews than all of Latin America and more than any city in the world other than New York. By the 1970s, all three of the major American rabbinical seminaries—Hebrew Union College (Reform), the Jewish Theological Seminary (Conservative), and Yeshiva University (Orthodox)—had established branches in Los Angeles. The branch of the Jewish Theological Seminary was not merely an institution for the training of rabbis but a "University of Judaism," boldly modeled after the Hebrew University in Jerusalem. It was perched on Mulholland Drive, atop the hills separating Los Angeles from the San Fernando Valley to the north. It did not look east toward New York. The largest Orthodox synagogue west of the Mississippi was in Beverly Hills not far from Rodeo Drive, and one of the most successful of all American Jewish charitable institutions was the

Simon Wiesenthal Center of Los Angeles. Los Angeles also contained many kosher restaurants, including one specializing in vegetarian dishes owned by the mother of the Hollywood director Steven Spielberg.

By the 1980s, more than eight hundred thousand Jews lived in the South, over half along the eighty miles of Florida coast stretching from Miami to Palm Beach. Totaling over half a million Jews by the 1980s, Florida's Jewish population was greater than that of any other state except New York and California and, on a percentage basis, ranked just behind New York and New Jersey.

The center of Florida Jewry was in the Miami–Fort Lauderdale area. Here lived 40 percent of southern Jews, more Jews than in any other American metropolis except New York and Los Angeles. The Miami–Fort Lauderdale Jewish population had been less than fifty thousand in 1948. Most of Miami's newcomers originated in the North and Midwest. A few thousand Jews from Cuba also arrived in southern Florida after the 1959 revolution. During the 1970s and 1980s, the congressman from the North Miami Beach–Hollywood region was Jewish, and one of Florida's United States senators at this time was a Jew from the Miami area. Miami Beach even boasted a two-hundred-sixty-pound Jewish police chief from the Bronx with the unlikely name of Rocky Pomerance, who was probably the only police chief in the world with a daughter in the rabbinate. His situation was no stranger, however, than that of Charleston, South Carolina's, first black police chief: Reuben Morris Greenberg. Greenberg was also a member of the board of trustees of Congregation Emanu El, a Conservative congregation in Charleston, and the cochairman of its adult education committee. Greenberg's paternal grandfather was a Jew; his other three grandparents were blacks.[18]

Jews were not loath to advertise their presence in Florida's "Garden of Yidn." One Jew involved in the hotel industry took umbrage at the suggestion that the massive influx of Jews into Miami Beach in the winter should be broadened to include other groups. "I'm sick of hearing that," he remarked. "We made Miami Beach a corned-beef and dill-pickle stand and that's the way it's going to be!" An airline even provided blintzes, cheesecake, and celery tonic on its flights between New York and Miami. One entrepreneur contemplated going much further in proclaiming the Jewish conquest of Miami Beach. He planned to name his restaurant "Kleine Momser," which means *little bastard* in Yiddish. Only the protests of an angry rabbi dissuaded him.[19]

In truth, Miami Beach Jewry was not southern but an outpost of northern Jewry. The Jewish shopping district in North Miami Beach resembled similar districts in Brooklyn, Queens, and Skokie, Illinois. Southern Florida's Jews had less sense of being southern than did Jews in the South's small towns. Rabid segregationists correctly perceived that Jews living in the urban areas of the South were less attuned to regional racial mores than Jews in the small towns. During the civil rights protests of the 1950s, synagogues in Miami, Atlanta, and other large cities were defaced and even bombed. For the segregationist, the urban southern Jew symbolized the hostile outside and urban forces bent on overturning southern racial patterns. The small-town Jew, in contrast, was viewed as a loyal child of the Confederacy, a Jewish southerner rather than a southern Jew.

Just as American Jews were confronted with the question of whether they were American Jews or Jewish Americans, so southern Jews (except for those living in southern Florida and northern Virginia) were confronted with the question of whether they were southern Jews or Jewish southerners. This matter of identity was complicated by the fact that the experiences of the southerner and the Jew were, in certain respects, similar. Both groups realized they once were viewed with some disdain by the rest of society. From the perspective of the Christian and the northerner, the Jew and the southerner were both part of exotic and even outlandish cultures. Anti-Semitism had its counterpart in the northern image of the South as a land of hookworm, ranting fundamentalist preachers, sheet-wearing bigots, and ignorant sharecroppers. Jews and southerners alike had strong memories of tragedy and defeat. Jews had their Holocaust, and southerners had their Civil War.

Both groups strongly felt the pull of place. The Jewish place was several thousand miles away in the Middle East, while the southern sense of place was hallowed by memories of the Confederacy. If Jews instinctively became excited when news flashes on the Middle East were broadcast over the radio, so southerners, as William Faulkner noted, instinctively knew what it was like on that hot day in July 1863 when Pickett made his doomed charge toward northern lines at Gettysburg. Eli Evans wrote,

> I am not certain what it means to be both a Jew and a Southerner, to have inherited the Jewish longing for a homeland while being raised with the southerner's sense of home. The conflict is deep in me—the Jew's involvement in history, his deep roots in the drama of man's struggle to understand deity and creation. But I respond to the Southerner's

commitment to place, his loyalty to the land, to his own tortured history, to the strange bond beyond color that Southern blacks and whites discover when they come to know one another.[20]

In contrast to other parts of the South, the Jewish presence in the Miami area was ubiquitous. In Miami, Jewish programs were aired on local radio and television stations, Jews supported several weekly newspapers, and shops catering to Jews were located throughout the area, particularly in Miami Beach and North Miami Beach. One of the world's most elegant kosher restaurants (specializing in Chinese cooking) was located in the Eden Roc Hotel on Miami Beach's gold coast. In years when the Miami Dolphins played at home during the eight-day Jewish festival of Hanukkah, Lubavitch Hasidim lit a menorah at the game. Thus seventy thousand cheering fans in the football-crazy South, the vast majority of whom were not Jews, vicariously participated in a rite marking a Jewish victory over Hellenism and paganism. The Lubavitchers also placed menorahs on the median strip of one of the state's major north-south highways, on Collins Avenue in Miami Beach, and on Hallendale Beach Boulevard, a major east-west thoroughfare on the border between Dade and Broward counties. All of these were main thoroughfares for visitors seeking to partake of the fleshpots of southern Florida.[21]

The Jews of Miami Beach were sui generis, not only in relation to American Jewry but also in relation to the other Jews of southern Florida. Most of Miami Beach's year-round Jewish residents were northerners who had migrated south to spend their remaining years in the sunshine. The average age of Miami Beach's residents, over half of whom were Jews, was sixty-eight, the highest of any American city. Carl Fisher, who founded Miami Beach in the 1920s, had not intended for it to become a geriatric shtetl. "Fisher wasn't anti-Jewish," a business associate recalled. "He was anti-kike. Some of his best friends were Jews." Except for wealthy Jews such as John D. Hertz, head of the Yellow Cab company, and Albert D. Lasker, president of the Lord and Thomas advertising agency, Fisher hoped to exclude Jews from his sunshine paradise. Since Miami Beach was to be a city without cemeteries, the Jewish dead were not welcome either. This did not create a major problem for elderly Jews since most had arranged for their interment in Jewish cemeteries in the North, and Jewish funeral parlors in southern Florida took care of all the transportation details.[22]

One other aspect of the demography of Miami Beach Jewry was noteworthy. In certain neighborhoods in heavily Jewish southern Miami Beach there were no Jewish children. And in some of the senior citizen communities in Dade and Broward counties the visiting of young children for more than a few hours was discouraged. For perhaps the first time in history, a community of Jews eschewed the responsibilities of being parents and grandparents for the delights of playing canasta and pinochle, listening to the latest news analyses, and involvement in the various committees of the condominium association. *Life Is with People* was the title of a popular anthropological study of eastern European Jewish culture. In the southern Florida leisure world definition of *people,* status was reserved for those with varicose veins and Medicare cards.

For community activists in southern Florida, the condition of Jews in Miami Beach, especially the thirty-five thousand living in the efficiency and one-bedroom apartments in the thirty square blocks of South Beach, was a scandal. They first became concerned with the poor of South Beach during the 1960s as a result of President Lyndon B. Johnson's War on Poverty. The city officials, hotel owners, and real estate promoters of Miami Beach, in contrast, would have preferred that the poor of South Beach remain invisible. For them, anything that marred the image of their tropical fairyland was sacrilegious. In fact, many of South Beach's residents barely scraped by on inadequate pensions, Social Security, and food stamps, and they worried about the inflation that was constantly undermining their skimpy standard of living. Their poverty was particularly galling, because it existed only a couple of miles from the gold coast of northern Miami Beach and Bal Harbour, where conspicuous consumption had been developed into an art form. It was one thing to be poor in New York or Chicago, but quite another to be poor in a city catering to the fantasies of the affluent.[23]

The postwar growth of Jewish tourism to southern Florida was one of the causes of the decline of that other great Jewish watering hole, the borscht belt of Sullivan and Ulster counties in upstate New York. With the coming of jet commercial transportation in the late 1950s, flight time from the New York airports to southern Florida, Disney World, the islands of the Caribbean, and Bermuda had been shortened to approximately the same as the driving time from Brooklyn and Long Island on Route 17, "the derma road," to Grossinger's, the Concord, and the other Jewish resort hotels in the Catskills. Travel to Europe and Israel had also become less onerous. The hotels of the Catskills now found themselves competing with Club Med, Miami Beach, Paris, and Jerusalem, a competition they could not win.

Beginning in the late 1970s, the Catskills faced yet another rival in the gambling casinos of Atlantic City.[24]

Jet transportation was not the only problem facing the Catskills resorts. They had originally been established to provide relief from the sweltering heat of New York's streets. The air conditioning that now made New York livable during the summer also eliminated some of the appeal of the Catskills. The most famous aspect of the Catskills hotels was the entertainment they provided for their guests. The borscht belt was a training ground for some of America's greatest singers and comedians. Red Buttons, Danny Kaye, Jerry Lewis, Milton Berle, Henny Youngman, and many other comics had begun their trek from "gags to riches" in the mountains in the 1930s and 1940s. By the 1980s, however, television and video cassette machines were providing even better entertainment, including sporting events, without the viewer having to leave the living room.

The Catskills resorts were victims of changing life-styles as well as of modern technology. Many Jews were able, because of the postwar economic boom, to purchase second homes in Florida, in the mountains in New York and Pennsylvania, or on the New York and New Jersey shore. Different employment patterns also hurt the hotels and bungalow colonies. It had been common for mothers and children to spend one or two of the summer months in the mountains, with husbands joining them on the weekends. This became impossible when the wives joined the work force.

A more diet-conscious population made the traditional heavy Jewish cuisine of the Catskills less appealing. With thin being in, the resorts provided a more varied menu, including macrobiotic cooking. Milton Kutsher of Kutsher's Country Club called borscht "a relic of the antediluvian age." One of his guests agreed. "Borscht went out about twenty-five years ago. We're into vichyssoise and pasta primavera." Grossinger's, where plentiful, delicious, and kosher food was the major attraction, had to modify its fare to accommodate a more sophisticated and less ethnic palate. Elaine Etess, the daughter of the fabled Jennie Grossinger, noted that "our cuisine is not just Jewish. We have the most incredible Chinese food." Other hotels also modified their offerings. "We don't even use the word 'borscht' on our menu," the owner of the Pines Hotel said. "We just call it beet soup, because otherwise people wouldn't know what it was."

For younger and unattached Jews of the sixties and seventies, the meat-market atmosphere of the singles' weekends in the Catskills had little appeal. The mass matchmaking practices of the hotels were too crude and

From *Miss America, 1945: Bess Meyerson's Own Story* by Susan Dworkin (New York: Newmarket Press, 1987). Used by permission of Bess Meyerson and Newmarket Press, 18 East 48 Street, New York, NY 10017

Bess Myerson comforting two wounded soldiers.

Courtesy of the American Jewish Historical Society

Refugees arriving in Boston shortly after World War II.

The Wall of the Martyred Millions in Temple
Beth Am, Los Angeles.

Protest by Philadelphia Jews in 1946 against British Palestine policy.

Paying homage
at Auschwitz to
victims of the
Holocaust.

The formal opening of the new building of the American Jewish Historical Society
on the campus of Brandeis University.

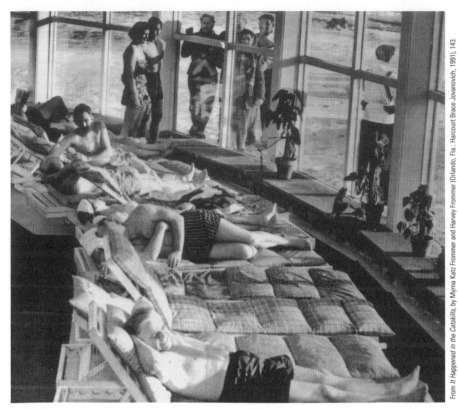

From *It Happened in the Catskills*, by Myrna Katz Frommer and Harvey Frommer (Orlando, Fla.: Harcourt Brace Jovanovich, 1991), 143.

Enjoying the winter sun at a Catskill resort.

Courtesy of the American Jewish Historical Society

Supporters of anti-Semitic Fr. Leonard Feeney protest the presence of a Catholic chapel at Brandeis University.

The New York Times

Hank Greenberg hits a home run to win the 1945 pennant for the Detroit Tigers.

The Museum of Modern Art Film Stills Archive

Dave Goldman (John Garfield) explains to Phil Green (Gregory Peck) in
Gentleman's Agreement what it means to be a Jew.

Marjorie Morningstar hovering behind Herman Wouk.

A bemused John Harvard observes the carrying of Torah scrolls across the Harvard Yard to the new Harvard Hillel Society building.

Irving Shapiro in Du Pont's boardroom.

Harold Shapiro addressing the Princeton University community.

Chief Justice Warren Burger swears in Henry Kissinger as Secretary of State, while Kissinger's mother holds the Bible and President Richard Nixon looks on.

Women accompanying men in a synagogue choir.

The Frank Lloyd Wright-designed Beth Shalom Congregation in Elkins Park, Pa.

Marjorie Morningstar (Natalie Wood) brings Noel Airman (Gene Kelly) home to a seder.

The Jewish Community Center of Trenton, New Jersey, located in suburban Ewing Township.

Students at a Jewish day school watching the lighting of the Hanukkah menorah.

American Jewish organizations strongly protested the television show *Bridget Loves Bernie*.

Photofest

The failure of
Jewish organiza-
tions to object to
thirtysomething
reflected a more
permissive attitude
toward exogamy.

Courtesy of Brandeis University

The three chapels at Brandeis University. The chapels are placed so that none can
ever cast a shadow on another.

Rabbi Sally J. Priesand,
the first woman
ordained by Hebrew
Union College.

Governor Nelson Rockefeller and other dignitaries pay tribute to Golda
Meir and Israel.

American Jews protesting the treatment of Soviet Jewry.

Rabbi Alexander Schindler, president of the Union of American Hebrew Congregations, carrying a Torah during the dedication of Kibbutz Yahel.

Michael Lerner, editor of *Tikkun*.

Norman Podhoretz,
editor of *Commentary*
and a leading
neoconservative
intellectual.

Elie Wiesel receives the Medal of Freedom from President Reagan.

blatant for a college-educated generation. Besides, the opening of dozens of singles' places in New York City also meant that one no longer had to travel ninety miles for romance, sex, and potential spouses.

The most important problem facing such resorts was that the number of Jews who wanted to vacation within a totally Jewish ambience was constantly decreasing and the hotels were unable to develop a new clientele. The children and grandchildren of the hotels' original clientele were "less Jewish" and did not respond to Jewish entertainers and Jewish food with the same enthusiasm. For them, a weekend in the Hamptons was more chic than one in the mountains. The hotels had to think up new devices to keep the rooms full. In the 1960s, for example, the Monticello Raceway (which was owned by a Jewish hotelman) staged the Elephantonian, a race between elephants, and the Mammaltonian, a race between an elephant and a camel.

As the clientele of the hotels changed, religious Jews found their religious atmosphere less uplifting. "How can you expect to have a solemn religious service in a converted nightclub," one rabbi complained, "where the whole congregation was dancing the Watusi just the night before?" The New York Board of Rabbis strongly urged Jews to stay at home instead of celebrating the Jewish holidays in such pagan surroundings.

With increasing land values and fewer guests, it made more economic sense for the hotel owners to sell out to developers or, as in the case of Brown's Resort Hotel, to build condominiums themselves. Hundreds of hotels, motels, and bungalow colonies in the Catskills went out of business in the 1970s and 1980s. Some became Buddhist retreats or drug rehabilitation centers, while others were converted into Jewish schools and Hasidic summer communities. Two developers transformed the Evans Hotel in Loch Sheldrake into Vacation Village, a modern Orthodox community with over two hundred families and a kosher Chinese restaurant.

The public became fully aware only in 1985 that a chapter in American Jewish history was ending. In that year developers purchased Grossinger's, the crown jewel of the Jewish Catskills, and announced plans to refurbish the faded hotel and to build condominiums nearby. It was soon revealed that the hotel's occupancy rate had fallen below 50 percent and that it had been running a deficit for years. The hotel's debts were in seven figures. It was a sad day for the hotel's employees and other onlookers when the wreckers came in the spring of 1986 to level some of its buildings. The Grossinger family, for its part, was nowhere to be found, having taken the money and run—seemingly without regret. Four years later the new Grossinger's declared bankruptcy, and one of the greatest of all Jewish pleasure palaces was now officially dead. "All day people stop by to see the place," a security guard at Grossinger's said. "Their grandparents vacationed here. Their parents were married here. They want to pay tribute."

In order to survive, the remaining hotels prayed for the legalization of gambling and worked to broaden their customer base. "My parents came for cards, shows and eating," one of the owners of Brown's explained. "But I'm trying to give the Catskills a different face, to broaden the cultural base and make it more modern." The remaining hotels survived only because of conventions. Encouraged by the hotels, others—blacks, Poles, Irish, and Italians—discovered the glories of the Jewish Alps. Brown's, Jerry Lewis's favorite hotel, organized Irish and Greek heritage weekends. The Women's Christian Temperance Union held conventions in the Catskills. The Nevele Hotel discarded its kosher menu and served bacon and shrimp cocktails, while the Concord, although still kosher, provided its guests with a Japanese translation of its menu.

In 1989, after a Korean-American real estate entrepreneur named Michael Chung purchased the Imperial Hotel, Asian Americans had their own Catskills resort. The kitchen remained kosher since the hotel still had Jewish guests, but now the menu included *kim-chee* and Korean rice. Chopsticks were available at every meal. The Imperial also offered a summer camp for Asian American teenagers that included SAT preparation and a punk music night.

While the Catskills hotels became less Jewish, an increasing percentage of the Jews who lived during the summer in the mountain bungalow colonies were ultra-Orthodox Jews from Brooklyn. With their earlocks and black coats, they presented a strange sight to the area's year-round residents. The major gathering place for the mountains' Orthodox population was the one-block hamlet of Woodbourne. Here on Saturday nights could be found a cross section of American Orthodoxy, ranging from the modern Orthodox with their knitted skullcaps to the more traditional with their white stockings and black hats. It was an ethnographers' paradise.[25]

In its decline, the Jewish Catskills culture was a microcosm of metropolitan Jewry. Both experienced a fading of ethnicity, a tendency to define Jewishness in religious terms, the impact of acculturation on Jewish values and the family, and the movement of other ethnic groups into Jewish areas as Jews moved up the social and economic ladder. By the 1970s and 1980s, most of the leading entertainers at the remaining Catskills hotels were not even Jewish. Symptomatic of the fate of the Jewish Catskills was the fact that *Dirty Dancing,* a popular film of the 1980s that portrayed the mating habits of the guests at a Catskills hotel, was filmed at a resort in North Carolina, five hundred miles south of the borscht belt.

The most important aspect of the postwar mobility of America's Jews was their relocation to the suburbs and their movement into the middle class. While mirroring national currents, these demographic trends were more intense among Jews. Historian Arthur Hertzberg estimated that, in the two decades between 1945 and 1965, one out of every three Jews left the big cities for the suburbs, a rate higher than that of other Americans. Jews tended to cluster together in suburbia, but some brave pioneers moved into suburbs that contained few if any Jews. One of the first analyses of the impact of suburbanization on Jews was Albert I. Gordon's 1959 book *Jews in Suburbia,* which concerned Newton, Massachusetts. Gordon had a Ph.D. degree in anthropology from the University of Minnesota. More important, he was the rabbi of Temple Emanuel in Newton, an exclusive suburb of Boston, which had a large and growing Jewish population by 1959. The nickname of Newton was "the garden city." Old-timers claimed this was because of its many parks and flower beds. Others claimed it was because there was a Rosenbloom on every corner.[26]

There were many reasons for the explosive growth of suburbia after 1945. They included the increased use of automobiles, postwar prosperity, the pent-up demand for housing created by the depression and the war, the desire of veterans to resume a normal family life after the dislocations of wartime, the baby boom of the late 1940s and 1950s, government programs that encouraged the building and purchase of houses by veterans, and the postwar cult of domesticity that defined women's highest calling as mother and wife. The ability to deduct local property taxes and interest payments on mortgages from one's income in computing federal income taxes made suburban homes more affordable. The postwar housing boom was concentrated in suburbia. Pre–World War II suburbs increased in population, while new suburbs were created from scratch on tracts of land that had been woods, desert, and marsh. The great pioneer in this postwar suburban housing boom was Jewish builder William L. Levitt. By using the techniques of mass production that he had developed in constructing bases for the military during the war, Levitt built tens of thousands of affordable homes for families eager for a taste of the American dream after the deprivations of the 1930s and the war years.

By 1960, a plurality of Americans were living in suburbia and demographers were predicting that by the 1990s a majority of Americans would be suburbanites. This mass exodus to what one historian called the "crabgrass frontier" took many students of American and Jewish demography by surprise. Coming mostly from cities or small towns, demographers were unable to appreciate the appeal of the new suburban lifestyle, which combined the convenience of living close to the economic and cultural opportunities of the city with the opportunity of participating in an ersatz rural life of "country wagons," picture windows, mini-gardens in the backyard, and weekend barbecues.

Prominent demographer Sophia M. Robison illustrated the difficulty of demographers in comprehending the impact of suburbia. Her 1948 study, *The Jewish Population of Essex County,* predicted that the Jewish community of Newark, New Jersey, then numbering close to sixty thousand, would remain relatively stable. This stability, she wrote, "revealed both in the length of residence and the age distribution suggests that it may well provide an integrating and stabilizing force in the community at large." Her 1949 examination of Trenton Jewry was more perceptive. Here Robison suggested that "the decentralization of the population, an emptying out of the old Ghettos, following the trend in the general community, suggests another topic of interest not only in the provision of special Jewish services but in the integration of Jews into the general community life and activities as well."[27]

Despite Robison's forecast of stability for Newark Jewry, by the late 1960s the city's Weequahic section, the center of Newark Jewry and the neighborhood made famous by Philip Roth's novel *Portnoy's Complaint,* was virtually all black. By then the Jewish population of Newark was well under a thousand, and most of these were elderly people living in two housing projects near the airport. Roth, the laureate of Newark Jewry, had described in his novella *Goodbye, Columbus* (1959) how Newark's Jews "had struggled and prospered, and moved further west, towards the edge of Newark, then out of it, and up the slope of the Orange Mountains, until they had reached the crest and started down the other side, pouring into Gentile territory as the Scotch-Irish had poured through the Cumberland Gap."[28]

The statistics on American Jewish population published in the annual *American Jewish Year Book* reveal the extent of this migration. It estimated that as of 1948 six hundred Jews lived in Millburn and sixteen hundred in

West Orange. Ten years later, it listed the Jewish population of Millburn as two thousand and that of West Orange as seven thousand. Livingston had less than one hundred Jews in 1948. Ten years later it had over twenty-five hundred. In this same ten-year period the Jewish population of Newark declined from fifty-eight thousand to forty-one thousand.

The suburbanization of Newark Jewry began during the late 1940s, before the exacerbation of race relations and white flight. It was completed shortly after the bloody race riot of 1967 caused most of the city's remaining Jews to run for their lives. Jewish store owners remained in the city a while longer, but eventually most of them also relocated to safer and more lucrative locations in the suburbs. The history of Newark's Jews was paradigmatic. The same pattern occurred in Cleveland, Detroit, Boston, St. Louis, and other northeastern cities. The Jewish working-class neighborhoods in the West Side of Chicago, the East Bronx, and Dorchester and Roxbury in Boston became dismal and dangerous slums.

By the 1970s, the suburbanization of Newark Jewry had spread beyond Essex County. By then Morris County to the west had a large Jewish population, and Jews were pushing inexorably into Somerset County and other "Gentile territory" stretching to the Delaware River. Exurbanization had replaced suburbanization, and the D-factor—dispersion, diffusion, and decentralization—had replaced the M-factor. This diffusion decreased the proportion of the state's Jewish population that lived in or around Newark from one-third to one-fourth. In order to meet the needs of a now scattered Jewish population, the Jewish federation of Essex County (Newark) broadened its geographical scope. In the 1980s it merged with the much smaller and younger federation of Morris County. At that time it changed its name from the Jewish Federation of Metropolitan New Jersey to the Jewish Federation of Metro-West.

Located just across the Hudson River from New York City's two million Jews, New Jersey was a center of Jewish suburbanites. New Jersey's northern suburbs became a favorite refuge for New York's Jews escaping the city. In the 1970s alone, the Jewish population of New York City declined by one-third, to slightly over one million. Prior to the war, the Bronx had over half a million Jews and Brooklyn over eight hundred and fifty thousand. By 1977, there were less than one hundred and fifty thousand Jews in the Bronx and a little more than half a million in Brooklyn. The greatest concentration of Jews prior to the war had been in the Brownsville–East New York section of Brooklyn. Here, rabbis, scholars, prizefighters, future industrialists, and members of Murder Incorporated lived side by side. Pitkin Avenue, its main thoroughfare, was a major shopping area for central Brooklyn. By 1960, Jewish Brownsville had disappeared, and in its place stood one of the dreariest and most drug-infested slums in New York City.[29]

Bergen County in northern New Jersey along the Hudson River bene-fited more than any other New Jersey county from this Jewish exodus from New York City, exhibiting an extreme case of suburbanitis. Before World War II, Bergen County did not have one major city, including the county seat of Hackensack; its population lived in dozens of midsized towns and villages. The county contained few Jewish families until the completion of the George Washington Bridge in 1931 made commuting to Manhattan a viable option, but the depression and the war slowed down this Jewish exodus. By 1950, the county had only twenty thousand Jews (the Jewish Federation of Community Services of Bergen County was not established until 1953). By the 1980s, however, over one hundred thousand Jews lived in Bergen County, more than in any other county in the state. The cities of Teaneck and Englewood in Bergen County were over one-quarter Jewish. This rise in Bergen County's Jewish population led to the establishment of synagogues, Jewish day schools, and stores and restaurants in Englewood, Fair Lawn, and Teaneck that catered to Jewish religious needs and diets.

Suburbanization was important in other parts of the state, too. In Passaic County, Jews deserted Paterson and Passaic for Wayne and Fair-lawn. In Fairlawn, a suburb of Paterson, the Jewish population increased from one thousand in 1948 to four thousand in 1958. Wayne, in Passaic County, had one of the most rapid increases in Jewish population of any city. Less than twenty Jewish families lived in Wayne in 1958. Ten years later there were eight hundred and fifty families. During a school board election campaign in the mid-1960s, one of Wayne's Gentile politicians deplored the rise in the community's Jewish population, claiming that it would result in larger school budgets and higher property taxes. Further south, Trenton's Jews moved north and west to Ewing Township and other suburbs, while Cherry Hill, Haddonfield, and Haddon Township on the eastern side of the Delaware River attracted Jews from Philadelphia. The flow of Jews into New Jersey from Philadelphia and New York increased the proportion of American Jewry living in the Garden State and raised the percentage of New Jersey's residents who were Jews.[30]

The problems of postwar American Jewry were primarily the problems of suburbia. The diffusion of Jewish population into the suburbs and exurbs diluted Jewish identity. In the compacted Jewish neighborhoods of the cities, Jewish identity was absorbed through osmosis. In suburbia, it had to be nurtured. Jewish suburbanites lived in localities where, in contrast to the city, most of the people were not Jews, the local store did not sell Jewish newspapers, there were no kosher butchers, synagogues were not numerous, and corned beef sandwiches were not readily available.[31]

The Jewish identity of suburbanites was both weaker and narrower than in the cities. Here there were no bitter quarrels between the religious and the secularists, Yiddishists and Hebraists, communists and socialists, and Zionists and Bundists. Pessimists feared that suburbia would be a graveyard for Jewishness. In his religious apologia *This Is My God* (1959), Herman Wouk painted the prospect of Jewish oblivion in American suburbia. It was "the threat of pleasantly vanishing down a broad highway at the wheel of a high-powered station wagon, with the golf clubs piled in the back." Mr. Abramson, our golfer, had not disappeared. "When his amnesia clears, he will be Mr. Adamson, and his wife and children will join him, and all will be well. But the Jewish question will be over in the United States."[32]

The situation, however, was not as bleak as Wouk imagined. The most important and surprising fact about suburban Jews was how many wished to continue identifying as Jews. This was demonstrated by the fact that the first generation of suburban Jews tended to congregate together. Some suburbs such as Silver Spring outside of Washington and Great Neck and Scarsdale outside of New York City had large Jewish communities, while neighboring suburbs had relatively few Jews. Suburban social life was divided along religious lines. While anti-Semitism was generally not a problem in suburbia, Jews and Gentiles socialized within their own group. Sociologists referred to the "five o'clock shadow" to mark the separation of Jews and Gentiles in their own social worlds once the workday had ended. Suburban Jews, despite their cultural assimilation, felt more comfortable among fellow Jews.

By far the most common expression of Jewishness in suburbia was membership in a synagogue. Suburban Jews might not believe in God, as Albert I. Gordon noted, but they believed in God's people and wanted to be part of it. The easiest and most popular way of doing this was by joining a synagogue. One survey of a suburban Los Angeles congregation revealed that less than 2 percent of the respondents said they had joined because they were religious. Synagogues benefited almost by default from the lack of rival forms of Jewish identity in suburbia.[33]

Jewish suburbanites had fled from neighborhoods that were strongly Jewish in an ethnic sense, and where synagogue membership was often the exception and not the rule. As second- and third-generation Americans, they did not feel the pull of Jewish ethnicity as strongly as their parents and grandparents. To be Jewish in suburbia largely meant affiliating with Judaism, whatever the nature of that affiliation might be. "The securely American status of the third generation and its increasing mobility have released it from old ties and community sentiments," the sociologists Judith R. Kramer and Seymour Leventman wrote in 1961. "Searching for new social anchorage, young Jews frequently turn to religion as the source of their identity. Although their 'non-Jewish' social behavior belies their religious intent, they choose to be Jews. As other ethnic factors fail to provide satisfactory grounds for social identity, religion increases in significance—and utility." A religious definition of Jewishness was also more compatible with American values. In a nation of over three hundred different religious groups, Americans viewed religious pluralism as natural and desirable. They expected the children of immigrants, however, to be free of ethnic impurities and to be fully Americanized. Suburbanization was largely responsible for the increase in synagogue affiliation from 20 percent of American Jewish families in 1930 to nearly 60 percent in 1960.[34]

The suburbanites were not attracted to Orthodox synagogues, which they identified with the lower-class, immigrant ghettos from which they had escaped. Rather, they wanted to affiliate with synagogues that would be compatible with their new social and economic status. Suburban Jews joined or created non-Orthodox synagogues and encouraged erstwhile Orthodox synagogues to drop their Orthodox affiliation when they relocated to the suburbs. The history of Newark's synagogues illustrates the social dynamics. There were forty-eight congregations in the Newark area in 1945. Of the thirty-four congregations in the city itself, thirty-one were Orthodox. The fourteen congregations in the suburbs were either Conservative or "modern" Orthodox. By 1976, there were forty-six congregations in the Newark area. Eighteen were Orthodox, twenty were Conservative, and eight were Reform. Eleven of the Orthodox congregations were in Newark and the inner suburbs of Hillside and Irvington. Of the seven Orthodox suburban congregations, only the one in West Orange had a sizable membership. The other Orthodox congregations were small and served mainly as places of worship. The Conservative and Reform congregations, in contrast, were large and dynamic. Several had memberships that were equal to the membership of all of Newark's Orthodox congregations combined.

The weakening of Jewish ethnicity accounted for one of the most puzzling phenomena in the history of postwar American Jewry—a largely secular population exhibiting a respect for religion. "God and faith are not part" of the vocabulary of the suburban Jew, Judd L. Teller wrote in 1968. "He gives them fleeting thought at best and may even be said to be unaligned in the eternal debate between believers and agnostics." And yet suburban Jewry experienced a synagogue "edifice complex" during the 1950s, 1960s, and 1970s. Hundreds of millions of dollars were raised to build elaborate synagogues equipped with catering halls, classrooms, game rooms, and even miniature gymnasiums. In the New York area, these multipurpose synagogues were often named "centers." Rabbi Morris Werb of the Conservative synagogue of Caldwell, New Jersey, noted that the synagogue-center had become "a focal point of group interest . . . and for the inculcation of Jewish values for the children." Arthur Hertzberg, who had been a rabbi of a congregation in Englewood, New Jersey, and knew the suburban ethos well, called these synagogues temples of Jewish togetherness.[35]

These "shuls with pools and schools" were generally located on heavily traveled streets. It was as if suburban Jews were using these structures to advertise their newfound pride in being Jewish and their new economic and social status. "We need a synagogue so they'll have more respect for us, to show that we have arrived, that we're not merely a bunch of individuals," one suburbanite told sociologist Herbert Gans. Rabbis and sociologists, however, were unable to detect any increase in Jewish knowledge or ritual observance among the members of these congregations. On the contrary, the number of Jews who kept kosher, observed the Sabbath, and had a serious interest in Jewish ideas and books declined during the building boom. Suburban Jews were eclectic in their Jewish practices.[36]

For most suburban Jews, the major role of Judaism was now the celebration of life-cycle events. Births, confirmations, Bar Mitzvahs, weddings, and deaths required the presence of rabbis and a modicum of Jewish ritual. Prayer, as one rabbi ruefully noted, "is fast becoming a lost art." The sanctuaries of the synagogues were full for the High Holy Days—the Jewish New Year and the Day of Atonement. They were vacant on the remaining days of the year except for a smattering of the faithful who attended Sabbath services and the other holidays. This was the case even though, according to Jewish law, the Sabbath was far more important than the New

Year. In many suburban synagogues, the raison d'être of Sabbath morning services was providing a suitable religious setting so that families could celebrate the Bar Mitzvahs of their thirteen-year-old sons. Bar Mitzvah means "son of the commandment" and signifies the age when a young man becomes an adult according to Jewish law. At this time he is obligated to observe all Jewish rituals. (During the 1970s, Bat Mitzvah celebrations for girls became popular among the non-Orthodox.) In fact, few suburban families wanted their children to assume these responsibilities. The rabbis of these Bar Mitzvah factories might have felt that they were participating in a farce, but there was little they could do.[37]

The families, for their part, got what they wished. They had passed on to their children their own already attenuated sense of Jewish identity, and they had ensured that their children's peers would be Jews. They had not, however, made them *too* religious, which they associated with the lower-class Orthodoxy of the inner-city neighborhoods they had deserted. Jewish observance, the parents realized, was designed to segregate Jews from the rest of society. This was the last thing Jewish suburbanites wanted for their children, now that they had elevated themselves economically and socially. Being a member of a synagogue was acceptable, since religion was a fundamental aspect of the suburban life-style. Taking seriously what the synagogue preached was something else. Suburban rabbis, Gordon reported, were troubled because their congregants desired "an easy, relaxed kind of country club atmosphere, rather than a house of worship with a positive philosophy for Jewish life, with a strong belief in God and His purposiveness at its very center."[38]

Suburban Judaism largely involved rituals oriented toward children and the home, such as lighting Hanukkah candles and participating in a Passover seder. Hanukkah assumed greater importance on the Jewish calendar. Coming in December, it enabled parents to assuage the regrets of their children for not being able to celebrate Christmas. Purim also became more important since it came at approximately the time of Easter, the other great Christian holiday.

The synagogue itself was valued because of the educational, social, recreational, and religious activities provided for the family, particularly for the children. The synagogue was suburban Jewry's main instrument for the transmission of Jewish identity to the young, and Hebrew school was its most important activity. Suburban Jewish families often joined synagogues when it was time for their children to begin Hebrew school and then quit after the children stopped going to classes. The parents wanted to instill in the children a sense of Jewish history and peoplehood and enough Hebrew so that they would not embarrass themselves during the Bar Mitzvah celebration. Knowing their clientele, congregational schools put minimal demands on their students. An intensive curriculum would have alienated the parents, who did not want the schools to isolate their children from the rest of society or to put obstacles in the way of their social and economic ascent.

Jewish life in suburbia was a favorite target of Jewish intellectuals and sociologists. They described Jewish suburbia as bland, conformist, and materialistic and suburban Judaism as gaudy and anti-intellectual. They contrasted the Jewishness of Shaker Heights and Scarsdale with that of eastern Europe prior to the Holocaust or of the areas of first settlement in America. In their popular 1952 book *Life Is with People,* Mark Zborowski and Elizabeth Herzog praised the piety, simple dignity, and sense of community of Jews living in the small towns of eastern Europe. A decade later the same image was presented to a wider audience in the enormously successful Broadway musical (and later popular movie) *Fiddler on the Roof.* Those who had actually lived in these shtetls were not so nostalgic, remembering them as backward, poor, and dominated by the well-to-do and the rabbis. In fact, *Fiddler on the Roof* was based on short stories of the Yiddish writer Sholom Aleichem, who was severely critical of the ignorance and superstition of small-town eastern European Jewish life.[39]

The shtetl's appeal derived from the fact that Zborowski and Herzog pictured it as an antisuburb. Immigrant neighborhoods, especially the Lower East Side, were also romanticized and for the same reason. In movies such as *Lies My Father Told Me, Crossing Delancey,* and *Hester Street,* the process of Americanization is portrayed as a movement away from honesty and cultural authenticity.

Based on Abraham Cahan's 1896 novella *Yekl: A Tale of the New York Ghetto, Hester Street* emphasized the conflict between the spiritual values of Europe and the attractions of a materialistic America. The major goal of Jake, the movie's central figure, is to be accepted as a "real American fella." In spite of having lived in the United States only three years, he has been thoroughly Americanized. He has changed his name from Yekl to Jake, wears a derby, is familiar with the world of American sports, and spends his evenings at a dance hall in the company of the beautiful and Americanized Mamie. Jake's life is complicated by the arrival of his wife, Gitl, and his son, Yossele. Although he is able to change his son's name to Joseph and to cut off his earlocks, he can't convince Gitl to give up the religious customs and superstitions of Europe. Jake's embarrassment with Gitl soon turns to loathing. Jake is also contemptuous of his boarder and fellow worker Bernstein. He teases Bernstein for studying the Talmud and for being a "greenhorn." Bernstein, in turn, curses Columbus, and says that when a Jewish immigrant leaves for the United States he should cry out to God, "Goodbye, O Lord, I'm going to America." The film concludes with Jake and Gitl divorcing, Mamie and Jake going to city hall (not to a synagogue) to be married, and Gitl and Bernstein planning marriage after Gitl has fulfilled the waiting period required by Jewish law of a divorcee. They talk of opening a grocery store that she will run while he studies the Talmud. Their life will be idyllic.

Hester Street and the other films of Jewish immigrant life failed to convey any sense of the poverty and filth of these neighborhoods. As Stanley Kaufmann noted in his review of *Hester Street,* it was "phony to the eye." Viewers are left wondering why immigrant Jews worked night and day in order to move to different surroundings. Instead of presenting viewers with the real circumstances of the Lower East Side or the Montreal ghetto, they portray life in a mythic antisuburb.[40]

In *World of Our Fathers,* Irving Howe contrasted the moral and political passion of the immigrant communities with the spiritual vacuity of the suburbs. While admitting that vulgarity was not a monopoly of the suburbs, Howe surmised that "there may be some truth in the view often expressed by older Yiddishists and younger intellectuals that something about the vulgarity of the suburb was more troubling than the immigrant variety." By becoming part of the American mainstream, American Jewry had lost the most distinctive traits of the Jewish spirit—"an eager restlessness, a moral anxiety, an openness to novelty, a hunger for dialectic, a refusal of contentment, an ironic criticism of all fixed opinion." Judith R. Kramer and Seymour Leventman's 1961 volume *Children of the Gilded Ghetto* was also suffused with a nostalgia for an authentic and wholesome immigrant Jewish culture that had been overwhelmed by the sterility and materialism of suburbia. "Subject to the judgment of its heirs," they predicted, "the gilded ghetto may be tarnished by rejection."[41]

The most bitter critics of suburban Jewry were the radical Jews of the 1960s and 1970s. Many were in flight from the affluence, vulgarity, and spiritual emptiness that they had experienced in suburbia. As one Jewish coed said during the 1960s, you don't know how bad Scarsdale really is until you live there. Jewish-oriented radicals wished to rescue authentic Judaism from the decadence it had undergone in suburbia. Young Jews had been alienated from Judaism, one radical claimed, because "it has given young people no help in their search for alternatives to what has become the life-style of the Jewish suburb." The Jewish community of suburbia "has traded its soul and creativity for the power of consumption."[42]

One instrument in the greening of American Jewry was the *havurot,* the small groups that came together for worship, the study of Jewish texts, and social and political action. The radicals hoped that, in contrast to Jewish suburbia and academia, the *havurot* would satisfy their hunger for spiritual nourishment and their quest for community. This Jewish contribution to the greening of America, their members made clear, was to be an antisuburb. Instead of being impersonal, politically passive, and rational, the Judaism of the *havurot* was to be communal, socially involved, and spiritual. Few young Jews, however, were prepared to forsake the creature comforts of suburbia for the dubious benefits of the *havurot,* and only the most viable of the *havurot* survived once the excitement caused by the Vietnam War and the civil rights movement dissipated.

Not all Jews, of course, were affluent or living in suburbia. Americans had become sensitized to the problem of poverty in the 1960s and 1970s as a result of the War on Poverty. The lure of government money proved irresistible. Jewish activists emphasized that, despite the prosperity and middle-class status of most Jews and notwithstanding the claims of Pollyannas, there still existed a sizable number of poor aged Jews. The most important year in the Jewish war on poverty was 1972, when the Office of Economic Development provided the first of several grants to alleviate Jewish poverty. In that year, also, Ann G. Wolfe published her seminal essay, "The Invisible Jewish Poor," in the Spring 1972 issue of the *Journal of Jewish Communal Service.* Wolfe claimed that affluence and complacent Jewish leadership had obscured widespread Jewish poverty, which she estimated at anywhere from seven hundred thousand to eight hundred thousand, two-thirds of whom were elderly. In New York alone, she asserted, there were a quarter of a million poor. If Wolfe was correct, the rate of poverty among Jews was greater than among non-Jews. This was highly unlikely since average Jewish family income was much larger than that of Americans generally.

Jewish communal leaders greeted Wolfe's figures with skepticism. Although they realized there were Jewish poor, they believed she had greatly exaggerated their numbers, that poverty was less prevalent among Jews than among other groups, and that the Jewish federations had not ignored the Jewish poor. They noted that she had committed a crucial methodological error by not taking into account the size of families of the Jewish poor. As Saul Kaplan, the research director of the Jewish federation of Chicago pointed out, Jews were the only ethnic group in which unrelated individuals constituted a majority of the poor. Jewish leaders argued that the number of Jewish poor was less than half of Wolfe's estimate. Wolfe had considered only cash income in calculating the number of Jewish poor. When food stamps, rent supplements, public housing, Medicaid, and other income transfers were factored in, it was likely that there were less than two hundred thousand Jewish poor.[43]

For the student of American Jewish history, the most interesting question about Jewish poverty, however, was not its extent but what it meant to be poor in America in the 1960s and 1970s. At a time when Jews were the richest ethnic group in the richest country in history, it was particularly galling to be poor. The poor were aberrant and, in their own eyes, failures. The success of other Jews made their own failure that much more difficult to live with. At a time when economists talked about the affluent society, the poor could not fall back on the excuse that poverty was the normal condition. In a fluid and individualistic society such as America, success and failure were seen as the result of personal and not communal factors. Any child, Americans commonly (and mistakenly) believed, could end up as president, but that also suggested that any child could end up a failure. It was up to the individual. Even more harmful than any material deprivation experienced by the poor was the psychological damage resulting from the realization that they, and not society, were responsible for their own condition. More than anything, it was the feeling of loneliness, the belief that they had been forgotten by family and deserted by the Jewish community, that angered poor Jews.

Perhaps the most important characteristic of the Jewish poor was that they were mostly elderly. According to Wolfe and other students of the Jewish poor, two-thirds of them were aged. Many were first-generation Americans who had never overcome their cultural disabilities and who had the misfortune of becoming adults prior to World War II, when there were fewer economic opportunities for Jews. Because of the age of the Jewish poor, it was inevitable that Jewish poverty would diminish.

There was no evidence that a significant number of younger Jews, except for some of the extremely religious in Brooklyn and upstate New

York and a growing number of single-parent families, were growing up in conditions of poverty. There was nothing in American Jewish experience akin to what the sociologist Oscar Lewis called "the culture of poverty," in which destitution was perpetuated from one generation to the next. Few American Jews were part of what sociologists termed the *underclass*. Drug addiction, family breakdown, criminality, poor scholastic performance, and high unemployment were not prominent among the Jewish poor.

The Jewish migration into suburbia resulted from the massive movement of Jews into the ranks of the middle class. This phenomenon took place in Canada, England, and other Western countries besides the United States. In 1982 W. D. Rubinstein, an Australian, prophesied that the Jews could become "the first ethnic group in history without a working class of any size." By the 1950s, American Jewry already consisted of mostly small businessmen, professionals, and members of government and business bureaucracies. With the passage of time, the American Jewish profile became increasingly elitist. Going to college became virtually universal among Jewish youth, and a Jewish dropout was now defined as a person with only a bachelor's degree. The ranks of Jewish businessmen diminished and the percentage of Jewish academicians and professionals increased. (An accountant was defined as a Jewish boy who stuttered and couldn't stand the sight of blood.) In one of Lenny Bruce's most memorable skits, he admitted Jewish responsibility for the death of Jesus: "We killed him because he didn't want to become a doctor, that's why we killed him."[44]

By every possible social and economic measure—education, percentage of white-collar workers and professionals, income—Jewish mobility was the wonder of American sociology. Jews, Catholic sociologist Andrew Greeley said in 1974, were "America's most impressive success story." Black economist Thomas Sowell agreed, terming Jewish economic and social mobility "unprecedented and unparalleled." Sociologists debated the source of this success but not its existence. There was little doubt that Jews, along with Asians, had become the most middle-class of American ethnic groups. The affluence of Jews made it difficult for them to sympathize with other groups that were less successful in pulling themselves up by their own bootstraps. A minority of Jews even argued that, in light of their social and economic position, Jews should reevaluate their political ties with disadvantaged groups such as blacks and Hispanics.[45]

As a result of the metamorphosis of the Jewish economic profile, the Jewish working class in America virtually disappeared, and fewer Jews were skilled craftsmen and members of labor unions. Less than one-third of 1 percent of employed American Jews in 1970 were laborers, compared to 4 percent of white Americans. Conversely, 60 percent of employed Jews were professionals, technical managers, and administrators, compared to 26 percent of white Americans. The figures for family income revealed the same disparity. Sociologist Steven M. Cohen estimated in 1988 that income among American Jews was close to double that of Gentiles, with twice as many Jews as non-Jewish whites reporting annual household incomes of more than $50,000.[46]

Although Jews did not like to dwell on their affluence for fear of stirring up the resentment of Gentiles, they were fully aware of Jewish prosperity. Public opinion polls, however, did not indicate that most Americans begrudged their success. On the contrary, one of the reasons they admired Jews was because of their financial achievement. Pepperidge Farm Products even ran an advertisement in 1988 in *Jewish Action,* the quarterly published by the Union of Orthodox Jewish Congregations of America, stating that its products were now kosher and thus suitable for an upscale clientele. Dr. Anthony Ranalli, the company's vice president of quality assurance and technical service, explained that Pepperidge Farm had been anxious to receive kosher certification because its products "are popular with the upper mobile, 'yuppie' consumer—and many kosher consumers fill that description."

The rise of Jews out of the working class decreased the number of Jews who were members of labor unions and diminished support for unions among the Jewish rank and file. Prior to World War II, Jews were a significant segment of the labor force of the garment industry in New York, Philadelphia, Rochester, and other cities, and they had been instrumental in founding the International Ladies' Garment Workers' Union, the Amalgamated Clothing Workers of America, and the other garment industry unions. Jews remained in positions of leadership in these unions well into the 1980s, even though their membership was now largely black, Hispanic, and southern white. The head of the ILGWU in the 1980s was a Jew whose own son was a clothing manufacturer. The movie *Norma Rae* portrays this transformation of the garment unions. The labor organizer of a Carolina textile factory is a New York Jew, and the workers he tries to organize are poor southern whites and blacks. This ethnic contrast between the union leadership and the rank and file led to unsubstantiated accusations by black militants in the 1960s of racism within the garment unions. Most Jewish union members were not to be found in the garment unions but in "middle-class" unions of social workers, teachers, and government employees, and they had little in common with steel and automobile workers.

By the 1950s a fundamental change had occurred in the social and economic position of American Jews and in the image that Gentiles had of them. For centuries, the contrast between light hair and dark hair had been used by novelists to emphasize the differences between Gentiles and Jews. In Sir Walter Scott's *Ivanhoe,* for example, Rowena, the Gentile blonde, symbolized family and normality, while Rebecca, the Jewish brunette, represented mystery and sensuality. In the 1950s, however, a decade after Bess Myerson became Miss America, a brown-haired Jew became the personification of female suburban middle-class existence. Her name is Marjorie Morningstar (Morgenstern), the eponymous heroine of Herman Wouk's 1955 best-selling novel. In its cover story on Wouk, *Time* magazine, the journal of the American middle class, described his heroine as "an American Everygirl who happens to be Jewish." Singer Linda Ronstadt remembered the impact the novel had on her as a teenager growing up in Arizona, far from the fabled Catskills Mountains and New York City where Morningstar came of age. "It screwed me up about love and romance and everything," Ronstadt said, "But I loved it then, and it made me wish I was Jewish."[47]

In an age of Marlon Brando, James Dean, Elvis Presley, and the Beats, *Marjorie Morningstar* was remarkable for its conventionality. Wouk, *Time* said, was "a Sinclair Lewis in reverse." The theme of the novel is the conflict between Marjorie's two selves, the aspiring actress Marjorie Morningstar, who rejects Jewish middle-class values, and Marjorie Morgenstern, who wants to marry and have children. Her conventional self wins out. She longs for Noel Airman, a lascivious Bohemian and unsuccessful playwright, but accepts the social and moral canons of the middle class. She allows herself to be seduced by Airman, although she does not believe in premarital sex. The experience is accompanied by "shocks, ugly uncoverings, pain, incredi-ble humiliation." After it is over, Marjorie accidentally breaks a glass, a symbol of Jewish mourning. The chapter in which this occurs is titled "Another Glass Breaks."[48]

By the end of the novel, Marjorie is an aging sedate suburban matron. As Mrs. Milton Schwartz, she lives in a large house in Mamaroneck in Westchester County with her four children and successful lawyer husband. Marjorie, *Time* wrote, had "yearned for Don Juan and settled for Steady

John." She presides over a traditional Jewish home and a kosher kitchen, attends synagogue services regularly, and is active in Jewish communal life. She is contented with the way things turned out. Life with Noel Airman (i.e., air man) would have been insubstantial.

Jewish intellectuals were dismayed by Wouk's encomium to suburbia and the bourgeois life. Norman Podhoretz, for example, described *Marjorie Morningstar* as a protest against the "appetite for diverse areas of experience . . . [and the] refusal to surrender one's demands on the world without a fight." Morningstar was a middle-class heroine who had "flirted with the risk of life and given it up for submission to law." She had "seen Montmartre and settled in Mamaroneck." For Podhoretz, *Marjorie Morningstar* was a story of frustrated achievements and gloomy defeat. American Jews should lament, Podhoretz concluded, "if the Jewish personality can indeed only flourish by rooting itself in a parochial, insulated way of life, and if the suburbs of New York are to become another kind of ghetto, to protect the Jew from the assaults of Greenwich Village."49

At the same time that Americans were reading *Marjorie Morningstar,* Gerald Green's *The Last Angry Man* was also on the best-seller lists. Green's novel described the last years of a Jewish doctor living in central Brooklyn, an area that had once been a vibrant Jewish community but was now rapidly becoming a black slum. It resembled the neighborhood where Podhoretz himself had been raised. By 1956, there were few Jews left in Brownsville, East New York, and Ocean Hill to be angry. The families of Podhoretz and the other Jews from the working-class Jewish neighborhoods of Brooklyn, the Bronx, and Manhattan had worked their way up the economic ladder, migrated to better areas within the city or to the suburbs, and continued their transformation from American Jews into Jewish Americans. This process of acculturation was felt particularly in the area of religion, the aspect of Jewish identity that most clearly distinguished the Jew from other Americans.

CHAPTER SIX

JUDAISM, AMERICAN STYLE

No ASPECT of postwar American Jewish life was more paradoxical than the condition of religion itself. At least outwardly, American Judaism appeared to be flourishing. The number of congregations, their budgets, and their membership rolls peaked after 1945. In 1937, the 237 Conservative congregations in the United States had around 75,000 member families, and the 290 Reform congregations had 50,000 families on their rolls. Twenty years later, there were over 500 Conservative congregations with 200,000 member families and 520 Reform congregations with 255,000 member families. The number of Orthodox synagogues and their families also increased dramatically. More important than the new congregations and their buildings was the fact that an increasing percentage of American Jews now defined their Jewishness within a religious context. In 1930 only 20 percent of American Jewish families belonged to a synagogue. By 1960, 60 percent were affiliated with a synagogue, and the synagogue had become the most important of all American Jewish institutions. For the majority of American Jews, the most important manifestation of identity and of survivalist impulses was paying dues to a synagogue. "American Judaism," historian Naomi W. Cohen wrote, had "fused the religious and nationalist elements of the tradition under a religious rubric and Americanized format."[1]

Judaism benefited from the great respect accorded religion by the general society. Religion was particularly valued after 1945 because of America's worldwide confrontation with the Soviet Union and atheistic communism. There was no easier way for Jews to demonstrate that they were fully Americanized than to profess a faith in God, since nowhere else in the Western world was the status of religion as elevated as in America. Postwar surveys revealed that among Americans the clergy was the most respected profession, even more than medicine and the law, while religious figures such as Billy Graham, Fulton J. Sheen, and Norman Vincent Peale were consistently found on lists of the most admired Americans. The popularity of religion was due in part to the belief that it was a cure-all for what ailed America and Americans. Not only would it guarantee victory in the struggle with atheistic communism, but, as Rabbi Joshua Loth Liebman argued in his best-selling book of 1946, *Peace of Mind,* it would also bring mental health to a nation that was recovering from the impact of World War II and had to live with the threat of nuclear war.[2]

Popular culture reflected this climate of opinion. During the fifties, Mickey Spillane became a Jehovah's Witness and gangster Mickey Cohen was converted to Christianity by Billy Graham; Fulton J. Sheen was a media star; the songs "Vaya con Dios," "I Believe," and "Big Fellow in the Sky" made the charts; Norman Vincent Peale's *The Power of Positive Thinking* broke every American record for nonfiction sales; and films with religious themes were commercial successes. For those with specific problems, the bookstores offered *The Power of Prayer on Plants* and *Pray Your Weight Away.* Jane Russell, a movie actress of the 1940s and the star of *The Outlaw,* described God as a "living doll." The 20 September 1954 issue of *Time* magazine reported that religion had even reached the toy market. "In response to the 'resurgence of religious feeling and practice in America today,' the Ideal Toy Co. is putting on sale a knee-jointed doll that can be made to 'kneel in a praying position.'"[3]

With their fingers on the public pulse, politicians went out of their way to assure the electorate of their piety and religiosity. In 1954, the words "under God" were added to the Pledge of Allegiance, and the next year "In God We Trust" was put on all American currency. Although not a church-goer before becoming president, Eisenhower became the nation's leading apostle of religion. "Recognition of the Supreme Being," he told the American Legion when he launched their "Back to God" campaign in 1955, "is the first, the most basic expression of Americanism. Without God, there could be no American form of government, nor an American way of life." Twenty-one years later the country elected Jimmy Carter as president. His major claim to fame, besides being a one-term governor of Georgia, was that he was a "born-again" Christian with fundamentalist leanings.[4]

After 1945 even intellectuals took religion more seriously. Theologians such as Reinhold Niebuhr, Paul Tillich, Martin Buber, and Jacques Maritain and religious movements such as neo-orthodoxy and theistic existentialism enjoyed a brief moment in the academic sun. Enrollments in seminaries and in college religion courses increased. Historian H. Stuart Hughes reported in 1951 that "the avant-garde is becoming old-fashioned; religion is now the latest thing." In the previous year, *Partisan Review* had run a symposium on "Religion and the Intellectuals," in which half of the twenty-nine participants expressed either sympathy or a benevolent neutrality toward religion. Even Jewish intellectuals, who before the war had viewed religion in general and Judaism in particular with skepticism if not contempt, now spoke at least respectfully of the claims of Judaism and read books by Abraham Joshua Heschel, Martin Buber, the late Franz Rosenzweig, and other Jewish religious thinkers. In 1951, Will Herberg's *Judaism and Modern Man* and Heschel's *Man Is Not Alone* heralded a miniboom in Jewish theology.[5]

Judaism profited from the demographic transformation of American Jewry that took place after 1945. With the emergence of the second and third generations, the thick ethnic component of Jewishness diminished. While not wishing to deny their Jewish background or separate themselves from the Jewish community, the younger generations realized that their Jewishness would inevitably differ from that of their immigrant ancestors. The tendency to answer the question, What does it mean to be Jewish in America? in nonethnic terms was encouraged by the pressures for Americanization. While the general population might consider ethnicity to be quaint and colorful, as in the case of the popular radio and television show *The Goldbergs,* they did not believe ethnicity should extend beyond the first generation. The children of the immigrants were expected to dive into the American melting pot and to purge themselves of their ethnic dross. As a result, upwardly mobile Jews quickly and quietly dropped much of the remaining ethnic trappings of Jewish identity.

Besides Yiddish culture, the other secular forms of Jewish identity brought from Europe also had little appeal to the second and third generations. Few American Jews were sufficiently Zionistic to settle in Palestine or Israel, fewer still took any interest in Hebraic culture except for learning a smattering of Hebrew necessary for worship, and Jewish socialism had little relevance for a population that was becoming suburban and overwhelmingly middle class. For most Jews, then, Judaism remained the major link to their heritage.

The postwar American religious revival encouraged this tendency to conflate Judaism and Jewish identity. The socialist, Zionist, Yiddish, and communist antireligious movements had little drawing power after 1945. The communitywide federations also had to come to terms with the power of the synagogues. The rivalry between the synagogues and the federations ultimately derived from differing definitions of Jewish identity. The rabbis argued that the glue binding Jews to one another was their religion, while the federation leaders emphasized ethnic and secular elements of Jewish identity. The rabbis believed the synagogue was the central Jewish institution, while the secular federation leaders claimed it was the community center.

After 1945, the major responsibility for Jewish education shifted from the communitywide Talmud Torahs funded by the annual federation fund-raising campaigns to congregational schools and to the growing day school movement. By the 1960s, Reform, Conservative, and Orthodox congregational schools were educating over half a million children, and the expenditures for these schools made up a large percentage of congregational budgets. The synagogue had become the most important institution for socializing the young into the Jewish community. Local congregations sponsored chapters of national religious youth organizations such as the National Federation of Temple Youth (Reform), United Synagogue Youth (Conservative), and the National Conference of Synagogue Youth (Orthodox). These became more important than the youth organizations funded by B'nai B'rith and the various Zionist groups. Some congregations even hired full-time youth leaders to coordinate the activities of the young.[6]

Generally located in suburbia, these congregations also provided a wide range of cultural and social activities for adults, with worship often seeming to be the least important and popular of the activities of these Jewish centers. Observers of the American Jewish scene in the 1940s and 1950s thus had good reason for believing that the future of American Jewry rested with the rabbis and the synagogues. "If the past is to guide us," one historian wrote in 1954, "we may fairly affirm that the American Jewish community must be . . . essentially a religious community, or it will not be at all."[7]

After the war, as Will Herberg's 1955 volume, *Protestant-Catholic-Jew,* noted, the general population now considered Judaism to be one of America's three great faiths. The interfaith movement, with its assumption that Protestantism, Catholicism, and Judaism were equally valid expressions of American religion, helped elevate the status of Judaism. Popular culture accorded Judaism a place alongside that of Protestantism and Catholicism, despite the fact that Jews were never more than 3 percent of the population after 1945. Various aspects of Jewish ritual, including marriages, Bar and Bat Mitzvahs, holidays, and even circumcisions, were favorably and frequently depicted in the movies and on television.

In an ecumenical age in which one religion was supposedly as good as any other, Jewish rituals were often pictured in incongruous settings. In one segment of television's *The Flying Nun,* for example, a rabbi performs a Jewish wedding, complete with the breaking of the glass and a bridal canopy, within the confines of a convent. In *M*A*S*H,* a Christian chaplain officiates at a ritual circumcision. He repeats the Hebrew prayers relayed to him by a rabbi at sea. On *Cheers,* the circumcision of a son born of a mixed marriage takes place in the saloon's poolroom. In the Blue Ridge Mountains, the television family, the Waltons, participate in a Bar Mitzvah celebration, hear the Jewish memorial prayer for a dead relative, and dance the horah. American Judaism can truly be said to have come of age when Archie Bunker, that lovable bigot, hosts a traditional Sabbath evening dinner.[8]

This legitimization of American Judaism, however, was not accompanied by any upsurge among American Jews of religious observance or passion. The widely heralded return to the synagogue did not result in an increase in observance, the most important index of religious commitment. Nor were there any startling changes during the postwar years in the percentage of Jews attending weekly synagogue services and eating only kosher food. In *The Religious Factor,* his famous 1961 examination of religious behavior in Detroit, sociologist Gerhard Lenski noted that less than one-third of Detroit's Jews attended synagogue services more than once a month. "In the case of Judaism," Lenski concluded, "we are confronted with a group in which the religious associations have been seriously weakened." The religious behavior of Detroit's Jews was not unusual. In the 1980s, three-quarters of American Jews did not observe kashrut within the home, two-fifths did not fast on Yom Kippur, and 90 percent did not attend a religious service once a month or more.[9]

American Jews seemed to have opted for a Judaism of affiliation without ritual observance or synagogue attendance. Nor did they take seriously the intellectual dimensions of Judaism. Few Jews read weighty books in Jewish theology, philosophy, or history. They preferred instead the pop religious psychology of Harold Kushner and Joshua Loth Liebman, simplistic guides to instant Judaism, second-rate novels with Jewish themes and Jewish characters, and coffee-table books on Jewish history.

Not surprisingly, Jewish religious leaders were not optimistic regarding the future of American Judaism. Heschel, the most influential of the postwar religious figures, noted that "our services are conducted with pomp and precision. The rendition of the liturgy is smooth. Everything is present: decorum, voice, ceremony. But only one thing is missing: Life." Sociologists were also pessimistic regarding the future of American Judaism, none more so than Charles S. Liebman, an American-born scholar who had settled in Israel, where he taught at Bar Ilan University, an Orthodox institution. In his appropriately titled book *The Ambivalent American Jew,* Liebman distinguished between the "elite" religion of the rabbis and the "folk" religion of the laity. The laity, Liebman claimed, were little concerned with the traditional ritualistic demands of Judaism preached from the pulpit. For them Judaism was primarily a means to interact with other Jews and to pass on to their children a sense of Jewishness. Their Judaism was superficial and simplistic, merely "the public facade for the essentially communal content of Jewish identification."[10]

By the 1970s, the majority of American Jews immigrating to Israel were, like Liebman, either Orthodox or sympathetic to Orthodoxy. Push and pull factors had shaped their decision to relocate. They wished to live in a land they believed was promised to Jews by God, and they despaired of the future of Judaism in America. Even nonreligious American Jews who had moved to Israel frequently criticized the spiritual vacuity of American Judaism. Thus Hillel Halkin, the scion of a prominent American Zionist family, argued in *Letters to an American Friend: A Zionist's Polemic* (1977) that, apart from the Orthodox minority, American Judaism had little to offer and no future. The Judaism of the Conservative and Reform movements was a "pathetic charade," an "insipid seven-layer substitute" for traditional Judaism. They had modeled themselves on upper-class Protestantism. Their decorous and dispassionate services had debased Judaism and left their congregants spiritually bereft. They were "religious movements in name only."[11]

The most important influence shaping the Conservative and Reform movements came from the laity. Except for a small minority of right-wing Conservative Jews, few members of the Reform and Conservative laity took seriously the demands of their denominations. They were as casual in religious observance as their Christian countrymen. While both professed a belief in God, there was little evidence that this had a significant influence on their daily lives. Despite the hopes of American Jewish and Christian religious leaders, Jew and Gentile alike after 1945 responded largely to secular impulses.

Most American Jews believed the primary role of piety was not to shape their daily behavior but rather to help guarantee Jewish survival, however they might define it, and to sanctify various life-cycle events—births, conversions, confirmations, Bar and Bat Mitzvahs, weddings, and funerals. The appeal of the synagogue stemmed from its virtual monopoly over the celebration of these events. Sabbath attendance at the typical postwar synagogue was unimpressive except on the occasion of a Bar or Bat Mitzvah. The laity either ignored or replaced those rabbis who insisted on the observance of Jewish rituals even at the expense of social and economic ascent.

After an initial period of anger and frustration stemming from their congregants' apathy, most pulpit rabbis made an uneasy compromise with reality. Most of their hours were taken up with visiting hospitals, preparing sermons, sharing in the life-cycle events of their congregants, participating in civic, interfaith, and Jewish activities, and meeting with other rabbis. These were all valuable activities, but they were less exalted than the traditional role of the rabbi as teacher and scholar. Because of the limited power of the American rabbinate over the laity, and because the Reform and Conservative laity asked so little from its leadership, American Jewry did not exhibit the militant anticlericalism found in eastern Europe in the late nineteenth and twentieth centuries. There was no need to protest a nonexistent rabbinical tyranny or obscurantism. "No longer negative toward Judaism," Daniel J. Elazar wrote about his fellow American Jews in 1976, "the reaction of many is best characterized as apathetic."[12]

Symptomatic of the attitude of American Jewry toward Judaism was its response during the 1970s and 1980s to the widely publicized phenomenon of Christian and Asian religious cults. While only a small percentage of young American Jews were attracted to the cults, they made up a large percentage of the cults' membership. Some of the cults' leaders were of Jewish birth, including the head of the American Moonies (followers of Korean evangelist Sun Myung Moon). American Jewish leaders believed that the only possible explanation for the appeal of the cults was that they were totalitarian organizations that had "brainwashed" the gullible. These leaders warned parents about the cults and supported attempts to deprogram those Jews who had been seduced.

Such an approach was highly questionable, since it risked violating the freedom of religion of cult members, who had a perfect right to belong to them if they so chose. The brainwashing charge also diverted attention away from the real reason why young Jews were initially attracted to the cults. Raised in secular homes, they sought out the cults because of a spiritual hunger, which their families and synagogues had been unable to satisfy. The brainwashing charge resulted from the inability of Jewish leaders to take religion seriously. "What other religious groups in America," Reform Rabbi Eugene B. Borowitz complained in 1968, "can boast of men who are zealously committed to interfaith activities, but who have no faith of their own, who worship in no church with any degree of regularity, and who observe no commandments but those that their organizational participation requires or common American decency requires?"[13]

Perhaps nothing was more revealing about the religious outlook of postwar American Jewry than its elevation of the erstwhile minor holiday of Hanukkah into one of the most widely observed celebrations on the Jewish calendar. Even the Lubavitch Hasidim emphasized the celebration of Hanukkah. Ironically, this most nationalistic of all Jewish holidays enabled Jews to adapt more comfortably to American culture. Coming in December, Hanukkah was transformed into a Jewish counterpart to Christmas. The manner in which Jews observed Hanukkah resembled the Christians' celebration of Christmas. Hanukkah was a time for lighting candles by windows and giving gifts to children. In an effort to capitalize on the holiday spirit, manufacturers produced candies and other items for Jewish homes that resembled those produced for the Christmas market. Banks, particularly in the Northeast, encouraged their customers to open Hanukkah and Christmas savings programs, implying that the two holidays were comparable, at least insofar as they both required the spending of money.

The lighting of Hanukkah candles was one of the most widely observed Jewish religious practices in postwar America. The lighting of the candles and the giving of gifts took place at home, not in the synagogue, and the holiday was family oriented. Hanukkah put minimal demands upon Jews compared to the less widely observed but far more important festivals of Shavuot and Succot. Hanukkah did not place any barriers between Jews and Christians, nor did it require any fundamental change in behavior on the part of Jews. Yet it was perceived as an easy and important means for instilling Jewish identity in the young. The celebration of Hanukkah also benefited from the fact that, in commemorating the triumph of the Jews over the Hellenists in Palestine some two thousand years ago, it enabled American Jews to identify vicariously with the Israelis. This was at a time when the most important item on the American Jewish agenda was the survival of the state of Israel.

Hanukkah indicated that Jews respected Judaism as long as it did not interfere with their continuing acculturation and social mobility. This was particularly true in suburbia, where by 1960 a majority of America's Jews lived. The dominant values of suburbia were those of middle-class respectability, and part of middle-class respectability was religious affiliation. By establishing a synagogue, Jews, in effect, conveyed to their Christian neighbors that they accepted suburbia's standards of behavior, even though they themselves were generally not religious.

As Philip Roth's famous short story "Eli, The Fanatic" (1957) emphasized, suburban Jews are more interested in assimilating the dominant Protestant ethos of suburbia than in perpetuating anything approximating traditional Judaism. Roth's suburban Jews identify traditional Judaism with the urban Jewish neighborhoods that they had deserted as they ascended the social and economic ladder. The fears and insecurities of suburban Jewry are revealed when a European-born rabbi purchases a mansion in their quiet paradise in order to establish a yeshiva. "If I want to live in Brownsville," one of the town's Jews declares, "I'll live in Brownsville." Another predicts that a yeshiva could destroy the pleasant life that the community's Jews had made for themselves. "There's a good healthy relationship in the town because it's modern Jews and Protestants," he says, "people who respect each other, and leave each other be. Common sense is the ruling thing. . . . I'm for common sense. Moderation."[14]

Roth's analysis of Judaism in suburbia was echoed by rabbis and sociologists. In his *Jews in Suburbia* (1959), Rabbi Gordon of Newton noted that rabbis in suburbia were "sorely troubled because many of their congregants appear to want an easy, relaxed kind of country club atmosphere, rather than a house of worship with a positive philosophy for Jewish life, with a strong belief in God and His purposiveness at its very center." Kramer and Leventman's *Children of the Gilded Ghetto* (1961) emphasized that the Judaism of suburbia was highly acculturated. It resembled "a specialized voluntary association in the manner of Protestant denominations."[15]

The Protestantization of American Judaism, which had begun prior to World War II, accelerated after 1945. This was particularly manifested in the changing role of the congregational rabbi. The Protestant Reformation had transformed Christian worship in England and other countries in northern and western Europe. The central drama in the liturgy of the Roman Catholic Church was the saying of mass, and the most significant function of its priests was administering the sacraments. Protestant worship, by contrast, emphasized the sermon, and the most important role of the Protestant clergy was preaching. The highlight of traditional Jewish liturgy was the reading of the Torah on Saturday morning, and the major task of the Orthodox rabbi was explicating Jewish law. Traditional rabbis did not administer sacraments, and their infrequent sermons were generally discourses on a recondite aspect of Jewish law.

In order to meet the needs of an increasingly acculturated laity, the Conservative and Reform movements modified Jewish worship. Congregations instituted late Friday night services, which, although not well attended, were the most popular event on the weekly religious calendar. Such services did not interfere with shopping, work, or playing golf and tennis, and they provided an opportunity for the congregants to socialize during the collation following the service. The highlight of these services was a guest lecture or a well-prepared sermon by the rabbi focusing on social and political issues. These addresses frequently warned about the dangers of anti-Semitism, assimilation, and intermarriage. The congregants knew their rabbis primarily through their preaching, and homiletics became as highly prized among Jews as among Protestants.

The influence of Protestantism on Judaism was also seen in the growing number of congregations with choirs and highly paid cantors. Worship in non-Orthodox congregations increasingly became a spectator rather than a participant activity. Other changes in the synagogue accentuated the transformation of the congregants into passive spectators. It had been the custom in Europe for the rabbi and cantor to face the ark when leading services. With their backs to the congregants, their prayers were directed to the Almighty. By 1945, however, Reform and Conservative rabbis faced their congregants, just as the Protestant clergy and professional entertainers faced their audiences. The location for reading the Torah also changed. Instead of reading the Torah in the middle of the congregation while facing the ark, the Torah was read on a stage in the front of the synagogue with the reader facing the congregation. This change was more than a matter of convenience. It symbolized a change in the role of the Torah in American Jewish life. Instead of being an integral part of the entire community, it was now the exclusive responsibility of the congregation's elite, with the rest of the congregation relegated to the role of observers.

Nowhere after 1945 was the paradoxical condition of American Judaism—surface prosperity and spiritual decline—more evident than within Conservatism, the most popular branch of American Judaism. Conservative Judaism entered the postwar era with an optimism fueled by its own recent history and by the bleak prospects of Orthodoxy. Emerging in America during the first two decades of the twentieth century, Conservatism's historic mission had been not to replace traditional Judaism, but to make it relevant to America. Its leaders believed that as the eastern European immigrant generation died out, the Conservative movement would inherit the mantle of traditional Judaism. European-style Orthodoxy, they felt, would never flourish in America.

Except for the seating of men and women together in the synagogue—Conservative Judaism sanctioned family pews—it was often difficult prior to World War II to distinguish between the ritualistic patterns and religious ideology of Conservative and native-born Orthodox Jews. As Rabbi Israel Goldstein, a prominent Conservative rabbi, wrote in 1927, "there are some among us who are puzzled to understand wherein we conservatives, so-called, differ from this revamped orthodoxy which permits decorum in the service and English in the sermon." Both groups were responding to the same imperatives of acculturation. There was even some consideration given during the 1920s to merging the Jewish Theological Seminary with Yeshiva University. This was at a time when the orientation of native American Orthodoxy was more liberal and Conservative Judaism more traditional than they would be after 1945. American-trained Orthodox rabbis agreed with their Conservative counterparts that traditional Judaism would have to be Americanized if it was to maintain the loyalties of the upwardly mobile and college educated. Their differences with the Conservative leaders were a matter of degree, not of kind.[16]

The optimism of Conservative leaders seemed to be confirmed in the postwar years by the increase in the number of families affiliating with the movement, the development of the Conservative Ramah summer camps, the growth of the movement's Solomon Schechter parochial school system, the weighty position of the Jewish Theological Seminary in American Jewish intellectual life, and the important role of Conservative Judaism within American Zionism. Conservative synagogue centers, with their athletic, social, cultural, and spiritual activities, had become the model for Orthodox and Reform congregations, particularly in suburbia. "By choice and by necessity," Ruth R. Wisse wrote in 1979, "Conservatism remains the proving ground of American Judaism, reflecting its patterns of change and its degree of stability." Conservatism even made inroads during the 1970s and 1980s in Israeli religious life, and Conservative leaders fervently—and un-successfully—sought a recognition of their movement's legitimacy from Israel's Orthodox religious establishment, a recognition that they believed was deserved because of their contributions to Zion and their preeminent status within American Judaism.[17]

Most students of American Jewry writing in the years after the war expected Conservatism to remain the most popular of the three branches of American Judaism. Jacob Agus's *Guideposts in Modern Judaism* (1954), Robert Gordis's *Judaism for the Modern Age* (1955), and Joseph Blau's *Modern Varieties of Judaism* (1964) all argued that the future belonged to Conservatism. This was also one of the themes of Nathan Glazer's impor-tant 1957 volume, *American Judaism,* which emphasized the appeal of Conservatism to middle-class acculturated suburbanites.

These indications of prosperity within Conservatism, however, coex-isted with a growing pessimism both within and outside the movement regarding its contemporary significance and its long-term viability. Law-rence J. Kaplan, a McGill University colleague of Wisse, emphasized that Conservative leaders during the 1970s had been "plagued by self-doubt, disquiet, and gloom." Indicative of this "crisis of confidence" was the split of the movement into two antagonistic ideological factions, each with its own distinctive approach to Jewish law. According to Kaplan, the Conservative Left had repudiated the time-tested process of revising Halakhah (Jewish law) and wished the rabbinate to interpret the law so that it would conform to current social needs. The Conservative Right, on the other hand, sought to defend the traditionalist Conservative approach to Halakhah, even if it meant ignoring these needs. This unraveling of the Conservative move-ment's tenuous and ambiguous ideological posture, Kaplan claimed, re-flected a broader and deeper crisis within Conservatism. He was not alone in forecasting a possible split within the Conservative ranks, with the Right drifting toward Orthodoxy and the Left drifting toward Reform.[18]

The growing pessimism regarding Conservatism's future was reflected in the writings of Marshall Sklare, the leading authority on the sociology of postwar American Jewry. When Sklare published *Conservative Judaism: An American Religious Movement* in 1955 in the midst of the postwar American religious revival, he was rather hopeful about the movement's prospects. The volume's concluding chapter claimed that Conservatism had "made a notable contribution to survivalism and . . . provides a significant institutional framework for a possible revivified Judaism." There was no reason, Sklare claimed, why "the vitality of Conservatism should not continue for quite some time." He did not anticipate any large-scale defections from Conservatism. Instead he wondered whether Conservatism would "come to play a new and as yet unforeseeable role in the Jewish life of the future."

A second edition of *Conservative Judaism* appeared in 1972 with a new chapter titled "Recent Developments in Conservative Judaism." Sklare now spoke of a "crisis" within Conservatism, which he attributed to three factors: (1) the postwar revival of Orthodoxy, (2) the inability of Conservatism to retain the loyalty of its young, and (3) the lack of ritual observance among the Conservative laity. Prewar Conservative leaders had predicted that Orthodoxy would roll over and die, and this would leave them as the sole spokesmen for traditional Judaism in America. Unfortunately for Conservatism, the supposedly ossified Orthodoxy experienced a surprising rebirth after 1945 in both numbers and élan. American Orthodox notables vigorously rejected the claim of Conservatism to represent traditional Judaism. Conservative rabbis were now confronted by rivals who described them as religious charlatans and betrayers of traditional Judaism.[19]

The second edition of *Conservative Judaism* appeared at a time when many people still anticipated the "greening of America." Sklare believed that the middle-class ethos of Conservative Judaism had little attraction for young Jews, who presumably had been influenced by the counterculture of the 1960s. While all branches of Judaism had difficulty in appealing to what Sklare called the "Woodstock nation," the problem was particularly acute for Conservatism because of "its stress on cultural reconciliation and the blending of Jewish and general culture."

More important than the revival of Orthodoxy or the estrangement of the young was the absence of a ritually observant laity. Conservatism had assumed that ritual observance and synagogue attendance would become more widespread if the Halakhah was modified to conform to modern enlightened standards. But, as the Orthodox had predicted, the modernization of Halakhah had not resulted in any increase in ritual observance. As Sklare wrote, Conservative Judaism had been "an abysmal failure" in this area. "The belief among Conservative leaders that the movement's approach to *halachah* had the power to maintain observance, as well as to inspire its renewal, has proved illusory."[20]

In 1950, the Rabbinical Assembly, the organization of Conservative rabbis, responded to the decline in Sabbath attendance by approving the use of automobiles on the Sabbath for the sole purpose of traveling to the synagogue. The assembly's members believed that low attendance was due to the postwar dispersion of the Jewish population into the suburbs rather than to religious apathy. The rationale of the assembly's Committee on Jewish Law and Standards for modifying the restrictions against the use of automobiles indicated a mood of despair. "Unless [this declining trend is] halted and reversed," the committee stated, Sabbath observance "will soon reach an absolute nadir and the single greatest Jewish religious institution will have passed out of the lives of the great mass of the members of our congregations." The 1950 change did not have any appreciable effect on the Conservative laity. The same indifference to Jewish rituals and Jewish law was seen in other areas. A 1979 survey revealed that less than 7 percent of Conservative Jews claimed to be "totally kosher," and in less than one-third of Conservative homes was kiddush recited on Friday night. There was "not a Conservative synagogue in the country," Sklare noted, "where most congregants practiced the *mitzvoth* according to the Conservative regimen."[21]

By the 1970s, few Conservative leaders believed any longer that their movement possessed the formula for bringing American Jewry back to Jewish observance. Outsiders were skeptical that Conservatism could even be described as a movement since it lacked a mass membership committed to the official doctrines of the organization. There were Conservative organizations, but there were not many true Conservative Jews within these organizations. Institutional inertia seemed to be the primary force perpetuating Conservatism. Neither Orthodoxy or Reform exhibited to the same extent this dissonance between its official ideology and the behavior of its members. The Orthodox leadership and laity agreed that the essence of Judaism lay in the traditions handed down from one generation to another (although many self-styled Orthodox Jews were hardly observant), and the Reform leadership and laity agreed that tradition and Jewish law could be granted a vote but certainly not a veto over contemporary Judaism. Only within Conservative Judaism was there a sharp dichotomy between the behavior and orientation of the pulpit and the pew. In fact, for most Conservative Jews, being Conservative was merely vicarious. They were Conservative Jews because their rabbis kept kosher, observed the Sabbath, and were graduates of the seminary, or because they paid dues to a synagogue that identified with the Conservative movement. They were not Conservative Jews because their religious behavior differed from that of

Reform Jews or because they themselves took seriously the various statements of Jewish practice issued by the Conservative gurus.

Many parents resisted the efforts of Conservative congregational schools to instill in their children the tenets of Conservative Judaism. Because of parental pressures, these schools were forced to reduce the number of hours they met per week. They considered themselves lucky if they conveyed to their charges a sense of Jewish identity and enough Hebrew so that they could stumble through their Bar and Bat Mitzvah ceremonies without embarrassment. The students generally fled these holding pens with alacrity after the age of thirteen.[22]

Starting in 1916, Conservative leaders have been continually involved in an effort to establish the ideological parameters of Conservatism and to define what it means to be a Conservative Jew. These efforts have failed for two reasons. First, the left-wing and right-wing elements within Conservatism have been unable to agree on its most basic tenets, with the division between the two groups widening in the 1970s and 1980s. Second, and even more important, the Conservative laity has consistently refused to take seriously any ideological formulation or ritualistic demands by the movement's leadership. With few pangs of conscience, they have blissfully ignored their rabbis and the scholars at the seminary, who periodically emphasized the importance of kashrut, the sanctity of the Sabbath, and the role of prayer. Instead, Conservatism gratified the status needs of an upwardly mobile ethnic group, and its imposing temples provided a Jewish ambience that satisfied their survivalist instincts. Conservative Judaism enabled a laity consisting largely of secular Jews to believe that they were somewhat traditional. The Rabbinical Assembly's *Sabbath and Festival Prayer Book* (1946) reflected this combination of acculturation and tradition. The book contained Hebrew prayers (with English translations) as well as "America the Beautiful."

No one grasped Conservatism's basic appeal more clearly or predicted its future course more accurately than Mordecai Kaplan, the movement's greatest innovator. Kaplan taught at the Seminary from 1909 through 1963, developing a distinctive interpretation of American Jewish identity. A naturalist, Kaplan rejected the concept of a personal God, questioned the reality of God's revelation at Mount Sinai and His covenant with the Jewish people, and stressed the cultural aspects of Judaism. As indicated by the title of his most important book—*Judaism as a Civilization: Toward a Reconstruction of American Jewish Life* (1934)—he believed Judaism to be part of a culture rather than simply a religion. Kaplan viewed the attenuation of theism as an inevitable outgrowth of modern secularism, urbanization, and naturalism. Judaism could appeal to modern Jews, he claimed, only if it shed much of its excess supernatural baggage and recognized that Jewishness and the Jewish people were more important than Judaism. Kaplan even maintained that an atheist could be a rabbi. One of his books was appropriately titled *Judaism without Supernaturalism* (1958). Kaplan articulated a formula that enabled Jews to combine rationalism and Jewish survivalist instincts.

Approximately a hundred Conservative and Reform rabbis sympathetic to Kaplan's approach organized the Reconstructionist Rabbinical Fellowship in 1950. Eight years later the Fellowship of Reconstruction Congregations was established, and in 1968 the Reconstructionist Rabbinical College in Philadelphia opened its doors. Its purpose was to train rabbis, both male and female, for the small but growing number of Reconstructionist congregations.

Few Conservative congregations and Conservative rabbis accepted Reconstructionism's radical break with theistic Judaism. And yet while rejecting Kaplan's theology, Conservatism accepted his sociology. Kaplan wished to turn the synagogue into a center in which Jewish civilization would be manifested in a continual round of cultural, educational, social, and religious events. The synagogue center would enable Jews to identify with the Jewish people and to remain part of Jewish civilization. The history of the synagogue centers was hardly what Kaplan sought. Their bingo games, basketball, and art auctions demonstrated a much thinner and narrower understanding of Jewish civilization than Kaplan's. It is doubtful, however, that fully acculturated third- and fourth-generation Jews would be attracted to Kaplan's original conception of the synagogue center. America provided them with enough of a civilization.

By 1985, Conservatism included over eight hundred congregations, a youth movement with the largest membership of any American Jewish youth organization, sixty-five Solomon Schechter day schools, a half dozen Ramah summer camps, and a seminary in Israel. Despite this growth, Conservative leaders were afflicted with a serious morale problem. Rabbi Wolfe Kelman, the chief executive officer of the Rabbinical Assembly, was surprised by this pessimism. "No other group of committed professionals in recent Jewish history has been more successful in achieving those goals to which it has been *unequivocally* committed," he remarked in 1975, and yet there was no other group in Jewish life "which has developed such a tendency to believe the best about others and the worst about themselves." Kelman had inadvertently put his finger on the issue troubling his colleagues. Conservative rabbis were not concerned with their own professional attainments. Their major problem and the source of their disquietude was what it had been since 1945—their inability to instill in their congregants a commitment to the tenets of Conservative Judaism.[23]

Referring to the Reform custom of not wearing skullcaps during services, Mordecai Kaplan supposedly once quipped that many Conservative Jews became Reform "at the drop of a hat." In 1954, Rabbi Theodore Friedman somberly asked whether Conservatism was "merely a stopover of Jews on the way from Orthodoxy to Reform." Conservative leaders realized, of course, that their laity differed little from the Reform laity in terms of worship and ritual, and that their centrist ideology had little mass appeal. Professor Neil Gillman of the seminary pithily described the situation of Conservatism. It was a movement that consisted of "an Orthodox faculty teaching Conservative rabbis to minister to Reform Jews." The same complaint was heard in the field. As one Conservative rabbi noted in 1970, "Both the Orthodox and the Reform have a significant following. We don't. . . . We preach to congregants about *kashrut, Shabbat, halakhah* in general, knowing that the vast majority neither keeps them or feels any compunctions over ignoring these rules. The fraud is open, mutually recognized, with all the implicit contempt and self-contempt it engenders."

Conservative leaders questioned how long the movement could remain vibrant when its most cherished beliefs were the exclusive possession of a small number of professors in New York City and Los Angeles and a limited number of rabbis in the field. Conservative Judaism had seemingly lost its raison d'être. What reason was there for Jews to affiliate with Conservatism when they could just as easily join a Reform congregation, particularly since Reform had dropped its previous opposition to Zionism and was more sympathetic to the ethnic dimension of Judaism? And how could Conservatism claim to be the voice of traditional Judaism in America when it was challenged after the war by a resurgent and aggressive Orthodoxy? As early as 1927 Rabbi Israel Goldstein had anticipated the dilemma in which Conservatism would evetually find itself. "As Orthodoxy becomes more de-Ghettoized and Reform more conservatized, what is left for the Conservative Jew to do?"[24]

By the 1960s it had become clear that Conservative Judaism was floundering. The number of its affiliated families and congregations had ceased growing. In 1965, 44 percent of American Jews had identified themselves as Conservative and 27 percent as Reform. A decade later, 35 percent identified themselves as Conservative and 34 percent as Reform. Younger Jews who had been raised in families affiliated with Conservative synagogues seemingly had little loyalty to the movement.

In his 1965 presidential address to the Rabbinical Assembly, Rabbi Max Routtenberg voiced the fear that Conservatism was in disarray. Conservative Jews, he claimed, were "haunted by the fear that somewhere along the way we have become lost; our direction is not clear, and the many promises we made to ourselves and to our people have not been fulfilled." And yet only five years earlier Routtenberg's mood had been decidedly upbeat. "The future belongs to us," he told his fellow Conservative rabbis. "The tide of Conservative Judaism is still running strongly and will yet increase in the next generation or two. It meets the needs of American Jews better than Reform or Orthodoxy. It holds within it promise of an abundant and meaningful life, and there are many who believe that this promise will be fulfilled."[25]

The turmoil within Conservatism even invaded the halls of the Jewish Theological Seminary. For decades the seminary had been a force for tradition and continuity. Beginning in the 1970s, however, this was no longer true. In 1972, Gerson D. Cohen succeeded Louis Finkelstein as chancellor of the seminary. A historian and the seminary's librarian, Cohen was the first chancellor of the JTS whose field of specialization was not rabbinics. His selection presaged a more flexible attitude within the seminary toward Jewish law and a smaller role for its rabbinics department in determining the policies of the Conservative movement. The central issue in the seminary's transformation involved women's rights, particularly the ordination of women, which Cohen fervently supported.

Probably no ideological issue more sharply distinguished Conservatism from Orthodoxy after World War II than the role of women in the synagogue. While Orthodoxy stood firm against tampering with Jewish law regarding women's place within the synagogue, Conservative Judaism drew closer to Reform in obliterating any differences between male and female roles within Judaism. A 1955 ruling of the Rabbinical Assembly sanctioned the calling of women to the Torah, and a 1973 ruling permitted them to be counted for a minyan, the quorum required for services. By 1983, nearly sixty per cent of Conservative congregations were calling women to the Torah and counting them as part of a minyan.

In that same year the decision to ordain women came before the seminary faculty, eleven years after the Reform movement had ordained its first female rabbi. Despite a long responsum by Professor Joel Roth arguing that Jewish tradition did not preclude the ordination of women, the five senior Talmudists at the seminary declared the proposal ran counter to Jewish law. They even refused to participate in the faculty's deliberations regarding the ordination of women, not wishing to dignify a process that might lead to a violation of Jewish law. Despite the objections of the movement's leading Halakhic authorities, the seminary faculty on 24 October 1983, by a vote of thirty-four to eight, approved the ordination of women. In May 1985, Amy Eilberg, the daughter of a former United States congressman from Philadelphia, became the first woman ordained by the seminary and was soon accepted for membership in the Rabbinical Assembly. Two years later, the seminary graduated its first female cantor.

The supporters of the ordination of women claimed that it was perfectly compatible with Conservative Judaism's customary approach to Jewish law. Cohen declared that "without controverting Jewish law, we have adapted it to the religious and ethical norms of a new generation. . . . I believe deeply that . . . we behaved as our ancestors did on occasion when they found new forms of response for new challenges." Ismar Schorsch, who replaced Cohen as the seminary's chancellor in 1986, also strongly favored the ordination of women. A historian like his predecessor, Schorsch asserted that the decision to ordain women was an example of evolutionary Halakhah, the hallmark of Conservative Judaism. "This is how Judaism ultimately works," he said in 1986. "The change in the status of woman began with the Emancipation, and it is still going ahead."[26]

But other advocates of the 1983 decision agreed with the movement's leading Talmudists that feminism could not be reconciled with Halakhah. This led Seymour Siegel, a theologian at the seminary, to argue that this was simply too bad for Halakhah. Jewish law would have to be ignored if it could not be made to conform to current sociological demands, particularly if it prevented the elimination of sexism and misogyny. "When Jewish law makes us insensitive, less human and more prone to withhold human rights from our fellow man," Siegel said, "then it has lost its primacy in Jewish life. *Halacha* is a means, not an end in itself. The means should be judged by the ends. . . . For it is clear . . . that if strict halachic conformance frustrates our highest and best human instinct, then the *halachic* considerations should be secondary and yield to ethics and *menshlichkeit*." This was a radical reading of the traditional role of Conservative Judaism, which, Conservative spokesmen had always claimed, was the harmonizing of modernity and Halakhah.[27]

For critics of Conservative Judaism, the Seminary's overriding of its Department of Talmud and Rabbinics confirmed their belief that Conservatism was less concerned with maintaining the historical integrity of Jewish law than with appearing to be modern and relevant. Ruth Wisse argued that the debate over the ordination of women reflected an intellectual emptiness within Conservatism, an excessive pragmatism "not very likely to inspire." Orthodox spokesmen scorned the Conservative movement for deserting Jewish law and claimed that the decision to ordain women demonstrated the intellectual bankruptcy of Conservatism.[28]

Even ardent supporters of Conservative Judaism admitted that Halakhah had been stretched almost to the breaking point. It was difficult to see how Conservatism, once it rejected the sentiments of its leading legal scholars, could claim that it remained committed to the continuity of Jewish law. And if it could not make that claim, then what kind of movement was it, and how did it differ from Reform, particularly when Reform was moving to the right ritually and ideologically? Orthodox scholar Michael Wyschogrod predicted that a fusion between Reform and Conservatism was now possible because of the liberties Conservative Judaism had taken with Jewish law—which, he claimed, would "only lead to tragic results."[29]

There were, however, dissident elements within Conservatism who rejected the innovations of the 1980s and sought to restore the movement to its historic path. In 1984, traditionalist elements within Conservatism founded the Union for Traditional Conservative Judaism. David Weiss Halivni, Conservative Judaism's most eminent Talmudist and an esteemed member of the seminary's faculty, was the leading intellectual force in the establishment of the union. He left the seminary a few years later and took a position in the Department of Religion at neighboring Columbia University. A small but prominent group of Conservative rabbis affiliated with the union. They included David Feldman of Teaneck, New Jersey, a noted authority on Jewish law and medical ethics, and David Novak, a Conservative scholar on the faculty of the University of Virginia.

The most noteworthy of the union's efforts was the establishment of a rabbinical school—the Institute of Traditional Judaism—in 1989 to train traditionalist male Conservative rabbis. Halivni was selected as rector of this potential rival to the Jewish Theological Seminary. Supporters of the new seminary included Elie Wiesel, the distinguished Brandeis biblical scholar Nahum Sarna (whose own daughter-in-law was an ordained Reform rabbi), and Orthodox philosopher Eliezer Berkovits. They hoped the institute could help unify American Judaism, which was becoming increasingly polarized between an inflexible and intolerant Orthodoxy and the large majority of American Jews who were indifferent, and even hostile, to Halakhah. The institute's dean, Ronald D. Price, defined its goal as "strengthening open-minded observant Judaism." The school's motto was "Genuine Faith and Intellectual Honesty."[30]

Members of the union stressed that they, not their opponents within Conservatism, had remained faithful to the teachings and outlook of what Price termed "traditional modernism." Price argued that the union was necessary because the Conservative movement had turned away from the original vision of its founders. While the members of the union took Halakhah seriously, their opponents favored a Jewish life-style "grounded in secularism." In a broadside directed at members of the Rabbinical Assembly, the union encouraged those members of the Conservative rabbinate who believed in the "historic mission" of Conservatism to join the union and "build for the future." There were few signs that this call was successful. Despite the support of some of Conservatism's leading lights, the union was unable to attract a mass following.[31]

One of the reasons for the plight of Conservative Judaism, as Sklare noted, was the refusal of Orthodoxy to roll over and die. Although the number of Orthodox Jews was never large—between 5 and 10 percent of American Jewry—the strength of Orthodoxy did not lie in size. "The only remaining vestige of Jewish passion resides in the Orthodox community" Charles S. Liebman wrote in 1965. While this was an exaggeration, since it overlooked the fervent commitment of many American Jews to Israel and the United Jewish Appeal, it was probably correct regarding American Judaism. This passion manifested itself in the Orthodox conviction that it was the only true form of Judaism. From the perspective of the Orthodox, Conservatism and Reform were heresies that, like previous heresies, would disappear in time. There was no more surprising aspect of American Judaism after 1945 than this mood of Orthodox triumphalism, a mood that confounded the most basic assumptions of Conservative and Reform leaders and sociologists regarding the future of American Judaism.[32]

Conservative spokesmen had assumed prior to World War II that Orthodoxy smacked too much of Europe and the immigrant ghetto to appeal to the Americanized and upwardly mobile offspring of the immigrants. With the demise of Orthodoxy, Conservatism would be left to carry the banner of tradition. "Given due sacrifice and willingness on our part," Louis Finkelstein had said in 1927, "the Judaism of the next generation will be saved by us. Certainly it can be saved by no other group." Sociologists echoed this prognosis of the inevitable death of Orthodoxy in America. The history of Orthodoxy, Sklare wrote in 1954, "can be written in terms of a case study of institutional decay." Catering to isolated groups of Jews, the Orthodox synagogue led "*an attenuated existence.*"33

The incongruity of Orthodoxy in America was one of the themes of Nathan Glazer's 1957 survey, *American Judaism.* Written by a sociologist destined to become one of America's leading authorities on ethnicity and American Jewry, *American Judaism* reflected the fundamental assumptions of American sociologists regarding Judaism in general and Orthodoxy in particular. Glazer's book was the latest in a line of studies that went back at least to 1928 when Louis Wirth published *The Ghetto,* an examination of Chicago's immigrant Jewish neighborhood. An assimilationist, Wirth identified the ghetto with the worst aspects of Jewish life. He described Orthodoxy as "an intolerant medieval theology" that had imprisoned European Jewry in intellectual darkness until the Enlightenment "began to shine" its rays. Jews, Wirth predicted, would inevitably desert Orthodoxy as they moved up the social and economic ladder. Wirth's assertion that education, social mobility, and acculturation were incompatible with Orthodoxy became the jumping-off point for students of American Judaism. Even the Orthodox themselves were pessimistic regarding the future of Orthodoxy. Rabbi Samuel Rosenblatt of Baltimore noted in 1940 that Orthodoxy, despite being "the sole correct version and the most satisfying form of the Jewish religion," had failed in America.34

The popularity of modernization theory, one of the most important themes of postwar social science, strengthened the tendency to view Orthodoxy and other forms of traditional religion as fossils. Modernization enthusiasts stressed the sharp distinction between traditional and modern societies and claimed that the rural, static, and traditional order was being overwhelmed by the secularism, egalitarianism, centralization, rationalization, and industrialization accompanying economic and social modernization. Modernization supposedly undermined fundamentalist religious ideas and charismatic practices and encouraged rationality and intellectual sophistication.35

In *American Judaism,* Glazer asserted that there was little future for Orthodoxy in America and that it had retained its appeal only among the poorer and less Americanized Jews who had not yet risen into the middle class. Thus in examining Orthodoxy he focused on the Hasidim living in the Williamsburg section of Brooklyn. But, as Glazer recounted, the Judaism of Williamsburg had very little appeal to Americanized Jews. Glazer did not realize, however, that traditional Judaism in the postwar years was not restricted to European sects residing in Brooklyn's declining neighborhoods. By 1957, Orthodoxy was in the process of transplanting itself to suburbia and attracting a new clientele.

Glazer's sociological model, which identified Orthodoxy with exotic Hasidic sects and the poor, had no place for the growing number of Orthodox who were college-educated, quintessentially middle class, and financially successful. These modern Orthodox, as they came to be known, made up a majority of American Orthodoxy. They were not mentioned in *American Judaism,* even when a new edition of the book appeared in 1972 with a thirty-page epilogue. Glazer was not alone in failing to note the postwar Orthodox renaissance and the presence of the modern Orthodox. In his influential 1964 book, *Assimilation in American Life,* sociologist Milton Gordon drew attention to the decline of Orthodoxy and claimed that kashrut, "except on ceremonial occasions, is fast disappearing."[36]

In fact, far from vanishing, kashrut was becoming more popular. A year prior to the publication of Gordon's book, a *Wall Street Journal* headline of 8 April 1963 proclaimed "Kosher Label Covers More Name Brands from Aspirin to Pizza" (the article's subtitle was "Gentiles Help Boost Sales of Matzo Balls"). Food manufacturers were eager to capture the kosher market, which had become a multibillion-dollar business. General Foods Corporation even prepared a short coloring book for young children titled *Brachos for Breakfast,* which listed the proper blessings to be said over breakfast foods. Food companies manufactured a variety of kosher products from bubblegum cigars and aspirin to kosher ersatz bacon and cheeseburgers. By 1990, sixty organizations and private individuals were certifying over eighteen thousand products as kosher, and kosher products made up more than 30 percent of all packaged goods sold in supermarkets. The Buitoni Company, for example, advertised its Italian marinara sauce as a substitute for "old-fashioned horseradish" as a spread for gefilte fish. "This zesty and tangy Italian 'sauce of the sea' brings out all the subtle flavors of gefilte fish. And it never makes your eyes water! . . . You can serve this delicious change-of-pace sauce . . . with peace of mind. Buitoni Marinara is OU and Pareve." In 1990, the first federal kosher consumer bill was introduced in the United States Congress by Stephen J. Solarz of Brooklyn. The bill's purpose was to protect the Orthodox against the fraudulent labeling of nonkosher products as kosher.[37]

A particularly noteworthy aspect of the revival of kashrut and Orthodoxy was the opening of dozens of kosher restaurants in Los Angeles, Boston, Miami, New York, and other cities with large Jewish populations. As late as 1968, Judd Teller had predicted the decline of Jewish restaurants. Suburban middle-class Jews, he argued, did not wish to eat in kosher and Jewish-style restaurants. Not only did they remind Jews of the lower-class ethnic neighborhoods from which they had fled, but they also served a cuisine considered unhealthy.[38]

Teller did not anticipate that kosher restaurants specializing in non-Jewish food would find a market among the religious. These restaurants were a revealing barometer of changes within Orthodoxy. The new affluence of the post–World War II Orthodox enabled them to pay the often exorbitant prices of these elegant establishments. The restaurants catered to Orthodox yuppies—doctors, lawyers, accountants, bankers, and other professionals—who were not inhibited by the numbers on the right side of the menu. In addition, the restaurants revealed a willingness to display one's Orthodoxy outside the confines of the home. Eating at kosher restaurants indicated, along with the wearing in public of skullcaps and other distinctive Orthodox clothing, a greater confidence in American pluralism. Finally, the restaurants disclosed an impulse toward cultural amalgamation as the Orthodox strove to combine the best of the Jewish and outside worlds. The consumption of haute cuisine, even if kosher, was in itself essentially a secular act.

The food offered by these restaurants ran the gamut from French, Mexican, and Italian to vegetarian and macrobiotic. For those unmarried Orthodox reluctant to attend movies and other secular entertainments for religious reasons, the restaurant was an important arena for courting. In Cheers—a Manhattan kosher Italian restaurant—a couple could begin their meal with funghi e vitello (marinated mushrooms and shredded veal in a vinaigrette), move on to fusilli alla puttanesca (tender chunks of chicken stewed in a rich sauce of tomatoes, olives, capers, and garlic served with homemade twists of pasta), and wash it down with a cup of caffe de caffeinato. In 1989, the Levana restaurant in New York advertised a seventy-five dollar meal complete with a glass of Pinot Brut champagne, Irish salmon mille-feuille for appetizer, smoked breast of duck for the second course, and then a filet of beef flambé for the main course. In 1990, a new wrinkle was added to eating out kosher style in New York when an entrepreneur hired a boat to transport diners around Manhattan Island. Dinner for two on the Glatt Yacht, as it was named, came to one hundred and fifty dollars. The most bizarre of these kosher restaurants was New York's Shalom Japan, a supper club owned by Miriam Mizakura, a native of Japan and a convert to Orthodox Judaism. Its menu included tempura, sake, sushi, cholent, and corned beef on rye. Its owner was, as she told her customers, a real JAP. One of her favorite stories concerned Mr. Yakki who built a succah and now "people come to eat sukiyaki in Yakki's succah."39

The symbiosis between Jewish and non-Jewish cultures manifested by these eateries caused Rabbi Menashe Klein, the leading Hasidic *posek* (authority on Jewish law) in America, to issue a ruling forbidding Jews from eating in such restaurants. Rabbi Klein would certainly have been dismayed by a kosher Chinese restaurant in Brooklyn named Yunkee, which appealed to Jews wishing to be cosmopolitan, kosher, and red, white, and blue Yankees all at the same time. He would have been even more aghast at a nightclub in New York City providing kosher food to its customers while they enjoyed the gyrations of belly dancers. In his collection of responsa entitled *Mishneh Halakhot* (vol. 10), Klein emphasized that these restaurants were defeating one of the major purposes of kashrut—to separate Jews from non-Jews. While Jews might not be walking in the ways of Gentiles, he emphasized, they certainly were eating in their ways, and consequently "it is forbidden to enter restaurants that have non-Jewish names and non Jewish styles of cooking and food which is given non-Jewish names. It is also forbidden to participate in weddings and other affairs where this style of food and drink are served."

One can only imagine what Rabbi Klein would have thought of a group of Orthodox Jews called the Kosher Dining Club, who gathered every six weeks in Baltimore to eat a kosher dinner consisting of dishes from throughout the world. "This just goes to show you don't have to eat crummy to keep kosher," one participant said. "We're not here just to share an experience. we're doing something to make people see how beautiful Judaism is." Beauty, as the saying goes, is in the eye of the beholder.40

The most important bulwark of American Orthodoxy was not its restaurants but its extensive parochial school system. Although there was a drop-out phenomenon among those educated in Orthodox schools, most remained within the Orthodox fold. By the 1980s, there were over one hundred thousand students enrolled in over five hundred Orthodox day schools, and every city with more than five thousand Jews had a day school. Most of these were under modern Orthodox auspices. Some, such as Ramaz in Manhattan, Maimonides in Brookline, Massachusetts, and Frisch in Bergen County, New Jersey, resembled upper-class prep schools. The Orthodox day school movement was aided by the National Society for Hebrew Day Schools (Torah Umesorah). Torah Umesorah was created to encourage the founding of Orthodox day schools and to help provide them with instructional material, faculty, and administrators.[41]

In contrast to the sectarian Orthodox, the modern Orthodox were Orthodox up to a point. Their life-style, to quote Charles Liebman, was "half-pagan, half-halakhic." Orthodox couples went to racy movies and Playboy clubs, as did other Americans. One meeting of the Association of Jewish Studies in the 1980s even featured a paper that discussed the Halakhic implications of vacationing at Club Med. (The paper subsequently appeared in *Tradition,* a journal published by Yeshiva University.) The modern Orthodox, sociologist Samuel C. Heilman concluded, "stand between two sources of stigmatization: the contemporary, which considers their Orthodoxy a stigma, and the traditional Orthodox community, which looks upon their modernity with disapproval. As such, modern Orthodox Jews have only themselves." The title of one book on the modern Orthodox described them in oxymoronic terms as "cosmopolitan parochials."[42]

The classic sociological relationship between Orthodoxy and social status and affluence seemed to have been turned on its head in suburbia. The laity of suburban modern Orthodox communities became known as *fruppies*—frum (i.e., religious), young professionals. Few of them were in business, the most important occupation for first- and second-generation Jews. Instead, they gravitated to the high status professions. In the typical modern Orthodox community of West Orange, New Jersey, there was such a shortage of poor people that the faithful were unable to carry out directly the religious obligation to provide food for them at Purim and Passover. Instead, money was given to the rabbi, who then distributed it to poor Jews in Brooklyn and Israel.[43]

The second edition of Sklare's *Conservative Judaism* reflected the new importance of Orthodoxy. There was no talk of Orthodoxy's "institutional decay" as there had been in the first edition. Instead, Sklare now spoke of "the renaissance of American Orthodoxy." "Unaccountably, Orthodoxy has refused to assume the role of invalid," Sklare wrote. "Rather, it has transformed itself into a growing force in American Jewish life. It has reasserted its claim of being *the* authentic interpretation of Judaism." And far from being a religion of the poor and immigrant, Orthodoxy had even relocated to "upper-class and upper-middle-class areas." Orthodoxy, Sklare concluded, had repealed "the laws of religious gravity."[44]

By the 1970s, Conservative leaders clearly recognized the challenge of modern Orthodoxy. No longer could they assume that Orthodoxy was an American anachronism. While there was not a significant growth in the number of those identifying themselves as Orthodox, the hemorrhaging within Orthodoxy had been reduced, and the Orthodox birth rate was considerably higher than the non-Orthodox. Louis Bernstein, an Orthodox rabbi, described the Orthodox birth rate as "the only positive population factor on the American Jewish scene."[45]

In addition, the prestige of Orthodoxy had risen, and the number of those described as "card-carrying" Orthodox, as distinguished from the "fellow-traveling" Orthodox, increased. "To be Orthodox," wrote Stuart E. Rosenberg, was "no longer regarded as 'un-American.'" Some Conservative rabbis felt the challenge of Orthodoxy most directly in the contrast between their sparsely attended services and the larger attendance at Orthodox congregations. Traditionalist Conservative Jews often joined the modern Orthodox synagogues springing up in suburbia, leaving Conservative congregations with just a handful of the ritually devout. Conservative leaders also realized that some of the Orthodox viewed them with condescension, if not contempt, for the many compromises they had made with Jewish law and ritual.[46]

The media became interested in an Orthodoxy that refused to die. The *New York Times Magazine* (30 September 1984) ran an article entitled "American Jews Rediscover Orthodoxy," *New York* magazine (17 November 1986) published one called "The New Orthodox," and Channel 13 in New York City presented a half-hour show describing the courting and marriage of a newly Orthodox young couple. The *New Yorker* even published in the mid-1980s a lengthy three-part series on the Lubavitch Hasidim of Brooklyn. Far from being anachronisms, the Orthodox were now viewed as the guardians of Judaism and participants in a vibrant religious tradition. The non-Orthodox tended to admire them for their intense Jewish commitment and for the warmth and vitality of their communities.

The non-Orthodox also had to deal with a more assertive Orthodoxy in communal matters, particularly in the allocation of communal funds. As they became more affluent, Orthodox Jews played a larger role in communal organizations, such as the local federations and the United Jewish Appeal. In order to attract the Orthodox to their banquets, these organizations began using kosher caterers. Orthodoxy, Conservative rabbi Mordecai Waxman wrote, had "finally come to grips with the American scene," and now had a laity and a rabbinate capable of assuming major roles in Jewish organizational life.[47]

Despite their confidence that the future of American Judaism belonged to them, the Orthodox were not without problems of their own. The most important of these was an incessant divisiveness. The spirit of triumphalism within Orthodoxy increased the importance of the intra-Orthodox competition over who represented the faithful. The Orthodox were constantly looking over their right shoulder, fearful that someone might challenge their religiosity. Just as modern Orthodoxy assailed Conservative Judaism for its compromises, so yeshiva leaders attacked modern Orthodoxy for its concessions to modernity and its refusal to isolate itself from modern culture. Only the complete immersion in Torah, the yeshivas avowed, could ensure that undiluted Orthodoxy would be passed on to future generations.

The term *modern Orthodoxy* itself was used by the traditionalists in a derogatory manner to describe the more acculturated Orthodox. The implication was that they were outside the authentic Orthodox mainstream of "Torah-true" Judaism. Recognizing that *modern Orthodoxy* often had a negative connotation, its spokesmen preferred to describe themselves as *Centrist Orthodox*. But, as Rabbi Walter Wurzberger lamented, "the mere fact that the term 'Modern Orthodoxy' is no longer in vogue and has been replaced by an expression that deliberately avoids any reference to modernity speaks volumes" about the rightward drift of American Orthodoxy.[48]

For the modern Orthodox, their differences with the sectarian Orthodox involved more than merely the interpretation of Jewish tradition. It was also a conflict between different stages in the process of Americanization. While the modern Orthodox "thought Yiddish but dressed British," the sectarian Orthodox tended to wear distinctive clothing—black suits, white shirts, and black hats. Although financially successful and acculturated, the modern Orthodox were still afflicted with that most Jewish of all conditions—guilt. The sectarian Orthodox were a constant reminder to them of the extent to which they had deviated from Torah-true Judaism. Hypocrisy—defined by Duc de la Rochefoucauld as the tribute that vice pays to virtue—characterized modern Orthodoxy. The constitution of the modern Orthodox synagogue of West Orange, for example, stated that the congregation must follow the *Shulhan Arukh,* the code of Jewish law compiled by Joseph Caro in the sixteenth century. This, however, was not taken seriously since its observance would have entailed too sharp a break with modernity and would have violated the community's fragile religious consensus. Thus children in diapers were allowed in the sanctuary, despite the fact that this violated Jewish law.

During the 1970s and 1980s the Orthodox consensus moved steadily to the right because of the pressure from the sectarian Orthodox. The most common congregational manifestation of this rightward drift within modern Orthodoxy concerned the height and configuration of the *mehitzah,* the barrier separating men and women during prayer. Controversies over mehitzahs erupted in modern Orthodox congregations throughout America. This was not fortuitous. With Conservatism eliminating all restrictions on women participating in services, maintaining and even raising the height of the mehitzah was a relatively painless way for the modern Orthodox to demonstrate their fidelity to Jewish tradition and to engage in religious one-upmanship without fundamentally changing their life-style. The fact that the issue of the mehitzah was often symbolic did not detract from the intensity with which it was debated. Breakaway congregations were even established by dissident elements unable to convince their synagogues to change their mehitzahs.[49]

The divisiveness within Orthodoxy was most clearly seen in the conflict between the sectarian Orthodoxy of the yeshivas and the centrist Orthodoxy of Yeshiva University, the most prominent institution of modern Orthodoxy. Since the establishment of Yeshiva College in the 1920s, Yeshiva University's educational goal has been the synthesizing of Judaism and the best of Western civilization. In contrast to the yeshivas, the university did not disdain the study of modern science, literature, political thought, and history. It sought to prepare its students for productive careers in the mainstream of academia, the professions, and business. Samuel Belkin, the president of Yeshiva University, denied that "integration in the American community in any way implies the abrogation of even one iota of our sacred tradition. More than two generations of our people have been lost to us because of the erroneous belief that there exists a serious conflict between our spiritual heritage and the American way of life, which is itself deeply rooted in Hebraic spiritual values." Yeshiva University's motto was "Torah U-mada"—Torah and secular knowledge.[50]

From its very beginning, right-wingers, some of whom even taught in the university's own rabbinical seminary division, have accused Yeshiva University of building a modern university at the expense of the study of Torah. These critics argued that the university's emphasis on synthesis was a cloak for compromise and secularism. There are, after all, only so many hours in the day, and every hour spent reading Milton is one less hour that can be devoted to the Talmud. From the perspective of the Orthodox Right, a Jewish university was a contradiction in terms. A post–high school Jewish school that did not devote itself to the exclusive study of the Talmud did not deserve to be called Jewish, and an institution for the study of the Talmud was a yeshiva and not a university.

The Orthodox Right did not believe Yeshiva University's philosophy of synthesis was possible. In crucial areas, Orthodoxy and Western civilization were simply incompatible. Furthermore, they feared that an immersion in a university atmosphere would result in assimilation. The heads of yeshivas sanctioned higher education only if done for purely vocational purposes, and only if it did not interfere with the study of the Talmud. By the 1970s there were approximately ten thousand men studying the Talmud in yeshivas in the United States. Many attended college, but generally at night and usually in vocationally oriented programs such as computer science and accounting.[51]

Besides differing in their approaches to higher education, right-wing and centrist Orthodoxy differed over the proper stance toward Reform and Conservatism. For the Orthodox Right, these movements were abominations and their rabbis were frauds. The sectarian Orthodox disdained any official contacts with the non-Orthodox out of fear of granting them legitimacy, and they warned their followers not to set foot in non-Orthodox synagogues. In 1945, a group of Orthodox rabbis publicly burned Mordecai Kaplan's *Sabbath Prayer Book,* a decade after the Nazis had begun their burning of Jewish books. Ten years later, Aaron Kotler, Moshe Feinstein, and nine other prominent right-wing rabbis forbade cooperation with the Synagogue Council of America, the New York Board of Rabbis, and other organizations containing non-Orthodox rabbis. Feinstein even declared that the blessing of a non-Orthodox rabbi was not a true blessing and that it was forbidden to honor these heretics by inviting them to recite a blessing. He also stated that religious divorces were not required to end marriages performed by these so-called rabbis since they were not true Jewish marriages to begin with.

The modern Orthodox, in contrast, were more open-minded. "Centrist Orthodoxy holds that one must indeed disagree with the non-Orthodox," Norman Lamm, president of Yeshiva University, said in 1988, "but we must do so respectfully. That means lowering the temperature of the polemical rhetoric, acknowledging that they are valid groupings, and, indeed, in granting that if they are sincere in their convictions, they possess spiritual dignity." In his grudging toleration of the non-Orthodox, Lamm was careful to distinguish between spiritual dignity and spiritual truth. The graduates of Yeshiva University reflected this ecumenical outlook. They were, Liebman wrote, "church-oriented, communally involved, and very much aware of the necessity for compromise."[52]

By the 1980s, the attacks from the Right had weakened the morale of the modern Orthodox. Modern Orthodox leaders now spoke of a crisis of confidence and a failure of nerve within centrist Orthodoxy. A modified version of Gresham's law seemed to be operating within Orthodoxy. Fanaticism and authoritarianism were driving out conciliation and tolerance. Increasingly, the Right was defining the terms and context of religious discourse within Orthodoxy both in America and Israel. Centrist Orthodoxy seemed to be sharing the fate common to all moderate movements— the difficulty of creating a deeply committed following. Extremist movements are better at attracting what philosopher Eric Hoffer called "the true believer."

The most intriguing question confronting students of American Orthodoxy concerned the reasons for its postwar resurgence. Observers of the Jewish scene emphasized that its growth was due to general as well as specifically Jewish factors. As was true of other Americans, some Jews turned to religion as an answer to the problems engendered by an increasingly mobile and consumption-oriented society. Orthodoxy also benefited from the immigration of hundreds of thousands of Jews from Europe during the 1930s and late 1940s. Many were militantly Orthodox, and their numbers included prominent rabbis. Even Holocaust survivors who were not themselves devout identified with Orthodoxy. For them, Orthodoxy was an integral part of the Jewish culture that Hitler had sought to destroy, and perpetuating Orthodoxy became a sacred obligation.

Orthodoxy also benefited from the growing tendency to define Jewishness in religious and not in ethnic terms. If Judaism was a religion, and if the Orthodox were the most religious, then Orthodoxy was the most authentic form of Judaism. In the final analysis, the most appealing aspect of Orthodoxy was not its theology but its practice. Outsiders were generally drawn to Orthodoxy not because they were convinced that God had handed down the oral and written law to Moses on Mount Sinai, but because of the vigor of Orthodox communities and the lower rates of drug addiction, delinquency, and divorce among the Orthodox.

By the 1980s, the fastest-growing segment of American Judaism was neither Orthodoxy or Conservatism but Reform. After 1945, the leaders of the Reform movement had embarked upon an aggressive campaign to eliminate its elitist image and to increase the number of its member families. Prior to World War II the center of the Reform movement had been Cincinnati. In 1948, the Union of American Hebrew Congregations decided to move from Cincinnati to New York City, and two years later Hebrew Union College merged with Stephen S. Wise's Jewish Institute of Religion to create a New York campus. Defending the move of the UAHC to New York, Rabbi Maurice N. Eisendrath, the UAHC's executive director, declared that Reform leaders "must come out of our provincial shell and accept this challenge rather than . . . leave these masses, by our default, to others who do dwell closer to them."[53]

In contrast to Conservatism, its major competitor, there was no disagreement between the tenets of the Reform movement and the deportment of its members regarding Jewish law. Neither believed it to be authoritative. In fact, one 1972 survey revealed that only 10 percent of Reform rabbis even believed in a personal God. For the overwhelming majority of American Jews who were nonobservant and secular, Reform was an attractive option that placed few obstacles in the way of their upward social and economic mobility. Many members of Reform congregations had attended Conservative synagogues in their youth. Their decision to affiliate with Reform was logical in view of their own religious behavior.[54]

Reform's freedom from the restraints of Jewish law enabled it to respond to feminist demands that gender distinctions within Judaism be eliminated. The Hebrew Union College—the Reform seminary in Cincinnati—graduated its first female rabbi in 1972. The feminist movement did not split Reform as it did Conservatism. The Reform movement had for a long time accepted the principle of sexual equality within the synagogue and had counted women for a religious quorum since the nineteenth century.

The most controversial postwar manifestation of Reform's latitudinarian attitude toward Jewish law and tradition was its 1983 decision to recognize as Jews the offspring of Jewish fathers and Gentile mothers. Conservative and Orthodox spokesmen had not strenuously objected to the ordination of female Reform rabbis, viewing it as an internal matter of the Reform movement. They did, however, strongly protest the patrilineal decision because of its potential impact on Jewish unity. Since the codification of Jewish law two thousand years ago, a person had been considered Jewish only if his mother was Jewish or if he had undergone a traditional conversion. With the patrilineal decision, the Reform movement accepted as Jews persons whom Orthodoxy and Conservatism denied were Jewish. This meant that non-Reform Jews could never be sure that potential spouses were in fact Jewish. It also meant that the right of Reform Jews to immigrate to Israel under the Law of Return might be challenged since the Israeli government accepted the traditional definition of Jewish identity. The Israeli rabbinate accepted conversions to Judaism only if performed by Orthodox rabbis. Even some Reform leaders, disturbed by the implications of the patrilineal decision, urged caution.

In areas other than gender and personal status, however, the Reform movement adopted a more traditional stance after World War II. It published a manual for Sabbath observance and a book titled *Gates of Mitzvah* (1979), which discusses some of the religious commandments mandated by Jewish law. The mitzvah, the book asserted, "is the key to authentic Jewish existence and to the sanctification of life." *Gates of Mitzvah* was a sharp break with Reform's traditional attitude toward the mitzvot, which emphasized ethical rather than ritual commandments. It saw the mitzvot, including the dietary prohibitions, as a catalyst of ethical impulses. In 1975, the Reform movement came out with *Sha'are Tefilah* (Gates of Prayer) to replace the *Union Prayer Book*. *Sha'are Tefilah* had more Hebrew, contained a prayer for Israel's Independence Day, and included references to the destruction of the Temple in Jerusalem by the Romans some two thousand years ago. Such books probably would not have been published with a Reform imprimatur before World War II. In addition, some Reform congregations encouraged the wearing of skullcaps and prayer shawls during services, practices that the nineteenth-century founders of Reform had rejected. This tentative turn to tradition also manifested itself in the growing popularity of religious circumcisions, the Bar and Bat Mitzvah ceremony, and weddings with canopies and other traditional elements. Students at Hebrew Union College encouraged this emphasis on tradition. They successfully pressured the college to change the name of the chapels at its Los Angeles and New York branches to "synagogue."[55]

This new traditionalism resulted partially from the belief that the Reform ideology of the nineteenth and early twentieth centuries was irrelevant in a post-Holocaust era. Classical Reform had rejected those elements in Judaism, such as the dietary laws and the Sabbath restrictions, that could not be justified on the basis of reason and science. It had dismissed Zionism and other elements of Jewish life that hindered the full integration of Jews into their host societies and had stressed the ethical and rational components of Judaism at the expense of the emotional and ritualistic.

Nothing challenged Reform's faith in rationality, progress, and science more than the Holocaust, which had demonstrated the demonic side of human nature. The Holocaust had also demonstrated that the Zionists were correct in arguing that, in an era of virulent nationalism, Jews must have a land of their own. The murder of European Jewry and the establishment of the state of Israel in 1948 help explain the emergence of what was termed neo-Reform. In contrast to classical Reform, neo-Reform emphasized Jewish peoplehood. As early as the 1930s, neo-Reform spokesmen were stressing the ethnic as well as the religious component of Jewish identity and enthusiastically supporting a Jewish homeland in Palestine. Their numbers increased after the war.

In 1963, Hebrew Union College established a branch in Jerusalem, and beginning in 1970 each rabbinical student had to spend a year studying in Israel. In 1968, one year after the Six-Day War, the World Union of Progressive Judaism, for the first time in its history, held its international convention in Jerusalem, and five years later the headquarters of the union itself relocated to Jerusalem. The Reform movement also established two Reform kibbutzim in Israel, created the Association of Reform Zionists of America in 1977, encouraged Reform Jews who were so inclined to settle in the Jewish state, and made Israel Independence Day a holiday on the Reform calendar.[56]

This Zionization of Reform resulted in the use of more Hebrew in religious services and greater emphasis on Hebrew in its religious schools. The Sephardic pronunciation used in the Reform liturgy and taught in its schools was the same as that in Israel. Reform also introduced Hebrew singing and Israeli dancing into the curriculum of its schools. The statement of principles adopted by the American Reform movement in 1976 clearly revealed the influence of Israel. The one-thousand-word San Francisco

Platform emphasized the importance of Israel and Hebrew as well as Judaism in shaping Jewish identity. Reform Jews, it declared, "have both a stake and a responsibility in building the State of Israel, assuring its security, and defining its Jewish character."[57]

The realization that people did not live by reason alone led to a new emphasis within the Reform movement on those aspects of Judaism that defined Jews as a people—their history, customs, emotions, and traditions. Reform Jews, one Reform rabbi declared, were rediscovering "the warmth and meaning of Jewish tradition," which had been obliterated by the austerity of classical Reform. Rabbi Samuel Freehof attempted to assimilate Jewish tradition into Reform by publishing a series of volumes of Reform responsa, including *Recent Reform Responsa* (1963) and *Reform Responsa for Our Time* (1977). Even more surprising for a movement that had always vigorously championed the public school system was its support for Reform day schools. By 1981, nine such schools had been established.[58]

On the surface at least, the Reform movement appeared to be vigorous. The number of Reform congregations had grown rapidly (from 300 in 1943 to 656 in 1964), and most of these new congregations were located in the burgeoning suburbs. Its youth movement—the National Federation of Temple Youth—was larger than its Orthodox and Conservative counterparts, Hebrew Union College was flourishing, and Reform Judaism had a growing presence in Israel. The flow of Jewish population from the snowbelt to the sunbelt was from areas where Orthodoxy and Conservatism were strong to regions where Reform was dominant. Reform Judaism increasingly was becoming the denomination of choice for American Jews. Reform, one spokesman claimed, "represents for most Jews the authentically American expression of Judaism."[59]

Not all Reform leaders, however, were so optimistic about their movement's future. They bemoaned the high intermarriage rate, the low synagogue attendance, and the widespread indifference to Judaism and to the synagogue on the part of the Reform laity. The only thing that distinguished many self-styled Reform Jews as Reform was paying dues to a Reform congregation. They could just as easily be members of a Conservative synagogue, as many of them had been. They identified with Reform for social reasons or for the welfare of their children. They did not identify with Reform because they were attracted to any distinctive theology or program.[60]

Part of this Reform malaise also stemmed from growing doubts within the movement regarding its strain of prophetic Judaism. The traditional liberal political agenda of Reform resonated less strongly after 1970. Fewer supported the movement's official positions regarding race relations, the economy, and foreign affairs. Onlookers wondered what could give Reform a sense of purpose if it should lose its raison d'être of social action. A survey of the Reform rabbinate released in 1972 presented some disturbing conclusions. It revealed that nearly two-thirds of the rabbis wished to move closer to Conservative Judaism, while nearly 30 percent wanted to move in the direction of religious humanism. Reform Judaism itself seemed to have little appeal for its pulpit practitioners.[61]

One of the more somber of the Reform leaders was Daniel Jeremy Silver, who had succeeded his father, Abba Hillel Silver, as rabbi of a large and prestigious Reform congregation in Cleveland. Silver believed that Reform was facing a crisis stemming from the movement's lack of intellectual coherence. Reform, he argued in 1984, had became a "theological smorgasbord," a "movement without a message." It needed to be transformed from "a community of fate into a community of faith." This, of course, could also be said of Conservatism. Silver's lament was understandable coming as it did from a man who had written several significant works in Jewish theology.

It is doubtful, however, that the largely irreligious Reform laity would respond to Silver's call for a renewal of "religious obligation." For them the appeal of Reform was institutional rather than theological or ideological. They might have hungered for community, but there was no indication that they were prepared for a life of spiritual commitment and discipline. In this respect, they were typical of American Jewry, for whom being Jewish was a matter of identifying experientially with the Jewish people and not of observing ritual or Jewish tradition.[62]

CHAPTER SEVEN

FROM CULTURE TO CAUSES

THE declining Jewish immigration after 1945—combined with the diminution of anti-Semitism, the growing acceptance of Judaism as a legitimate aspect of the American cultural and religious landscape, and the social and economic mobility of American Jews—transformed the nature of American Jewish identity. For those born and raised in tightly segregated Jewish communities in central and eastern Europe (or in North Africa and the Middle East), being Jewish was almost as natural as breathing. They spoke and read Yiddish (or Ladino), they ate distinctive foods, and they felt more comfortable within a Jewish ambience. Even those immigrants most estranged from Judaism and the Jewish community were generally products of an intensely European Jewish culture.

This was not true, however, of their children and grandchildren, who had been shaped by the American culture they had learned about in school, in the street, on the playground, or from the media. The American-born did not speak Yiddish, avoided European-style Orthodox synagogues, were not attracted to the working-class world of Yiddish socialism, and had only a passing acquaintance with Hebrew and Yiddish writers and thinkers. Their relationship with the Jewish world of their ancestors was largely nostalgic. They flocked to the musical show *Fiddler on the Roof* and made Irving Howe's *World of Our Fathers* (1976) a best-seller. Howe believed the popularity of his book stemmed from the readiness of Jews "to say farewell in a last fond gesture . . . an affectionate glance at the world of their fathers before turning their backs forever and moving on, as they had to." They had been raised as Americans and had no desire to remain within isolated Jewish ethnic and religious enclaves. Often there was little, culturally, to distinguish them from non-Jews.[1]

This was particularly evident among Jewish intellectuals, who prided themselves on their freedom from parochial ethnic and religious loyalties. Jewish intellectuals—Daniel Bell, Nathan Glazer, Irving Howe, Sidney Hook, Alfred Kazin, Irving Kristol, William Phillips, Norman Podhoretz, Harold Rosenberg, Meyer Schapiro, and Lionel Trilling—and their magazines—*Commentary, Partisan Review,* and the *New York Review of Books*—assumed in postwar America a preeminent position among the American intelligentsia. Controversies involving the meaning of literary modernism, socialism, and neoconservatism that wracked American intellectual circles were essentially intramural debates within what Podhoretz called "the family," the circle of second-generation Jews who dominated New York intellectual life after the war.

One of the reasons for the important position of those who came to be known as the New York intellectuals was the fact that—as Jews, intellectuals, and New Yorkers—they lived on the margins of American and American Jewish cultures. As historian Terry A. Cooney wrote, it was precisely the Jewishness of New York intellectuals that provided them with "a double exile that promised exceptional insight." The New York intellectuals rejected the "particularisms of nationality, race, religion, or philosophy, and they celebrated richness, complexity, and diversity." Their "cosmopolitanism was by nature suspicious of dogma and quick to lash out against the narrowing of cultural possibilities." This emphasis on the relationship between Jewish creativity and marginality and alienation was not original. Sociologists and economists such as Robert A. Park and Thorstein Veblen had previously said much the same thing, but they had written before Jewish intellectuals had assumed such an important role in American culture.[2]

The New York intellectuals themselves stressed their alienation from the parochial world of their parents and their indifference to Jewish concerns. In 1944, at the nadir of the Holocaust, Isaac Rosenfeld declared that being Jewish "should occupy no more of a man's attention than any ordinary fact of his history." In his autobiography, fittingly entitled *A Margin of Hope,* Irving Howe remembered the estrangement from Jewish concerns that young Jewish radicals such as himself felt during the early 1940s. Jewishness, he remarked, "was not regarded as a major component of the culture I wanted to make my own, and I felt no particular responsibility for its survival or renewal. It was simply *there*. While it would be shameful to deny its presence or seek to flee its stigma, my friends and I could hardly be said to have thought Jewishness could do much for us or we for it." He was, he wrote, excited then by "the idea of breaking away, of willing a new life." American literature provided the precocious and ambitious Howe entry into a culture of infinite possibilities. How could life in the East Bronx compete with Melville's search for the great white whale, the excitements of radical politics, or the glories of William Faulkner and Sherwood Anderson?[3]

The flight of these intensely American intellectuals from Jewishness was not particularly traumatic. There had been little in their homes or schooling to convince them that Jewish culture was worth preserving in America. They had received a brief Jewish education in dreary heders where, Sidney Hook wrote, "Judaism seemed mainly a mass of superstitions taught by tyrannical old men who brooked no contradiction or honest doubt." These schools and their parents represented a world that the intellectuals desperately sought to escape. "The day my father died," Howe recalled, "I felt almost nothing. . . . I knew myself to be unworthy, a son with a chilled heart." As was true of most immigrant Jewish families of the twentieth century, the parents of the New York intellectuals were intensely Jewish in an ethnic sense but were poorly educated, not particularly religious, and consumed with hopes of escape from poverty. Kazin's father was radical and irreligious, and Howe's father was "hardly pious." "Sometimes the family was about all that was left of Jewishness," Howe remembered, "or, more accurately, all that we had left of Jewishness had come to rest in the family." The parents of the neophyte agnostic Sidney Hook convinced him to go through with his Bar Mitzvah ceremony not by appealing to tradition or by demonstrating the truths of Judaism, but by pleading with him not to embarrass them before their relatives and neighbors.[4]

But not even the seemingly estranged and deracinated New York intellectuals were able to sever their ties to Jewish memory and concern. Howe's autobiography contained a chapter entitled "Jewish Quandaries," which noted that what the New York intellectuals felt regarding Jewishness "was rarely quite in accord with what we wrote or thought. . . . This was a kind of culture lag, recognition behind reality." Even the most emancipated and cosmopolitan were reluctant to reject their Jewish background in toto and, even if they could, World War II did not allow them that luxury. As Norman Podhoretz remarked, the Holocaust had demonstrated "the inescapability of Jewishness." The Alfred Kazin who had revolted against "sentimental chauvinism" would later describe in *New York Jew,* one of the volumes of his autobiography, how the Holocaust became the consuming event of his life. "In my private history of the world I took down every morsel of fact and rumor relating to the murder of my people. . . . The line-up was always before my eyes. I could imagine my father and mother, my sister and myself . . . fuel for the flames, dying by a single flame that burned us all up at once." *New York Jew* also contains a moving description of Kazin's trip to Israel after the Six-Day War.[5]

Howe also was unable to free himself from his past. The Holocaust affected him in the same way it had Kazin. It was, he wrote, "the most terrible moment in human history." Howe rejected attempts to universalize the Holocaust. The murder of European Jewry, he emphasized, was first and foremost a Jewish tragedy, "the culminating ordeal in the sequence of ordeals which comprises the experience of the Jewish people. One's first response—not the sole response, but the first—had to be a cry of Jewish grief." As a result of the Jewish catastrophe, Howe began reflecting on what it meant to be Jewish in America.[6]

Howe admitted that a concern with Jewish suffering "wasn't, of course, a very forthright way of confronting my own troubled sense of Jewishness, but that was the way I took." Jewishness, he realized, had always been an integral part of his life. An advocate of secular Jewishness, Howe now described himself as a "partial Jew." Unsympathetic toward either Judaism or Zionism, his Jewish identity existed in "a state of prolonged interregnum, between the denied authority of total faith and the sterile prospects of assimilation." Howe's road back to Jewishness had arrived at "a historical end," but "there, at ease or not," he chose to remain. Along the way he had edited several volumes of Yiddish literature and wrote *World of Our Fathers,* his prize-winning elegy to the left-wing working-class culture of his parents' generation.[7]

Howe's situation was not unique. Feeling Jewish, the Jewish intellectuals were unable to define precisely what that involved. The acrimonious debate over Hannah Arendt's *Eichmann in Jerusalem: A Report on the Banality of Evil* (1965) played a major role in their evolving Jewish consciousness. Her emphasis on the "banality of evil" and on Jewish passivity in the face of barbarism was extremely troubling. It forced the intellectuals to consider the extent to which the culture of Europe's Jews had facilitated their own slaughter, and whether American Jewry had done enough to rescue European Jewry. The passions aroused in the intellectuals, Howe wrote, were "overwhelming. I cannot think of anything since then that harassed me as much except perhaps the Vietnam War. You might say that it was a tacit recompense for our previous failure to respond."[8]

Despite the fact that the New York intellectuals were not sympathetic to Jewish nationalism, they looked to Israel to bolster their fragile sense of Jewishness. In an act that amazed his friends, the childless Philip Rahv bequeathed his estate to Israel upon his death in 1973, two months after the Yom Kippur War. During the 1970s and 1980s, Howe wrote brooding essays from a non-Zionist and leftist perspective on Israeli politics and society. Hook, in contrast, supported the 1982 Israeli invasion of Lebanon, attacked elements within the media for criticizing Israel, and blamed the Palestine Liberation Organization and not Israel for the turmoil in the Middle East.

Hook's support for Israel was particularly noteworthy: in the 1930s and 1940s, he had been too good a socialist to support Zionism. "Having transcended American nationalism by our allegiance to a universalist ideal, in which all men were brothers, we were not going to settle for a more parochial national ideal," Hook recalled. "The Jewish problem—and we all knew what that was—would be solved when the economically classless society of the future was established." For him, the essence of American Jewish identity lay not in nationality, language, custom, literature, religion, or history, but in the affinity of American Jews for democratic, secular, and egalitarian values. "As I interpret Jewish culture," he wrote before the war, "its noblest traditions have fused passion for social justice with respect for scientific method and knowledge. When Jews forsake this method, they forsake a precious part of their tradition." Socialism, he said, was the most acceptable social philosophy for Jews since it alone wedded "the ideals of the good life in the good society to the methods of intelligent analysis and action." After the war, Hook favored a binational state in Palestine and warned American Jews not to become intoxicated by Israel's military victories during its War of Independence. "A people that has, by and large, been rational and pacific," he lamented, now sought through militarism, ultranationalism, and "the *mystique* of action . . . to prove that they are like everyone else—inconsistent, fanatical, atavistic."[9]

After 1945, Hook and other American Jewish intellectuals were less likely to give credence to the anti-Zionist bugaboo of dual loyalty. Columnist Dorothy Thompson made precisely that accusation in a 1950 *Commentary* essay titled "America Demands a Single Loyalty." She was answered in the same magazine by Harvard historian Oscar Handlin. "America Recognizes Diverse Loyalties" did not take the traditional tack of denying that Jews had dual loyalties. Rather, it rejected the assumption that American nationality involved a "rigorous tribalism." Handlin reassured American Jews that their support of Israel did not imply disloyalty to America. Jews were simply one of many American ethnic groups concerned with the security and prosperity of other countries. This was not the eccentric thinking of unassimilated aliens but "the normal outcome of the freedom of group life in a democracy." Multiple loyalty was not a problem because America's concept of nationality was "broad and expansive" and did not demand that its citizens love only the United States.[10]

The most surprising fact about the second and third generations—intellectuals as well as nonintellectuals—was that, despite their acculturation, most continued to identify as Jews. Their understanding of what Jewishness involved was, however, far thinner than that of the immigrants. For them, Jewish identity was not cultural but primarily associational. In *Assimilation in American Life* (1964), Milton M. Gordon argued that in this "distinction between cultural behavior and social structure lies one of the major keys to the understanding of what the assimilation process has actually been like in the American experience." This was perhaps more true of Gordon's fellow Jews than of any other ethnic group. Jews joined Jewish organizations, contributed to the United Jewish Appeal and other Jewish causes, lived in Jewish neighborhoods, sent their children to Jewish schools and summer camps, and had Jewish friends. Not only did they feel more comfortable with Jews, but associational Jewishness was the best way, and for some the only way, they knew of assuring Jewish continuity.[11]

The social transformation of American Jewry modified the nature of Jewish identity. The immigrant generation for whom Jewish identity was primarily cultural was replaced by American-born Jews who defined Jewish identity primarily in political and philanthropic terms. They perceived American Jewry not to be a distinct cultural entity but an interest group with distinctive claims that Jews were obligated to defend. Reversing the advice of nineteenth-century German Jewish leaders to be Germans on the street and Jews at home, American Jews were Americans at home and Jews in the street. As Leonard Fein argued, "The core method of Judaism is community. Ours is not a personal testament, but a collective and public commitment. . . . What defines the Jews *as Jews* is community; not values, not ideology." One was Jewish not because of theological categories but because one chose to identify as a Jew and to affiliate with other Jews. This new view of Jewish identity affected the role of rabbis. Congregations believed their rabbis' major function was to defend such Jewish interests as the security of the state of Israel and the struggle against anti-Semitism, not to be a source of Jewish learning.[12]

Of all American Jewish interests, none was more important in the postwar years than Israel. After 1967, support for Israel became the common denominator of American Jewish life, and no Jew who was not a staunch supporter of Israel could expect to occupy a responsible position in a major Jewish organization. Jewish leaders could be intermarried, but they could not question the legitimacy of Israel or be unduly critical of its foreign policy. Jews who attacked the Jewish state, such as members of the American Council for Judaism, risked ostracism from the Jewish community. Founded in 1943, the American Council for Judaism represented the views of those within Reform Judaism who had remained true to their movement's longstanding opposition to Zionism. Never a mass organization, the council limped along in the 1950s and 1960s until it became a casualty after the Six-Day War of 1967, when even its staunchest defenders finally realized that it no longer had a constituency.[13]

Even non-Zionist American Jewish organizations that had not been directly concerned with Israel attempted to benefit from the popularity of the Jewish state. They broadened their programming to include Israeli-oriented activities. The Conference of Presidents of Major Jewish Organizations even located its offices in the American headquarters of the Jewish Agency for Israel on Park Avenue in New York City. "Insuring the survival of Israel has become the heart of the defense function of the American Jewish community," Daniel J. Elazar wrote in 1974. "Even the community-relations agencies are now spending a high proportion of their time and resources trying to increase support for Israel in the United States. As a result, the most important decision makers in the community are those who are related to the defense of Israel, namely the federation and UJA leadership, voluntary and professional." Hadassah, the women's branch of the American Zionist Organization, became the largest Jewish organization in the United States. Its membership was several times larger than that of the National Organization for Women.[14]

So intense was the involvement of Jews with Israel that some sociologists argued that the real religion of most American Jews was "Israelism." Israel, Charles S. Liebman wrote in 1973, "provides the major symbolic content for the American Jewish religion today." Elazar agreed. "Even the most peripheral of American Jews are touched by the Jewish authenticity of

Israel, while the more committed find the power of Israel . . . almost irresistible." This was substantiated by polls taken in the 1980s that revealed that over 80 percent of American Jews would consider the destruction of Israel as the "greatest personal tragedy in their lives." This support remained constant despite the Israeli invasion of Lebanon, the struggle between the Orthodox rabbinate and non-Orthodox elements regarding the definition of "who is a Jew," and Israel's response to the *intifada,* the revolt of the Arabs living in occupied territory. Israel became the major component of American Jewish identity, influencing all aspects of Jewish life, including Judaism.[15]

On Yom Kippur, the most important day of the Jewish calender, when more American Jews were at prayer than at any other time of the year, appeals were made in synagogues throughout the country for the purchase of Israeli bonds. In the modern American version of Yom Kippur, personal atonement for one's sins was linked to a financial commitment to the well-being of the Jewish state. Most synagogues also had gift shops in which the most popular items were Israeli-made items for the home. Synagogue Hebrew schools taught Israeli dances and songs and attempted to inculcate in their students a close identification with Israel. American Jewry's romance with Israel was responsible for the large number of American Jewish tourists who visited Israel after 1967. Visiting Israel was not an ordinary vacation. It resembled a pilgrimage in which American Jews identified themselves personally with the people and the land of Israel. This was particularly evident among American Jewish leaders. Their missions to Israel, Rabbi Arthur Hertzberg wrote, "are to be understood as part of a religious phenomenon, the modern equivalent of Hassidim traveling in exultation to see their rebbe and to spend some time in the uplifting precincts of his court."[16]

Israel resembled a screen upon which American Jews projected their most fervent dreams and aspirations; it became a panacea for relieving their anxieties and frustrations. Israel enabled the nonreligious to express their Jewish identity, although within a secular context. For some, Israelism became a surrogate for Judaism. For those secular Jews whose major affiliation with the Jewish community was through the various self-defense organizations such as the Anti-Defamation League, Israel was the most important reason for fighting anti-Semitism. The establishment of Israel was fortuitous because the decline of American anti-Semitism after 1945 deprived secular Jews of a domestic focus for their Jewish identity, and Israel gave them a reason for continuing to identify as Jews. Rightly or wrongly, they believed that critics of the Jewish state in America and elsewhere were motivated by anti-Semitism and not by considerations of realpolitik.[17]

Israel also provided American Jews with an outlet for expressing their patriotism. By describing Israel as the only democracy in the Middle East, as a barrier to the spread of Marxism, Soviet influence, and Moslem fundamentalism, and as a staunch ally of the United States, Jews asserted that American and Israeli interests were, if not identical, then at least similar. They also argued that Israel resembled the United States in its commitment to democracy, industrialization, technology, and modernization. Supporters of Israel turned the classic argument against Zionism—that it led to dual loyalties and prevented the full acceptance of Jews into the host society—on its head. For a Jew to be an American patriot, it was now argued, he must also be pro-Israel, since American national interests required a strong Israel.

Leftist Jews, although embarrassed by the role of Orthodoxy in Israel and critical of what they perceived to be expansionist, chauvinist, and militarist tendencies within the Jewish state, nevertheless praised the Israel of the 1950s and 1960s as the most successful example of a modern democratic and socialist state. A good example of the tendency of American Jews, including academicians, to see in Israel what they wanted to see was Irving Louis Horowitz's 1974 book *Israeli Ecstasies/Jewish Agonies*. Horowitz, a then-radical sociologist at Rutgers University, reassured "those of the younger generation possessing a radical persuasion" of Israel's radical credentials. He particularly wished to respond to those on the Left who accused Israel of being a bastion of Western imperialism and capitalism. Not only was Israel "dedicated to principles of social egalitarianism as well as to a higher degree of public ownership of basic means of production," Horowitz wrote, but it also shared with Third World countries "a deep and desperate sense of national autonomy and national liberation." Israel's natural home, he avowed, was actually within the Third World, and it was only because of its abnormal security needs that it had such close economic and military ties with the United States.[18]

Horowitz argued that Israel's character as a secular and socialistic state whose natural allies were the struggling nations of Asia and Africa was disguised by the artificial ties between the Jewish state and the affluent, bourgeois Jewish communities of the West. "It is more important," he wrote, "that a Uganda ruler opens up a legation in Jerusalem than that ninety conferences between American Jews and Israeli Jews are held in

Israel. The State needs legations more than conferences, needs Africans at least as much as Americans, needs support from poor nations no less than from wealthy Jews." Horowitz advised Israel to treat its Arab minority fairly, to eliminate all vestiges of the Orthodox religious establishment, and to remain faithful to the goals of its socialist founders. If these were not done, he said, "the unique place of Israel in the covenant of nations will become sheer myth, lost in the rubble of geographical determinism." Israel was also important, Horowitz avowed, because its example could strengthen the social concern and compassion that had traditionally characterized American Jewry. Thus he recommended closer ties between Israel and black Africa not only because it was good in and of itself, but also because it would strengthen "the ties between American Jews and American black people . . . to a considerable degree."[19]

Enthusiasm for the idea and reality of a Jewish state was widespread among American Jews after 1945. This had not always been the case. Prior to the 1930s, Zionism had little appeal for American Jews. They believed that they were already living in what Zionism hoped to create—a nation in which there would be no restrictions on the social, economic, and intellectual advancement of Jews. When American Jews referred to the golden land, they meant the United States, not Palestine. "The United States is our Palestine," Rabbi David Philipson asserted in 1895, "and Washington our Jerusalem." Evidently European Jews agreed. Between 1880 and 1920, for every one who migrated to the Promised Land, over forty crossed the Atlantic to the land of promise. American Jewish leaders feared that Zionism would lead to legitimate suspicions among Gentiles regarding the loyalty of America's Jews.[20]

The destruction of European Jewry combined with the refusal of the Western nations, particularly the United States, to do anything meaningful to rescue the remnants convinced American Jews that a Jewish state was necessary. The Zionism of American Jews was, however, sui generis. It did not encompass the most important element in Zionist ideology—aliyah. Despite the claim of Israeli Zionists that every Jew was obligated to relocate to Israel, less than 100,000 American Jews settled in Israel, and most of those who did eventually returned to the United States. More American Jews chose to be buried in Israel than to live there. Israeli spokesmen viewed this refusal of American Jews to leave the fleshpots of the West with a mingling of contempt and fear. It not only deprived the Jewish state of the large Jewish population that would guarantee its existence, but it also denied the fundamental tenet of Zionist ideology regarding the abnormality of Diaspora life once a Jewish state had been established. The result was, as Zionist Nahum Goldmann stated in 1954, that Israel was the only state in the world where 90 percent of its people lived outside its borders.[21]

For Israelis, American Zionism was refugeeism, not true Zionism. From the perspective of those who had been influenced by classical Zionism, American Zionism was an oxymoron. Abba Eban quipped that, after the establishment of Israel in 1948, American Zionism had demonstrated one of the great truths of religion—that there can be life after death. Israelis were convinced that, with the establishment of the Jewish state, America's Jews were living in exile and should move to Israel. American Jewish leaders feared that such talk cast doubts on their loyalty as American citizens. American Jews also objected to the Zionist claim that Jews could not survive as Jews in America because of anti-Semitism and assimilation and that their psyches were being maimed by living outside of Israel. For them, America was both a haven and a home.

In the late 1940s, the American Jewish Committee threatened to withdraw support for Israel if the Jewish state's leaders did not stop calling for a massive immigration of Jews from the United States to Israel. The issue came to a head in Jerusalem in August 1950 at a meeting between David Ben-Gurion, Israel's prime minister, and Jacob Blaustein, president of the AJC. Realizing the political importance of American Jews, Ben-Gurion backed down. He released a statement asserting that "the Jews of the United States, as a community and as individuals, have only one political attachment and that is to the United States of America. They owe no political allegiance to Israel. . . . The government and the people of Israel fully respect the right and integrity of the Jewish communities in other countries to develop their own mode of life and their indigenous social, economic and cultural institutions in accordance with their own needs and aspirations." Jacob Blaustein of the American Jewish Committee responded that "to American Jews, America is home. There, exist their thriving roots; there, is the country which they have helped to build; and there, they share its fruits and its destiny. They believe in the future of a democratic society in the United States under which all citizens . . . can live on terms of equality." While the American Jewish Committee won this round, Israel's leaders remained convinced that the place for America's Jews was in the Jewish state.[22]

American Jews did not believe that their reluctance to exchange Brooklyn for Jerusalem and Los Angeles for Tel Aviv meant that they were less than wholehearted champions of the Zionist undertaking. Reinterpreting Zionism, they preferred to view Israel as a refuge for persecuted Jews and not as a national homeland for all Jews. There was much truth to the joke that defined American Zionism as a movement in which one person gave money to a second person to send a third person to Israel. As Daniel Elazar noted, fund-raising for Israel had become "the most visible Jewish communal activity." This was especially noticeable after 1967. Even Jews who did not belong to synagogues or Jewish organizations contributed to the United Jewish Appeal. "I am because I give" became the existential definition of American Jewishness, and status within American Jewry depended to a large extent on one's annual gift to the United Jewish Appeal campaign.[23]

This was particularly true of the lay leadership of the Jewish federations and the United Jewish Appeal. Jonathan S. Woocher perceptively titled his examination of the ideology of these leaders *Sacred Survival: The Civil Religion of American Jews.* Few of these leaders were religious in a traditional sense, and their involvement in the federations and the UJA was for them a substitute religion. "What are sometimes referred to as secular activities, because they are not directly under synagogue auspices, are not only necessary, but they, too, are Torah, for they were born of and are informed and infused by our religious faith," one of these leaders declared. "Judaism as a religion has always been a social force—it is the application of timeless principles to timely problems." This civil religion had its own educational system (leadership development programs), annual rites (the fund-raising campaign), pilgrimages (missions to Israel), communal activities (fund-raising dinners and telethons), weekend retreats, and norms of behavior (acceptable financial commitments to the UJA). Civil Judaism, Woocher wrote, "is not essentially a Judaism of the home, the synagogue, and the school. . . . It is a Judaism of the historical-political arena, of an elaborated polity and of public activism. And, though it has no Temple, it does once again have a Jewish commonwealth to serve as its focal symbol."[24]

For American Jews, Zionism was a philanthropy, the most important of all Jewish philanthropies, and one to which they were tied largely by charitable contributions and by the purchase of bonds issued by the Israeli government. Jews voted with their wallets, if not with their feet, for Israel. Fund-raising became the most important barometer of the relationship between American Jews and the state of Israel. During his first term as

Israel's prime minister, Ben-Gurion made only one visit outside of Israel, and that was in May 1951 to the United States to launch the first Israel bonds campaign. Fund-raising in America for Israel increased during periods of crisis in the Middle East and subsided during times of quiet. Contributions to the United Jewish Appeal, the major fund-raising campaign for Israel, rose dramatically in the years prior to the establishment of Israel and in 1956, the year of the Sinai war between Israel and Egypt. Previous fund-raising efforts were dwarfed, however, by the contributions of Jews in 1967 to help pay for the Six-Day War.[25]

Nineteen sixty-seven was a watershed year in the history of American Jewry. While Jews had supported Israel from its founding in 1948, the depth of their emotional involvement with the Jewish state only became fully evident nineteen years later. Not even they themselves realized just how important Israel had been to them. There had been clues. One of these was the incredible popularity of *Exodus* (1958), Leon Uris's potboiler about the establishment of Israel. It sold more than twenty million copies in hardcover and paperback and was probably read by more Jews during the 1950s than any other book. Those Jews who did not read the novel saw the movie version by Otto Preminger. But not even the most astute observers of American Jewry were prepared for 1967. "American Jews, try as they may," Morris N. Kertzer wrote on the eve of the Six-Day War, "find difficulty in feeling the peoplehood of Israel, the mystical bond that unites them with their coreligionists outside the United States. . . . The boundaries of America are the limits of their creative Jewish concerns."[26]

Feelings toward Israel that had been suppressed or ignored by American Jews gushed forth because of the particular circumstances preceding the June 1967 Six-Day War. With Israel surrounded by Arab enemies threatening genocide, American Jewry faced the prospect of witnessing a Holocaust for the second time. For American Jewry, Israel had been a tragically belated and partial answer to Auschwitz. The establishment of the Jewish state meant that the martyrdom of the six million European Jews was not totally in vain and that Jewish history still had meaning. Should Israel be overrun by the Arabs, the psychological blow to American Jews would have been devastating.

They were determined to do whatever was possible to prevent it. Rabbi Arthur Hertzberg, writing two months after the war with its memories still fresh, noted that the crisis had united American Jews "with deep Jewish commitments as they have never been united before, and it has evoked such commitments in many Jews who previously seemed untouched by them. . . . There are no conventional Western theological terms with which to explain this," he said, "and most contemporary Jews experience these emotions without knowing how to define them. . . . Israel may . . . now be acting as a very strong focus of worldwide Jewish emotional loyalty and thereby as a preservative of a sense of Jewish identity."[27]

The response of American Jewry to the Six-Day War surprised even those most sanguine about the depth of American Jewish identity. In June 1967 alone, more than seventy-five hundred American Jews volunteered to take over the civilian jobs of Israelis serving in the armed forces. One man accompanied by his two sons approached an official of the Jewish Agency in New York on 5 June, the day the war broke out. "I have no money to give but here are my sons," he said. "Please send them over immediately." The outpouring of money by American Jews (and some Gentiles) to help Israel pay for the war was unprecedented in the history of Jewish and American philanthropy. In 1966, over $136 million had been pledged to the various Jewish community fund drives, and an article in *Fortune* magazine discussed "the miracle of Jewish giving." In 1967, the figure was $317 million: $15 million was raised in fifteen minutes at one luncheon, and over $100 million was raised in a month. Money came in faster than it could be tabulated; and donors, overcome by the urgency of the situation, often insisted on giving cash rather than checks. Numerous persons donated the cash-surrender value of life insurance policies. Contributions were made to the United Jewish Appeal in lieu of anniversary, birthday, graduation, Bar Mitzvah, and Father's Day gifts. Jewish youth organizations turned their treasuries over to the UJA. In Essex County, New Jersey, the golf course at a Jewish country club was closed on a Sunday morning so that a fund-raising meeting could take place, while in Washington, D.C., a Jewish belly dancer at an Arabic night club donated several nights' pay to the cause. The purchase of Israel bonds by Americans also increased, from $76 million in 1966 to $190 million in 1967.[28]

The reaction of American Jews to the Yom Kippur War of 1973 dwarfed their response to the Six-Day War, as once again American Jewry was engulfed by memories of World War II. American Jews were particularly angered by the fact that Egypt and her allies chose Yom Kippur, the most solemn day of the year, to launch a surprise attack. In 1973, in contrast to 1967, Israel was thrown on the defensive early in the war and faced a far more difficult economic and military situation than six years earlier. American Jews responded accordingly. This time over thirty thousand American Jews volunteered to work in Israel. $107 million was pledged to the UJA during the first week of the war, and a total of $675 million was pledged during the entire campaign. This included $1,000,000 raised by Jewish university students, three gifts of $5 million and forty gifts of $1 million or more.[29]

While the level of fund-raising of 1973 could not be sustained, the United Jewish Appeal continued to be one of America's most extraordinary philanthropies. It raised more money per year than the combined efforts of the American Heart Association, the American Cancer Society, the Muscular Dystrophy Association, the March of Dimes, and the National Easter Seal Society. Over half of American Jews contributed either to the UJA or to federation campaigns. And these gifts were supplemented by contributions to individual Israeli institutions such as the Technion, the Weizmann Institute, and Hebrew University, which ran separate fund-raising campaigns, and by the annual purchase of hundreds of millions of dollars of Israeli bonds. "Organized activity—often philanthropic in character," Daniel Elazar said, "has come to be the most common manifestation of Judaism, replacing prayer, study, and the normal private intercourse of kin as a source of being Jewish." The United Jewish Appeal even reached within the walls of Sing Sing. Rabbi Irving Koslowe, the Jewish chaplain at the prison, recounted the response of a member of the Collection Committee when asked to explain the fact that 100 percent of the Jewish inmates contributed. "Honestly, Rabbi, we didn't use any strong-arm tactics."[30]

There were Jews both in Israel and America critical of this "checkbook" Judaism. William Zuckerman argued that American Jewishness had degenerated into "campaign Judaism." American Jewry, Zuckerman said, "has almost consciously emptied itself of all higher aspirations and spiritual needs and has willingly limited itself to the role of a financial milk cow for others. . . . How can a community . . . whose highest ideal is mechanical fund-raising, be the source of nobility and greatness?" Writing checks might be a salve for the conscience of Jews who felt guilty that they were not better Jews, but they were no substitute for making aliyah, observing the Sabbath, and keeping kosher. While true, these complaints missed the point. People pay for those things they value, and the vast sums contributed in 1967 and 1973 demonstrated, as nothing else could demonstrate, the priority of many American Jews. They also illustrated how closely American Jews had tied their own fates to Israel.[31]

Israel made American Jews feel good. After World War II and the stories of Jews going to the slaughter like sheep, Israel had redeemed Jewish honor. Jews were now victors as well as victims. Ari Ben Canaan, the hero of *Exodus,* had little in common with the scholars and pietists of eastern Europe who had perished in the Holocaust. Nor did he have anything in common with the schlemiels in the films of Woody Allen and in the novels of Philip Roth. He was brave, tough, and familiar with warfare. One poster produced in the aftermath of the Six-Day War showed a Hasid in a telephone booth taking off his long black coat to reveal a Superman costume.

The new image of Super Jew resulted in a spate of novels such as *Black Sunday,* which pictured the Israelis as superspies and supercounterespionage agents. Paul Breines called these books "Rambowitz" novels. In one of these literary masterpieces, the hero is an Israeli who fights American neo-Nazis. He "wore a thin silver chain under an open khaki shirt, bush shorts, and lug-soled hiking boots. In his hand was a smoking Uzi automatic carbine." The plot of Harry Arvay's cheap paperback thriller *Operation Kuwait* is described on its back cover.

> On the edge of an oil-rich desert, Black September has established X19, a secret base where the art of sky sabotage is taught to paramilitary terror troops. While it operates, no plane can fly anywhere in the world free of fear. But Israel's Security Branch has other ideas. Their daredevil team of counterspy commandos has launched an operation that will smash X19 bullet by bullet, gun by gun, terrorist by terrorist.

The publisher also promised another novel by Arvay entitled *The Piraeus Plot,* described as "another dynamic adventure of the undercover war in the Middle East, matching the crack Israeli Secret Service vs. International Terrorists!" This Rambowitz stereotype even carried over to the portrayal of American Jews. In the movie *Private Benjamin* (1980), for example, Judy Benjamin, a prototypical Jewish American princess, gives up a life of affluence and indulgence and enlists in the army, where she performs heroically.[32]

American Jews wished to become vicarious Israelis. At Jewish communal banquets it became customary to sing the Israel national anthem, "Hatikvah" (Hope), along with "The Star Spangled Banner." Jews also flocked to the Israeli nightclubs that sprouted up in New York City during the 1970s and 1980s. Even the most bizarre events involving American Jews often had an Israeli aspect. One such event took place in May 1974 in New York City.

A man named David F. Kamaiko hijacked a helicopter and demanded that two million dollars in ten-dollar bills be placed in valises and delivered to him by a bikini-clad woman. The pilot of the helicopter later related that Kamaiko had been quite distraught by a recent massacre of Israeli children in the town of Maalot by Arab terrorists and planned to use the money to buy guns for the Jewish Defense League.[33]

Marshall Sklare, a leading authority on contemporary Jewry, noted that Israel "had a profound effect on the American Jew, particularly on his psychological make-up. It has given him a heightened sense of morale—morale that enables him to abide newer challenges of the American scene to Jewish status and security." Pride in Israel and fear for its security spurred intense American Jewish political activity on its behalf. By the 1980s, American Jews supported over seventy political action committees throughout the country, to help fund the campaigns of sympathetic politicians, and financed the American-Israel Public Affairs Committee (AIPAC), an effective pro-Israel lobby in Washington.

Jews were generous contributors to political campaigns, particularly to those of Democratic candidates. But the spigots would be turned off, as George McGovern, the 1972 Democratic presidential candidate, discovered, if a candidate's position on the Middle East was not completely supportive of Israel. Richard Nixon, McGovern's opponent, received an unprecedented amount of money from Jewish sources because he was viewed as reliable regarding the Middle East. Jewish political activity in 1972 was so intense and prominent that the journalist Stephen D. Isaacs dubbed it the "Year of the Jew."[34]

After 1967, political activity in behalf of Israel became another way to manifest Jewish identity. "Jews who maintain only the most pro forma links with the Jewish religious tradition, who know little or nothing of Jewish culture," Daniel Elazar said, "increasingly express themselves Jewishly in connection with Jewish political causes or interests." After 1967, the dues-paying membership of AIPAC increased rapidly, and in the 1980s the Jewish Institute for National Security Affairs was established to lobby for a strong military and close links between the Israeli and American defense establishments.[35]

Not surprisingly, American Jews did not welcome criticism of the Jewish state. People are less tolerant about matters that mean the most to them, and this was certainly true of Jews and Israel. There was far more criticism of the policies of the Israeli government and the Israeli social

system within Israel than from American Jews. In the 1960s, Jewish notables were horrified by the phenomenon of the New Left, largely because
some of its most prominent leaders were Jews hostile to Israel. American
Jews concluded, not in all cases accurately, that this hostility must stem
from anti-Semitism. An egregious example was the response to a 1970
document published by the American Friends Service Committee. Titled
Search for Peace in the Middle East, it suggested that Jewish political pressure had inhibited public debate regarding the Middle East and had worked
against the cause of peace. "No one who is truly concerned about the long-
term fate of Israel and the long-term threats to inter-faith harmony," the
Quaker document said, "can be indifferent to these dangers."

A group of Jewish academicians published a rejoinder under the title
*Truth and Peace in the Middle East: A Critical Analysis of the Quaker
Report.* They accused the Quakers of having "displayed a blatant bias,
repressed facts, distorted history and presented a slanted and one-sided set
of conclusions." They attributed this to Christian theological anti-Semitism
disguised as anti-Zionism. "The basic attitude of some Christians, theologians as well as laymen," the Jewish professors charged, "is still deeply
rooted in the postulate that because the Jews refused to accept Jesus as the
Messiah, they are eternally damned and condemned to wander the earth as
homeless witnesses to their sins."[36]

The role of Israel in American Jewish life was shaped by memories of
the Holocaust. When American Jews talked about the survival and security
of Israel, the Holocaust was still fresh in their minds. They constantly worried that the United States was going to betray Israel for the sake of Arab oil
and American influence in the Arab lands, just as Neville Chamberlain had
betrayed Czechoslovakia in 1938. For American Jews, the position of Israel
resembled that of the helpless Jews of eastern Europe. They overlooked the
fact that Israel had demonstrated on several occasions that it was more than
equal to the task of defending its interests. American Jews were impressed
not by evidence of Israeli military supremacy, but by fear of another Holocaust. And the genocidal rhetoric of the Arabs confirmed for American
Jews what they had always assumed to be the Arabs' ultimate objective.

Jews were bitterly disappointed with the indifference of Quakers and
other Christian groups to the plight of Israel, particularly during the crisis
of 1967 when it appeared that Israel could be destroyed. Neither the National Conference of Catholic Bishops nor the National Council of Churches
made forthright statements in Israel's behalf at that time. This was far more

revealing to Jews of Christianity's real attitudes toward Jews and Judaism than the numerous interfaith dialogues and the frequent declarations by Christians in the 1950s and 1960s of their goodwill. Calls by Christian groups after 1967 for an even-handed policy toward the Middle East were viewed by American Jews as manifestations of their underlying anti-Semitism.

"To be a Jew in America," Leonard Fein wrote in 1988, "is to carry with you the consciousness of limitless savagery. It is to carry that consciousness with you not as an abstraction, but as a reality; not, God help us all, only as a memory, but also as a possibility." Among American Jews, the relationship between Israel and the Holocaust was symbiotic. Memories of the Holocaust strengthened the ardor of American Jews for Israel, while the perilous situation of Israel in the 1960s encouraged Jews to bring into the open the hurt they carried because of the Holocaust.[37]

For the first decade and a half after the end of World War II, Jews were reluctant to discuss the Holocaust. They had not even preempted the use of the word: a 1959 book entitled *Holocaust* did not deal with the destruction of European Jewry but with a lethal fire in 1942 in a Boston nightclub. During the 1950s, Jewish communities did not sponsor Holocaust commemorations, the Jewish lecture circuit did not feature speeches on the Holocaust, no Holocaust centers existed in the United States, and there was little public discussion among Jews regarding the fate of European Jewry.

Holocaust survivors hesitated to speak about their experiences, perhaps because they did not wish to burden their children with their horrific memories. This natural reticence was encouraged by the guilt of the survivors for having survived while relatives perished. The image of Jews being led without protest to the gas chambers at Auschwitz, Treblinka, Chelmno, and the other Nazi murder factories was naturally distasteful to American Jews. They were not sympathetic to the argument that, besides taking up arms, there were other ways of opposing the Nazis, such as prayer and the refusal to become dehumanized.

This reluctance to confront openly the meaning of the Holocaust ended in the 1960s. That decade began with the Eichmann trial and the publication of Raul Hilberg's *The Destruction of the European Jews* and Leon Uris's *Mila 18* and ended with the publication of Saul Bellow's *Mr. Sammler's Planet*. In the 1950s, Elie Wiesel, a survivor of Auschwitz, had been unable to find publishers for his books. In 1960 he published an English edition of *Night,* his memoir of the Holocaust, and began attracting public notice.

Beginning in the 1960s, remembrance of the Holocaust became an important Jewish interest and a significant aspect in the shaping of American Jewish identity. Yom HaShoah (Holocaust Remembrance Day) became part of the Jewish calendar. Jews funded the erection of Holocaust memorials—most notably Nathan Rapoport's statue "Liberation" in Liberty State Park in New Jersey across the water from the Statue of Liberty—and helped finance museums for the study of the Holocaust. The most important of these were to be located in New York City and Washington, D.C., and were to cost at least three hundred million dollars. The federal government's Holocaust museum in Washington, located near the Mall and a stone's throw from the Washington Monument, is scheduled to open in the spring of 1993. In 1987, the United States Holocaust Memorial Council published a directory of Holocaust institutions in America. It listed nineteen museums, forty-eight resource centers, twelve memorials, twenty-six research institutes, and five libraries. Courses on the Holocaust were often the most popular offerings of departments of Judaica at American universities.[38]

One result of this new public concern with the Holocaust was a new interest, also beginning in the 1960s, in the fate of Russian Jewry. Prior to then, American Jews had largely written off the two million Russian Jews who, it was believed, must be nearly completely assimilated as a result of a half-century of communism. Elie Wiesel's *The Jews of Silence* (1966) challenged this indifference. He emphasized that Jewish identity in the Soviet Union had not been destroyed, and that the Jews of silence were actually those living in the United States who continued to ignore the plight of Russian Jewry. He dared American Jewry to do for the Russian Jews what they had not done for those who had been caught up in the Holocaust. He was successful. By the late 1960s, the issue of Russian Jewry had become an important item on the American Jewish agenda. Initially, American Jews sought to ensure equal economic, educational, and religious opportunities for Jews in the Soviet Union. This changed in the 1970s. American Jews now endeavored to secure the right of Jews to emigrate from the Soviet Union to the West and to Israel.[39]

By the 1980s, Auschwitz, the largest of the Nazi murder camps, was a place for pilgrimages of American Jews. Every year delegations of American Jewish leaders and Jewish youth visited Auschwitz before proceeding on to Israel. When President Reagan paid a brief visit in 1985 to a German military cemetery in Bitburg that contained the graves of SS soldiers, American Jews were naturally outraged. They were equally outraged by the proposal of Polish Catholics to build a Carmelite convent at Auschwitz, believing that it would desecrate the memories of the millions of Jews who had died at Auschwitz simply because they were Jewish. "Within the American Jewish community," wrote Michael Berenbaum, the project director of the United States Holocaust Memorial Museum, "the Holocaust has entered the domain of shared sacrality." Rabbi Emil Fackenheim, himself a survivor, even proposed that, as a result of the Holocaust, Jews must assume another religious obligation along with the traditional six hundred and thirteen commandments. The six hundred and fourteenth commandment was to never provide Hitler with a posthumous victory through assimilation.[40]

The unexpected emergence in the 1960s of the Holocaust into the forefront of American Jewish consciousness was partially due to the importance of the survivors within the American Jewish community. The survivors and their children constituted approximately 8 percent of American Jewry and their influence on American Jewish life was much greater than their numbers. The survivors were now willing to tell their story, fearing that, with the passage of time, their experiences would fade from memory. The survivors were particularly eager to pass on their histories to their children. "I have an occasional nightmare now," Elie Wiesel said. "I wake up shivering, thinking that when we die, no one will be able to persuade people the Holocaust occurred." One reason for Wiesel's nightmare was the surfacing during the 1970s of a group of crackpot anti-Semitic "revisionist" historians who claimed that the Holocaust never occurred. For the survivors, this was the ultimate obscenity.[41]

The new absorption in the Holocaust was also due to events in the Middle East, particularly the Six-Day War. Repressed memories of the Holocaust sprang out in the open during the dark days of May and early June 1967, when Jews had to confront the very real possibility of a second Holocaust. The murder of Europe's Jews no longer appeared to be idiosyncratic. Instead it was a paradigm of the modern Jewish condition. Arthur D. Morse's *While Six Million Died: A Chronicle of American Apathy* appeared in the same year as the Six-Day War. His sensationalistic claim that the indifference of the Roosevelt administration to the Nazi killings made it an accessory to the Holocaust received a favorable hearing among American Jews. The extremism of Morse's accusations would be tempered and made more credible by scholarly books by Henry L. Feingold, Saul Friedman, and David Wyman, and Wyman would broaden the list of villains to include the American Jewish establishment. Jews were not slow in drawing the relationship between the events of the 1930s and 1940s and those of the 1960s and 1970s, and Israeli leaders, particularly Menachem Begin, continually reminded them of the fate of the Jews in World War II. American Jews were determined that no future historian would be able to charge their generation or their generation's government with partial responsibility for the destruction of another Jewish community. And Jews were not reluctant to use the Holocaust to plead Israel's case before non-Jews.

For some American Jews, the Holocaust became central to their own image of themselves as Jews. With often only a tenuous relationship to Judaism, they clung to the Holocaust as the core element in their Jewish identity. As sociologist Chaim I. Waxman emphasized, such Jews were determined that the Holocaust experience be reserved exclusively for Jews: no Armenians, Gypsies, or Cambodians need apply. For them to minimize the unique Jewishness of the Holocaust "would be to deprive them of what they perceive to be their uniqueness as Jews. . . . While for other Jews, the Holocaust was another confirmation of Jewish uniqueness, for these Jews the Holocaust is the source of Jewish uniqueness."[42]

This often obsessive concern with the Holocaust was not without its critics, who feared that the underlying message that Jews were getting from what came to be called the "Holocaust industry" or "Shoah business" was that Jewish identity involved suffering. This was the premise, for example, of Bernard Malamud's novel *The Assistant*. If Jewish identity was to be passed on to future generations, it needed a more positive and affirmative definition than martyrdom. Historian Deborah Lipstadt feared that "if our image is only of suffering, we will have robbed ourselves of the joy and replenishment that Jewish tradition has always fostered." Others pointed out that the major role of Jews in the Holocaust was as victim and that Holocaust commemorations solemnized death. This, they argued, was not appropriate for a religion and a people who had always valued life, and it was particularly inappropriate for American Jews who were citizens of a nation that had never experienced anything remotely similar to the virulent anti-Semitism of eastern Europe. Injustice, Leon Wieseltier wrote,

> retains the power to distort long after it has ceased to be real. It is a posthumous victory for the oppressors, when pain becomes a tradition.

> And yet the atrocities of the past must never be forgotten. That is the unfairly difficult dilemma of the newly emancipated . . . an honorable life is not possible if they remember too little and a normal life is not possible if they remember too much.[43]

The overwhelming majority of American Jews were not survivors or descendants of survivors. Their decision to continue identifying themselves as Jews would have to rest on more than memory of the Holocaust (or pride in Israel). "The Holocaust-Israel symbols," Rabbi Eugene B. Borowitz said in 1990, "for all their remaining potency, have lost their recent authority." Other religious leaders, dismayed by the condition of American Judaism, echoed Borowitz. They believed American Jewry had lost its way when a 1988 survey of the American Jewish Committee could reveal that five times as many American Jews believed the Holocaust and Israel were more important to them as Jews than the Exodus and the receiving of the Torah on Mount Sinai. The Holocaust, Rabbi Daniel Jeremy Silver wrote, "*cannot, and does not, provide the kind of vitalizing and informing myth around which American Jews could marshal their energies and construct a vital culture. Martyrs command respect, but a community's sense of sacred purpose must be woven of something more substantial than tears*" (italics in original). Jews who had a sense of "sacred purpose," such as Hasidim, felt no need to dwell on the Holocaust.[44]

By the 1980s, serious questions were being raised about the impact of Israelism on American Jewry. Some came from rabbis who were dismayed by the extent to which Israel had become a substitute for Judaism. "Israelo-centrism," Rabbi Borowitz wrote, "no longer can be the engine driving American Jewish life, keeping us ahead of the assimilation threatening to overtake us." Jacob Neusner of Brown University gained a measure of notoriety in the 1980s for asserting that, for American Jews, the United States was the Promised Land, and that Jews could lead as authentic a Jewish life in the Diaspora as in Israel. This issue involved dollars and cents since domestic Jewish institutions competed with Israel in the allocation of funds raised by the federations. But even more important than this was the matter of American Jewish identity, the perception of American Jews of what it meant to be Jewish in America. Those who questioned Israelism were skeptical that American Jewry could flourish if it depended on American Jews being vicarious Israelis. Not only did Israelism depend on a romanticized image of Israel that bore little relationship to reality, but it implied that American Jewry lacked indigenous sources of strength. It was unrealistic to expect Jews to remain Jews because of an attachment to another country some six thousand miles away (or because of memories of events that took place during the 1940s). But if Israel could not continue indefinitely to be the core of American Jewish identity, what would replace it? In view of the apathy of most American Jews toward Judaism, it was doubtful that religion could fulfill that role.[45]

During the 1970s and 1980s, serious doubts were also being raised about another important component of Jewish identity—political liberalism. Many Jews had believed that the essence of Jewish existence was having a Jewish heart and that the essence of Jewish obligation was social action. Persons with Jewish hearts would necessarily support the civil rights movement, civil liberties, abortion rights, foreign aid, social welfare legislation, the strict separation of church and state, and the other elements of modern liberalism. From this perspective, a Jewish conservative was a contradiction in terms.[46]

Jewish leaders continually warned their flocks during these decades that it would be un-Jewish to desert liberalism. In an op-ed piece in the 2 November 1984 *New York Times,* Arthur Hertzberg, a former president of the American Jewish Congress, cautioned Jews that voting for Ronald Reagan would mean forsaking their Jewish political souls. Entitled "Behind Jews' Political Principles," Hertzberg's essay argued that Jews in the past had rebuffed the blandishments of the Right to vote their pocketbooks. Jews knew then that politics was about "life and death," the creation of a "world of justice," and "the nature of democracy." For Hertzberg, the emphasis of conservative Jews on Jewish self-interest was "ignoble" and reduced "the meaning of the Jewish struggle in America to a quest for success and abandons those who are still friendless and foreign to fend for themselves." Hertzberg accused Reagan's Jewish supporters and the opponents of affirmative action of desecrating the memories of the victims of the Holocaust who died because they lived in an unjust world. "We cannot today join the forces of selfishness," he said. According to Hertzberg, the most valuable aspect of Jewish culture, the one most worthy of being passed down to future generations, was not Judaism but the passion for social justice.

Except for blacks, no group voted so consistently for liberal Democratic candidates. In 1960, for example, a larger percentage of Jews than Irish Catholics voted for John F. Kennedy. Jews were the only major American ethnic or religious group in which voting was not correlated with class. "Jews," Irving Louis Horowitz wrote, "have proven to be a unique force in American politics in that, despite their class backgrounds or interests, they have exhibited the capacity to vote and act beyond their class and interest group constraints." In a famous aphorism, Milton Himmelfarb noted that Jews lived like Episcopalians and voted like Puerto Ricans. Indeed, liberalism seemed to be more potent among the Jewish economic and social elite than among the Jewish middle class. Ronald Reagan, for example, got a larger percentage of Jewish votes in Brooklyn than he did in Scarsdale, Short Hills, and Shaker Heights. In Orthodox areas of Brooklyn, the vote for Republican candidates was closer to American norms than in non-Orthodox Jewish areas, where Democrats consistently received over 80 percent of the vote. Paradoxically, the Orthodox appeared politically "more American" and "less Jewish" than the non-Orthodox.

During the 1960s, 1970s, and 1980s, Republicans, sociologists, and political scientists predicted a transformation of Jewish voting patterns—only to be consistently proven wrong. Thus in April 1973, in the wake of Nixon's reelection, Irving Kristol forecast that the Jews would move to the right politically. "This is not a temporary phenomenon. Jewish politics in the decades to come are going to be very different from what Jewish politics have been in the past century and a half."[47]

Save for the election of 1980, when John Anderson ran as an independent candidate, over two-thirds of the Jewish electorate continued to vote for Democratic presidential candidates. This had even been true in 1972, when George McGovern was the Democratic candidate. The Jewish voting pattern for liberal Congressional and mayoral candidates was equally skewed. The 1984 election revealed the idiosyncratic nature of Jewish voting patterns. Except for blacks and the unemployed, Walter Mondale got a higher percentage of votes among Jews than among any other group. Jews were the only group to give Reagan less support in 1984 than in 1980, even though Reagan's margin of victory increased and the Republicans ardently courted Jews.[48]

Sociologists, historians, and political scientists offered various explanations of American Jewish liberalism. In *The Political Behavior of American Jews* (1956), Lawrence Fuchs argued that liberalism emerged ineluctably from Jewish values, which stressed the importance of charity and social justice. Fuchs's interpretation, as many critics pointed out, ignored the fact that there was no correlation between the intensity of Jewish commitment and liberalism. Jews living in the shtetls of eastern Europe or in Orthodox neighborhoods in Brooklyn were less liberal than more assimilated Jews. Prominent Jewish leftists were often contemptuous of Jewish tradition and interests. The explanation of Jewish liberalism as a fulfillment of Judaism also downplayed the fact that Jewish leftism was intensely secular and rejected the Orthodox definition of Jewish identity. It is not surprising that the Jewish socialist labor movement (and YIVO) emerged in Vilna, the Jerusalem of Europe, as opposing definitions of Jewish identity in the midst of the most intensely Orthodox Jewish community in eastern Europe.

Another interpretation looked not to Judaism but recent history to explain this Jewish commitment to liberalism. Prior to the late nineteenth century, the Jewish political orientation in Europe and the Arab lands was passive. Jews feared the state and were detached from political involvement. Since the parties of the Left in Europe in the nineteenth and twentieth centuries favored Jewish emancipation and opposed anti-Semitism, Jews naturally supported the political Left and distrusted the political establishment, which was often anti-Semitic. In addition, the growth in Europe of an urban Jewish proletariat in the late nineteenth century encouraged Jews to look to various forms of socialism as panaceas for their economic and social difficulties.

These liberal and leftist political impulses were reinforced when Jews migrated to America. The *Forward,* the most important Yiddish daily paper, was a socialist journal. It had on its masthead the slogan, "Workers of the World Unite." The political Left in America, particularly during the 1930s, identified itself with the interests of what were termed the "urban masses," which included Jews. In addition, the fact that Franklin D. Roosevelt led America into war against Hitler intensified Jewish support for the liberal wing of the Democratic party. Jews, Judge Jonah Goldstein jested, had three *velts* (worlds): *die velt* (this world), *yene velt* (the other world), and Roosevelt.

With good reason, Jews identified anti-Semitism with the Right. This accounted for their interpretation of Nazism as a right-wing, reactionary movement, despite the fact that the word Nazism stood for National Socialism. In addition, they attributed the rise of Hitler to the economic and social dislocations caused by the Great Depression. A society that provided good housing, jobs, unemployment insurance, health care, and educational opportunities would, they believed, be less immune to anti-Semitic demagogues. Liberalism was thus a bulwark against anti-Semitism.

While favoring the amelioration of social and economic problems by a strong central government, the Jewish approach to politics also contained an anarchistic strain. Jews had a deep distrust of authority because established political and social authority had threatened Jewish interests. The Jewish approach to politics was expressed by the rabbi's response in *Fiddler on the Roof* when asked to compose a prayer for the czar. "Oh God," the rabbi prayed, "please keep the czar . . . far away from us." Jews had a knee-jerk sympathy for dissenters challenging the legitimacy of constituted authority. This was exhibited in the many Jewish members of the American Civil Liberties Union, the distrust of Jews of the police, and their willingness to give the benefit of the doubt to the powerless in any conflict with government or powerful economic interests.

In contrast to the Irish, Jews tended to view politics in terms of social and economic redemption rather than as an opportunity for personal advancement. Largely excluded from the politics of eastern Europe, most Jews did not believe politics was a place where a nice Jewish boy could or should pursue a career. Jews were influential in postwar American politics as intellectuals, contributors, and voters, but not as politicians. Skeptical toward politicians, Jews are not skeptical toward the political process. For them, it is the means to create a better world.

Whatever its origins, liberalism remained a major component of American Jewish identity after 1945. The most eloquent postwar defense of Jewish liberalism was Leonard Fein's 1988 volume *Where Are We? The Inner Life of America's Jews*. Fein, the founder of *Moment* magazine and a former professor at Brandeis University, wrote this book at a time when Jewish liberalism was under increasing attack from Jews. Viewing assimilation as unfaithful to American and Jewish tradition, but cognizant that less than 10 percent of American Jews observed the traditional commandments of Judaism, Fein argued that only a commitment to economic and social justice "can serve as our preeminent motive, the path through which our past is vindicated, our present warranted, and our future affirmed."[49]

Few phenomena troubled Jewish liberals and socialists in the 1970s and 1980s as much as the emergence of a small group of neoconservative Jewish intellectuals and the metamorphosis of *Commentary* from a staunchly liberal magazine into America's leading conservative monthly. In their essay "Are American Jews Turning to the Right?" Bernard Rosenberg and Irving Howe declared that this question was a matter of some concern since "the overwhelming thrust of Jewish thought and writing in America . . . has been liberal and whatever radicalism we have had in America has found disproportionate support among Jews." They were optimistic that Jews would remain faithful to Jewish values of moral compassion and social commitment and that liberalism would retain its popularity within the Jewish community.[50]

In *Breaking Ranks,* the second volume of his autobiography, Norman Podhoretz, the editor of *Commentary,* confronted critics of neoconservatism and the rightward drift of his magazine. *Breaking Ranks* chronicled Podhoretz's split from the American Left during the 1960s. He pointed to Howe, an editor of the socialist quarterly *Dissent,* as an example of the intellectual bankruptcy of modern socialists. Howe's socialism, Podhoretz claimed, resembled a religion. The less he believed in socialism, "the more desperate he was to affirm his socialist faith. And since there was so little of a positive nature left to affirm, what he mainly did was to attack other intellectuals for deserting the true faith."[51]

Dissent's answer was not long in coming. Its Spring 1981 issue contained a long "special feature" by Bernard Avishai, a left-wing professor at the Massachusetts Institute of Technology and a future editor of the *Harvard Business Review.* Entitled "Breaking Faith: *Commentary* and the American Jews," it confirmed Podhoretz's argument that left-wing politics was a surrogate religion for some Jewish intellectuals. Avishai contrasted the self-indulgent conservatism of *Commentary* with "*the civil religion to which we try to make converts*" (italics in the original). Avishai attributed *Commentary*'s fall from grace to the Six-Day War. *Commentary* had thrown its lot in with Jewish chauvinists and had broken ranks with "the radically democratic view of politics with which *Commentary* had justifiably tried to identify American Jews for a decade." For Avishai, *Commentary* had been guilty of apostasy, and it was the responsibility of right-thinking Jews to "repudiate the politics that the magazine claims to be pursuing for our 'own good.'" Only by remaining true to authentically Jewish "urbane, communitarian values of the left" could American Jews remain intellectually relevant.[52]

As if to answer Avishai's accusation that it did not speak for Jewish interests and values, *Commentary* published Murray Friedman's "A New Direction for American Jews" in its December 1981 issue. Friedman, the Middle Atlantic director of the American Jewish Committee, called for a radical change in the activities and goals of Jewish community relations organizations such as the American Jewish Committee, the American Jewish Congress, and the Anti-Defamation League of B'nai B'rith. Friedman asserted that the "liberal-left perspective" of these organizations was based on the misconception that the fate of liberalism and Jews were inextricably bound together. According to Friedman, the commitment of modern liberalism to racial quotas, the expansion of the welfare state, and the strict separation of church and state no longer served Jewish interests. His "new direction," in contrast, called for a "moderate conservatism" aimed at strengthening private enterprise and reversing the "breakdown of the orderly norms of our society." Friedman's sensible program would have brought the politics of American Jews more in line with that of the rest of the country. For most of American Jewish officialdom, however, it was too sharp a break with conventional liberal wisdom.[53]

The most severe challenge to the Jews' perception of themselves as liberals concerned civil rights. Joel Spingarn and other Jews had been involved in the civil rights movement since the beginning of the twentieth century. This stemmed from a combination of benevolence and self-interest. As members of a persecuted minority, Jews could more readily empathize with blacks than could other white Americans. This partially explained why many of the most prominent recent students of American black history—Herbert Aptheker, Stanley Elkins, Eric Foner, Herbert G. Gutman, Gerda Lerner, Lawrence W. Levine, Leon F. Litwack, Gilbert Osofsky, and Allan H. Spear—were Jews. Jews also believed that they themselves would benefit if all forms of prejudice were removed from American society.

Whatever its source, Jews had been an important presence in the civil rights movement. About half of the white civil rights attorneys in the South in the 1960s were Jews. More than half of the white freedom riders in the 1960s were Jews, and nearly two-thirds of the white volunteers involved in Freedom Summer in Mississippi in 1964 were Jews. Two of them—Andrew Goodman and Michael Schwerner—were murdered. Jews also provided much of the funds for the National Association for the Advancement of Colored People, the Congress of Racial Equality, and other civil rights organizations.[54]

Jews were flabbergasted when, beginning in the 1960s, they discovered that not all blacks appreciated their efforts and that anti-Semitism was growing within the black community. In the 1980s, Jews were particularly disturbed by evidence that Jesse Jackson, a candidate for the Democratic nomination for president, had a reflexive dislike of Jews and Israel, and by the failure of Jackson and other black leaders to forcefully repudiate Louis

Farrakhan and other black anti-Semites. The Jewish community relations agencies concluded that anti-Semitism within the ghettos of Chicago, New York, and other large cities was far greater than they had previously assumed. This had already been deduced by Jews who lived near the ghetto or had businesses in black areas.

The split between Jews and blacks did not result from a weakening of Jewish support for a color-blind society. It stemmed rather from changes within the civil rights community. While Jews continued to champion the principle of merit, black leaders insisted on affirmative action to redress past grievances. In practice, affirmative action meant racial discrimination in behalf of blacks and other aggrieved minorities. Affirmative action evoked among Jews memories of the quotas that had limited their economic and educational opportunities in Europe and in the United States prior to 1945. Jews were also offended by radical blacks who accused Israel of being a colonialist society oppressing the Palestinians, a supposedly Third World people.

Jews were unprepared for the souring of black-Jewish relationships in part because they misunderstood the history of these relationships. Jews perceived the years prior to 1967 as a golden age of amity between two minorities facing common dangers. Jews believed they were immune from the virus of racism because of their experience with anti-Semitism and the Holocaust. Because Jews believed that they, along with blacks, were among the persecuted, it was difficult for them to comprehend the real nature of black-Jewish relationships and the source of black anti-Semitism. In 1967, for instance, left-wing journalist I. F. Stone blamed it simply on "over-wrought blacks" and cautioned Jews not to exaggerate its extent. In truth, Jews had ceased being an oppressed American minority, and their relations with blacks had never been marked by equality. Blacks had been the employees, tenants, debtors, students, and welfare supplicants, while Jews had been the employers, landlords, creditors, teachers, and welfare bureaucrats. Jews had done things *for* blacks but rarely *with* blacks. Occasionally, as in Harold Cruse's anti-Semitic volume *The Crisis of the Black Intellectual* (1967), blacks protested this servile relationship. For blacks, the most important thing about Jews was that they were white, not that they had once exhibited paternalism toward blacks.[55]

Stone and other radicals downplayed the significance of black anti-Semitism because they believed the natural place of Jews was alongside the dispossessed and the powerless and because they tended to romanticize the oppressed, believing they had cornered the market on virtue. A prominent example of such thinking was *Jews of the Left* (1979), written by Arthur Liebman, a socialist. The bulk of *Jews and the Left* chronicled the decline of the American Jewish radical subculture. In his concluding chapter, however, Liebman reversed direction and predicted that the "Jewish community's harsh confrontation with capitalism will result in a renewed Jewish commitment to socialism." This, he claimed, would come about as a result of the erosion of the economic position of Jewish businessmen due to the expansion of the giant corporations and the shrinkage in the income and numbers of Jewish lawyers, accountants, actuaries, and other professionals economically dependent on Jewish businessmen. For Liebman, the crucial facts about America's Jews were their economic marginality and lack of power. Jews will eventually realize that "their interests as Jews, downwardly mobile persons, as members of an exploited working class, and as an impoverished, or early impoverished, strata of petty traders and merchants are antithetical to the powerful American bourgeoisie." Jews will then take their place within "an ethnically heterogenous socialist movement capable of converting the United States into a humane, democratic socialist society." Liebman left unexplained the role of the Jewish petty bourgeoisie within a movement supposedly dedicated to the interests of the proletariat.[56]

Liebman's analysis echoed what the Jewish Left had been saying since the radical heyday of the 1960s regarding the economic and cultural oppression of America's Jews. The Jewish Left had emerged after 1967 as one aspect of the New Left. Concentrated on the university campus, radical Jews founded dozens of magazines with titles such as the *Jewish Radical* (Berkeley), *Rock of Ages Review* (Chicago), *Chutzpah* (Chicago), *Genesis 2* (Boston), and *Voice of Micah* (Washington). They worked in behalf of Soviet Jewry, demanded Jewish studies programs, criticized the priorities of the American Jewish establishment, and insisted that American Jewry take the social and economic teachings of Judaism seriously. The Jewish Left, two of their number wrote, feared that "if the Jews do not assert their own uniqueness, then others will ultimately define the Jews' uniqueness for them. They fear America's capacity to absorb its minorities, whether political or cultural. They fear the spiritual poverty of the so-called affluent society. They fear being overwhelmed by the grinding machine of technology, consumption, and bureaucratic impersonality."[57]

The most important issue for the Jewish Left was Israel. Even Abbie Hoffman, who was otherwise estranged from Jewishness, called himself a Zionist after the Six-Day War. Radical Jews were militant in defending Zionism and Israel against the charge of colonialism. "In dealing with those who oppose Israel, we are not reasonable and we are not rational. Nor should we be," Michael J. Rosenberg, a Brandeis student, said. "There is nothing for us to apologize about. What is called for is unabashed pride. The accomplishments of Zionism are singular and can well serve as a model for every oppressed and downtrodden people." For radical Jews, Zionism was a movement of national liberation, and Israel's natural place was with the Third World.[58]

Radical Jews with a spiritual bent gravitated to the *havurot* movement, the Jewish counterpart to the commune development of the 1960s. Here they hoped to create the mysticism, joy, and sense of community of Hasidic sects, but without their sexism, fundamentalism, and authoritarianism. The first *havurah* was Havurot Shalom in Somerville, Massachusetts, organized in 1968 by Rabbi Arthur Green, who would later become president of the Reconstructionist Rabbinical College in Philadelphia.[59]

Spokesmen for establishment Judaism greeted the *havurot* with skepticism, seeing them as more pagan than Jewish. The leaders of Conservative Judaism were particularly troubled by the *havurot* movement since it consisted mainly of persons who had grown up in Conservative synagogues. Rabbi Wolfe Kelman predicted in 1971 that "this artificially inflated dimension of the youth culture will prove to be a passing fad remembered nostalgically by those who are easily seduced by slogans and fashions which promise instant eschatology, and by schools where students and teachers are interchangeable, love is God, and the greening of America is inevitable." Kelman's forecast was confirmed in the 1970s when the *havurot* movement went into a sharp decline, along with most of the other manifestations of the counterculture and the New Left.[60]

The most important attempt by radical Jews to define a radical American Jewish identity occurred in 1986 with the founding of the quarterly (later bimonthly) magazine *Tikkun* by Michael Lerner. Lerner's own life anticipated the radical Jewish thrust of *Tikkun*. A significant figure within the New Left during the 1960s, he created the Seattle Liberation Front while teaching philosophy at the University of Washington. He was arrested (and later released) in 1970 for organizing a demonstration in behalf of the Chicago Eight, which Seattle newspapers described as the biggest in that city since the general strike of 1919. Lerner was a radical Jew rather than a Jewish radical. He was raised in an intensely Zionist family in New Jersey, studied in the 1960s at the Jewish Theological Seminary where he fell under the spell of Heschel, and served as national president of Atid, the Conservative movement's national college organization. Alienated from the comfortable Judaism of suburbia, Lerner suggested in 1969 that "the synagogue as currently established will have to be smashed." His religious search would eventually lead him to Orthodoxy.[61]

Lerner hoped that *Tikkun* could rescue American Jews and Judaism from the complacency and materialism of the American Jewish political and religious establishment. "The universalistic dream of a transformation and healing of the world, the belief that peace and justice are not meant for heaven but are this-worldly necessities that must be fought for, *is* the particularistic cultural and religious tradition of the Jews," Lerner declared in *Tikkun*'s first issue. From the beginning, Lerner trumpeted *Tikkun* as a left-wing alternative to *Commentary*. *Tikkun* would speak for those who, contrary to *Commentary*'s editors, were "still moved by the radical spirit of the Prophets and who insist on keeping their message alive."[62]

Tikkun almost immediately became the voice of the Jewish Left, particularly those nostalgic about the 1960s. It supported feminism, gay rights, disarmament, the campaign against apartheid, ecology, animal rights, and affirmative action. Its major concern was the Middle East, and the outbreak of the *intifada* one year after the appearance of its first issue was grist for its mill. *Tikkun* strongly supported the Israeli peace movement and a Palestinian homeland, and published articles with such provocative titles as "Israel: Our Collective Guilt" and "Rabin as Pharaoh." "Certainly when we see Israel engaging in activities that are not only morally inappropriate but actually self-destructive, we must cry out in anguish," Lerner wrote. *Tikkun*'s attacks on Israeli policy were often eloquent, but they were frequently vitiated by a lack of political realism and by an unwillingness to give the Israeli government the same benefit of doubt granted the Israeli peace movement.[63]

Not surprisingly, American Jews who did not share the magazine's radical perspective soon came to view it as the enfant terrible of American Jewry. Norman Podhoretz, the editor of *Commentary,* refused to appear on the same platform with Lerner. Hershell Shanks, the editor of *Moment* magazine, found Lerner's "stridency and moral posturing" to be "insufferable." "There is a messianic arrogance to Lerner and his self-appointed quest," Shanks wrote. "A relic of the '60s, he bursts out of the blue, flags waving, shotgun blasting, peppering the smug and victorious gatekeepers with a steady stream of buckshot."[64]

The fundamental difference between Lerner and Podhoretz did not concern the specifics of Israeli government policy or the latest radical cause. Rather, it stemmed from differing approaches to American Jewish life. Lerner believed that being Jewish ineluctably meant a commitment to radical politics. Podhoretz assumed that the American Jewish community would flourish best in a society in which conservative values and policies were ascendant. Both, however, implicitly agreed that the focus of American Jewry involved not culture but interests, whether they be radical or conservative. Jewish survivalists, however, feared that a community in which interests rather than culture were paramount had little future, particularly in light of the acculturation of American Jewry.

CHAPTER EIGHT

THE QUESTION OF SURVIVAL

DURING his twelve years as mayor of New York City (1978–89), Edward I. Koch would often walk the streets of his city and ask pedestrians, "How am I doing?" He would continue asking this question until his defeat in 1989. By the 1990s, this was also the most important and troubling question that Jews were asking about themselves. While Koch was concerned with his individual political survival, Jews were concerned with their group survival. On the face of it, their prospects as Americans were bright. The economic and social profile of America's Jews was the envy of other ethnic groups, anti-Semitism had diminished almost to the point of insignificance, and the political influence of Jews was at its peak.

The future of American Jews as Jews was, however, another matter. Sociological data had raised serious questions regarding the prospects for American Jewish survival. Intermarriage was widespread, the birth rate was far lower than that of Gentiles, the median age of American Jews was much higher than that of non-Jews, and the Jewish divorce rate and other signs of family breakdown were rapidly approaching national norms. The Jewish family—supposedly the guarantor of Jewish survival—was under siege, and there was nothing on the horizon promising relief.

In other areas of Jewish life as well, pessimism seemed to be the order of the day. Apathy perhaps best described the attitude of American Jews toward Judaism. Although Israel had become the most important cement of American Jewish identity, a majority of American Jews had never visited the Jewish state. Their relationship with Israel was largely vicarious, and some Jewish leaders questioned whether a strong American Jewish identity could rest on political lobbying and philanthropy in behalf of what, after all, was a foreign country.

The possibility of building Jewish identity and group cohesiveness around the struggle against anti-Semitism or around leftist politics was also problematic. While many American Jews remained convinced that anti-Semitism was a serious threat, half of American Jews by the 1990s no longer were concerned about domestic anti-Semitism. As two leading sociologists of American Jewry noted, "The conceptions of the Jew as distinct from the non-Jew and of the reality of anti-Semitism have been eroded, at least among major segments of American Jews. . . . The traditional images of Jews and Gentiles are not as powerful as they once were, nor are they compatible with America's integrationist and pluralist ethos."[1]

In an age when many Americans considered *liberal* to be a mark of opprobrium, the continuing support of American Jews for left-of-center politics appeared anachronistic. Despite the 1983 claim of Rabbi Albert Vorspan, the head of the Reform movement's Social Action Commission, that "a commitment to social justice is inherent in Judaism," many Jews believed that liberalism was not an intrinsic trait of Jewishness or Judaism. The politics of American Jews stemmed rather from the unique historical circumstances of Jews in eastern Europe and the United States in the nineteenth and twentieth centuries. Liberalism, they maintained, was not an intrinsic component of the Jewish identity of Jews in Israel or North Africa. Nor was there anything exclusively Jewish about liberalism. Non-Jews could also favor civil rights, social welfare programs, civil liberties, the separation of church and state, a nonmilitaristic foreign policy, and the other major components of modern liberalism.[2]

The left-wing stance of American Jews was an example of what sociologists call cultural lag. The Jews differed from other major American ethnic or religious groups in not moving politically to the right as they ascended the social and economic ladder. An example of this cultural lag was Ellen Willis, a columnist for the left-of-center weekly *Village Voice*. Jewishness for Willis meant being part of "a persecuted minority." "To me," she said, "the status of Jews as . . . persecuted outsiders is at the core of what Judaism and Jewishness is all about. It's what all Jews—religious and secular, Zionist and non-Zionist, conservative and radical—have in common." But by the 1980s most contemporary Jews did not see themselves in such terms. The three-quarters of the world's Jews who lived in the United States, Great Britain, and Israel were not "persecuted outsiders." Indeed, if *Tikkun* and the *Village Voice* could be believed, the persecuted outsiders of Israel were the Palestinians and not the Jews. It was questionable whether the attenuated Jewish identity of a secularist and radical such as Willis could survive the recognition of Jewish *embourgeoisment.*[3]

Edward Koch's own life illustrated the glittering accomplishments as well as the clouded future of postwar American Jewry. The child of immigrants, he grew up in a poor neighborhood in the Bronx. His political career—both as a congressman from Greenwich Village and then as the second Jewish mayor of New York—personified the opportunities of American life for the children and grandchildren of those impoverished Jewish immigrants from central and eastern Europe who had settled in America's cities during the late nineteenth and early twentieth centuries. For twelve years, Koch dominated the city's politics. He became mayor at a time when New York was near bankruptcy, and he benefited from the city's economic boom of the 1980s. He also gained advantage from his willingness to exploit his Jewish background.

Beginning in 1977, when Bess Myerson campaigned at his side, Koch emphasized his Jewishness, and he rolled up large pluralities in Jewish districts. Koch was the most visibly Jewish politician of the 1980s. If his public success gratified New York's Jews, his private life did not gladden Jewish survivalists. Koch was consumed by politics and, despite the best efforts of New York Jewry's matchmakers, remained a bachelor. From the survivalist perspective, it would have been preferable had he married and become a father.

At least Koch did not intermarry. The growing rate of intermarriage was the most troubling aspect of contemporary American Jewish life for Jewish survivalists. Intermarriage presented an insoluble dilemma since it stemmed from diminishing anti-Semitism and rapid social and economic mobility, which Jews welcomed. With Jews now living in suburbia, attending residential colleges rather than urban commuter institutions, and working in corporate and academic bureaucracies, social contacts with Gentiles became closer and more frequent. Surveys taken in the 1980s revealed that a large majority of Jews had close relationships with Gentile colleagues and neighbors and that they had a more positive attitude toward non-Jews. No longer did Jews perceive all Gentiles to be closet anti-Semites. In such an atmosphere, an increase in intermarriage was inevitable. Jews who decried intermarriage proposed such panaceas as improving Jewish education and strengthening the Jewish family. None of these held out much prospect for slowing the rate of intermarriage, particularly since those most prone to intermarriage were the least likely to be enrolled by their parents in Jewish schools or to be the products of intensely Jewish families.[4]

Jewish parents were often unable to convey to their offspring the reasons for their opposition to intermarriage. The ethnic and religious loyalties that they took for granted did not resonate to the same extent among their children. Furthermore, the liberalism that Jewish parents had passed down to their children encouraged intermarriage. Liberalism warned against intolerance, encouraged people to judge others as individuals and not as members of a group, and argued that religious and ethnic differences were anachronisms. How could liberal Jews attribute to anti-Semitism the reluctance of Gentiles to marry Jews and at the same time oppose Jews selecting Gentile spouses without appearing to be bigots themselves? The answer that many Jews gave to their children for opposing intermarriage was sociological and psychological.

Marriage was difficult even in the best of circumstances, they argued, and marriage across religious and ethnic lines reduced the possibility for its success. The mental health of the couple and not the threat to Jewish survival became the basis for rejecting intermarriage. Such an argument was self-defeating when it became apparent by the 1980s that the success or failure of a marriage often had little to do with religious and ethnic differences. When this became evident, parents were left without an effective weapon for opposing intermarriage. For the young, intermarriage simply took the liberalism of their parents to its logical conclusion, and they viewed parental opposition to intermarriage as hypocritical, particularly in those cases when their parents had not previously exhibited any strong religious or ethnic attachments.

Another reason for the Jewish difficulty in opposing intermarriage was that it was a by-product of a development that Jews otherwise favored—the willingness of Gentiles to have closer social relationships with Jews. A Gallup poll in the 1970s revealed that over two-thirds of Americans approved of marriages between Jews and Christians. While Jews might have been gratified that Caroline Kennedy, the only daughter of President John F. Kennedy, would marry Edwin Schlossberg, they could not have been pleased that it took place in a Roman Catholic church. That Caroline Kennedy's paternal grandfather, Joseph P. Kennedy, had been an anti-Semite made her choice of a husband particularly noteworthy. The Kennedys were not the only prominent American family that had a Jewish member. Lee Radziwill, the sister of Jackie Kennedy, married Herbert Ross; Maria Cuomo, the daughter of Governor Mario Cuomo of New York, married Kenneth Cole; and Laura Delano Roosevelt, the granddaughter of President Franklin D.

Roosevelt and Eleanor Roosevelt and the daughter of Congressman Frank-lin Delano Roosevelt, Jr., married Charles H. Silberstein. In weddings of Jews and prominent Gentiles, the background of the Jewish spouse was not disguised, and it was not unusual for rabbis to officiate.[5]

Until the 1960s, few American Jews saw intermarriage as a threat to Jewish survival, in part because the intermarriage rate was low. Less than one out of fourteen Jews who married prior to the 1960s had a non-Jewish spouse. It was also due to the expectation that anti-Semitism would prevent widespread intermarriage and that Jewish community norms would con-tinue to discourage it. Surveys indicated that the overwhelming majority of Jewish parents strongly opposed intermarriage. The following joke from the 1950s indicates the popular attitude of Jews toward intermarriage. A Jewish soldier calls his mother to inform her that he is coming home from the Korean War. "That is wonderful," she replies. "I have survived the war without being wounded." "That is good," she responds. "I am bringing home a Korean wife," he then says. "That is also good." The soldier then says that he and his bride don't have a place to live. "That's okay. You can stay in my apartment," his mother tells him. "But you live in a one-bedroom apartment!" "That's no problem," the mother retorts. "After I put the phone down I am going to jump out of the window, and you will have the entire apartment to yourself."[6]

Such an attitude toward intermarriage was soon overtaken by events. The intermarriage rate increased so dramatically that by the 1980s few Jewish families, except for the Orthodox, had not been affected by it. Over one-third of American Jews who married in the 1980s had a non-Jewish spouse. In New York City the figure was lower, while in the hinterland the intermarriage rate was higher. In Denver, nearly three-quarters of the Jews had wed non-Jews. Jews did not know how to deal with what David Singer in 1979 described as "the single most pressing problem confronting the organized Jewish community." As intermarriage snowballed, Jews were less willing to object to it, particularly when many of the leaders of Amer-ica's most prominent Jewish organizations and their children were them-selves intermarried. If intermarriage was not viewed as a curse, neither was it viewed as a blessing. American Jews, Singer noted, were now condemned to "living with intermarriage."[7]

In the early 1970s, the protests of Jews regarding the television series *Bridget Loves Bernie* had caused the program to be taken off the air. Loosely based on the 1920s play *Abie's Irish Rose, Bridget Loves Bernie* concerned the tribulations of an intermarried couple played by David Birney and Meredith Baxter Birney, who in real life were an intermarried couple. In the late 1980s, these same Jewish organizations did not protest when the television shows *thirtysomething, Chicken Soup,* and *L.A. Law* portrayed romantic involvements and marriages between Jews and Christians. By the 1980s, most American Jews grudgingly accepted intermarriage since there was little they could do about it in any case. As Americans, they lived in a culture that believed that love could overcome all cultural barriers. Among Jews surveyed in Boston, the number of those who strongly opposed or would discourage their children from intermarrying had shrunk from 70 percent in 1965 to 31 percent in 1987. A national survey revealed that almost as many Jewish parents would be disturbed by a marriage between their child and a Hasid as would be upset by a marriage between their child and a Gentile.[8]

The writings of Marshall Sklare, the most distinguished American sociologist of American Jewry, reflected the growing concern of American Jewry with intermarriage. There was not one reference to intermarriage in his famous 1957 anthology, *The Jews: Social Patterns of an American Group.* Sklare's 1964 *Commentary* article, "Intermarriage and the Jewish Future," was among the first significant examinations of what up to that point had not been a decisive aspect of American Jewish sociology. It appeared in the same year that *Look* magazine published its famous cover story, "The Vanishing American Jew." Sklare noted that Jews had a reputation for resisting intermarriage, that the Jewish rate of endogamy was far higher than that of any other white ethnic or religious group, and that American Jewish leaders and scholars complacently believed the threat of intermarriage had been contained. The most widely accepted figure for the rate of intermarriage at that time was a low 7.2 percent.[9]

Sklare, however, was not optimistic about the future. He noted that the 7.2 percent figure was based on Jewish marriages among all ages, and that the figure for recent marriages might be twice as high. He warned that attributing intermarriage among Jews to self-hatred, cowardice in the face of anti-Semitism, or social climbing misread its etiology and conveyed to the Jewish community the mistaken message that intermarriage was the result of neurotic behavior. The desire to escape anti-Semitism or to rise on the social ladder could not have been important causes of intermarriage, Sklare argued, because marriages with Gentiles had increased while anti-Semitism was dwindling and many of the traditional status distinctions were being swept away. With Jews entering into the highest echelons of American society, there was no longer any reason for a status seeker to disguise a Jewish background.

He was also skeptical that intermarriage could be explained as the result of a conscious revolt of Jewish children from the ways of their parents. Such a revolt did take place among the children of the immigrants, he noted, but intermarriage did not surge until the emergence of the third generation. With their belief that intermarriage was a deviant act, Jews found it difficult to accept the reality that intermarriage was no longer an aberration. "Assumptions of pathology—social or personal—no longer explain either the rate or the reasons for exogamy among Jews," Sklare concluded. "From the evidence that has begun to accumulate, it is becoming impossible to view intermarriage as an indication either of personal aberration or of social persecution."

Sklare attributed the increase of intermarriage to the greater willingness of Gentiles to consider Jews as suitable marriage partners, to the massive movement of Jews out of Jewish neighborhoods and traditional Jewish occupations, to acculturation, to the diminished Jewish loyalties of the third (and fourth) generations, and to the high rate of college attendance among Jews, where they were exposed to the values of secularism, universalism, and egalitarianism that ran counter to the parochial impulses discouraging intermarriage. Intermarriage was an inevitable result of living in a free society. The dropping of social and economic barriers against Jews also led to the lowering of romantic barriers between Jews and Gentiles. Intermarriage, Sklare correctly noted, cast into doubt "American Jewry's dual ideal of full participation in the society and the preservation of Jewish identity."[10]

In 1964, Sklare was not yet convinced that the situation was irreparable, and he did not rule out the possibility that the threat of intermarriage could be countered. This hopeful note was missing from Sklare's next *Commentary* article on intermarriage, which appeared in 1970, one year before a major study revealed that the current Jewish intermarriage rate was over 31 percent. Sklare's essay bore the far more somber title "Intermarriage and Jewish Survival" and argued that, despite some hopeful signs of American Jewish renewal, the survival of the American Jewish community was imperiled. Sklare was concerned here not only with the increase in the intermarriage rate but also with its growing acceptance within American Jewry. The stance of parents and Jewish spokesmen toward intermarriage was in the process of changing from opposition to accommodation. "The Jewish community as a whole is soon bound to find itself embroiled in a bitter debate over what this new development portends for its survival as a distinctive group."[11]

By the 1980s, the impact of intermarriage had become pervasive within American Jewry. One indication was Mixed Blessing Inc. The company, founded in 1988 by Philip and Elise Okrend, a Jewish couple, produced greeting cards for intermarried couples that combined Jewish and Christian messages. One card had on its cover a figure that was half Christmas tree and half Star of David. Another pictured Santa Claus spinning a dreidel, a Hanukkah toy top with Hebrew lettering. A third card pictured a Christian angel lighting candles on a Hanukkah menorah. "Interfaith marriages can be a bit awkward at times," Philip Okrend said. "These cards preserve the joyful memories and feelings of both holidays." Unconvinced, Jewish and Christian leaders objected to the conflating of Judaism and Christianity. "It's a travesty to both faiths," one rabbi said. The Okrends were not dissuaded. "We're trying to promote unity more than anything else," Philip Okrend responded. For Jewish survivalists, it was precisely this dilution of Jewish distinctiveness manifested by interfaith greeting cards that was the major threat facing American Jews.[12]

The offspring of intermarriages often found themselves in limbo, not knowing whether they were Jews or Christians. Two such children founded Pareveh, the Alliance for Adult Children of Jewish-Gentile Intermarriage. The Jewish dietary laws divide food into three broad categories: meat, dairy, and pareveh, or nondairy and nonmeat items. According to kosher laws, while meat and dairy foods cannot be eaten at the same meal, pareveh foods can be consumed at any time. For the founders of the alliance, the use of the word pareveh signified that they felt themselves to be, in modern terminology, neither fish nor fowl. The logo of their organization was one half of a Jewish star surrounded by a circle. Of Pareveh's thirteen hundred members in 1990, 44 percent considered themselves to be Jewish, another 29 percent viewed themselves as Christians, and the remaining 27 percent described themselves as neither. Pareveh was, in essence, a support organization for those who had difficulty coming to terms with their mixed background. It provided to its members audiotapes such as "You're Not Alone: Our Lives as Children, Grandchildren and Great-grandchildren of Intermarriage," "But We're in Love! Thinking About a Happy Intermarriage," and "What About Our Grandchildren? Parents of Interfaith Couples." It also published in 1991 a guide for the children of intermarriages titled *Between Two Worlds*.[13]

By the 1980s, Jewish attitudes toward intermarriage had shifted, in Egon Mayer's words, "from outrage to outreach." Intermarriage manuals and pop sociological volumes describing the bliss of intermarriage were now available. They had such upbeat titles as *Mixed Blessings: Marriage between Jews and Christians*; *Intermarriage: The Challenge of Living with Differences between Christians and Jews*; *Intermarriage Handbook: A Guide for Jews and Christians*; *Happily Intermarried: Authoritative Advice for a Joyous Jewish-Christian Marriage*; and *Mixed Marriage: Between Jew and Christian*. Another, *When a Jew and Christian Marry*, was written by Samuel Sandmel, Distinguished Service Professor of Bible and Hellenistic Literature at Hebrew Union College, and was published by a Catholic press. For Rabbi Samuel Silver, the author of *Mixed Marriage*, intermarriages are "harbingers of a new kind of world unity, in which not only couples but ideologies and theologies will 'live happily ever after.'" They signal "the emergence of people who are determined to transcend the limitations of adherence to one branch of the Judeo-Christian family." Also available were guides to child rearing. An advertisement for one of these— Lee F. Gruzen's *Raising Your Jewish Christian Child: Wise Choices for Interfaith Parents*—stated that it showed how parents could enrich the spiritual lives of their children by providing them with the best from both the Jewish and Christian heritages. "This year's holidays can be the richest, most harmonious ones your family has ever celebrated." The advertisement appeared in *Commentary*.[14]

Jewish-Christian romances and intermarriage were grist for the mills of Philip Roth, Bernard Malamud, and other Jewish novelists. The eponymous protagonist of Chaim Potok's *My Name Is Asher Lev* does not intermarry, but he does have an urge to paint crucifixes. Hollywood movies also featured intermarriage. *The Heartbreak Kid* was a modern version of the theme of Jewish-Irish marriage that had been popular in such films of the 1920s as *Kosher Kitty Kelly, Abie's Irish Rose,* and *The Cohens and the Kellys.* In *The Heartbreak Kid,* Len Cantrow (Charles Grodin) marries Kelly Corcoran (Cybill Shepherd), while in *Play It Again, Sam,* Allan Felix (Woody Allen) is romantically involved with Linda Christie (i.e., Christ), played by Diane Keaton.

During the 1970s and 1980s, intermarriage became a major topic of investigation at the Petschek National Jewish Family Center of the American Jewish Committee, the Maurice and Marilyn Cohen Center for Modern Jewish Studies at Brandeis, and other Jewish think tanks, and sociologists produced significant works on intermarriage. The most important of these was Egon Mayer's *Love and Tradition: Marriage Between Jews and Christians* (1985). Mayer believed that the traditional Jewish opposition toward intermarriage would have to be modified if American Jewry was to survive the crisis of intermarriage.[15]

This crisis particularly affected the Reform movement, because intermarriages were more prevalent among its members than within Orthodoxy or Conservatism. Orthodox and Conservative rabbis would not officiate at an intermarriage since it was a violation of Jewish law. Although the Reform movement did not accept the binding power of Jewish law, it nevertheless had opposed intermarriage. As late as 1973, the Central Conference of American Rabbis, a Reform organization, reaffirmed this position. This resolution, however, was not binding on the CCAR's members, since no sanctions were imposed on dissenting rabbis. This was in keeping with the Reform movement's tradition of allowing its rabbis the autonomy to interpret Jewish tradition as they saw fit. Furthermore, the 1973 resolution was not a manifestation of any increased opposition to exogamy. Rather it was a last-ditch effort to hold the fort against the increasing sentiment within the Reform rabbinate in favor of participating in intermarriages.[16]

The growth in the intermarriage rate and the desire of the prospective Jewish spouse and his or her parents to have a rabbi participate resulted in Reform rabbis receiving an increasing number of requests to solemnize such marriages. This presented them with a dilemma. On the one hand, they realized that participating in an intermarriage was viewed as aberrant by the majority of their colleagues and that it ran counter to Jewish tradition. On the other hand, they sympathized with the idea of having a Jewish presence at an intermarriage, and they were often pressured by their congregants to participate in such weddings. They also feared that a refusal would lessen the possibility that the couple would ultimately identify with the Jewish community. Thus Rabbi Irwin Fishbein urged his colleagues in 1973 "not to slam a door that may be only slightly ajar" by refusing to officiate at intermarriages. Fishbein claimed that "rabbinic participation in mixed marriages is in the best tradition of Reform Judaism. It is an attempt to respond in a positive way to the increasing incidence of mixed marriage in a mobile and open society." As a result, not only did the number of

Reform rabbis willing to perform intermarriages increase, but they also became less defensive about doing so. By the time of the 1973 CCAR convention, at least 10 percent of America's approximately one thousand Reform rabbis were willing to officiate at intermarriages, and their numbers would escalate rapidly over the next two decades. One survey in the late 1980s estimated that half of Reform rabbis participated at mixed marriages.[17]

The Reform movement responded to a sense of despair regarding the demographic hemorrhaging of American Jewry in other ways as well. Rabbi Alexander Schindler, a leading Reform spokesman, proposed that Jews abandon their traditional resistance toward conversions and embark on a vigorous missionary campaign. In 1983, the Reform movement established the Commission on Reform Jewish Outreach to encourage "both the non-Jewish parents in mixed marriages and their children, along with the 'unchurched,' to convert to Judaism to become Jews by choice." Soon American Jews were distinguishing between "Jews from birth" and "Jews by choice." Orthodox and Conservative leaders opposed these proselytizing efforts. They feared that persons responding to a Reform-sponsored missionary program effort would be lukewarm Jews at best and that their conversions would not be conducted according to Jewish law. They were also not sympathetic with the proposal of Egon Mayer, perhaps the leading authority on intermarriage, to establish "conversion outreach centers." Mayer, however, did not believe that a large number of Gentile spouses would convert because of religious reasons even though many had a positive attitude toward various aspects of secular Jewish life. This led to his radical suggestion to change the nature of Jewish identity by creating a new category of Jew. These would be members of the Jewish "people" but not of the Jewish "faith." This "ethnic conversion" would confirm the Jewishness of individuals who "are Jews through the alchemy of sociology, not of *halachah*."[18]

Beginning in the 1950s, the number of converts to Judaism increased, from about three thousand to ten thousand per year in the 1980s. These, however, were more than counterbalanced by those Jews who became Christians or, more often, simply assimilated into the general society. Almost all converts to Judaism were individuals contemplating marriage with Jews. They included such celebrities as Sammy Davis, Jr., Lynda Carter ("Wonder Woman"), Marilyn Monroe, and Elizabeth Taylor. Conversions by prominent Americans revealed the higher status of Jews and Judaism in postwar America, but they also demonstrated that, as in the case of Davis, Monroe, and Taylor, such conversions often had to be taken with a grain of salt. When Monroe's marriage to playwright Arthur Miller and Taylor's marriages to impresario Mike Todd and singer Eddie Fisher ended in divorce, the two actresses resumed their lives with no evidence of any continuing Jewish identity they had presumably assumed upon conversion.[19]

Jews by choice, as the converts referred to themselves, were a different type of Jew. The vast majority of their conversions resulted from the desire to please a prospective Jewish spouse. A small minority of converts were attracted to Judaism. In neither case, however, did the converts have any feeling for the ethnic or historical dimensions of Jewishness. Coming from Christian backgrounds, the converts saw Judaism simply as a faith community similar to that of Christianity, and, as a result, they embraced a watered-down version of Jewishness. One example was *Choosing Judaism* (1981), a Reform guide to conversion written by Lydia Kukoff, a convert. This book paid no attention to the Jews' relationship to the Holocaust or to Israel. Many of the Jews by choice realized that the Orthodox in the United States viewed their conversions with skepticism and that the Orthodox rabbinate in Israel did not consider them to be Jews. The desire of the Reform and Conservative movements to have the Israeli religious establishment legitimize non-Orthodox conversions and a non-Orthodox rabbinate was one factor in the bitter Israeli political struggle in the 1980s over the question of who is a Jew.

Even more controversial than the Reform's decision to undertake a proselytizing campaign was the 1983 resolution of the Central Conference of American Rabbis that a child with one Jewish parent would be classified as Jewish if the child, "through appropriate and timely public and formal acts of identification with the Jewish faith and people," indicated a wish to identify with Judaism and the Jewish people. These acts included attending religious school and participating in religious services. By implication, a child with a Jewish mother and a Gentile father would not be considered Jewish if these "formal acts of identification" were not performed. The 1983 decision resulted in part from pressure on the part of the Reform lay leadership that such children—their own children and grandchildren—not be written off. The Reform rabbinate was also eager for these children to remain within the Jewish community and the Reform fold, and it wished to eliminate from Judaism distinctions based on gender. The patrilineal decision was not a radical break with Reform practice since in many Reform congregations the children of non-Jewish mothers were already considered "cultural" Jews. Ideologically, however, it was a sharp break with the conventional definition of a Jew based on matrilineal descent or traditional conversion.[20]

Conservative and Orthodox rabbis, as well as a minority of Reform rabbis, feared that the patrilineal decision could split American Jewry. They warned that this sharp break with Jewish tradition would force Jews to investigate the family pedigree of prospective spouses to ensure that they were actually Jewish. They also asserted that the 1983 decision granted a certain legitimacy to intermarriages. Finally, they noted that it had de-legitimized children with Jewish mothers and non-Jewish fathers who were unwilling, for whatever reason, to perform "formal acts of identification." Jewish law had always considered such persons to be Jewish based on the principle of matrilineal descent.

Jewish survivalists were concerned both with the quantitative and qualitative aspects of intermarriage. Intermarriage reduced the size of the American Jewish population. Furthermore, the Jewish identity of intermarried families was not as strong as that of endogamous families. Handwringing regarding intermarriage generally missed the point: intermarriage was not the cause of acculturation and assimilation but its result. Jews did not intermarry in order to assimilate; they intermarried because they were already largely assimilated. This triumph of love over tradition indicated the extent to which they were Jewish Americans rather than American Jews.

The rise in intermarriage helped exhume the debate of the 1950s over whether Jewish continuity was compatible with freedom. Sociologist Charles Liebman did not believe so and, as a result, had immigrated to Israel. In *The Ambivalent American Jew,* Liebman warned that, "if the Jewish community is to survive, it must become more explicit and conscious about the incompatibility of integration and survival" and "at least to some extent, reject the value of integration, which I see as sapping its very essence." The problem, as Liebman well knew, was that except for the growth of the Jewish day school movement, there were few signs that American Jews agreed with him."[21]

Intermarriage was merely one element of the demographic stagnation of American Jewry that troubled Jewish survivalists. From a high of 3.7 percent of the American population in 1937, the Jewish population declined to 3.01 percent in 1961 and to about 2.5 percent by the early 1990s. This shrinkage was not merely relative. In 1984, Marshall Sklare estimated that America's Jewish population had declined somewhere between 250,000 and 400,000 since 1970. "What's worse," he added, "it should snowball from here." Sidney Goldstein, a prominent Jewish sociologist, predicted in 1981 that there would be no more than four million American Jews by the year 2100. Nathan Glazer agreed with Sklare and Goldstein. "American Jews," he said in 1986, "stand at a point where the maintenance of their absolute numbers in the United States, let alone their proportion in the general population, is unlikely." Demographer Elihu Bergman's forecast was the most pessimistic. In a famous article in 1977 in *Midstream* magazine, "The American Jewish Population Erosion," he claimed that by 2076 the American Jewish population could be as little as ten thousand and no more than a million. "If present trends are not arrested or reversed, the American Jewish community faces extinction as a significant entity, and by its own hand" by the middle of the twenty-first century. While no other scholar accepted Bergman's figures, most shared his long-term pessimism.[22]

A smaller American Jewish population had important implications for fund-raising, political influence (particularly as it pertained to Israel), and the viability of communal institutions. The leveling off of the Jewish population at somewhere between five and a half and six million and the likelihood of its decline was particularly distressing because of the loss of one-third of world Jewry in the Holocaust. American Jewry, the largest Jewish community in the world, was not contributing to the replenishing of Jewish numbers.

Previously in American history, immigration had boosted the Jewish population, but this had not taken place to the same extent after 1945. The postwar waves of Jewish immigrants were small in comparison to those of the nineteenth and early twentieth centuries, and the Jewish identity of the Israelis and Soviets who made up the majority of the Jewish immigration of the 1970s and 1980s was often attenuated. Much to the amazement of American Jews, many of the Israeli and Russian immigrants were Jewish in name only. The most important waves of immigration to America during the 1970s and 1980s were from Latin America and Asia, and these contained few Jews. Even if the Jewish and non-Jewish birth rates had been comparable, the percentage of Jews in the general population would have declined because of immigration. By 1990, there were more Asians living in the United States than Jews.[23]

American Jews were ignoring the first commandment of the Bible to "be fruitful and multiply." Since the 1930s the Jewish birth rate had been approximately one-quarter to one-third less than that of Gentiles, and this disparity continued into the 1960s, when the birth rate among Jews declined to below the zero population growth (ZPG) rate of 2.1 births per woman. The Jewish birth rate remained below ZPG throughout the 1970s and 1980s. "For American Jewry," sociologist Chaim I. Waxman said, "the issue is not that of zero population growth, but of negative population growth." The prognosis was particularly bleak because the intermarriage rate was increasing, and intermarried couples have fewer children. Furthermore, every year more Jews were becoming part of that segment of society that has a low fertility rate—the college-educated, upwardly mobile, affluent residents of metropolitan regions.[24]

Some American Jews were not only troubled by the overall low Jewish birth rate but also by the disparity between it and the much higher birth rate of the Orthodox. If the current trends in birth rates continued into the twenty-first century, the power of the Orthodox in the United States (and in Israel) would inevitably increase. This was not a comforting prospect for those fearful of Orthodox hegemony within American Jewry.

No other major ethnic or religious group had as low a birth rate as American Jews. By the 1970s, alarmists were decrying the impact this was having on the prospects for long-term Jewish survival in America and were pleading with Jewish couples to have one more child per family. Such cheerleading had little effect. The Jewish birth dearth was determined by social and economic factors, not by appeals to conscience. The social characteristics of Jews were precisely those that demographers associate with low birth rates and late marriages. Episcopalians and Presbyterians living in Scarsdale and Short Hills also had low birth rates and a high number of single people. Conversely, the Jewish birth rate was highest in the least acculturated segment of American Jewry—the Orthodox communities of Brooklyn and upstate New York.[25]

The low birth rate of Jews helped account for another significant element in the American Jewish demographic crisis—the greying of American Jewry. American Jews were considerably older than the rest of the population and, as a result, their mortality rate was higher. In 1980, 15.5 percent of the Jewish population was over sixty-five, compared to 11.8 percent for the total American white population. In response to the growth of the Jewish elderly, Jewish federations established new vocational, social, and medical programs to service the aged, and Jewish old-age homes were expanded and new residential facilities were constructed.[26]

Except among the Orthodox, the traditional Jewish American family seemed to be in serious trouble in the 1970s and 1980s. Steven Bayme, the Director of the American Jewish Committee's Jewish Communal Affairs Department, asserted in 1989 that "the increasing numbers of Jews found in alternative family constellations threaten to undermine traditional ideas and replace them with a family value system in which all alternatives become equally valid." Jewish spokesmen and scholars emphasized that Jews living in "alternative family" situations were less affiliated with Jewish organizations and their Jewish identity was weaker than those residing in traditional two-parent families with children at home. Not only did the traditional family socialize their children into becoming Jews, but this process of socialization in turn increased the parents' Jewish consciousness. Thus parents often joined synagogues and began attending religious services when it was time for their oldest child to attend Hebrew school. This process, however, did not have the same effect on alternative families. Unconventional families, Steven M. Cohen noted, "constitute a challenge to an organized Jewry that to this day is built largely around the conventional two-Jewish-parents-with-children family."[27]

During the 1970s and 1980s, the divorce rate among Jews approached that of Gentiles, and the percentage of Jewish children living in one-parent families rose steadily. In addition, the Jewish marriage rate decreased. For the first time in its history, American Jewry had a large number of singles. According to one study, in 1965 73 percent of Jewish adults in Boston were married. Only 56 percent were married ten years later. "It's a huge problem," Sylvia Barack Fishman of Brandeis's Cohen Center said. "People in general are marrying later, but Jewish people are marrying even later. This works against the communal interest. It becomes a Jewish issue because whatever may be adaptive in the general community, may be maladaptive in the Jewish community, a minority community which already suffers from intermarriage." Between 1967 and 1979 the percentage of never-married Jews in their thirties increased by over two and a half times, and the percentage of separated and divorced Jews in the same age group quadrupled. One survey of over six thousand Jewish males found that half of all the men under forty were either intermarried or divorced, and many of the remaining men were single. This, of course, was one element in the low Jewish birth rate.[28]

Synagogues and Jewish secular organizations such as the Ninety-second Street YM-YWHA in New York developed programs to deal with what was described as the singles problem. The Lincoln Square Synagogue in Manhattan was particularly renowned in this respect. It came to be known as the "wink-and-stare synagogue" because of its extensive efforts in matchmaking among New York yuppies. Jewish professionals were well aware of the sociological literature demonstrating that singles tended to have weaker Jewish identities than those who were married and had children. If Jewish teachings encouraged marriage, marriage in turn encouraged Jewishness.

One of the most important factors influencing the American Jewish family was the higher career aspirations of American women. Social trends such as suburbanization, the growth in white-collar employment, and the emergence of a feminist movement that emphasized individual self-fulfillment encouraged women to acquire job skills, to marry later, and to have fewer children. This became noticeable in the mid-1960s with the ending of the postwar baby boom and an increase in the percentage of women attending college and professional schools. Within two decades, over 40 percent of law school and accounting graduates would be women. The mass media reflected this change. The enormously successful television series *L.A. Law,* for example, featured four female attorneys, only one of whom was married.

One of the reasons that some Jewish organizations gave for opposing affirmative action during the 1970s and 1980s was the fear that favoritism for blacks and Hispanics might adversely affect the prospects for college-educated Jewish women. As members of the middle and upper-middle class and as the offspring of parents who had high career aspirations for their children, Jewish women were particularly well situated to take advantage of these new economic opportunities. In addition, a higher percentage of Jewish women went to college than their Gentile counterparts, and there was a positive correlation between education and female labor force participation. Jewish women increased their involvement in the labor force during the 1970s and 1980s more rapidly than did the women of probably any other ethnic group. One 1985 survey reveals that only one out of three Jewish women believed that women who stay at home make better mothers than those who work outside of the home. Not surprisingly, a disproportionate number of the leading feminists, including Betty Friedan, Shulamith Firestone, Susan Brownmiller, Andrea Dworkin, and Robin Morgan, were Jews.[29]

The women's movement affected other aspects of the American Jewish community besides the family. With more women working, there was a shortage of hands to do the volunteer work that was the lifeblood of the federations, synagogue sisterhoods, and local and national organizations. After spending a day at the office, women were less willing to attend meetings at night, and as a result, the memberships of the women's branch of B'nai B'rith, Hadassah, and of other organizations declined. One Hadassah leader described the crisis in voluntarism as "the panty hose syndrome." "If we can find a way to have a meeting when a woman has her panty hose on, she'll go. But the minute she comes home and they're off, that's it." Hadassah, by far the largest and most successful Jewish women's organization, ran a full-page advertisement in the *New York Times* seeking members. The average age of its members was then about fifty. Hadassah and other Jewish organizations were adversely affected by the feminist movement's denigration of voluntarism as unworthy of the time and attention of the liberated and economically self-sufficient new woman. "Jewish women's organizations and sisterhoods are being phased out," Trude Weiss-Rosmarin, the editor of the *Jewish Spectator,* asserted. "Women's 'auxiliaries' are obsolete. They do not fit into our culture at the time when men and women share the same concerns and commitment and are equally well educated and informed."[30]

Beginning in the 1970s, feminists attacked traditional Judaism for its sharp gender distinctions. In Jewish law, women have different rights and obligations from those of men. Thus women are exempt from the requirement of morning prayer because of their family responsibilities, are unable to be a witness in a religious trial, cannot initiate a divorce, cannot lead the congregation in prayer or read from the Torah, and cannot sit alongside men in the synagogue. For Jewish feminists, this smacked of misogyny, and they demanded change. Women, Weiss-Rosmarin wrote in 1970, "resent the legal inferiority and disabilities to which Jewish law subjects them. They want legal equality, especially with respect to the laws of marriage and divorce." The influence of the feminists was felt throughout American Judaism, even within Orthodoxy.[31]

The discontent of Jewish feminists led to the founding of the Jewish Feminist Organization (1974–77), to the issuing of feminist haggadahs (the book read during the Passover seder), to the establishing of Jewish women's consciousness-raising groups, to the publishing (beginning in 1976) of *Lilith,* a Jewish feminist magazine, to the development of nonsexist Jewish liturgies, and to the publication of books on women and Jewish law and the history of Jewish women. The Statement of Purpose of the Jewish Feminist Organization eloquently laid out the goals of those who sought to synthesize Jewishness with feminism.

> We, Jewish feminists, have joined together here in strength and joy to struggle for the liberation of the Jewish woman. Jewish women of all ages, political, cultural and religious outlooks and sexual preferences, are all sisters. We are committed to the development of our full human potential and to the survival and enhancement of Jewish life. We seek nothing less than the full, direct and equal participation of women at all levels of Jewish life—communal, religious, educational and political. We shall be a force for such creative change in the Jewish community.[32]

Jewish feminism stemmed from the women's movement of the 1960s and the stirring of Jewish consciousness of the late 1960s and early 1970s. As feminist Ellen M. Umansky noted, Jewish feminism emerged "as a means of asserting both *Jewish* visibility within the feminist movement and *feminist* consciousness within the U.S. Jewish community." According to the feminists, Jewish women were victims of a conspiracy to keep them pampered, protected, and powerless. "The issue is not *Halakha* at all," one feminist declared. "The issue is male fear and rage at the idea of autonomous women defining their own relationship to the Jewish tradition. The issue is power: Who will have power over Jewish women's lives?"[33]

Under feminist pressure, the Reform and Conservative movements sought to purge themselves of sexism by ordaining women as rabbis and cantors, by counting them for a minyan, and by granting them all religious honors available to men. Reform went further in eliminating gender distinctions, including redefining Jewish identity to encompass patrilineal as well as matrilineal descent. By the 1980s, one-third of the rabbinical students at Hebrew Union College were women, and in 1986 the entire class of cantors at HUC consisted of women.[34]

Even the Orthodox were affected by feminism. Modern Orthodox leaders, while remaining faithful to Jewish law, allowed women to organize themselves into prayer groups and to study the Talmud. They also encouraged Shalom Bat and Bat Torah ceremonies—feminine counterparts to the Shalom Zachor and Bar Mitzvah ceremonies for boys—marking the birth of a girl and her reaching the age of religious maturity. Within Orthodox circles, it became common for girls as well as boys to spend a year studying in Israel after high school graduation. In Boro Park, an Orthodox neighborhood in Brooklyn, women established an organization called Getting Equal Treatment (GET) to compel husbands to grant their wives *gets* (Jewish divorces). Orthodox women also sought rabbinical sanction for minyans at which women would pray apart from men and read from the Torah. Among the most interesting examples of this syncretism between Orthodoxy and feminism was Esther Jungreis. A female Jewish Billy Graham, this attractive and well-dressed Long Island wife and mother conducted revival meetings in order to bring Jews back to tradition. Blu Greenberg, a modern Orthodox feminist and the wife of Rabbi Irving Greenberg, predicted that her lifetime would see the ordaining of women Orthodox rabbis, a forecast shared by few other observers of contemporary Orthodoxy.35

Besides religion, the other area of major concern for Jewish feminists was the paucity of women in positions of power in Jewish federations and national organizations, both on lay and professional levels. The title of one article in *Lilith* declared, "The Jewish Establishment Is Not an Equal Opportunity Employer." This, the feminists argued, stemmed from a pervasive sexism within American Jewry and not from the career choices or interests of American Jewish women. Women had been relegated to menial tasks, such as preparing the collations after Sabbath services and collecting money for Hadassah; they could be found in positions of power in large numbers only in exclusively women's organizations.36

Beginning in the 1970s, women made gains in Jewish organizational life, particularly in the area of voluntarism. By the end of the decade, women were presidents of five of the thirty-two Jewish cultural organizations, of seven of the twenty-four community relations agencies, and of two of the sixteen overseas aid organizations. Ten of the 137 executive officers of religious and cultural organizations were women. This ratio increased during the 1980s. By the mid-1980s, the proportion of women on the boards of federations and federation-funded agencies had increased to 40 percent, and women were federation presidents in Baltimore, Boston, Los Angeles, and New York.37

Women did not make as much progress as professionals in Jewish organizations. A 1981 survey conducted by the Conference of Jewish Communal Service revealed that women comprised only 8 percent of the executive directors and assistant directors of 273 agencies. Women professionals found it difficult to reach the highest echelons of Jewish organizations and, as a result, had lower salaries. Chaim Waxman predicted in 1983 that, "given this pattern of exclusion, women who seek leadership positions will probably find them outside Jewish organizational life and increasing numbers of Jewish women . . . will . . . feel alienated from American Jewish communal life." Feminists were concerned with more than merely opening up the ranks of Jewish organizations to women. They also objected to the fact that the most important of their concerns—providing day care under Jewish auspices and the high price of Jewish education—were not very high on the priorities of these Jewish philanthropies.[38]

Feminist complaints regarding Jewish organizations were of direct interest to only a small minority of women. This was not true of another area of feminist concern—combating the negative images of Jewish women, particularly the notion of the Jewish American princess (JAP). Feminists believed that the liberation of Jewish women could not occur until they became fully aware of the extent to which they had internalized this image of the JAP. Even women who normally did not think of themselves as liberated were sensitized into protesting the stereotype. Disseminated by comedians and JAP joke books, "Slap a JAP" sweatshirts, movies such as Paul Mazursky's *Down and Out in Beverly Hills,* and novels such as Philip Roth's *Goodbye, Columbus,* the stereotype portrayed Jewish women, particularly those who had grown up in the gilded ghettos of suburbia, as materialistic, frigid, emasculating, and self-centered. One of the effects of the JAP stereotype, it was feared, was increased intermarriage, since it presented Gentile woman as far more appealing, which in turn reduced the number of potential mates for Jewish women.

By the 1980s, much of the Jewish feminist agenda had been achieved. The Reform and Conservative seminaries were graduating female rabbis and cantors; the American Jewish Congress and other Jewish organizations supported such feminist concerns as affordable day care and abortion rights; and women had a larger role in Jewish organizational life. For Jewish survivalists, however, the crucial question concerned the long-term impact of feminism on American Jewish life and not the personal fulfillment of individuals. Charles E. Silberman was among the optimists. "In the long run," he said, "the energy being released by the Jewish women's movement is likely to provide the most important source of religious renewal." Other persons, however, argued that, insofar as feminism encouraged late marriages, lower birth rates, and careerism among women, it had had a negative impact on Judaism and Jewish survival. Historian Lucy Dawidowicz warned of the incompatibility between some feminist objectives and "the Jewish communal need for stability, security, and survival." Blu Greenberg suggested that feminist goals be tempered by Jewish needs and that couples have children before moving on to dual careers.[39]

Most Jewish sociologists prior to the 1980s were gloomy regarding the future of American Jewry. In the 1940s and 1950s they worried that the vicissitudes of the business cycle and anti-Semitism threatened American Jewry, while during the 1960s and 1970s they emphasized the threat of affirmative action, acculturation, and assimilation. In his 1985 *Commentary* essay "On Jewish Forebodings," Nathan Glazer asserted that, while Jews would continue to identify as Jews, "little by way of custom, belief, or loyalty will be assumed as a result of their identity as Jews. . . . The sociologists who have persistently feared for the American Jewish future may . . . have feared for the wrong reasons; but I believe they have been right to be fearful."[40]

In the 1980s, however, a few Jewish sociologists dissented from this pessimism. The most important aspect of the study of contemporary American Jewish sociology during the 1980s was the debate between transformationists such as Steven Cohen, Calvin Goldscheider, and Alvin Zuckerman, who believed the American Jewish community was in the process of being transformed but not weakened, and assimilationists such as Charles Liebman, Marshall Sklare, William B. Helmreich, and Glazer, who asserted that American Jewry was assimilating culturally and declining numerically.

The transformationists acknowledged that America had greatly modified Jewish life during the twentieth century, but they argued that this did not threaten Jewish continuity. They claimed that new criteria must be used for judging the vitality of American Jewish life, criteria that were appropriate for Jews living in modern rather than premodern times. The ebbing of the customs and observances that Jews brought with them from Europe and the Arab lands has been counterbalanced by the emergence of new practices, such as the celebration of Hanukkah, and of new concerns, such as Russian Jewry and the security of the state of Israel.

Thus the transformationists were not unduly disturbed by the low percentage of American Jews who observed the Sabbath and maintained a kosher household. The transformationists also argued that intermarriage was actually increasing the Jewish population because of the many Gentile spouses who converted to Judaism and because, they contended, at least half of the children in intermarried families were being raised as Jews. These assertions were highly problematic. Even more important for the transformationists was that Jews even into the fourth generation continued to identify themselves as Jews, to live in Jewish neighborhoods, and to have Jews as their closest friends. Finally, the transformationists were not convinced that Jewish schools had failed in imparting a sense of Jewish identity to their students.[41]

The bête noire of the transformationists was a sociological paradigm that argued that modernization was incompatible with the maintenance of strong ethnic and religious loyalties. This paradigm was strongly challenged, particularly by Goldscheider and Zuckerman in their *The Transformation of the Jews* (1984). For them, the modernization process had modified but not attenuated Jewish identity. Industrialization, urbanization, and nationalism had undermined traditional religious mores, but they also led to the emergence of new religious ideologies, to the birth of modern Zionism and then Israel, and new bases of ethnic and religious cohesion such as Jewish cultural organizations and Jewish suburban neighborhoods. According to Goldscheider and Zuckerman, modernization had actually strengthened Jewish cohesion.[42]

As modern social scientists, the transformationists relied on survey research for their information. The transformationists' critics were skeptical of the accuracy of sampling techniques, since individuals disaffected from the Jewish community would probably not be reached by such surveys. Even more important was the transformationists' reliance on computer printouts. Statistics can measure, but they cannot evaluate. Thus they could reveal how many Jews attended a Passover seder, but they could not disclose what took place at the seder and what significance it had for those attending. Statistics could also not distinguish between peripheral and important Jewish involvements. Lighting Hanukkah candles was put on the same level with not riding on the Sabbath since both are ritual observances. But observing the Sabbath connoted a depth of Jewish commitment that was far greater than lighting candles.

For the transformationists, the key issue was cultural cohesiveness and survival. For assimilationists such as Glazer, the key issue was whether there was anything worth preserving in American Jewish culture. From the assimilationist perspective, the manner in which the transformationists framed their questions and defined Jewish identity confirmed their fears that American Jewish culture had been trivialized. In the final analysis, the difference between the transformationists and the assimilationists did not concern the question merely of whether the glass of American Jewish identity was half empty or half full. It also involved the issue of whether the liquid was worth drinking in the first place.

The assimilationists dismissed the transformationists as Pollyannas, particularly regarding intermarriage. The assimilationists emphasized traditional standards of Jewish identity such as religious observance and endogamy and contended that, based on such touchstones, the image of a declining American Jewry was accurate. In his strongly argued essay "Misguided Optimism," Helmreich asserted that the transformationist claim that Jewish identity had remained strong while taking on new forms was "rather weak and unimpressive." The reality was that large numbers of Jews had drifted away from communal affiliation. "Can a minority comprising less than 2.5 percent of the total American population," he rhetorically asked, "lose so many of its coreligionists without suffering irreparable damage? Perhaps the optimists can answer that question."[43]

The argument between the transformationists and the assimilationists received popular attention in 1985 with the publication of Charles Silberman's *A Certain People*. A well-known journalist and author of a series of books on contemporary American problems, Silberman strongly argued the transformationist position. For him, the issue was not Jewish survival, which he assumed as a given, but rather the quality of the Jewish community. Silberman viewed the openness of America as an opportunity rather than a danger to Jewish identity. He stressed that the overwhelming majority of American Jews were choosing to remain Jews, a creative intellectual ferment permeated American Jewish life, new religious rites and new forms of Jewish identity had emerged, and Jews gave generously of their time and money to Jewish causes. *A Certain People* claimed that postwar America resembled previous golden ages of Jewish life in which there was fruitful cross-fertilization between Jewish culture and that of the general society. Even though they were thoroughly American, Jews had remained "a certain people."

Silberman was an active member of the Reconstructionist movement. He was a member of the Board of Governors of the Reconstructionist Rabbinical College and chairman of the Reconstructionist Prayerbook Commission. Silberman's stress on the validity of diverse forms of Jewish expression and his definition of a Jew as anyone who identified with the Jewish people echoed the Reconstructionist emphasis on Jewish peoplehood.

Silberman had little patience for the Orthodox claim that only Jews born to a Jewish mother or converted according to Orthodox standards could be considered Jews. His frame of reference was sociological, the willingness of people to identify as Jews. Silberman (and the other transformationists), however, refused to pass judgment on the precise nature of this identity or to speculate on the impact of Jewish values and ideas on the daily lives of America's Jews. No distinction was drawn between the Jewishness of a first-generation immigrant and that of his Jewish great-grandchild. Both were Jewish.

For critics of the transformationists, there was more to being Jewish than writing a check to the UJA, attending a seder, and belonging to a synagogue. As Glazer noted in his review of *A Certain People,* the book ignored the fact that the "characteristic wholeness and density of Jewish life has been radically broken." Jewishness has become largely "symbolic and gestural," an inheritance that Jews respect but that has little influence in their daily lives. While American Jews might be a certain people, they no longer saw themselves as a chosen people or a separate people. American Jews were becoming Jews in the way that other Americans were Presbyterians, Masons, and Republicans. Had Silberman been more concerned with the interior life of America's Jews, Glazer concluded, he might have tempered his optimism.[44]

Silberman and the other transformationists discounted the pessimistic conclusions found in most of the sociological literature regarding contemporary American Jewry. They ignored, for example, overwhelming evidence pointing to a Jewish fertility rate below replacement level and the demographic hemorrhaging caused by intermarriage. In contrast to the figures of the transformationists, the statistics of most students of intermarriage indicated that by the 1980s no more than 20 percent of the Gentile spouses in intermarriages were converting to Judaism. Only one quarter of the children in mixed marriages where the Gentile spouse did not convert were being raised as Jews, and very few of these children themselves were marrying Jews. According to two prominent Jewish demographers, the transformationists had put forward "unfounded claims, formulated in sweeping terms and with internal contradictions—although the fragmentary data that do exist go far to disprove" their arguments.[45]

For American Jewish survivalists, the important question of Jewish numbers was subsidiary to that of the quality of Jewish life. Jewish survival was justified, they believed, only if the quality of that life was worth preserving. While the optimists pointed to the minority of American Jews who had become more Jewish, the pessimists emphasized the growing number of Jews who had little contact with things Jewish. The postwar Jewish renewal evidenced by the growth of the day school movement, the flourishing of Orthodoxy, the love affair with Israel, a greater concern with tradition within Reform, the increase in Jewish philanthropy, and Jewish studies in academia affected only a minority of America's nearly six million Jews. Perhaps a quarter of America's Jews were Jews in name only. Jewish educators concluded that Jewish parents were getting for their children the pathetic Jewish education they wanted and deserved. Of the major American religious groups, the Jews consistently placed last in surveys of religious attendance and belief.

"Acculturation without assimilation" was one sociologist's apt description of Chicago Jewry, a description equally appropriate for the Jewish population of other cities. American Jews did not wish to assimilate, and they had built an elaborate institutional structure to prevent this. But they were fuzzy as to what being Jewish should mean. There was much truth to the sardonic comment of Ze'ev Chafets, who had moved to Israel from Michigan, that "in most places, Judaism doesn't seem to be about anything. It is a holding operation—an effort to wring one more generation of allegiance from people who are no longer sure what being a Jew is all about. In Israel, the national anthem is 'Ha-Tikvah,' the hope; in America it is 'We're Here Because We're Here.'"[46]

The most important aspect of recent American Jewish history has been the transformation of American Jews into Jewish Americans. The price of their remarkable economic and social ascent had been the attenuation of Jewish identity. This process had been slowed down by recollections of the Holocaust and anti-Semitism and by Israel's seemingly precarious position. As time goes on, however, there are fewer and fewer American Jews who have personally experienced the Holocaust or serious anti-Semitism. Only Israel has the ability to evoke deep passion among American Jews, but it is doubtful that a strong American Jewish identity could be based on a vicarious identification with a foreign country by third- and even fourth-generation Americans. The problem facing American Jewry in the 1990s—the largest Jewish community in history—is apathy and not the hostility of the host society. "In a free and open society the drift away from Jewish life is not surprising," Daniel J. Elazar wrote. "Indeed, the way it occurs—so casually and without deliberate intent, so unlinked to ideology, and certainly not to any ideology of assimilationism—is . . . a reflection on the character of American society."[47]

This thinning of Jewish identity was reflected in the growing number of persons who were not affiliated with the Jewish community. During the 1970s and 1980s, synagogues, particularly Conservative synagogues, and secular organizations such as the American Jewish Committee, the American Jewish Congress, and B'nai B'rith experienced a shrinkage in membership despite strenuous efforts to stem this decline. The phenomenon of widespread nonaffiliation was particularly noticeable in metropolitan Los Angeles, where only one in four Jewish families belonged to a synagogue and less than 7 percent contributed to the local Jewish federation. The city's intermarriage rate and percentage of mixed marriages in which the Gentile spouse did not convert to Judaism was also growing. By the 1980s, mixed marriages in Los Angeles outnumbered conversionary marriages by three to one. The situation in Los Angeles was especially troubling because of the avant-garde reputation of southern California. It was assumed that social trends characteristic of Los Angeles would eventually spread to the rest of the country. Furthermore, the flow of Jewish population was to southern California and other sunbelt areas. "After all," Bruce Phillips, a Jewish demographer, noted, "how often do you meet someone in Michigan or Brooklyn who moved there from L.A.?"[48]

By the 1990s, American Jews faced a unique situation, one for which their history had not prepared them. "There are massive forces of attrition and hemorrhaging occurring in the Jewish community," Rabbi Henry Siegman said in 1977. If anything, these forces accelerated after 1977. While few American Jews formally repudiated Jewishness through apostasy, perhaps a third of America's Jews had concluded that being Jewish was a trivial element in their lives. Indifference and not anti-Semitism was the source of most of what ailed American Jews. Intermarriage, for instance, was the symptom; apathy was the disease. For the apathetic, being Jewish involved an annual contribution to the local federation, attendance at the synagogue on the Jewish New Year and Day of Atonement, and having Jewish friends.[49]

Viewed from the perspective of history and sociology, the future did not seem bright. "The momentum of Jewish experience in America is essentially spent," historian Arthur Hertzberg said in 1989. "Ethnicity will no doubt last for several more generations, but it is well on the way to becoming a memory. But a community cannot survive on what it remembers; it will persist only because of what it affirms and believes." And Hertzberg, who was also a rabbi, was impressed by the absence among American Jews of such affirmations, particularly regarding Judaism. According to Hillel Halkin, Jewish life in America was doomed. "Jewish life has a future, if at all, only in Israel; . . . Jewish and Israeli history are two converging lines that are ultimately bound to meet, so that whoever wishes to be a point on one must be one on the other as well."[50]

After 1945, American Jewry, the largest, wealthiest, and most powerful community in the history of the Diaspora, confronted the challenge of freedom and opportunity. There now seemed hardly any honor or position in American life for which they could not aspire. The question posed by Barbra Streisand in the film *Funny Girl* (1968)—"is a nose with deviations a crime against the nation?"—was answered after World War II with a resounding no. Gentiles enjoyed the movies of Woody Allen, they made bestsellers out of *Marjorie Morningstar, Exodus, Portnoy's Complaint,* and other books with Jewish themes, and they helped Harry Golden become a Jewish Will Rogers. A black comedienne by the name of Caryn Johnson even thought it would benefit her career if she changed her name to Whoopi Goldberg. This openness of American society also meant that there were few external influences forcing Jews to affirm a sense of Jewishness. Jews would continue being Jews because they wanted to, not because they were being forced to. The initiative for Jewish continuity would have to come from within.

Some Jews doubted that this would be enough. They continued to harp on the threat of anti-Semitism, fearing that otherwise the solvent of assimilation would be too powerful. That the major threat to Jewish identity came from the friendliness of American society and not its hostility was borne out in March 1991, when an event occurred that perhaps more than any other, illuminated the situation of Jews in postwar America. On Sunday, 24 March, Harvard University selected Neil L. Rudenstine as its twenty-sixth president to succeed the retiring Derek Bok.

The selection of Rudenstine took place six decades after the most famous anti-Semitic incident in American academic history. In 1922, A. Lawrence Lowell, Harvard's president, recommended that a quota be placed on Jewish enrollment in Harvard College in order to solve the university's "Jew problem." Lowell was a nativist and a supporter of the Immigration Restriction League. "I long ago came to the conclusion that no supposed democracy could be successful unless it was tolerably homogenous," he said in 1918. This concern with homogeneity included the democracy called Harvard University.[51]

Rudenstine's biography refuted the accusation that Jews could not fit in at Harvard and other elite institutions. He was born in Ossining, New York, where his father was a guard at Sing Sing prison. His family lived continually on the edge of poverty, and he was able to attend Wooster School, an Episcopalian prep school, only because of a full scholarship. He was class valedictorian and won varsity letters in baseball, football, and basketball. Rudenstine attended Princeton on a scholarship, graduating summa cum laude, and then studied for two years at Oxford on a Rhodes scholarship. In 1964, he received a Ph.D. degree in English literature from Harvard. After teaching at Harvard for several years, he moved to Princeton, where he advanced from dean of students to dean of the college and then to provost. At the time of his selection by the Harvard Board of Overseers, Rudenstine was the executive vice president of the Andrew W. Mellon Foundation. He had become a full-fledged member of the American establishment.[52]

Particularly noteworthy was the fact that Rudenstine was Harvard's first president who was not an Anglo-Saxon Protestant. His father, Harry, was a Jewish immigrant from Kiev. His mother, Mae, was from a large Italian family, and he grew up speaking Italian before he spoke English. Harry's marriage caused a rift in his family, and it wasn't until Rudenstine was fourteen that he met his paternal relatives and became conscious of his Jewish ancestry. His perspective, he said, was "very American, a microhistory of a large part of the last century: persecution, from the Jewish side, and poverty, from the Italian side." Rudenstine continued this ecumenism in his own marriage. His wife's father was a Russian Jew and her mother was a Dutch Protestant. Their household was devoid of any sense of Jewishness. One of their two daughters sang in an Episcopalian choir. The most Jewish of the Rudenstine family was his daughter Antonia. "I have ended up feeling more Jewish in my personal leanings," she said in 1991. "I am more tied to Judaism than to any Christian religion. I'm going to a seder this year. But it's never been a formalized thing. I am not familiar with the Jewish holidays or their meaning in any educated way."[53]

Jews could take scant pride in Rudenstine because of his tenuous relationship to things Jewish. His life seemed to mirror the inverse relationship between social mobility and Jewish identity. But, as Marshall Sklare pointed out in his essay "American Jewry—The Ever Dying People," the prospects of American Jewry have rarely appeared cheery. Jews have survived one crisis after another, and perhaps they will also survive the freedom and prosperity of America.[54]

NOTES

Chapter One. The Aftermath of the War

1. Meyer Levin, *In Search: An Autobiography* (New York: Horizon, 1950), 232; Robert M. Abzug, *Inside the Vicious Heart: Americans and the Liberation of Nazi Concentration Camps* (New York: Oxford University Press, 1985), 66–67.

2. Susan Sontag, *On Photography* (New York: Farrar, Straus, and Giroux, 1973), 19–20.

3. Charles H. Stember, "The Recent History of Public Attitudes," in *Jews in the Mind of America,* ed. Charles H. Stember (New York: Basic Books, 1966), 144–54.

4. Leonard Dinnerstein, *America and the Survivors of the Holocaust* (New York: Columbia University Press, 1982), 176; Theodore Solotaroff and Marshall Sklare, Introduction to Stember, *Jews in the Mind of America,* 9.

5. Dinnerstein, *America and Survivors of the Holocaust,* 176.

6. Solotaroff and Sklare, Introduction, 9.

7. Stember, "Recent History of Public Attitudes," 137–41.

8. Ibid., 53–59; Charles E. Silberman, *A Certain People: American Jews and Their Lives Today* (New York: Summit, 1985), 57; Lucy S. Dawidowicz, *On Equal Terms: Jews in America, 1881–1981* (New York: Holt, Rinehart, and Winston, 1982), 129–30.

9. John Morton Blum, *V Was for Victory: Politics and American Culture during World War II* (New York: Harcourt, Brace, Jovanovich, 1976), 172–75.

10. Wayne S. Cole, *Roosevelt and the Isolationists, 1932–1945* (Lincoln: University of Nebraska Press, 1983), 474–76.

11. *Congressional Record,* 28 February 1941, 1513–14; *CR,* 31 July 1941, 6498–99; Stember, "Recent History of Public Attitudes," 120–26; Ben Halpern, "Anti-Semitism in the Perspective of Jewish History," in Stember, *Jews in the Mind of America,* 291.

12. Stember, "Recent History of Public Attitudes," 116–20.

13. Ibid., 132–34; Glen Jeansonne, *Gerald L. K. Smith: Minister of Hate* (New Haven: Yale University Press, 1988), 155–56.

14. Jerome N. Frank, "Red, White, and Blue Herring," *Saturday Evening Post,* 6 December 1941, 9–11.

15. The circumstances surrounding Myerson's victory and its impact are discussed in Susan Dworkin, *Miss America, 1945: Bess Myerson's Own Story* (New York: Newmarket, 1987), 7–8, 106–11, 132.

16. The attitude of Jews and the general public toward Hank Greenberg are discussed in Hank Greenberg, *Hank Greenberg: The Story of My Life,* ed. Ira Berkow (New York: Times Books, 1989), 61–62, 82–117, 233–66; see also William M. Simons, "The Athlete as Jewish Standard Bearer: Media Images of Hank Greenberg," *Jewish Social Studies* 44 (Spring 1982): 95–112.

17. Andrew Kopkind, "Bess Bets," *Village Voice,* 12 November 1979, 19–20. *Litvak* is a Yiddish term designating a Jew from Lithuania.

18. Philip Gleason, "Americans All: World War II and the Shaping of American Identity," *Review of Politics* 43 (October 1981): 518; Dawidowicz, *On Equal Terms,* 129.

19. Silberman, *A Certain People,* 28–31.

20. Leonard Dinnerstein, *Uneasy at Home: Antisemitism and the American Jewish Experience* (New York: Columbia University Press, 1987), 181–85.

21. Arthur Hertzberg, *The Jews in America: Four Centuries of an Uneasy Encounter: A History* (New York: Simon and Schuster, 1989), 309.

22. There is a picture of the Four Chaplains stamp in the *Encyclopaedia Judaica* 11 (1972): column 1571.

23. Henry Popkin, "The Vanishing Jew of Our Popular Culture," *Commentary* 14 (July 1952): 51–55; Stuart Samuels, "The Evolutionary Image of the Jew in American Film," *Ethnic Images in American Film and Television,* ed. Randall M. Miller (Philadelphia: Balch Institute, 1978), 27–28; Alan Spiegel, "The Vanishing Act: A Typology of the Jew in the Contemporary American Film," in *From Hester Street to Hollywood: The Jewish-American Stage and Screen,* ed. Sarah Blacher Cohen (Bloomington: Indiana University Press, 1983), 260–61.

24. Patricia Erens, *The Jew in American Cinema* (Bloomington: Indiana University Press, 1984), 170–73.

25. Ibid., 173–75; Lester D. Friedman, *Hollywood's Images of the Jew* (New York: Frederick Ungar, 1982), 125.

26. Erens, *The Jew in American Cinema,* 176–80; Friedman, *Hollywood's Images of the Jew,* 125–30; K. R. M. Short, "Hollywood Fights Anti-Semitism, 1945-1947," in *Feature Films as History,* ed. K. R. M. Short (Knoxville: University of Tennessee Press, 1980), 174–80.

27. Herman Wouk, *The Caine Mutiny* (Garden City, N.Y.: Doubleday, 1952), 441–42.

28. Herman Wouk, *This Is My God,* rev. ed. (New York: Pocket Books, 1974), 32–33.

29. Jonathan Netanyahu, *Self-Portrait of a Hero: The Letters of Jonathan Netanyahu (1963-1976),* intro. Herman Wouk (New York: Random House, 1980), v–xi.

30. Elinor Grumet, "Elliot Cohen: The Vocation of a Jewish Literary Mentor," in *Studies in the American Jewish Experience,* ed. Jacob R. Marcus and Abraham J. Peck (Cincinnati: American Jewish Archives, 1981), 9–25.

31. Elliot E. Cohen, "An Act of Affirmation," *Commentary* 1 (November 1945): 1–3.

32. Norman Podhoretz, *Making It* (New York: Random House, 1967), 100, 134–35; Judd L. Teller, *Strangers and Natives: The Evolution of the American Jew from 1921 to the Present* (New York: Dell, 1968), 257–59.

33. Irving Howe, *A Margin of Hope: An Intellectual Biography* (New York: Harcourt, Brace, Jovanovich, 1982), 210–17; Richard H. Pells, *The Liberal Mind in a Conservative Age* (New York: Harper and Row, 1985), 352–53.

34. Howe, *Margin of Hope,* 234–39; Pells, *Liberal Mind in Conservative Age,* 381–83.

35. Pells, *Liberal Mind in Conservative Age,* 384–85.

Chapter Two. The Decline of Anti-Semitism

1. Arthur Hertzberg, *The Jews in America: Four Centuries of an Uneasy Encounter: A History* (New York: Simon and Schuster, 1989), 331.

2. Isaiah M. Minkoff, "Inter-Group Relations," in *American Jewish Year Book* (Philadelphia: Jewish Publication Society of America, 1947), 49:189.

3. Chaim I. Waxman, *America's Jews in Transition* (Philadelphia: Temple University Press, 1983), 116–18, 156. Kahane would be assassinated in 1990 by an Arab.

4. Ehrhard Bahr, "The Anti-Semitism Studies of the Frankfurt School: The Failure of Critical Theory," in *Foundations of the Frankfurt School of Social Research,* ed. Judith Marcus and Zoltan Tar (New Brunswick, N.J.: Transaction, 1984), 311–12.

5. Ibid., 313–20.

6. T. W. Adorno, "Scientific Experiences of a European Scholar in America," in *Perspectives in American History,* ed. Donald Fleming and Bernard Bailyn (Cambridge, Mass.: Charles Warren Center for Studies in American History, 1968), 356–64.

7. Victor S. Navasky, *Naming Names* (New York: Viking, 1980), 112.

8. Glen Jeansonne, *Gerald L. K. Smith: Minister of Hate* (New Haven: Yale University Press, 1988), 119–20; Charles Stember, "The Recent History of Public Attitudes," in *Jews in the Mind of America,* ed. Charles H. Stember (New York: Basic Books, 1966), 165–69; Thomas F. Pettigrew, "Parallel and Distinctive Changes in Anti-Semitic and Anti-Negro Attitudes," in Stember, *Jews in the Mind of America,* 389.

9. Ronald Radosh and Joyce Milton, *The Rosenberg File: A Search for Truth* (New York: Holt, Rinehart, and Winston, 1983), 348–55; Deborah Dash Moore, "Reconsidering the Rosenbergs: Symbol and Substance in Second Generation American Jewish Consciousness," *Journal of American Ethnic History* 8 (Fall 1988): 26.

10. Jeffrey M. Marker, "The Jewish Community and the Case of Julius and Ethel Rosenberg," *Maryland Historian* 3 (Fall 1972): 106–12.

11. Radosh and Milton, *Rosenberg File,* 355; Lucy S. Dawidowicz, "'Anti-Semitism' and the Rosenberg Case: The Latest Communist Propaganda Trap," *Commentary* 14 (July 1952): 41–45. *Commentary* also published Robert Warshow's essay "The 'Idealism' of Julius and Ethel Rosenberg" in its November 1953 issue.

12. Marker, "Jewish Community and Case of Julius and Ethel Rosenberg," 107–8.

13. Arthur Liebman, *Jews and the Left* (New York: Wiley, 1979), 518; Moore, "Reconsidering the Rosenbergs," 26.

14. Stember, "Recent History of Public Attitudes," 156–69.

15. Leonard Dinnerstein, *Uneasy at Home: Antisemitism and the American Jewish Experience* (New York: Columbia University Press, 1987), 182–84.

16. Stember, "Recent History of Public Attitudes," 65, 95–99, 121–26.

17. Ibid., 126–27; Dinnerstein, *Uneasy at Home,* 190.

18. Stember, "Recent History of Public Attitudes," 127–34; Earl Raab, "The Black Revolution and the Jewish Question," in *Black Anti-Semitism and Jewish Racism,* ed. Nat Hentoff (New York: Schocken, 1970), 15.

19. Edward S. Shapiro, "Anti-Semitism Mississippi Style," in *Anti-Semitism in*

American History, ed. David A. Gerber (Urbana: University of Illinois Press, 1986), 131–46.

20. Stember, "Recent History of Public Attitudes," 189–93; Melvin I. Urofsky, *We Are One! American Jewry and Israel* (Garden City, N.Y.: Anchor, 1978), 218.

21. Benjamin R. Ringer, "Jews and the Desegregation Crisis," in Stember, *Jews in the Mind of America,* 197–207.

22. Stember, "Recent History of Public Attitudes," 104–6; Nathan Perlmutter and Ruth Ann Perlmutter, *The Real Anti-Semitism in America* (New York: Arbor House, 1982), 72–78.

23. The fullest analysis of anti-Semitism during the Civil War is Bertram W. Korn, *American Jewry and the Civil War* (Philadelphia: Jewish Publication Society of America, 1951).

24. Stember, "Recent History of Public Attitudes," 69–70.

25. Waxman, *American Jews in Transition,* 154.

26. Stember, "Recent History of Public Attitudes," 91.

27. Thomas F. O'Dea, "The Changing Image of the Jew and the Contemporary Religious Situation: An Exploration of Ambiguities," in Stember, *Jews in the Mind of America,* 303. For a cogent critique of the methodology of polling and survey research regarding anti-Semitism, see Lucy S. Dawidowicz's essay "Can Anti-Semitism be Measured?" in her collection *The Jewish Presence: Essays on History and Identity* (New York: Holt, Rinehart, and Winston, 1977).

28. Ben Halpern, "Anti-Semitism in the Perspective of Jewish History," in Stember, *Jews in the Mind of America,* 285. The idiosyncratic nature of American anti-Semitism is explored in Henry L. Feingold, "Finding a Conceptual Framework for the Study of American Antisemitism," *Jewish Social Studies* 47 (Summer–Fall 1985), 312–26.

29. Perlmutter and Perlmutter, *Real Anti-Semitism in America,* 72–78; Seymour Martin Lipset, "Blacks and Jews: How Much Bias?" *Public Opinion* 10 (July–August 1987): 4.

30. Lipset, "Blacks and Jews," 5, 57–58.

31. Seymour Martin Lipset, "Jewish Fear, Black Insensitivity," *New York Times,* 9 March 1990. For a book arguing that American Jews are justified in fearing anti-Semitism, see Gary A. Tobin with Sharon L. Sassler, *Jewish Perceptions of Anti-Semitism* (New York: Plenum, 1988).

32. Steven M. Cohen, "Undue Stress on American Anti-Semitism?" *Sh'ma,* 1 September 1989, 113–15.

33. Arnold Forster and Benjamin R. Epstein, *The New Anti-Semitism* (New York: McGraw-Hill, 1974), 3–5, 324.

34. Perlmutter and Perlmutter, *Real Anti-Semitism in America,* 9, 32, 92–93, 221.

35. Urofsky, *We Are One!,* 445.

36. For the postwar history of Rocky Mountain anti-Semitic groups and the murder of Berg, see Kevin Flynn and Gary Gerhardt, *The Silent Brotherhood: Inside America's Racist Underground* (New York: Free Press, 1989).

37. Daniel Levitas, "Distress and Despair in Rural America," *Congress Monthly* 54 (May–June 1987): 5–7; Lipset, "Blacks and Jews," 57.

38. James B. Ringer, *The Edge of Friendliness: A Study of Jewish-Gentile Relations* (New York: Basic Books, 1967). See also Gerhard Lenski, *The Religious Factor: A Sociologist's Inquiry* (New York: Anchor, 1963), 36–37.

39. John Higham, *Send These to Me: Jews and Other Immigrants in Urban America* (New York: Atheneum, 1975), chap. 9.

40. O'Dea, "Changing Image of the Jews," 321.

41. Stember, "Recent History of Public Attitudes," 49–51.

42. Will Herberg, *Protestant-Catholic-Jew: An Essay in American Religious Sociology* (New York: Anchor, 1955, 1960), 84.

43. Mark Silk, *Spiritual Politics: Religion and America Since World War II* (New York: Simon and Schuster, 1988), 40–44.

44. Stember, "Recent History of Public Attitudes," 99–101.

45. Ibid., 179–80.

46. Jenna Weissman Joselit, *New York's Jewish Jews: The Orthodox Community in the Interwar Years* (Bloomington: Indiana University Press, 1990), 21.

47. David G. Dalin, "Leo Pfeffer and the Separationist Faith," *This World* 24 (Winter 1989): 136–40; David G. Singer, "One Nation Completely Under God? The American Jewish Congress and the Catholic Church in the United States," *Journal of Church and State* 26 (Autumn 1984): 475–90.

48. Wolf Blitzer, *Territory of Lies: The Exclusive Story of Jonathan Jay Pollard: The American Who Spied on His Country for Israel and How He Was Betrayed* (New York: Harper and Row, 1989), 282–84; Robert I. Friedman, "The Secret Agent," *New York Review of Books,* 26 October 1989, 8–12; Yosef Goell, "The Lessons of the Pollard Affair," *Congress Monthly* 54 (May–June 1987): 3–4.

49. Leonard Fein, *Where Are We? The Inner Life of America's Jews* (New York: Harper and Row, 1988), 111–13.

50. "The Strange Defense of Espionage in the Case of Jonathan Pollard," *Issues* (Summer–Fall 1989): 2. *Issues* is a newsletter published by the American Council for Judaism.

51. Friedman, "Secret Agent," 12.

52. David Biale, "J'Accuse: American Jews and L'Affaire Pollard," *Tikkun* 2 (May–June 1987): 10–12.

53. Charles E. Silberman, *A Certain People: American Jews and Their Lives Today* (New York: Summit, 1985), 360–66.

Chapter Three. Filling the Void

1. Lucy S. Dawidowicz, *The Golden Tradition: Jewish Life and Thought in Eastern Europe* (Boston: Beacon, 1967).

2. Moses Rischin, "Introduction," in *The Jews of North America,* ed. Moses Rischin (Detroit: Wayne State University Press, 1987), 19.

3. Salo Wittmayer Baron, *Steeled by Adversity: Essays and Address on American Jewish Life,* ed. Jeannette Meisel Baron (Philadelphia: Jewish Publication Society of America, 1971), 460, 468.

4. Sidney Hook, "The Plural Sources of Jewish Life in America," paper prepared for the Fortieth Annual Conference of the American Jewish Committee, 25 January 1947, Sidney Hook Papers, Hoover Institution, Stanford University.

5. Abraham J. Karp, "United Jewish Appeal," in *Jewish Voluntary Organizations,* ed. Michael N. Dobkowski (Westport, Conn.: Greenwood, 1986), 468.

6. Ibid., 469–70; Daniel J. Elazar, *Community and Polity: The Organizational Dy-*

namics of American Jewry (Philadelphia: Jewish Publication Society of America, 1976), 166–67.

7. Moshe Starkman, "Cultural Activities," in *American Jewish Year Book,* (Philadelphia: Jewish Publication Society of America, 1947), 49:175.

8. Arnold Shankman, "YIVO Institute for Jewish Research," in Dobkowski, *Jewish Voluntary Organizations,* 502–5.

9. Michael N. Dobkowski, "Congress for Jewish Culture," in Dobkowski, *Jewish Voluntary Organizations,* 1133–34.

10. Arthur Hertzberg, *The Jews in America: Four Centuries of An Uneasy Encounter: A History* (New York: Simon and Schuster, 1989), 157–58.

11. Michael N. Dobkowski, "Agudath Israel of America," in Dobkowski, *Jewish Voluntary Organizations,* 5–6.

12. Steven M. Lowenstein, *Frankfurt on the Hudson: The German-Jewish Community of Washington Heights, 1933–1983, Its Structure and Culture* (Detroit: Wayne State University Press, 1989), 98, 114–18.

13. Lowenstein, *Frankfurt on Hudson,* chaps. 3, 5, 10; Ernest Stock, "Washington Heights' 'Fourth Reich,'" *Commentary* 11 (June 1951): 581–88.

14. Michael N. Dobkowski, "Leo Baeck Institute," in Dobkowski, *Jewish Voluntary Institutions,* 309–11.

15. Hertzberg, *Jews in America,* 74; Nitza Rosovsky, *The Jewish Experience at Harvard and Radcliffe* (Cambridge: Harvard University Press, 1986), 46.

16. Abram L. Sachar, *A Host at Last* (Boston: Little, Brown, 1976), chaps. 2–3.

17. Gilbert Klaperman, *The Story of Yeshiva University: The First Jewish University in America* (New York: Macmillan, 1969), 150–51; Jeffrey S. Gurock, *The Men and Women of Yeshiva: Higher Education, Orthodoxy, and American Judaism* (New York: Columbia University Press, 1988), 92–93.

18. John A. Gliedman, "Brandeis University: Reflections at Middle Age," *American Jewish History* 78 (June 1989): 517; Sachar, *Host at Last,* 11.

19. Sachar, *Host at Last,* 14.

20. Gliedman, "Brandeis University," 521.

21. Irving Howe, *A Margin of Hope: An Intellectual Autobiography* (New York: Harcourt, Brace, Jovanovich, 1982), 184.

22. "Brandeis University—Neither Jewish, Nor American," *Jewish Forum* 33 (July 1950): 4.

23. Gordon Fellman, "Brandeis in the Balance," *Tikkun* 5 (November–December 1990): 28.

24. Hertzberg, *Jews in America,* 50.

25. Charles E. Silberman, *A Certain People: American Jews and Their Lives Today* (New York: Summit, 1985), 229–30; Ismar Elbogen, "American Jewish Scholarship: A Survey," in *American Jewish Year Book* (Philadelphia: Jewish Publication Society of America, 1943), 45:47–65.

26. Jacob Neusner, *The Public Side of Learning: The Political Consequences of Scholarship in the Context of Judaism* (Chico, Calif.: Scholars Press, 1985), 41.

27. Louis Finkelstein, ed., *The Jews: Their History, Culture, and Religion,* 3d ed. (Philadelphia: Harper, 1960), 1:xxvi.

28. Edmund Wilson, *A Piece of My Mind* (Farrar, Straus, and Cudahy, 1956), 151–58.

29. Arnold J. Band, "Jewish Studies in American Liberal Arts Colleges and Universities," in *American Jewish Year Book* (New York: American Jewish Committee, 1966), 67:3–30.

30. Samuel Sandmel, "Scholar or Apologist?" in *The Teaching of Judaica in American Universities: The Proceedings of a Colloquium,* ed. Leon A. Jick (New York: KTAV, 1970), 109–10.

31. Arnold J. Band, "Jewish Studies: A Generation Later," *Sh'ma,* 8 December 1989, 17–20.

32. Leon Jick, "Introduction," Association for Jewish Studies *Newsletter,* 2d ser., 2 (Spring 1989): 3–4; Michael N. Dobkowski, "Association for Jewish Studies," in Dobkowski, *Jewish Voluntary Organizations,* 73–75.

33. Gerald S. Strober, *America's Jews: Community in Crisis* (Garden City, N.Y.: Doubleday, 1974), 241–44; David Silverberg, "Jewish Studies on the American Campus," *Present Tense* 5 (Summer 1978): 52–56.

34. Robert Alter, "What Jewish Studies Can Do," *Commentary* 58 (October 1974): 73.

35. Gerson D. Cohen, "An Embarrassment of Riches: On the Condition of American Jewish Scholarship in 1969," in Jick, *Teaching of Judaica,* 135–50; Jick, Introduction to Jick, *Teaching of Judaica,* 3.

36. Marvin Fox, "Some Reflections on Jewish Studies in American Universities," *Judaism* 35 (Spring 1986): 143.

37. Cohen, "Embarrassment of Riches," 144.

38. Jacob Neusner, *The Academic Study of Judaism: Essays and Reflections* (New York: KTAV, 1975), 118. Robert Alter's essay "What Jewish Studies Can Do" is a particularly powerful warning against using Jewish studies for nonacademic purposes.

39. Leon Jick, "Tasks for a Community of Concern," in Jick, *Teaching of Judaica,* 84. Roughly translated, *derech eretz* means proper deportment.

40. Marshall Sklare, "Contemporary Jewish Studies," in Jick, *Teaching of Judaica,* 68–69.

41. Band, "Jewish Studies: A Generation Later," 17; Stuart E. Rosenberg, *The New Jewish Identity in America* (New York: Hippocrene, 1985), 259–60; Fox, "Some Reflections on Jewish Studies," 142.

42. Irving Greenberg, "Jewish Survival and the College Campus," *Judaism* 17 (Summer 1968): 260–81.

43. Norman Roth, "Jewish Studies in America—Present Problems and Future Prospects," *Judaism* 35 (Spring 1986): 169.

44. Paula E. Hyman, "Disciplinary Excellence's Jewish Effect," *Sh'ma,* 8 December 1989, 22–23.

45. Ismar Schorsch, "Wissenschaft and Values," *Tikkun* 2 (July–August 1987): 33; Neil Gillman, "Inside or Outside? Emancipation and the Dilemmas of Conservative Judaism," *Judaism* 38 (Fall 1989): 422.

46. Neusner, *Academic Study of Judaism,* 64.

47. Jacob Neusner, *Judaism in the American Humanities: Essays and Reflections* (Chico, Calif.: Scholars Press, 1981), 63–66.

48. Stanley F. Chyet, "American Jewish Archives," in Dobkowski, *Jewish Voluntary Organizations,* 30–33; Arnold Shankman, "American Jewish Historical Society," in Dobkowski, *Jewish Voluntary Organizations,* 50–52.

49. *New York Times,* 21 October 1954.

50. Lester D. Friedman, *Hollywood's Image of the Jew* (New York: Frederick Ungar, 1982), 305–8.

Chapter Four. A Tale of Two Shapiros

1. Charles E. Silberman, *A Certain People: American Jews and Their Lives Today* (New York: Summit, 1985),180.

2. Ibid., 99.

3. "U. of Chicago Provost Elected President Beginning Next Fall," *New York Times,* 15 September 1967.

4. Lawrence Bloomgarden, "Our Changing Elite Colleges," *Commentary* 29 (February 1960): 152; Stephen J. Whitfield, *American Space, Jewish Time* (Hamden, Conn.: Archon, 1988), 9.

5. Walter Goodman, "Bicker at Princeton: The Eating Clubs Again," *Commentary* 25 (May 1958): 406–10; Marcia Graham Synnott, *The Half-Opened Door: Discrimination and Admissions at Harvard, Yale, and Princeton, 1900–1970* (Westport, Conn.: Greenwood, 1979), 196.

6. Synnott, *Half-Opened Door,* 22.

7. Goodman, "Bicker at Princeton," 406–7.

8. Ibid., 409–15; Marianne Sanua, "Stages in the Development of Jewish Life at Princeton University," *American Jewish History* 76 (June 1987): 397.

9. *New York Times,* 28 and 29 April 1987.

10. Sanua, "Stages in the Development," 391–415.

11. Silberman, *A Certain People,* 52–53; Synott, *Half-Opened Door,* 15, 17, 128, 130.

12. Synott, *Half-Opened Door,* 155, 159; Bloomgarden, "Our Changing Elite Colleges," 152; Silberman, *A Certain People,* 30–31.

13. Silberman, *A Certain People,* 100–101.

14. Synnott, *Half-Opened Door,* xix–xx, 209.

15. Dan A. Oren, *Joining the Club: A History of Jews and Yale* (New Haven: Yale University Press, 1985), 243–45.

16. Synnott, *Half-Opened Door,* 209; Silberman, *A Certain People,* 119; Henry L. Feingold, *Zion in America: The Jewish Experience from Colonial Times to the Present* (New York: Hippocrene, 1974), 314.

17. James Yaffe, *The American Jews: Portrait of a Split Personality* (New York: Random House, 1968), 52.

18. Everett Carll Ladd, Jr., and Seymour Martin Lipset, *The Divided Academy: Professors and Politics* (New York: McGraw-Hill, 1975), 1–2, 56.

19. Arthur Hertzberg, *The Jews in America: Four Centuries of an Uneasy Encounter: A History* (New York: Simon and Schuster, 1989), 309; Ladd and Lipset, *Divided Academy,* 88–89, 344; Stephen Steinberg, *The Academic Melting Pot: Catholics and Jews in American Higher Education* (New Brunswick, N.J.: Transaction, 1977), 123.

20. Ladd and Lipset, *Divided Academy,* 150; Stuart E. Rosenberg, *The New Jewish Identity in America* (New York: Hippocrene, 1985), 252–56; Seymour Martin Lipset, "A Unique People in an Exceptional Country," in Seymour Martin Lipset, *American Plu-*

ralism and the Jewish Community (New Brunswick, N.J.: Transaction, 1990), 4; Silberman, *A Certain People,* 99.

21. Ladd and Lipset, *Divided Academy,* 150–53.

22. Silberman, *A Certain People,* 53.

23. Henry James, *The American Scene* (New York: Horizon, 1967), 130–39.

24. Edward S. Shapiro, "Jewishness and the New York Intellectuals," *Judaism* 38 (Summer 1989): 282–83.

25. Lionel Trilling, "Young in the Thirties," *Commentary* 41 (May 1966): 47.

26. Diana Trilling, "Lionel Trilling, A Jew at Columbia," *Commentary* 67 (March 1979): 40–46; Whitfield, *American Space, Jewish Time,* 62.

27. Trilling, "Lionel Trilling," 46.

28. Ibid.; Oren, *Joining the Club,* 260.

29. Peter Novick, *That Noble Dream: The "Objectivity Question" and the American Historical Profession* (Cambridge, Eng.: Cambridge University Press, 1988), 172, 369.

30. Novick, *That Noble Dream,* 172–74.

31. Carl Bridenbaugh, "The Great Mutation," *American Historical Review* 68 (January 1963): 323, 328–29.

32. Novick, *That Noble Dream,* 330.

33. Norman Podhoretz, "The Rise and Fall of the American Jewish Novelist," in *Jewish Life in America,* ed. Gladys Rosen (New York: Institute of Human Relations Press, 1978), 150.

34. Edward Alexander, "A Talmud for Americans," *Commentary* 90 (July 1990): 28; Edward S. Shapiro, "Anti-Semitism Mississippi Style," in *Anti-Semitism in American History,* ed. David Gerber (Urbana: University of Illinois Press, 1986), 143.

35. Ladd and Lipset, *Divided Academy,* 150; Charles Kadushin, *The American Intellectual Elite* (Boston: Little, Brown, 1974), 23–31.

36. Harriet Zuckerman, *Scientific Elite: Nobel Laureates in the United States* (New York: Free Press, 1977), 68–82.

37. Silberman, *A Certain People,* 152–54.

38. Whitfield, *American Space, Jewish Time,* 134–40.

39. Ladd and Lipset, *Divided Academy,* 156–61; Steinberg, *Academic Melting Pot,* 154.

40. Norman L. Friedman, "Orientation of Jewish Professors to the Jewish Community," *Jewish Social Studies* 35 (July–October 1973): 269; see also Henry Cohen, "Jewish Life and Thought in an Academic Community," *American Jewish Archives* 14 (November 1962): 107–28.

41. Ladd and Lipset, *Divided Academy,* 162–67; Steinberg, *Academic Melting Pot,* 135–46.

42. Whitfield, *American Space, Jewish Time,* 144.

43. Morris N. Kertzer, *Today's American Jew* (New York: McGraw-Hill, 1967), 23.

44. Silberman, *A Certain People,* 84.

45. Ibid., 85.

46. Ibid., 84; Hershel Shanks, "Irving Shapiro: 'You'll Never Build a Career with a Name like Shapiro,'" *Moment* 13 (September 1988): 34–37.

47. Silberman, *A Certain People,* 88.

48. Samuel Z. Klausner, "Anti-Semitism in the Executive Suite: Yesterday, Today, and Tomorrow," *Moment* 13 (September 1988): 33–39, 55.

49. Edward S. Shapiro, "Jews with Money," *Judaism* 36 (Winter 1987): 7–16.

50. Dyan Machan, "The *Financial World* One Hundred: The Highest Paid People on Wall Street," *Financial World,* 22 July 1986, 14–47. There is as yet no good book-length study of the contemporary Jewish presence on Wall Street. Judith R. Ehrlich and Barry J. Rehfeld, *The New Crowd: The Changing of the Jewish Guard on Wall Street* (Boston: Little, Brown, 1989) is more gossip than serious sociological and historical analysis.

51. Irving Howe, *World of Our Fathers* (New York: Harcourt, Brace, Jovanovich, 1976), 645–46.

52. Silberman, *A Certain People,* 58–59.

53. Stephen Birmingham, *"The Rest of Us": The Rise of America's Eastern European Jews* (Boston: Little, Brown, 1984), xvi, 357; Silberman, *A Certain People,* 329.

54. John Higham, *Send These to Me: Jews and Other Immigrants in Urban America* (New York: Atheneum, 1975), 179.

55. Alexis de Tocqueville, *Democracy in America,* ed. J. P. Mayer (Garden City, N.Y.: Anchor, 1969), 54, 615, 621; Shapiro, "Jews with Money," 11.

56. Jacob A. Riis, *How the Other Half Lives: Studies among the Tenements of New York,* ed. Sam Bass Warner, Jr. (Cambridge, Mass.: Belknap, 1970), 31.

57. Nathan Glazer and Daniel P. Moynihan, *Beyond the Melting Pot: The Negroes, Puerto Ricans, Jews, Italians and Irish of New York City* (Cambridge: MIT Press, 1963), 151–55.

58. G. William Domhoff and Richard Zweigenhaft, "Jews in the Corporate Establishment," *New York Times,* 24 April 1983.

59. Richard D. Alba and Gwen Moore, "Ethnicity in the American Elite," *American Sociological Review* 47 (June 1982): 377.

60. David Biale, *Power and Powerlessness in Jewish History* (New York: Schocken, 1986), 180; Milton Plesur, *Jewish Life in Twentieth-Century America* (Chicago: Nelson-Hall, 1982), 162.

61. Gerald Krefetz, *Jews and Money: The Myths and the Reality* (New Haven, Conn.: Ticknor and Fields, 1982), 14; Michael Gold, *Jews Without Money* (New York: Liveright, 1930), 13, 40, 57, 301, 309.

Chapter Five. Wandering Jews

1. Robert Gutman, "Demographic Trends and the Decline of Anti-Semitism," in *Jews in the Mind of America,* ed. Charles H. Stember (New York: Basic Books, 1966), 353–58.

2. William B. Helmreich, "Holocaust Survivors in American Society," *Judaism* 39 (Winter 1990): 14–27.

3. For the Russian immigration, see Sylvia Rothchild, *A Special Legacy: An Oral History of Soviet Jewish Emigrés in the United States* (New York: Simon and Schuster, 1985); and Steven Feldman, "How Jewish Are Soviet Immigrants?" *Moment* 14 (June 1989): 16–18.

4. Chaim I. Waxman, "The Emancipation, the Enlightenment and the Demography of American Jewry," *Judaism* 38 (Fall 1989): 501; Drora Kass and Seymour Martin Lipset, "Jewish Immigration to the United States from 1967 to the Present: Israelis and Others," in *Understanding American Jewry,* ed. Marshall Sklare (New Brunswick, N.J.:

Transaction, 1982), 272–94. For the identity problem of Israeli imigrants, see Moshe Shokeid, *Children of Circumstances: Israeli Emigrants in New York* (Ithaca: Cornell University Press, 1988); and Noah Elias and Judith Blanton, "Dimensions of Ethnic Identity in Israeli Jewish Families Living in the United States," *Psychological Reports* 60 (April 1987): 367–75.

5. George W. Pierson, "The M-Factor in American History," *American Quarterly* 14 (Summer 1962): 275–89.

6. Peter I. Rose, "Small-Town Jews and Their Neighbors in the United States," in *A Coat of Many Colors: Jewish Subcommunities in the United States,* ed. Abraham D. Lavender (Westport, Conn.: Greenwood, 1977), 42. See also Peter I. Rose, *Strangers in Their Midst: A Sociological Study of the Small-Town Jew and His Neighbors* (Ithaca: Cornell University Pres, 1959).

7. Rose, "Small-Town Jews and Their Neighbors," 41.

8. Lee J. Levinger, "The Disappearing Small-Town Jew," *Commentary* 14 (August 1952): 157–63.

9. Eugen Schonfeld, "Problems and Potentials," *Jewish Heritage* 15 (Winter 1974): 18.

10. Joseph Brandes with Martin Douglas, *Immigrants to Freedom: Jewish Communities in Rural New Jersey since 1882* (Philadelphia: University of Pennsylvania Press, 1971), 126–42; see also Gabriel Davidson, *Our Jewish Farmers and the Story of the Jewish Agricultural Society* (New York: L. B. Fischer, 1943); and Samuel Joseph, *History of the Baron de Hirsch Fund: The Americanization of the Jewish Immigrant* (Philadelphia: Jewish Publication Society of America, 1935).

11. Brandes, *Immigrants to Freedom,* 334–36.

12. Ibid., 326–332.

13. Daniel J. Elazar, "Developments in Jewish Community Organization in the Second Postwar Generation," in *American Pluralism and the Jewish Community,* ed. Seymour Martin Lipset (New Brunswick, N.J.: Transaction, 1990), 183–84. *Chai* is Hebrew for *life.*

14. Sidney Goldstein, "Jews in the United States: Perspectives from Demography," in *Jewish Life in America: Historical Perspectives,* ed. Gladys Rosen (New York: Institute of Human Relations Press, 1978), 64. For the difficulty of estimating Jewish population, see Sophia M. Robison, "How Many Jews in America?" *Commentary* 8 (August 1949): 185–92.

15. Daniel J. Elazar, *Community and Polity: The Organizational Dynamics of American Jewry* (Philadelphia: Jewish Publication Society of America, 1976), 164–65, 237.

16. Ibid., 39; Arthur A. Goren, "Jews," in *Harvard Encyclopedia of American Ethnic Groups,* ed. Stephan Thernstrom (Cambridge: Harvard University Press, 1980), 592.

17. Elazar, *Community and Polity,* 55–56; Chaim I. Waxman, *America's Jews in Transition* (Philadelphia: Temple University Press, 1983), 213–14.

18. Stephen J. Whitfield, "The Braided Identity of Southern Jewry," *American Jewish History* 77 (March 1988): 381–82; Seymour B. Liebman, "Cuban Jewish Community in South Florida," in Lavender, *Coat of Many Colors,* 300–301.

19. Harold Mehling, "Is Miami Beach Jewish?" in Lavender, *Coat of Many Colors,* 118–19, 122. This essay originally appeared in Harold Mehling, *The Most of Everything* (New York: Harcourt, Brace, World, 1960), 129–44.

20. Eli N. Evans, *The Provincials: A Personal History of Jews in the South* (New York: Atheneum, 1973), x.

21. Mehling, "Is Miami Beach Jewish?" 118.

22. Ibid., 120.

23. Elinor Horowitz, "Jewish Poverty Hurts in South Beach," in Lavender, *Coat of Many Colors,* 160–66.

24. *Derma* is a Jewish delicacy.

25. This discussion of the Catskills is based on personal observation; on Stefan Kanfer, *A Summer World: The Attempt to Build a Jewish Eden in the Catskills, from the Days of the Ghetto to the Rise and Decline of the Borscht Belt* (New York: Farrar, Straus, Giroux, 1989), 240–75; and on Lisa W. Foderaro, "Bankruptcy and Success Meet in Catskills Hotels," *New York Times,* 14 August 1990.

26. Arthur Hertzberg, *The Jews in America: Four Centuries of an Uneasy Encounter: A History* (New York: Simon and Schuster, 1989), 321.

27. Sophia M. Robison, *The Jewish Population of Essex County* (Newark: Jewish Community Council of Essex County, 1948), 117; Sophia M. Robison, *A Demographic Study of the Jewish Population of Trenton, N.J., 1949* (New York: Office for Jewish Population Research, 1949), 13.

28. Philip Roth, *"Goodbye, Columbus" and Five Short Stories* (New York: Bantam, 1963), 64.

29. Goldstein, "Jews in the United States: Perspectives," 64; Goren, "Jews," 593. For Jewish Brownsville, see Alter F. Landesman, *Brownsville: The Birth, Development and Passing of a Jewish Community in New York* (New York: Bloch, 1969).

30. Rodney Stark and Stephen Steinberg, *It "Did" Happen Here: An Investigation of Anti-Semitism: Wayne, New Jersey, 1967* (Berkeley, Calif.: Survey Research Center, 1967), 9–10.

31. For an incisive analysis of the role of New York neighborhoods in transmitting Jewish religion and culture, see Deborah Dash Moore, *At Home in America: Second Generation New York Jews* (New York: Columbia University Press, 1981).

32. Herman Wouk, *This Is My God* (Garden City, N.Y.: Doubleday, 1959), 251–57, 281–82.

33. Albert I. Gordon, *Jews in Suburbia* (Boston: Beacon, 1959), 109, 153.

34. Judith R. Kramer and Seymour Leventman, *Children of the Gilded Ghetto: Conflict Resolutions of Three Generations of American Jews* (New Haven: Yale University Press, 1961), 213–14; Hertzberg, *Jews in America,* 323.

35. Judd L. Teller, *Strangers and Natives: The Evolution of the American Jew from 1921 to the Present* (New York: Dell, 1968), 226; Morris Werb, "Jewish Suburbia—An Historical and Comparative Study of Jewish Communities in Three New Jersey Suburbs," Ph.D. diss., New York University, 1959, 244–45; Hertzberg, *Jews in America,* 327.

36. Herbert Gans, "The Origin and Growth of a Jewish Community in the Suburbs: A Study of the Jews of Park Forest," in *The Jews,* ed. Marshall Sklare (Glencoe, Ill.: Free Press, 1958), 224.

37. Gordon, *Jews in Suburbia,* 134.

38. Ibid., 126–27.

39. Marshall Sklare, "The Sociology of Contemporary Jewish Studies," in *The Jew in American Society,* ed. Marshall Sklare (New York: Behrman House, 1974), 19–25.

40. Stanley Kaufmann, "Women at Work," *New Republic,* 18 October 1975, 21; Robert F. Horowitz, "Between a Heartache and a Laugh: Two Recent Films on Immigration," *Film and History* 6 (December 1976): 75.

41. Irving Howe, *World of Our Fathers* (New York: Harcourt, Brace, Jovanovich, 1976), 619–21, 646; Kramer and Leventman, *Children of the Gilded Ghetto,* 168.

42. James A. Sleeper, Introduction to *The New Jews,* ed. James A. Sleeper and Alan L. Mintz (New York: Vintage, 1971), 3–23.

43. Saul Kaplan, "Comment: The Invisible Jewish Poor," *Journal of Jewish Communal Service* 48 (Summer 1972): 348–52.

44. W. D. Rubinstein, *The Left, the Right, and the Jews* (New York: Universe, 1982), 51.

45. Milton R. Konvitz, "Equality and the Jewish Experience," in Rosen, *Jewish Life in America,* 33–36; Thomas Sowell, *Ethnic America: A History* (New York: Basic Books, 1981), 88–98.

46. Seymour M. Lipset, "A Unique People in an Exceptional Country," in Lipset, *American Pluralism and the Jewish Community,* 3; Goldstein, "Jews in the United States: Perspectives," 89.

47. "Wouk Mutiny," *Time,* 5 September 1955, 48; Arnold Beichman, *Herman Wouk: The Novelist as Social Historian* (New Brunswick, N.J.: Transaction, 1984), 58.

48. Herman Wouk, *Marjorie Morningstar* (New York: Doubleday, 1955), 349.

49. Norman Podhoretz, "The Jew as Bourgeois," *Commentary* 21 (February 1956): 186–88.

Chapter Six. Judaism, American Style

1. Melvin I. Urofsky, *We Are One! American Jewry and Israel* (Garden City, N.Y.: Anchor, 1978), 211; Arthur Hertzberg, *The Jews in America: Four Centuries of an Uneasy Encounter: A History* (New York: Simon and Schuster, 1989), 323–24; Naomi W. Cohen, *American Jews and the Zionist Idea* (New York: KTAV, 1975), 146–47.

2. Will Herberg, *Protestant-Catholic-Jew: An Essay in American Religious Sociology* (New York: Anchor, 1955, 1960), 84.

3. Eric F. Goldman, *The Crucial Decade—and After* (New York: Vintage, 1960), 305–6; Martin E. Marty, *Righteous Empire: The Protestant Experience in America* (New York: Dial, 1970), 257–59; Herberg, *Protestant-Catholic-Jew,* 68.

4. Herberg, *Protestant-Catholic-Jew,* 258.

5. Ibid., 53–56.

6. Daniel J. Elazar, *Community and Polity: The Organizational Dynamics of America Jewry* (Philadelphia: Jewish Publication Society of America, 1976), 177–78; Jack Wertheimer, "Recent Trends in American Judaism," *American Jewish Year Book* (Philadelphia: Jewish Publication Society of America, 1989), 89:66.

7. Rufus Learsi, *The Jews in America: A History* (New York: KTAV, 1954, 1972), 356.

8. Jonathan and Judith Pearl, "As Others See Us: Jews on TV," *Moment* 15 (October 1990): 38–43, 58.

9. Gerhard Lenski, *The Religious Factor: A Sociologist's Inquiry* (New York: Anchor, 1963), 36; Nathan Glazer, "American Jewry or American Judaism," in *American Pluralism and the Jewish Community,* ed. Seymour Martin Lipset (New Brunswick, N.J.: Transaction, 1990), 32–33.

10. Heschel is quoted in Lucy S. Dawidowicz, *The Jewish Presence: Essays on*

Identity and History (New York: Holt, Rinehart, and Winston, 1977), 73; Charles S. Liebman, *The Ambivalent American Jew: Politics, Religion, and Family in American Jewish Life* (Philadelphia: Jewish Publication Society of America, 1973), 67–75.

11. Hillel Halkin, *Letters to an American Friend: A Zionist's Polemic* (Philadelphia: Jewish Publication Society of America, 1977), 128–35.

12. Elazar, *Community and Polity,* 16–17.

13. Charles Selengut, "American Jewish Converts to New Religious Movements," *Jewish Journal of Sociology* 30 (December 1988): 95–109; Eugene B. Borowitz, *A New Jewish Theology in the Making* (Philadelphia: Westminster, 1968), 46.

14. Philip Roth, *"Goodbye, Columbus" and Five Short Stories* (New York: Bantam, 1963), 184, 200–201.

15. Albert I. Gordon, *Jews in Suburbia* (Boston: Beacon, 1959), 126–27; Judith R. Kramer and Seymour Leventman, *Children of the Gilded Ghetto: Conflict Resolutions of Three Generations of American Jews* (New Haven: Yale University Press, 1961), 178.

16. Marshall Sklare, *Conservative Judaism: An American Religious Movement* (New York: Schocken, 1955, 1972), 217.

17. Ruth R. Wisse, "Women as Conservative Rabbis?" *Commentary* 68 (October 1979): 59.

18. Lawrence J. Kaplan, "The Dilemma of Conservative Judaism," *Commentary* 62 (November 1976): 44–47.

19. Sklare, *Conservative Judaism,* 250–82.

20. Ibid., 267–82.

21. Pamela S. Nadell, "Developing an American Judaism: Conservative Rabbis as Ethnic Leaders," *Judaism* 39 (Summer 1990): 361–62; Abraham J. Karp, "A Century of Conservative Judaism in the United States," *American Jewish Year Book* (Philadelphia: Jewish Publication Society of America, 1986), 86:57; Sklare, *Conservative Judaism,* 274.

22. Nadell, "Developing an American Judaism," 357.

23. Abraham J. Karp, "The Conservative Rabbi—'Dissatisfied But Not Unhappy,'" *American Jewish Archives* 35 (November 1983): 245.

24. Karp, "Century of Conservative Judaism," 61; Herbert Rosenblum, *Conservative Judaism: A Contemporary History* (New York: United Synagogue of America, 1983), 135; Neil Gillman, "Inside or Outside? Emancipation and the Dilemmas of Conservative Judaism," *Judaism* 38 (Fall 1989): 423; Karp, "Conservative Rabbi," 243, 245.

25. Karp, "Century of Conservative Judaism," 57; Rosenblum, *Conservative Judaism,* 44.

26. Karp, "Century of Conservative Judaism," 53; *Jerusalem Post,* 27 December 1986 (international ed.).

27. Karp, "Century of Conservative Judaism," 59. *Menshlichkeit* means to behave compassionately.

28. Wisse, "Women as Conservative Rabbis?" 62.

29. Karp, "Century of Conservative Judaism," 49, 60.

30. Ronald D. Price, "Good News for the Jewish World: A Rare Coalition Is Created," *Jewish News* (East Orange, N.J.), 5 April 1990.

31. Ronald D. Price, "I love Conservative Judaism but . . . ," *Sh'ma,* 29 May 1987, 116; Stuart E. Rosenberg, *The New Jewish Identity in America* (New York: Hippocrene, 1985), 216.

32. Charles S. Liebman, "Orthodoxy in American Jewish Life," in *American Jewish Year Book* (Philadelphia: Jewish Publication Society of America, 1965), 66:92.

33. Karp, "Conservative Rabbi," 255; Sklare, *Conservative Judaism,* 43–46.

34. Louis Wirth, *The Ghetto* (Chicago: University of Chicago Press, 1928), 82, 99, 210; Samuel Rosenblatt, *Our Heritage* (New York: Bloch, 1940), 149–50.

35. Daniel T. Rodgers, "Tradition, Modernity, and the American Worker: Reflections and Critique," *Journal of Interdisciplinary History* 7 (Spring 1977): 655–81; Raymond Grew, "The Crises and Their Sequences," in Raymond Grew, ed., *Crises of Political Development in Europe and the United States* (Princeton: Princeton University Press, 1978), 3–37.

36. Milton M. Gordon, *Assimilation in American Life: The Role of Race, Religion, and National Origins* (New York: Oxford University Press, 1964), 192–93.

37. Rosenberg, *New Jewish Identity in America,* 218; *Moment* 15 (February 1990): 16. *OU* is the symbol of the Union of Orthodox Hebrew Congregations, the major organization certifying the kosher character of food products.

38. Judd L. Teller, *Strangers and Natives: The Evolution of the American Jew from 1921 to the Present* (New York: Dell, 1968), 221–22.

39. Ze'ev Chafets, *Members of the Tribe: On the Road in Jewish America* (New York: Bantam, 1988), 145–47. *Glatt* is a more scrupulous manner of slaughtering animals according to Jewish law.

40. "International Kosher Cuisine in Baltimore," *New York Times,* 8 October 1989.

41. Chaim I. Waxman, *America's Jews in Transition* (Philadelphia: Temple University Press, 1983), 126; Rosenberg, *New Jewish Identity in America,* 198.

42. Solomon Poll, "The Persistence of Tradition: Orthodoxy in America," in *The Ghetto and Beyond: Essays on Jewish Life in America,* ed. Peter I. Rose (New York: Random House, 1969), 119; Liebman, "Orthodoxy in American Jewish Life," 91; Samuel C. Heilman, *Synagogue Life: A Study of Symbolic Interaction* (Chicago: University of Chicago Press, 1976), 266; Samuel C. Heilman and Steven M. Cohen, *Cosmopolitans and Parochials: Modern Orthodox Jews in America* (Chicago: University of Chicago Press, 1989).

43. For the West Orange community, see Edward S. Shapiro, "Orthodoxy in Pleasantdale," *Judaism* 34 (Spring 1985): 163–70.

44. Sklare, *Conservative Judaism,* 262–67.

45. Louis Bernstein, "Orthodoxy: Flourishing but Divided," *Judaism* 36 (Spring 1987): 174–78.

46. Rosenberg, *New Jewish Identity in America,* 35.

47. Mordecai Waxman, "Conservative Judaism Confronts Its Future," *Judaism* 36 (Spring 1987): 179.

48. Jenna Weissman Joselit, *New York's Jewish Jews: The Orthodox Community in the Interwar Years* (Bloomington: Indiana University Press, 1990), 147–50; Wertheimer, "Recent Trends in American Judaism," 118; "Modern Orthodox Rabbis Claim Assault from RCA Right Wing," *Jewish Week,* 13 July 1990.

49. For the issue of separate seating, see Lawrence H. Schiffman, "When Women and Men Sat Together in American Orthodox Synagogues," *Moment* 14 (December 1989): 40–49.

50. Rosenberg, *New Jewish Identity in America,* 192–93.

51. Liebman, *Ambivalent American Jew,* 77–83.

52. "Jewish Moderate Urges Believers to Take Stand," *New York Times,* 24 March 1988; Liebman, "Orthodoxy in American Jewish Life," 60.

53. Michael A. Meyer, *Response to Modernity: A History of the Reform Movement in Judaism* (New York: Oxford University Press, 1988), 356.

54. Gerald S. Strober, *America's Jews: Community in Crisis* (Garden City, N.Y.: Doubleday, 1974), 264.

55. "Reform Jews Are Returning to Tradition," *New York Times,* 26 June 1989; Wertheimer, "Recent Trends in American Judaism," 102–3; Meyer, *Response to Modernity,* 378.

56. Meyer, *Response to Modernity,* 348, 383. For the impact of Zionism and Israel on Reform, see Howard R. Greenstein, *Turning Point: Zionism and Reform Judaism* (Chico, Calif.: Scholars Press, 1981).

57. Marc Lee Raphael, *Profiles in American Judaism: The Reform, Conservative, Orthodox, and Reconstructionist Traditions in Historical Perspective* (New York: Harper and Row, 1985), 62–71.

58. "Reform Jews Are Returning"; Meyer, *Response to Modernity,* 378.

59. Meyer, *Response to Modernity,* 358; Wertheimer, "Recent Trends in American Judaism," 107.

60. Meyer, *Response to Modernity,* 369–71.

61. Ibid., 370; David Polish, "The Changing and the Constant in the Reform Rabbinate," *American Jewish Archives* 35 (November 1983), 314–15.

62. Daniel Jeremy Silver, "The Aging of Reform," in *Approaches to Modern Judaism,* ed. Marc Lee Raphael (Chico, Calif.: Scholars Press, 1984), 2:55–65.

Chapter Seven. From Culture to Causes

1. Howe is quoted in Leonard Fein, *Where Are We? The Inner Life of America's Jews* (New York: Harper and Row, 1988), 187–88.

2. Terry A. Cooney, *The Rise of the New York Intellectuals: "Partisan Review" and Its Circle* (Madison: University of Wisconsin Press, 1986), 242; Alexander Bloom, *Prodigal Sons: The New York Intellectuals and Their World* (New York: Oxford University Press, 1986). See also Alan Wald, *The New York Intellectuals: The Rise and Decline of the Anti-Stalinist Left from the 1930s to the 1980s* (Chapel Hill: University of North Carolina Press, 1987); David J. Hollinger, "Ethnic Diversity, Cosmopolitanism and the Emergence of the American Liberal Intelligentsia," *American Quarterly* 27 (May 1975): 133–51.

3. Cooney, *Rise of New York Intellectuals,* 14, 240; Fein, *Where Are We?,* 189; Stephen J. Whitfield, *American Space, Jewish Time* (Hampden, Conn.: Archon, 1988), 62; Irving Howe, *A Margin of Hope* (New York: Harcourt, Brace, Jovanovich, 1988), 151–61.

4. Sidney Hook, *Out of Step: An Unquiet Life in the 20th Century* (New York: Harper and Row, 1987), 33–34; Howe, *Margin of Hope,* 4, 337–39.

5. Howe, *Margin of Hope,* 251; Norman Podhoretz, *Making It* (New York: Random House, 1967), 118–22; Alfred Kazin, *New York Jew* (New York: Knopf, 1978), 26–34.

6. Howe, *Margin of Hope,* 247–51.

7. Ibid., 260–80.

8. Irving Howe, "The Range of the New York Intellectual," in *Creators and Disturbers: Reminiscences by Jewish Intellectuals of New York,* ed. Bernard Rosenberg and Ernest Goldstein (New York: Columbia University Press, 1982), 285–86.

9. Edward S. Shapiro, "The Jewishness of the New York Intellectuals: Sidney Hook, a Case Study," in *American Pluralism and the Jewish Community,* ed. Seymour Martin Lipset (New Brunswick, N.J.: Transaction, 1990), 161–64.

10. Dorothy Thompson, "America Demands a Single Loyalty," *Commentary* 9 (March 1950): 210–19; the quotations from Handlin are from "Israel and the Mission of America," which was published in Oscar Handlin, *Race and Nationality in American Life* (Garden City, N.Y.: Anchor, 1957), 193–200. Handlin made an even stronger case for multiple loyalties in this revised version of his original *Commentary* essay. The change in the essay's title is suggestive.

11. Milton M. Gordon, *Assimilation in American Life: The Role of Race, Religion, and National Origins* (New York: Oxford University Press, 1964), 67.

12. Fein, *Where Are We?,* 168.

13. Melvin I. Urofsky, *We Are One! American Jewry and Israel* (Garden City, N.Y.: Anchor, 1978), 447.

14. Daniel J. Elazar, "Decision-Making in the American Jewish Community," in *The Jewish Community in America,* ed. Marshall Sklare (New York: Behrman House, 1974), 103–4.

15. Charles S. Liebman, *The Ambivalent American Jew: Politics, Religion and Family in American Jewish Life* (Philadelphia: Jewish Publication Society of America, 1973), vii, 89–92; Daniel J. Elazar, *Community and Polity: The Organizational Dynamics of American Jewry* (Philadelphia: Jewish Publication Society of America, 1976), 85–86; Monty Noam Penkower, *At the Crossroads: American Jewry and the State of Israel* (Haifa: University of Haifa, 1990), 7; Steven M. Cohen, "Amoral Zionists, Moralizing Universalists and Conditional Doves," *Moment* 14 (August, 1989): 56–57.

16. Arthur Hertzberg, *Being Jewish in America: The Modern Experience* (New York: Schocken, 1979), 223.

17. Robert Silverberg, *If I Forget Thee O Jerusalem: American Jews and the State of Israel* (New York: William Morrow, 1970), 451–52; Liebman, *Ambivalent American Jew,* 88, 94–108; Marshall Sklare and Joseph Greenblum, *Jewish Identity on the Suburban Frontier: A Study of Group Survival in the Open Society* (New York: Basic Books, 1976), chap. 6.

18. Irving Louis Horowitz, *Israeli Ecstasies/Jewish Agonies* (New York: Oxford University Press, 1974), viii, 43, 75–85, 104.

19. Ibid., 79, 84–85.

20. Joseph P. Sternstein, "Reform Judaism and Zionism, 1895–1904," in *Herzl Year Book,* ed. Raphael Patai (New York: Herzl Press, 1963), 5:11–31; Melvin I. Urofsky, *American Zionism from Herzl to the Holocaust* (Garden City, N.Y.: Anchor, 1975), 78.

21. Silverberg, *If I Forget Thee,* 467–69.

22. Naomi W. Cohen, *American Jews and the Zionist Idea* (New York: KTAV, 1975), 116–17; Naomi W. Cohen, *Not Free to Desist: The American Jewish Committee 1906–1966* (Philadelphia: Jewish Publication Society of America, 1972), 310–13.

23. Elazar, *Community and Polity,* 80.

24. Jonathan S. Woocher, *Sacred Survival: The Civil Religion of American Jews* (Bloomington: Indiana University Press, 1986), 55, 160.

25. Urofsky, *We Are One!,* 202.

26. Morris N. Kertzer, *Today's American Jew* (New York: McGraw-Hill, 1967), 295.

27. Arthur Hertzberg, "Israel and American Jewry," *Commentary* 44 (August 1967): 72.

28. Lucy S. Dawidowicz, "American Public Opinion," in *American Jewish Year Book* (Philadelphia: Jewish Publication Society of America, 1968), 69:203–18; Silverberg, *If I Forget Thee,* 1–10, 574–77, 582; Robert Sheehan, "The Fund-Raising Businessmen: Eight Billion Dollars," *Fortune* 73 (January 1966): 148–50, 180–83; Marshall Sklare, "Lakeville and Israel: The Six-Day War and Its Aftermath," *Midstream* 14 (October 1968): 4–21; S. P. Goldberg, "Jewish Communal Services: Programs and Finances," *American Jewish Year Book* (Philadelphia: Jewish Publication Society of America, 1972), 73:238–39; Liebman, *Ambivalent American Jew,* 90–91.

29. Norman Podhoretz, "Now, Instant Zionism," *New York Times Magazine,* 3 February 1974; Daniel J. Elazar, "United States of America: Overview," in *The Yom Kippur War: Israel and the Jewish People,* ed. Moshe Davis (New York: Arno, 1974, 1–35; Stephen D. Isaacs, *Jews and American Politics* (Garden City, N.Y.: Doubleday, 1974), 267; Meir Moshe, "The Yom Kippur War in Middle America," *Midstream* 20 (June–July, 1974): 74–79; Elazar, *Community and Polity,* 341–77.

30. Whitfield, *American Space, Jewish Time,* 14; Arnold Dashefsky, "Sources of Jewish Charitable Giving: Incentives and Barriers," in Lipset, *American Pluralism and the Jewish Community,* 205; Elazar, *Community and Polity,* 12; Kertzer, *Today's American Jew,* 102.

31. Urofsky, *We Are One!,* 225–27.

32. Paul Breines, *Tough Jews: Political Fantasies and the Moral Dilemma of American Jewry* (New York: Basic Books, 1990), 186–200; Harry Arvay, *Operation Kuwait* (New York: Bantam, 1975).

33. "Helicopter Hijacked to Pan Am Building," *New York Times,* 24 May 1974.

34. Marshall Sklare, *America's Jews* (New York: Random House, 1971), 222; Isaacs, *Jews and American Politics,* passim.

35. Daniel J. Elazar, "The Jewish Context of the New Jewish Politics," in *The New Jewish Politics,* ed. Daniel J. Elazar (New York: University Press of America, 1988), 73.

36. American Friends Service Committee, *Search for Peace in the Middle East* (Philadelphia: AFSC, 1970), vi–vii; Arnold M. Soloway with Edwin Weiss and Gerald Caplan, *Truth and Peace in the Middle East: A Critical Analysis of the Quaker Report* (New York: Friendly House, 1971), 70–71.

37. Fein, *Where Are We?,* 60.

38. Judith Miller, *One, by One, by One: Facing the Holocaust* (New York: Simon and Schuster, 1990), 224–28.

39. Lewis H. Weinstein, "Soviet Jewry and the American Jewish Community, 1963–1967," *American Jewish History* 77 (June 1988): 600–613; William W. Orbach, *The American Movement to Aid Soviet Jewry* (Amherst: University of Massachusetts Press, 1979).

40. Michael Berenbaum, "The Nativization of the Holocaust," *Judaism* 35 (Fall 1986): 447.

41. Miller, *One, by One,* 220.

42. Chaim I. Waxman, *America's Jews in Transition* (Philadelphia: Temple University Press, 1983), 123.

43. Wieseltier is quoted in Miller, *One, by One,* 231–32, and in Jim Sleeper, *The Closest of Strangers: Liberalism and the Politics of Race in New York* (New York: Norton, 1990), 209.

44. Eugene B. Borowitz, "On the Passing of the Ethnic Era," *Sh'ma,* 21 September 1990, 123; Miller, *One, by One,* 231; Daniel Jeremy Silver, "Choose Life," *Judaism* 35 (Fall 1986): 462–63.

45. Borowitz, "On the Passing of the Ethnic Age," 122–24; Jacob Neusner, *Stranger at Home: "The Holocaust," Zionism, and American Jews* (Chicago: University of Chicago Press, 1981).

46. Henry Siegman, "Liberalism and the Jewish Interest," *Congress Monthly* 53 (September–October 1986): 3–5.

47. Horowitz, *Israel Ecstasies/Jewish Agonies,* 109; Irving Kristol, in *Congress Bi-Weekly* 40 (April 1973): 18–19.

48. Seymour Martin Lipset and Earl Raab, "The American Jews, the 1984 Elections, and Beyond," in Elazar, *New Jewish Politics,* 33–50.

49. Fein, *Where Are We?,* 199.

50. Bernard Rosenberg and Irving Howe, "Are American Jews Turning to the Right?" in *The New Conservatives: A Critique from the Left,* ed. Lewis A. Coser and Irving Howe (New York: New American Library, 1977), 64–89.

51. Norman Podhoretz, *Breaking Ranks* (New York: Harper and Row, 1979), 63–68.

52. Bernard Avishai, "Breaking Faith: *Commentary* and the American Jews," *Dissent* 38 (Spring 1981): 236–56.

53. Murray Friedman, "A New Direction for American Jews," *Commentary* 72 (December 1981): 37–44.

54. Jonathan Kaufman, *Broken Alliance: The Turbulent Times Between Blacks and Jews in America* (New York: Scribner's, 1988), 86–88.

55. Urofsky, *We Are One!,* 378.

56. Arthur Liebman, *Jews and the Left* (New York: John Wiley, 1979), 612–13.

57. Jack Nusan Porter and Peter Drier, eds., *Jewish Radicalism: A Selected Anthology* (New York: Grove, 1973), xlix.

58. Cohen, *American Jews and Zionist Ideal,* 144; Michael J. Rosenberg, "Israel without Apology," in *The New Jews,* ed. James A. Sleeper and Alan L. Mintz (New York: Vintage, 1971), 82, 86.

59. Alan Mintz, "Along the Path to Religious Community," in Sleeper and Mintz, *New Jews,* 25–34; Stephen C. Lerner, "The Havurot: An Experiment in Jewish Communal Living," in Porter and Dreier, *Jewish Radicalism,* 149–67.

60. Kelman is quoted in Gerald S. Strober, *America's Jews: Community in Crisis* (New York: Doubleday, 1974), 236.

61. Hershel Shanks, "Michael—His Magazine and His Movement," *Moment* 15 (June 1990): 30–31, 57; Michael Lerner, "The Editor: A Personal Note," *Tikkun* 4 (July August, 1989): 7–12.

62. Michael Lerner, "*TIKKUN:* To Mend, Repair and Transform the World," *Tikkun* 1 (1986): 3–13.

63. Lerner, "The Editor: A Personal Note," 12.

64. Hershel Shanks, "Michael—His Magazine and His Movement," 56–58.

Chapter Eight: The Question of Survival

1. Charles S. Liebman and Steven M. Cohen, *Two Worlds of Judaism: The Israeli and American Experiences* (New Haven: Yale University Press, 1990), 49–57.

2. Ibid., 111–17.

3. Ibid., 46–47, 103.

4. Ibid., 53–54.

5. David Singer, "Living with Intermarriage," *Commentary* 68 (July 1979): 48.

6. Fran Schumer, "Star-Crossed: More Gentiles and Jews Are Intermarrying—and It's Not All Chicken Soup," *New York Times,* 2 April 1990, 34.

7. Ibid.; Singer, "Living with Intermarriage," 48.

8. Liebman and Cohen, *Two Worlds of Judaism,* 53, 178.

9. Thomas B. Morgan, "The Vanishing American Jew," *Look,* 5 May 1964, 42–46. See also "A Threat to Survival," *Time,* 17 January 1964, 17.

10. Marshall Sklare, "Intermarriage and the Jewish Future," *Commentary* 37 (April 1964): 46–52.

11. Marshall Sklare, "Intermarriage and Jewish Survival," *Commentary* 49 (March 1970): 51–58; see also Marshall Sklare, *America's Jews* (New York: Random House, 1971), 180–209.

12. "Interfaith Cards for Holidays Irk Jewish Leaders," *Wall Street Journal,* 10 December 1990.

13. Charlotte Anker, "We Are the Children You Warned Our Parents About," *Moment* 16 (February 1991): 34–39.

14. Egon Mayer, "Intermarriage Research at the American Jewish Committee: Its Evolution and Impact," in *Facing the Future: Essays on Contemporary Jewish Life,* ed. Steven Bayme (New York: American Jewish Committee, 1989), 164; Singer, "Living with Intermarriage," 51–52.

15. Liebman and Cohen, *Two Worlds of Judaism,* 132.

16. Stuart E. Rosenberg, *The New Jewish Identity in America* (New York: Hippocrene, 1985), 171–72.

17. Jack Wertheimer, "Recent Trends in American Judaism," in *American Jewish Year Book* (Philadelphia: Jewish Publication Society of America, 1989), 89:93–94, 101, 105; Sklare, "Intermarriage and Jewish Survival," 56; Singer, "Living with Intermarriage," 50.

18. Rosenberg, *New Jewish Identity in America,* 132–33; Chaim I. Waxman, *America's Jews in Transition* (Philadelphia: Temple University Press, 1983), 177–78.

19. "One of 35 Jews in U.S. Adopted the Religion: 10,000 Convert Yearly," *Wall Street Journal,* 16 April 1984.

20. Wertheimer, "Recent Trends in American Judaism," 106.

21. Charles Liebman, *The Ambivalent American Jew: Politics, Religion, and Family in American Jewish Life* (Philadelphia: Jewish Publication Society of America, 1973), viii.

22. "As Jewish Population Falls in U.S., Leaders Seek to Reverse Trend," *Wall Street Journal,* 13 April 1984; Chaim I. Waxman, "The Emancipation, the Enlightenment and the Demography of American Jewry," *Judaism* 38 (Fall 1989): 492–94; Nathan Glazer, "New Perspectives in American Jewish Sociology," in Bayme, *Facing the Future,* 5; Elihu Bergman, "The American Jewish Population Erosion," *Midstream* 23 (October 1977): 9–19.

23. Robert Gutman, "Demographic Trends and the Decline of Anti-Semitism," *Jews in the Mind of America,* ed. Charles H. Stember (New York: Basic Books, 1966), 354.

24. Waxman, *America's Jews in Transition,* 168; U. O. Schmelz and Sergio Dellapergola, "Basic Trends in American Jewish Demography," in Bayme, *Facing the Future,* 75–76.

25. Sidney Goldstein, "Jews in the United States: Perspectives from Demography," *Jewish Life in the United States,* ed. Joseph B. Gittler (New York: New York University Press, 1981), 34–38.

26. Glazer, "New Perspectives in American Jewish Sociology," 10; "As Jewish Population Falls in U.S." For an overview of the condition of the Jewish elderly, see Alan Glicksman, *The New Jewish Elderly: A Literature Review* (New York: American Jewish Committee, 1991).

27. Steven Bayme, Introduction to Steven M. Cohen, *Alternative Families in the Jewish Community: Singles, Single Parents, Childless Couples, and Mixed-Marrieds* (New York: American Jewish Committee, 1989), iii; Cohen, ibid., 17.

28. Waxman, *America's Jews in Transition,* 162; William Petschek National Jewish Family Center, *Newsletter* 6 (Spring 1987): 5; *Jewish News* (East Orange, N.J.), 21 September 1989; ibid., 3 August 1989.

29. Sylvia Barack Fishman, "I'm Not a Feminist, but . . . ," *Brandeis Review* 10 (Summer 1990): 39; Sylvia Barack Fishman, "The Impact of Feminism on American Jewish Life," in *American Jewish Year Book* (Philadelphia: Jewish Publication Society of America, 1989), 89:28.

30. Estelle Gilson, "Will Today's Woman Join Hadassah?" *Moment* 15 (February 1990): 29–30, 55; Reena Sigman Friedman, "The Jewish Feminist Movement," in *Jewish Voluntary Organizations,* ed. Michael N. Dobkowski (Westport, Conn.: Greenwood, 1986), 595.

31. Friedman, "Jewish Feminist Movement," 576.

32. Ibid., 584.

33. Ellen M. Umansky is quoted in Fishman, "Impact of Feminism on American Jewish Life," 13; Judith Plaskow, "Up Against the Wall," *Tikkun* 5 (July–August, 1990): 25–26.

34. Fishman, "I'm Not a Feminist," 42; Fishman, "Impact of Feminism on American Jewish Life," 50.

35. Fishman, "Impact of Feminism on American Jewish Life," 54.

36. Amy Stone, "The Jewish Establishment Is Not an Equal Opportunity Employer," *Lilith* 4 (Fall–Winter, 1977–78): 25–26.

37. Fishman, "Impact of Feminism on American Jewish Life," 35; Waxman, *America's Jews in Transition,* 220–21.

38. Friedman, "Jewish Feminist Movement," 595; Waxman, *America's Jews in Transition,* 220–21.

39. Charles E. Silberman, *A Certain People: American Jews and Their Lives Today* (New York: Summit, 1985), 262; Dawidowicz is quoted in Fishman, "Impact of Feminism on American Jewish Life," 15, 29.

40. Nathan Glazer, "On Jewish Forebodings," *Commentary* 80 (August 1985): 36.

41. The most important statements of the transformationist position are Steven M. Cohen, *American Modernity and Jewish Identity* (New York: Tavistock, 1983); Steven

M. Cohen, *American Assimilation or Jewish Revival?* (Bloomington: Indiana University Press, 1988); Calvin Goldscheider, *Jewish Continuity and Change: Emerging Patterns in America* (Bloomington: Indiana University Press, 1986). *American Modernity and Jewish Identity* has a foreword by Charles E. Silberman. For a strong dissent from the transformationist position, see Schmelz and Dellapergola, "Basic Trends in American Jewish Demography," 72–111.

42. Calvin Goldscheider and Alvin Zuckerman, *The Transformation of the Jews* (Chicago: University of Chicago Press, 1984).

43. William B. Helmreich, "Misguided Optimism," *Midstream* 34 (January 1988): 30–32.

44. Nathan Glazer, review of Charles E. Silberman, *A Certain People: American Jews and Their Lives Today,* in *New York Times,* 1 September 1985.

45. Schmelz and Dellapergola, "Basic Trends in American Jewish Demography," 92–93, 104; Mayer, "Intermarriage Research at the American Jewish Committee," 173.

46. Erich Rosenthal, "Acculturation without Assimilation? The Jewish Community of Chicago, Illinois," *American Journal of Sociology* 66 (November 1960): 275–88; Ze'ev Chafets, *Members of the Tribe: On the Road in Jewish America* (New York: Bantam, 1988), 250.

47. Daniel J. Elazar, *Community and Polity: The Organizational Dynamics of American Jewry* (Philadelphia: Jewish Publication Society of America, 1976), 76.

48. Seymour P. Lachman and Barry A. Kosmin, "What Is Happening to American Jewry?," *New York Times,* 4 June 1990; Chaim I. Waxman, "Is the Cup Half-Full or Half-Empty? Perspectives on the Future of the American Jewish Community," in *American Pluralism and the Jewish Community,* ed. Seymour Martin Lipset (New Brunswick, N.J.: Transaction, 1990), 76; Chafets, *Members of the Tribe,* 251.

49. Joann S. Lublin, "The Crisis in Jewish Identity," *Wall Street Journal,* 4 November 1977.

50. Arthur Hertzberg, *The Jews in America: Four Centuries of an Uneasy Encounter: A History* (New York: Simon and Schuster, 1989), 386; Hillel Halkin, *Letters to an American Friend: A Zionist's Polemic* (Philadelphia: Jewish Publication Society of America, 1977), 25.

51. Marcia Graham Synott, *The Half-Opened Door: Discrimination and Admissions at Harvard, Yale, and Princeton, 1900–1970* (Westport, Conn.: Greenwood, 1979), 35, 69; Lawrence Bloomgarden, "Our Changing Elite Colleges," *Commentary* 29 (February 1960): 152.

52. Craig Lambert, "Renaissance President," *Harvard Magazine* 93 (May–June 1991): 31–36.

53. Judith S. Antonelli, "New Harvard President Reflects on Jewishness," *Jewish Advocate,* 29 March 1991.

54. Marshall Sklare, "American Jewry—The Ever Dying People," *Midstream* 22 (June–July 1976): 17–27.

BIBLIOGRAPHICAL ESSAY

General Works

There is no history of American Jews that focuses solely on the post–World War II era. The period after 1945 is discussed in the concluding chapters of several one-volume surveys of American Jewish history. These include Rufus Learsi, *The Jews in America: A History* (New York: KTAV, 1954, 1972); Judd L. Teller, *Strangers and Natives: The Evolution of the American Jew from 1921 to the Present* (New York: Dell, 1968); Henry L. Feingold, *Zion in America: The Jewish Experience from Colonial Times to the Present* (New York: Hippocrene, 1974); Henry L. Feingold, *A Midrash on American Jewish History* (Albany: State University of New York Press, 1982); Arthur A. Goren, *The American Jews* (Cambridge: Harvard University Press, 1982); Lucy S. Dawidowicz, *On Equal Terms: Jews in America, 1881–1981* (New York: Holt, Rinehart, and Winston, 1982); Abraham J. Karp, *Haven and Home: A History of the Jews in America* (New York: Schocken, 1985); and Arthur Hertzberg, *The Jews in America: Four Centuries of an Uneasy Encounter: A History* (New York: Simon and Schuster, 1989).

Among the most provocative analyses of postwar Jewry are Charles B. Sherman, *The Jew within American Society* (Detroit: Wayne State University Press, 1961); Morris N. Kertzer, *Today's American Jew* (New York: McGraw-Hill, 1967); James Yaffe, *The American Jews: Portrait of a Split Personality* (New York: Random House, 1968); David Sidorsky, *The Future of the Jewish Community in America* (New York: Basic Books, 1973); Milton Himmelfarb, *The Jews of Modernity* (Philadelphia: Jewish Publication Society of America, 1973); Eugene Borowitz, *The Masks Jews Wear: The Self-Deceptions of American Jewry* (New York: Simon and Schuster, 1973); Charles S. Liebman, *The Ambivalent American Jew: Politics, Religion and Family in American Jewish Life* (Philadelphia: Jewish Publication Society of America, 1973); Gerald S. Strober, *American Jews: Community in Crisis* (Garden City, N.Y.: Doubleday,

1974); Hillel Halkin, *Letters to an American Friend: A Zionist's Polemic* (Philadelphia: Jewish Publication Society of America, 1977); Arthur Hertzberg, *Being Jewish in America: The Modern Experience* (New York: Schocken, 1979); Chaim I. Waxman, *America's Jews in Transition* (Philadelphia: Temple University Press, 1983); Ben Halpern, *The American Jew: A Zionist Analysis* (New York: Schocken, 1983); Stuart E. Rosenberg, *The New Jewish Identity in America* (New York: Hippocrene, 1985); Charles J. Silberman, *A Certain People: America's Jews and Their Lives Today* (New York: Summit, 1985); Leonard Fein, *Where Are We? The Inner Life of America's Jews* (New York: Harper and Row, 1988); and Jerold S. Auerbach, *Rabbis and Lawyers: The Journey from Torah to Constitution* (Bloomington: Indiana University Press, 1990).

Three impressionistic works by journalists that emphasize the diversity of contemporary American Jewry are Israel Shenker, *Coat of Many Colors: Pages from Jewish Life* (Garden City, N.Y.: Doubleday, 1985); Ze'ev Chafets, *Members of the Tribe: On the Road in Jewish America* (New York: Bantam, 1988); and Howard Simons, *Jewish Times: Voices of the American Jewish Experience* (Boston: Houghton Mifflin, 1988). The changing image of the Jew in American popular culture is described in Lester D. Friedman, *Hollywood's Image of the Jew* (New York: Ungar, 1982); Sarah Blacher Cohen, ed., *From Hester Street to Hollywood: The Jewish-American Stage and Screen* (Bloomington: Indiana University Press, 1983); and Patricia Erens, *The Jew in American Cinema* (Bloomington: Indiana University Press, 1985).

Among the most valuable collections of essays on contemporary American Jewish culture, sociology, and politics are Peter I. Rose, ed., *The Ghetto and Beyond: Essays on Jewish Life in America* (New York: Random House, 1969); Abraham D. Lavender, ed., *A Coat of Many Colors: Jewish Subcommunities in the United States* (Westport, Conn.: Greenwood, 1977); Gladys Rosen, ed., *Jewish Life in America* (New York: Institute of Human Relations Press, 1978); Joseph B. Gittler, ed., *Jewish Life in the United States: Perspectives from the Social Sciences* (New York: New York University Press, 1981); Steven Bayme, ed., *Facing the Future: Essays on Contemporary Jewish Life* (New York: KTAV, 1989); and Seymour Martin Lipset, ed., *American Pluralism and the Jewish Community* (New Brunswick, N.J.: Transaction, 1990).

Stephen J. Whitfield, an astute student of contemporary Jewish life, has published two collections of his essays—*Voices of Jacob, Hands of Esau: Jews in American Life and Thought* (Hamden, Conn.: Archon, 1984), and *American Space, Jewish Time* (Hamden, Conn.: Archon, 1988)—that are in a class by themselves. They cover virtually the entire gamut of American Jewish life with the exception of religion.

Community Studies

The broad overviews of the American Jewish experience may be supplemented by communal studies. Among the best are Selig Adler and Thomas Connolly, *From Ararat to Suburbia: The History of the Jewish Community of Buffalo* (Philadelphia: Jewish Publication Society of America, 1960); Louis J. Swichow and Lloyd P. Gartner, *The History of the Jews of Milwaukee* (Philadelphia: Jewish Publication Society of America, 1963); Max Vorspan and Lloyd P. Gartner, *History of the Jews of Los Angeles* (San Marino, Calif.: Huntington Library, 1970); Lloyd P. Gartner, *The History of the Jews of Cleveland* (Cleveland: Western Reserve Historical Society, 1978); and Marc Lee Raphael, *Jews and Judaism in a Midwestern Community: Columbus, Ohio 1840–1975* (Columbus: Ohio Historical Society, 1979). Sidney Goldstein and Calvin Goldscheider, *Three Generations in a Jewish Community* (Englewood, Cliffs, N.J.: Prentice-Hall, 1968), is an important sociological study of the Jews of Providence, Rhode Island.

Naturally, more has been written about the Jews of New York City than any other community. Nathan Glazer's chapter on Jews in Nathan Glazer and Daniel P. Moynihan, *Beyond the Melting Pot: The Negroes, Puerto Ricans, Jews, Italians and Irish of New York City* (Cambridge: MIT Press, 1963), is an excellent brief overview of the political, economic, and social condition of the largest Jewish community in history. Egon Mayer, *From Suburb to Shtetl: The Jews of Boro Park* (Philadelphia: Temple University Press, 1979), discusses the postwar transformation of a Brooklyn neighborhood of approximately sixty thousand Jews into an outpost of right-wing Orthodoxy and describes its symbiosis of traditional Judaism and modern culture. Joseph A. D. Sutton, *Magic Carpet: Aleppo-in-Flatbush: The Story of a Unique Ethnic Jewish Community* (New York: Thayer-Jacoby, 1979), examines the growth of the Syrian Jewish community in the Flatbush neighborhood of Brooklyn. Marc Angel, "The Sephardim of the United States: An Exploratory Story," in *American Jewish Year Book* (Philadelphia: Jewish Publication Society of America, 1973), 74:77–138 is a good introduction to those American Jews who came from North Africa and the Middle East. Steven M. Lowenstein, *Frankfurt on the Hudson: The German-Jewish Community of Washington Heights, 1933–1983, Its Structure and Culture* (Detroit: Wayne State University Press, 1989), is the best work on what has been termed the *Fourth Reich*. Howard Brotz's *The Black Jews of Harlem: Negro Nationalism and the Dilemma of Negro Leadership* (New York: Schocken, 1970) is an excellent brief account of the most exotic part of New York's Jewish mosaic.

Two collections of essays on various aspects of southern Jewry are Leonard Dinnerstein and Mary Dale Palsson, eds., *Jews in the South* (Baton Rouge:

Louisiana State University Press, 1973), and Nathan M. Kaganoff and Melvin I. Urofsky, eds., *Turn to the South: Essays on Southern Jewry* (Charlottesville: University Press of Virginia, 1979). For an impressionistic account of growing up as a Jew in the South, see Eli Evans, *The Provincials: A Personal History of the Jews in the South* (New York: Atheneum, 1973). Evans's father was mayor of Durham, North Carolina, during the early 1960s at the time of the sit-ins. Evans's attempt to explain the nature of Jewish identity in the South led him to write a biography of perhaps the most enigmatic of all southern Jews, Judah P. Benjamin.

Communal Life

An excellent collection of brief histories of 120 national and local voluntary social service, philanthropic, religious, political, cultural, Zionist, and social agencies is Michael N. Dobkowski, ed., *Jewish American Voluntary Organizations* (Westport, Conn.: Greenwood, 1986). This volume also includes "The Jewish Federation Movement," by Deborah K. Polivy, and "The Soviet Jewry Movement in the United States," by Paul S. Appelbaum. Naomi W. Cohen, *Not Free to Desist: The American Jewish Committee, 1906–1966* (Philadelphia: Jewish Publication Society of America, 1972), and Deborah Dash Moore, *B'nai B'rith and the Challenge of Ethnic Leadership* (Albany: State University of New York Press, 1981), analyze the history of two of America's most important secular Jewish organizations.

The postwar history of Jewish charity and social work is covered in Herman D. Stein, "Jewish Social Work in the United States," in *American Jewish Year Book* (Philadelphia: Jewish Publication Society of America, 1956), 57: 1–48; Harry L. Lurie, *A Heritage Affirmed: The Jewish Federation Movement in America* (Philadelphia: Jewish Publication Society of America, 1961); Robert Morris and Michael Freund, eds., *Jewish Social Welfare in the United States, 1890–1952* (Philadelphia: Jewish Publication Society of America, 1966); Marc Lee Raphael, *Understanding American Jewish Philanthropy* (New York: KTAV, 1979); Abraham J. Karp, *To Give Life: The UJA in the Shaping of the American Jewish Community* (New York: Schocken, 1981); Marc Lee Raphael, *A History of the United Jewish Appeal* (Chico, Calif.: Scholars Press, 1982); and Ernest Stock, *Partners and Pursestrings: History of The United States Israel Appeal* (Lanham, Md.: University Press of America, 1987).

Jonathan Woocher, *Sacred Survival: The Civil Religion of American Jews* (Bloomington: Indiana University Press, 1986), is a superb analysis of the secular and religious motives impelling Jews who are involved in Jewish philanthropy. See also Arnold Dashefsky, "Sources of Jewish Charitable Giving: Incentives and Barriers," in Lipset, *American Pluralism and the Jewish Commu-*

nity, 203–25, and Milton Goldin, *Why They Give: American Jews and Their Philanthropies* (New York: Macmillan, 1976).

Beginning in the 1960s, the rescue of Soviet Jewry became an important item on the American Jewish agenda. It is discussed in William W. Orbach, *The American Movement to Aid Soviet Jewry* (Amherst: University of Massachusetts Press, 1979), and in Lewis H. Weinstein, "Soviet Jewry and the American Jewish Community, 1963–1987," *American Jewish History* 77 (June 1988): 600–613.

Daniel Elazar's *Community and Polity: The Organizational Dynamics of American Jewry* (Philadelphia: Jewish Publication Society of America, 1976) is an ambitious and successful exploration of the operations and assumptions of American Jewish life. Elazar continued his examination of Jewish organizational life in "Developments in Jewish Community Organization in the Second Postwar Generation," in Lipset, *American Pluralism and the Jewish Community,* 173–92.

Demography and Sociology

An early postwar effort to estimate the number of American Jews is Sophia M. Robison, "How Many Jews in the United States," *Commentary* 8 (August 1949): 185–92. The continuing flow of Jewish immigrants to America after 1945 is examined in Drora Kass and Seymour Martin Lipset, "Jewish Immigration to the United States from 1967 to the Present: Israelis and Others," in *Understanding American Jewry,* ed. Marshall Sklare (New Brunswick, N.J.: Transaction, 1982), 272–94; Sylvia Rothchild, *A Special Legacy: An Oral History of Soviet Jewish Emigrés in the United States* (New York: Simon and Schuster, 1985); and Moshe Shokeid, *Children of Circumstances: Israeli Emigrants in New York* (Ithaca: Cornell University Press, 1988).

An excellent introduction to the post-1945 sociology of America's Jews is Marshall Sklare, *America's Jews* (New York: Random House, 1971). In *The Jews: Social Patterns of an American Group* (Glencoe, Ill.: Free Press, 1958), Sklare brings together a collection of important essays on various aspects of the politics, economics, and sociology of American Jewry. Two other valuable collections of essays in American Jewish sociology are Marshall Sklare, ed., *The Jew in American Society* (New York: Behrman House, 1974), and Marshall Sklare, ed., *The Jewish Community in America* (New York: Behrman House, 1974). Because of the flow of Jewish population to the sunbelt, the information presented in Bruce A. Phillips, "Los Angeles Jewry: A Demographic Portrait," in *American Jewish Year Book* 86 (Philadelphia: Jewish Publication Society of America, 1986), 126–95, could be a harbinger of the future.

The argument between the pessimists and optimists over the future of

American Jewry is discussed in Chaim I. Waxman, "Is the Cup Half-Full or Half-Empty? Perspectives on the Future of the American Jewish Community," in Lipset, *American Pluralism and the Jewish Community*, 71–85. The case for optimism is strongly argued in Steven M. Cohen, *American Modernity and Jewish Identity* (New York: Tavistock, 1983), and Calvin Goldscheider, *Jewish Continuity and Change: Emerging Patterns in America* (Bloomington: Indiana University Press, 1986). The argument for pessimism is presented in Nathan Glazer, "On Jewish Forebodings," *Commentary* 80 (August 1985): 32–36; Nathan Glazer, "New Perspectives in American Jewish Sociology," in Bayme, *Facing the Future*, 3–22; U. O. Schmelz and Sergio Dellapergola, "Basic Trends in American Jewish Demography," in ibid., 72–111; and Charles S. Liebman, "The Quality of American Jewish Life: A Grim Outlook," in ibid., 50–71.

The best books on the postwar Jewish flight to suburbia include Albert Gordon, *Jews in Suburbia* (Boston: Beacon, 1959); Judith R. Kramer and Seymour Leventman, *Children of the Gilded Ghetto: Conflict Resolutions of Three Generations of American Jews* (New Haven: Yale University Press, 1961); Marshall Sklare and Joseph Greenblum, *Jewish Identity on the Suburban Frontier* (New York: Basic Books, 1967, 1979); and Benjamin Ringer, *The Edge of Friendliness: A Study of Jewish-Gentile Relations* (New York: Basic Books, 1967).

The impact of the women's liberation movement on American Jewry is examined in Sally Priesand, *Judaism and the New Woman* (New York: Behrman House, 1975); Anne Lapidus Lerner, "Who Has Not Made Me a Man: The Movement for Equal Rights for Women in American Jewry," in *American Jewish Year Book* (Philadelphia: Jewish Publication Society of America, 1977), 78:3–38; Reena Sigman Friedman, "The Jewish Feminist Movement," in Dobkowski, *Jewish Voluntary Organizations*, 575–601; and Sylvia Barach Fishman, "The Impact of Feminism on American Jewish Life," in *American Jewish Year Book* (Philadelphia: Jewish Publication Society of America, 1989), 89:3–62.

The upward social and economic mobility of Jews after 1945 is described in Lawrence Bloomgarden, "Our Changing Elite Colleges," *Commentary* 29 (February 1960): 150–54; Charles Kadushin, *The American Intellectual Elite* (Boston: Little, Brown, 1974); Everett Carll Ladd, Jr., and Seymour Martin Lipset, *The Divided Academy: Professors and Politics* (New York: McGraw-Hill, 1975); Stephen Steinberg, *The Academic Melting Pot: Catholics and Jews in American Higher Education* (New Brunswick, N.J.: Transaction, 1977); Harriet Zuckerman, *Scientific Elite: Nobel Laureates in the United States* (New York: Free Press, 1977); Marcia Graham Synott, *The Half-Opened Door: Discrimination and Admissions at Harvard, Yale and Princeton, 1900–70* (Westport, Conn.: Greenwood, 1979); Richard D. Alba and Gwen Moore, "Ethnicity in the

American Elite," *American Sociological Review* 47 (June 1982): 373–83; Dan A. Oren, *Joining the Club: A History of Jews and Yale* (New Haven: Yale University Press, 1985); and Edward S. Shapiro, "Jews with Money," *Judaism* 36 (Winter 1987): 7–16. Judith Ramsey Ehrlich and Barry J. Renfeld, *The New Crowd: The Changing of the Jewish Guard on Wall Street* (Boston: Little, Brown, 1989), fails to take its topic seriously.

The lingering presence of poverty, particularly among the elderly, is emphasized in Naomi Levine and Martin Hochbaum, eds., *Poor Jews: An American Awakening* (New Brunswick, N.J.: Transaction, 1974), and in Thomas Cottle's impressionistic *Hidden Survivors: Portraits of Poor Jews in America* (Englewood, Cliffs, N.J.: Prentice-Hall, 1980).

Joseph Brandes's superb *Immigrants to Freedom: Jewish Communities in Rural New Jersey Since 1882* (Philadelphia: University of Pennsylvania Press, 1971) explains the postwar decline of Jewish farm life in the state with the largest concentration of Jewish farmers. Small-town Jewry is examined in Lee J. Levinger, "The Disappearing Small-Town Jew," *Commentary* 14 (August 1952): 157–63, and in Peter I. Rose, *Strangers in Their Midst: A Sociological Study of Small-Town Jews and Their Neighbors* (Ithaca: Cornell University Press, 1959). Stefan Kanfer, *A Summer World: The Attempt to Build a Jewish Eden in the Catskills, from the Days of the Ghetto to the Rise and Decline of the Borscht Belt* (New York: Farrar, Straus, Giroux, 1989), is disappointing.

Religion

The most complete account of postwar American Judaism is Jack Wertheimer, "Recent Trends in American Judaism," in *American Jewish Year Book* (Philadelphia: Jewish Publication Society of America, 1989), 89:63–162. Marc Lee Raphael, *Profiles in American Judaism: The Reform, Conservative, Orthodox, and Reconstructionist Traditions in Historical Perspective* (New York: Harper and Row, 1985), and Joseph L. Blau, *Judaism in America: From Curiosity to Third Faith* (Chicago: University of Chicago Press, 1976), are two competent introductions to American Judaism. Will Herberg, *Protestant-Catholic-Jew: An Essay in American Religious Sociology* (New York: Doubleday, 1955, 1960), puts the history of American Jewry within the context of the religious revival of the 1950s. Jacob Neusner's two-volume collection, *Understanding American Judaism: Toward the Description of a Modern Religion* (New York: KTAV, 1975), contains many important articles on the contemporary sociological and theological condition of American Judaism. The final chapters of Nathan Glazer's *American Judaism* (Chicago: University of Chicago Press, 1957, 1972) are a pessimistic overview of post–World War II Judaism. Glazer, a prominent sociologist, focuses on the adaptation of Judaism to

American conditions. Several essays in the December 1987 issue of *American Jewish History* discuss *American Judaism* on the occasion of the thirtieth anniversary of its publication. The most relevant of these for the postwar period is Edward S. Shapiro, "The Missing Element: Nathan Glazer and Modern Orthodoxy," 77:260-76.

Charles S. Liebman, "Orthodoxy in American Jewish Life," in *American Jewish Year Book* (Philadelphia: Jewish Publication Society of America, 1965), 66:21-97, is the best introduction to American Orthodoxy. Also valuable are Gilbert Klaperman, *The Story of Yeshiva University: The First Jewish University in America* (New York: Macmillan, 1969); William B. Helmreich, *The World of the Yeshiva: An Intimate Portrait of Orthodox Jewry* (New York: Free Press, 1982); Jeffrey S. Gurock, "Resisters and Accommodators: Varieties of Orthodox Rabbis in America, 1886-1983," *American Jewish Archives* 35 (November 1983): 100-187; Jeffrey S. Gurock, *The Men and Women of Yeshiva: Higher Education, Orthodoxy, and American Judaism* (New York: Columbia University Press, 1988); M. Herbert Danzinger, *Returning to Tradition: The Contemporary Revival of Orthodox Judaism* (New Haven: Yale University Press, 1989); and Samuel C. Heilman and Steven M. Cohen, *Cosmopolitans and Parochials: Modern Orthodox Jews in America* (Chicago: University of Chicago Press, 1990). Solomon Poll, *The Hasidic Community of Williamsburg* (New York: Free Press, 1962) is an interesting work on the Satmar community of the Williamsburg area of Brooklyn, the most isolationist of America's Hasidic sects. Samuel Heilman, *Synagogue Life: A Study in Symbolic Interaction* (Chicago: University of Chicago Press, 1976), is an important sociological analysis of what takes place in a contemporary Orthodox synagogue.

The best study of Conservative Judaism is Marshall Sklare's brilliant *Conservative Judaism: An American Religious Movement* (Glencoe, Ill.: Free Press, 1955, 1972). Other important examinations of Conservative Judaism are Mordecai Waxman, ed., *Tradition and Change: The Development of Conservative Judaism* (New York: Burning Bush, 1958); Abraham J. Karp, "The Conservative Rabbi—'Dissatisfied But Not Unhappy,'" *American Jewish Archives* 35 (November 1983): 188-262; and Abraham J. Karp, "A Century of Conservative Judaism in the United States," in *American Jewish Year Book* (Philadelphia: Jewish Publication Society of America, 1986), 86:3-61. Charles S. Liebman, "Reconstructionism in American Jewish Life," in *American Jewish Year Book* (Philadelphia: Jewish Publication Society of America, 1970), 71:3-99, is the finest scholarly analysis of this Conservative "heresy."

For the history of Reform Judaism, see Sefton Temkin, "A Century of Reform Judaism in America," in *American Jewish Year Book* (Philadelphia: Jewish Publication Society of America, 1973), 74:3-75; David Polish, "The Changing and the Constant in the Reform Rabbinate," *American Jewish Ar-*

chives 35 (November 1983): 263 341; Mark L. Winer et al., *Leaders of Reform Judaism: A Study of Jewish Identity, Religious Practices and Beliefs, and Marriage Patterns* (New York: Union of American Hebrew Congregations, 1987); Gerald L. Showstack, *Suburban Communities: The Jewishness of American Reform Jews* (Ithaca: Cornell University Press, 1988); and Michael A. Meyer, *Response to Modernity: A History of the Reform Movement in Judaism* (New York: Oxford University Press, 1989). Leonard Fein, ed., *Reform Is a Verb: Notes on Reform and Reforming Judaism* (New York: Union of American Hebrew Congregations, 1972), is an important analysis of the status of contemporary American Reform written from a Reform perspective.

The *havurot* (fellowship) movement within American Judaism is discussed in James A. Sleeper and Alan Mintz, eds., *The New Jews* (New York: Random House, 1971); Jacob Neusner, *Contemporary Judaic Fellowship in Theory and Practice* (New York: KTAV, 1972); and Riv-Ellen Prell, *Prayer and Community: The Havurah Movement in American Judaism* (Detroit: Wayne State University Press, 1989).

Anti-Semitism

In "Finding a Conceptual Framework for the Study of American Anti-semitism," *Jewish Social Studies* 47 (Summer–Fall 1985): 312–26, Henry L. Feingold places American anti-Semitism within the context of American history. Leonard Dinnerstein's collection *Uneasy at Home: Antisemitism and the American Jewish Experience* (New York: Columbia University Press, 1987) contains several essays on the postwar period. Particularly relevant are "Southern Jewry and the Desegregation Crisis, 1954–1970" and "Antisemitism Exposed and Attacked, 1945–1980." Dinnerstein's forthcoming history of American anti-Semitism will fill a void in American Jewish historiography.

Sociologists have produced the most important works on postwar American anti-Semitism. The most significant include Charles H. Stember et al., *Jews in the Mind of America* (New York: Basic Books, 1966); Charles Glock and Rodney Stark, *Christian Beliefs and Anti-Semitism* (New York: Harper and Row, 1966); Gertrude Selznick and Stephen Steinberg, *The Tenacity of Prejudice: Anti-Semitism in Contemporary America* (New York: Harper and Row, 1969); and Rodney Stark et al., *Wayward Shepherds: Prejudice and the Protestant Clergy* (New York: Harper and Row, 1971). Lucy S. Dawidowicz's essay "Can Anti-Semitism Be Measured?" questions whether survey research of the type used in *Jews in the Mind of America* can accurately measure anti-Semitism. It is reprinted in Lucy S. Dawidowicz, *The Jewish Presence: Essays on Identity and History* (New York: Holt, Rinehart, and Winston, 1977).

Executives of the Anti-Defamation League of B'nai Brith wrote several popular books on postwar anti-Semitism, including three by Arnold Forster and Benjamin R. Epstein—*The Trouble-Makers: An Anti-Defamation League Report* (New York: Doubleday, 1952); *Cross-Currents* (Garden City, N.Y.: Doubleday, 1956); and *The New Anti-Semitism* (New York: McGraw-Hill, 1974)—and one by Nathan Perlmutter and Ruth Ann Perlmutter, *The Real Anti-Semitism in America* (New York: Arbor House, 1982). Ralph Lord Roy, *Apostles of Discord: A Study of Organized Bigotry and Disruption on the Fringes of Protestantism* (Boston: Beacon, 1953) is a popular study examining anti-Semitism within right-wing Protestantism. Gary A. Tobin with Sharon L. Sassler, *Jewish Perceptions of Anti-Semitism* (New York: Plenum, 1988), is concerned not with anti-Semitism itself but rather with Jewish perceptions of anti-Semitism. Tobin and Sassler argue that American Jews are not paranoid in believing that American anti-Semitism continues to be dangerous.

The Holocaust, Zionism, and Israel

Jacob Neusner's *Stranger at Home: "The Holocaust," Zionism and American Judaism* (Chicago: University of Chicago Press, 1981) discusses the impact of the Holocaust and Israel on American Jewish identity. For the history of postwar Zionism, see Robert Silverberg, *If I Forget Thee O Jerusalem: American Jews and the State of Israel* (New York: Morrow, 1970); Naomi W. Cohen, *American Jews and the Zionist Idea* (New York: KTAV, 1975); and Melvin Urofsky, *We Are One: American Jewry and Israel* (Garden City, N.Y.: Anchor, 1978).

Arthur D. Morse's portrayal of American and American Jewish indifference toward the Holocaust in *While Six Million Died: A Chronicle of American Apathy* (New York: Random House, 1967) was important in shaping a more activist Jewish political profile after the Six-Day War. Paul Breines's claim in *Tough Jews: Political Fantasies and the Moral Dilemma of American Jewry* (New York: Basic Books, 1990), that a militarist and expansionist Israel has undermined American Jewish liberalism, is unconvincing. The last chapter of Judith Miller's *One, by One, by One: Facing the Holocaust* (New York: Simon and Schuster, 1990) examines the influence of the Holocaust on American Jewish identity during the 1980s. This topic is also discussed in Michael Berenbaum, "The Nativization of the Holocaust," *Judaism* 35 (Fall 1986): 447–57; and in Daniel Jeremy Silver, "Choose Life," ibid., 458–66.

For the history of the Holocaust survivors who settled in America, see Dorothy Rabinowitz, *New Lives: Survivors of the Holocaust Living in America* (New York: Avon, 1976); Leonard Dinnerstein, *America and the Survivors of the Holocaust* (New York: Columbia University Press, 1982); and William B. Helmreich, "Holocaust Survivors in American Society," *Judaism* 39 (Winter 1990): 14–27.

Bibliographical Essay

Politics

The major concern of historians, political scientists, and sociologists who have studied the politics of American Jews has been to explain why Jews have consistently voted for liberal candidates. Lawrence H. Fuchs, *The Political Behavior of American Jews* (Glencoe, Ill.: Free Press, 1956), traces Jewish liberalism back to Judaism. But as critics of Fuchs have pointed out, this fails to expain why liberalism has tended to be more prominent among secular than religious Jews. For other explanations of Jewish liberalism, see Liebman, *The Ambivalent American Jew*; Werner Cohn, "The Sources of American Jewish Liberalism," in Sklare, *The Jews: Social Patterns of an American Group,* 614–26; Alan Fisher, "Continuity and Erosion of Jewish Liberalism," *American Jewish Historical Quarterly* 67 (December 1976): 322–49 (a premature obituary for Jewish liberalism); and Arthur Liebman, *Jews and the Left* (New York: John Wiley, 1979). Stephen Issacs, *Jews and American Politics* (Garden City, N.Y.: Doubleday, 1974), argues for the political importance of American Jews. Daniel J. Elazar, ed., *The New Jewish Politics* (New York: University Press of America, 1988), examines Jewish politics in the era of the political action committee.

Nathaniel Weyl, *The Jew in American Politics* (New Rochelle, N.Y.: Arlington House, 1968), and Alan J. Steinberg, *American Jewry and Conservative Politics: A New Direction* (New York: Shapolsky, 1988), claim that liberalism is antithetical to Jewish interests. Jack Nusan Porter and Peter Dreier, eds., *Jewish Radicalism: A Selected Anthology* (New York: Grove, 1973), attempt to conflate Jewishness with the radicalism of the 1960s; Bernard Rosenberg and Irving Howe, "Are American Jews Turning to the Right," in *The New Conservatives: A Critique from the Left,* ed. Lewis A. Coser and Irving Howe (New York: New American Library, 1977), 64–89, is a critical look at the supposed rightward drift of American Jews.

The support of Jews for the civil rights movement has been the most important element of Jewish liberalism. Tensions between Jews and blacks in the 1960s resulted in a spate of books on Jewish-black relations. They include Shlomo Katz, ed., *Negro and Jew: An Encounter in America* (New York: Macmillan, 1967); Nat Hentoff, ed., *Black Anti-Semitism and Jewish Racism* (New York: Richard W. Baron, 1969); Robert Weisbord and Arthur Stein, *Bittersweet Encounter: The Afro-American and the American Jew* (Westport, Conn.: Negro University Press, 1970); Louis Harris and Bert E. Swanson, *Black-Jewish Relations in New York City* (New York: Praeger, 1971); Ben Halpern, *Jews and Blacks: The Classic American Minorities* (New York: Herder and Herder, 1971); and Jonathan Kaufman, *Broken Alliance: The Turbulent Times between Blacks and Jews in America* (New York: Scribner's, 1988). Events have shown that Gary T. Marx, *Protest and Prejudice: A Study of Belief in the Black Com-*

munity (New York: Harper and Row, 1969), underestimates the extent of black anti-Semitism. Janet Dolgin, *Jewish Identity and the JDL* (Princeton: Princeton University Press, 1977), analyzes the response of lower-middle-class Jews living in declining urban neighborhoods to racial unrest.

Jewish Studies

The development of Jewish studies is described in Arnold J. Band, "Jewish Studies in American Liberal Arts Colleges and Universities," in *American Jewish Year Book* (Philadelphia: Jewish Publication Society of America, 1966), 67:3–30; Leon Jick, ed., *The Teaching of Judaica in American Universities: The Proceedings of a Colloquium* (New York: KTAV, 1970); Robert Alter, "What Jewish Studies Can Do," *Commentary* 58 (October 1974): 71–76; Jacob Neusner, *The Academic Study of Judaism: Essays and Reflections* (New York: KTAV, 1975); Jacob Neusner, *Judaism in the American Humanities: Essays and Reflections* (Chico, Calif.: Scholars Press, 1981); and Robert Gordis et al., "Jewish Studies in the Universities: A Balance Sheet," *Judaism* 35 (Spring 1986): 134–97.

Identity

The impact of World War II on the identity of American ethnic groups is explored in Philip Gleason's important essay "Americans All: World War II and the Shaping of American Identity," *Review of Politics* 43 (October 1981): 483–518. Charles S. Liebman and Steven M. Cohen, *Two Worlds of American Judaism: The Israeli and American Experiences* (New Haven: Yale University Press, 1990), is a provocative comparison of Jewishness in Israel and the United States. For the Jewish identity of American Jewish writers and intellectuals, see Daniel Bell, "Reflections on Jewish Identity," in Rose, *The Ghetto and Beyond*, 465–76; the symposium "Jewishness and the Younger Intellectuals," *Commentary* 31 (April 1961); Allen Guttmann, *The Jewish Writer in America: Assimilation and the Crisis of Identity* (New York: Oxford University Press, 1971); Alexander Bloom, *Prodigal Sons: The New York Intellectuals and Their World* (New York: Oxford University Press, 1986); and Edward S. Shapiro, "Jewishness and the New York Intellectuals," *Judaism* 38 (Summer 1989): 282–92.

INDEX

Index

I

Immigrants, 2, 197, 231, 253; accultura-tion, 66–67, 127; economic and social mobility, 118; farmers, 132, 133; fourth generation, 250–51, 254; German Jews, 31–32, 69–70, 133; from Israel, 127, 242; Russian Jews, 126–27, 242; second gen-eration, 14, 52, 66, 148, 161, 196, 200, 235; third generation, 52, 53, 66, 148, 161, 200, 235, 254; and traditional Juda-ism, 8, 169; urban neighborhoods, 102, 151, 152; war refugees, 3, 4, 125–26; and Yiddish culture, 66, 195, 200

Immigration: to Israel, 3, 29, 164, 204, 205; and Jewish survival, 125, 195, 242; nativist opposition to, 3, 5, 10, 102; Orthodox Judaism and, 67–68, 189; restrictive legislation, 3–4, 8

Indiana University, 95

Inside, Outside (Wouk), 23

Institute of Traditional Judaism, 178–79

Intellectuals, 101, 108; and Communism, 25, 26; eastern European, 60, 65; and fund-raising, 64; and Jewish culture, 111, 113, 196–97, 198–200; political ori-entation, 106, 110, 221; in publishing, 109; and religion, 111, 112, 160–61; and suburbanization, 151, 158

Interfaith movement, 53, 162, 166, 212–13

Intermarriage, 122, 193, 201, 255; ac-culturation and, 121, 231, 234–35, 241, 252; children of, 190–91, 236–37, 239, 240–41, 243, 249, 250, 253; and conver-sion to Judaism, 239–40, 250, 253, 255; efforts to counteract, 86, 231; Jewish opposition to, 232, 233–34, 235–36, 237; and Jewish survival, 86, 125, 229, 233, 235, 241, 243, 250, 252, 253; popular culture and, 233–34, 236, 237; rabbis and, 188–89, 233, 238–39, 241; and social acceptance, 43, 93, 231, 232–33, 235

"Intermarriage and the Jewish Future" (Sklare), 234

"Intermarriage and Jewish Survival" (Sklare), 235

Intifada, 202, 227

"Invisible Jewish Poor" (Wolfe), 153–54

Iowa, 49

Irish-Americans, 221

Irvington, N.J., 148

Isaacs, Stephen D., 211

Israel, 22, 93, 250, 255–56; American criti-cism of, 201, 202–3, 205, 211–12, 224, 227–28; American fund-raising for, 202, 206–7, 208, 209, 211; and Ameri-can Jewish identity, 29, 130, 166–67, 192–93, 201–2, 207–8, 210, 211, 217–18, 229, 254; American support for, 54, 55, 56, 201, 203–4, 205–7, 216, 225–26; Arab conflict, 52, 202, 204, 211, 212, 224, 227, 230; Conservative Judaism in, 170; definition of Jews, 191, 240; dual loyalty question, 42, 45, 199–200, 203, 205; espionage, 56, 58, 210; establishment of, 78, 82, 192, 202, 205, 251; Gentiles and, 47, 48, 212–13; immigrants to America from, 127, 242; immigration to, 127, 204, 214; immi-gration of Americans to, 29, 31, 92, 161, 164, 204–5; Jewish studies and, 78, 82, 85; Lebanon invasion, 199, 202; Reform Judaism and, 135, 192–93; Sinai War, 34, 41–42, 207; Six-Day War, 27, 201, 207–8; War of Independence, 63, 199; Yom Kippur War, 23, 208–9

Israeli Ecstasies/Jewish Agonies (Horo-witz), 203

Ivanhoe (Scott), 157

Ivry, Alfred, 80

J

"J'Accuse: American Jews and L'Affaire Pollard" (Biale), 58

Jackson, Rev. Jesse L., 109, 223–24

Jaffa, Harry, 110

James, Henry, 102, 103, 107

Japan, 8

ABOUT THE AMERICAN
JEWISH HISTORICAL SOCIETY

THE TWENTIETH CENTURY has been a period of change for the American Jewish community, bringing growth in numbers and in status and, most important, a new perception of itself as part of the history of the United States. The American Jewish Historical Society has also grown over the century, emerging as a professional historical association with a depth of scholarship that enables it to redefine what is *American* and what is *Jewish* in the American saga. To record and examine this saga and to honor its own centennial, the society has published this five-volume series, *The Jewish People in America.*

The society was founded on 7 June 1892 in New York City, where it was housed in two crowded rooms in the Jewish Theological Seminary. At the first meeting, its president Cyrus Adler declared that it was the patriotic duty of every ethnic group in America to record its contributions to the country. Another founding father emphasized the need to popularize such studies "in order to stem the growing anti-Semitism in this country." As late as the 1950s, the society was encouraging young doctoral students in history to research and publish material of Jewish interest, even though such research, according to Rabbi Isidore Meyer, then the society's librarian, would impede the writers' advancement in academia. In this climate, the early writings in the society's journal, *Publications of the American Jewish Historical Society,* were primarily the work of amateurs; they were narrowly focused, often simply a recounting of the deeds of the writers' ancestors. However, these studies did bring to light original data of great importance to subsequent historians and constitute an invaluable corpus of American Jewish historiography.

The situation has changed materially. One hundred years later, the society has its own building on the campus of Brandeis University; the building houses the society's office space, exhibit area, and library. The Academic Council of the society includes sixty-three professors of American history whose primary interest is American Jewish history. Articles in the society's publication, now called *American Jewish History,* meet the highest professional standards and are often presented at the annual meeting of the American Historical Association. The society has also published an extensive series of monographs, which culminates in the publication of these volumes. The purpose of *The Jewish People in America* series is to provide a comprehensive historical study of the American Jewish experience from the age of discovery to the present time that both satisfies the standards of the historical profession and holds the interest of the intelligent lay reader.

Dr. Abraham Kanof
Past President
American Jewish Historical Society
and Chairman
The Jewish People in America Project